The Apocalypse of the Sovereign Self

Miniature from the Monastery of Dionysius on Mount
Athos, painted in Constantinople in about 1059

GIL BAILIE

The
APOCALYPSE
of the
SOVEREIGN
SELF

*Recovering the Christian
Mystery of Personhood*

Angelico Press

First published in the USA
by Angelico Press 2023
Copyright © Gil Bailie 2023

All rights reserved:
No part of this book may be reproduced or transmitted,
in any form or by any means, without permission

Unless otherwise indicated, all Scripture quotations
are taken from the Revised Standard Version of
the Bible—Second Catholic Edition copyright
2006 National Council of the Churches of Christ
in the United States of America, except when they
occur in passages quoted from other works.

For information, address:
Angelico Press, Ltd.
169 Monitor St.
Brooklyn, NY 11222
www.angelicopress.com

ppr 978-1-62138-927-9
cloth 978-1-62138-928-6

Book and cover design
by Michael Schrauzer

The knowledge of what it means to be a person is inextricably bound up with the Faith of Christianity.
— Romano Guardini, *The End of the Modern World*

The world situation today shows clearly enough that whoever discards this Christian or at least biblical view must in one way or another find in a personless collectivism or individualism (which converge upon one another) his downfall.
— Hans Urs von Balthasar, "On the Concept of Person"

CONTENTS

PREFACE xi
1. The Triumph of the Will and the Twilight of Resolve 1
2. Mediation: "It was Like an Explosion Went Off" 11
3. A Mimetic Anthropology 21
4. Willy Loman: "The Man's Exhausted" 25
5. Hap and Biff Loman 29
6. Pale and Bloodless Emulation 39
7. "None of Them Are True" 54
8. A Small Mistake in Doctrine 62
9. Descartes: The Quest for Certainty 71
10. Rousseau: The Virtuoso of Vanity Victimhood 79
11. Nietzsche and the "Imitatio Christi" 91
12. Underground Man: Rebel Without a Cause 105
13. The Freudian Interlude 112
14. A Chameleon-like Disorder 126
15. "I Keep My Countenance, I Remain Self-possessed" 135
16. "Bug Off and Look at Me" 140
17. The Illness of Our Age 147
18. Multiphrenia 155
19. From Transgender to Transhuman 168
20. "Potential Mystics or Mystics in the Primitive State" . . . 173
21. Sylvia Plath: "A Mimicking Nothingness" 182
22. The Prodigal Son 189
23. The Absolute Opposite of All Hysteria 198

24	The Son Can Only Do What He Sees the Father Doing	217
25	"Anthropological Structures Prepared Beforehand"	229
26	The Mother's Smile	232
27	Misconceptions: Antinatal Rites	237
28	The Father's Patrimony	246
29	The School of Love and Responsibiity	256
30	*Pietas* and the Choreography of Forgetfulness	261
31	Mother Church	276
32	The Osmosis of Sanctity	282
33	The Eucharistic Meta-drama	288
34	The Acting Person: Not in One's Own Name	291
35	All the World's a Stage	301
36	Stage Fright	304
37	"I Live, Now No Longer I, But Christ Lives In Me"	312
	POSTSCRIPT	317
	INDEX	319

PREFACE

> To be lay is to write in the vernacular and speak to theological purpose by a deliberate, personal scanning of the contours of existence.[1]

BOOKS GIVE BIRTH TO BOOKS. THIS BOOK emerged from its immediate predecessor, *God's Gamble: The Gravitational Power of Crucified Love*, so much so that the précis of that book that appeared on its dust jacket can serve as an epigraph for the book it spawned.

> The Cross of Christ has left a crater at the center of history, an inflection of sacrificial love toward which everything before and after this event is ordered and properly understood. That Christ is the Alpha and Omega — the logic, the meaning of creation itself, from whom the drama of salvation emanates and toward whom it moves — is a central but often neglected doctrine of Catholic Christianity. Though it is a mystery that will ever elude rational explication, sufficient traces of it can be found.

No amount of argumentation or documentation can convince someone that this is true. Faith is ultimately a gift, and neither argumentation nor documentation can produce it in someone who has lost the sense of wonder, or someone reflexively on guard against being hoodwinked. The journey of faith, however, begins with that incipient form of faith that we call wonder. In fact, the growth of wonder is perhaps the best measure, not only of the health and vitality of faith, but of one's spiritual and moral health generally.

As I did in this book's immediate predecessor, with the exception of this preface I will be using the first-person plural, not to strike a lofty pose, but on the contrary as a slight grammatical reminder that

---

[1] Aidan Nichols, O.P., *The Word Has Been Abroad* (Washington, DC: Catholic University of America Press, 1998), 92.

virtually everything I am proposing is drawn from the great treasury of Christian thought. Put another way, the plural pronoun will stand as subtle testimony to the fact that I count myself among the gleaners who come after a great harvest has been gathered and stored but who are delighted nonetheless to find here and there overlooked fruits of that harvest worthy of retrieval and further evaluation. Moreover, this grammatical usage reinforces the theme of the book: the difference between the autonomous individual and the person properly understood, the latter being embedded in, and indebted to, a tradition.

For the same reasons, as I have in my previous books, I have chosen to quote liberally from the sources to whom I am indebted rather than going to the trouble of paraphrasing the wisdom of others. Those readers who wonder why I don't say everything in my own words will have stumbled upon the very argument I am making in this book. If the reader finds this tedious, I ask his indulgence. It seems to me only courteous to acknowledge my debt to those from whose writings I have benefited. If I can conduct an orchestra and chorus of voices, why attempt ventriloquy or pose as a virtuoso? The reader who grants any authority to what I have written should be reminded that this authority derives from its resonance with the work of that great cloud of witnesses on whom Christians necessarily rely. That is not to deny that the case I am making is in some sense my own, even if I neither arrived at it on my own nor claim any originality. I can only hope that the intellectual and moral force of the sources that I cite will compensate for any irritation my deference to these sources might provoke in the reader.

Let me express my heartfelt gratitude to those who have encouraged the writing of this book, and who have patiently waited as its author seemed forever to be discovering — to his own surprise — nuances that required further exploration. My wife Kathleen has been a constant source of encouragement. She embodies the faith for which her husband has tried to give an account. Without the countless ways in which my dear friend and colleague Randy Coleman-Riese has aided and encouraged me — not just during the writing of this book, but for many years — neither this book nor its immediate predecessor would have been possible. I also owe a debt of gratitude to my friend, Caroline Gissler, who patiently and lovingly poured over early drafts of the manuscript, offering inestimable advice and seasoned wisdom.

Preface

In keeping with the interdividual mystery of personhood which this book explores, I dedicate it to all those who gave me an example of a properly ordered and spiritually grounded life, most of whom were unaware of how blessed I was by their example. In gratitude for them I offer these few lines, written many decades ago, about one of the first people beyond the family who left an indelible mark on my life.

> I never knew I loved him; I was six,
> But hope he knew, though he's been dead these many years,
> What it meant when he took out those shears
> To cut the hedge and gave me a man to see,
> And let me run to fetch the ice and tea,
> Sit next to him, and while he'd slowly quench
> His measure of his worth: his thirst, I'd inch
> A little closer: "It's hot Jake, huh?" I'd say.
> He'd mumble: "God made it that-a'way;
> It's up to us to love the way it's made;
> He'll give us a little tea and ice and shade."
> And when the tea was gone, I'd grab the rake,
> Helping out again my old friend Jake. . . .
> He had even let me wear his smelly hat,
> And though he rarely talked, I remember that
> He'd pat me on the head and almost smile,
> As to say: "Not now, I'll tell you afterwhile."
> One summer he came to call me by my name.
> I leapt alive the way the preachers claim
> You're supposed to do when, despite the Fall,
> God's big enough to love you after all.

A word is in order about the image on the cover of this book. Rightly understood, it depicts the ecclesial circumstance in which mediated desire can function in accord with its divine provenance and ecclesial ordination: Christ is pointing to the Father; Peter is pointing to Christ, and the eyes of the apostles, prompted by Peter's example, are turned upward in recognition of the divine mystery that Christ came to reveal.

1 The Triumph of the Will and the Twilight of Resolve

> The apostate has seen, and then denied what he has seen. Through and through, he remains branded by the image he rejects: with terrible power this image leaves its imprint on his whole existence, which blazes brilliantly in the fire of denial.
> — Hans Urs von Balthasar[1]

> Balthasar can already look ahead to his final conclusion: one day, non-Christian humanity will stand before the "yawning abyss of reason and freedom," first opened up by Christians.... Staggered by the confrontation with this void, men will turn back for consolation to pagan antiquity, where a touch of true glory still bathed the cosmos. But when this fades, as fade it surely will, the decision will have to be made: nihilism or "self-surrender to the sign, in all its purity, of the glory of God's love revealed by Christ."
> — Aidan Nichols, O. P.[2]

THIS IS NOT A STORYBOOK, BUT IT IS A COLLECtion of stories—fictional and factual—and a running commentary on them. Both the factual stories and the literary ones will be read in an allegorical key, as a clue to the overall spiritual and existential predicament we will be exploring. Taken together, these stories limn the outlines of two more elusive stories: that of the autonomous *self* and that of the *person*, whose Christian origins and Christian connotations have too often been overlooked.

The tragically mistaken idea that the incalculable moral and cultural blessings of Christianity will survive the attenuation of the faith that

---

[1] Hans Urs von Balthasar, *The Glory of the Lord: A Theological Aesthetics*, Vol. I: *Seeing the Form*, trans. Erasmo Leiva-Merikakis (San Francisco: Ignatius Press, 1989), 524.
[2] Nichols, *The Word Has Been Abroad*, 150.

gave birth to these blessings is the predicate for much that happened in the Christian West over the last few hundred years. The cultural and confessional evisceration of Christianity, should it continue, will prove the validity of Christ's warning: "Apart from me you can do nothing" (Jn 15:5). For these words were addressed by Christ to his own followers — those most exposed to the revelation of which his life, death, and Resurrection consisted — and they now apply not only to Christians but even to those whose exposure to Christ has been merely cultural, and who may think the civilization shaped by Christian faith will survive the renunciation of that faith. As we shall see below, the most salient manifestation of the *nothing* of which Christ spoke is the nihilism that is ever more clearly becoming the distinguishing characteristic of the post-Christian world.

It might be said that there are two prominent forms of nihilism: the epistemological one exhibited by Pilate when he shruggingly asked Jesus, "What is truth?" and the socially contagious one exhibited by the mob when it shouted in unison, "crucify him." The proximity to one another of these two forms of nihilism in the Passion story is quite illuminating. Pilate's shrugging and dismissive remark sanctions a moral chaos, to the terrible consequences of which the mob spontaneously responds by regressing to the most primitive of moral certainties: the guilt of the unanimously accused victim. Neither the Roman prefect nor the crowd he would soon be obliged to appease exhibited that openness to truth of which the Old and New Testaments speak: a truth accessible only to a humble and contrite heart. It was just such a heart that made Augustine aware of the link between the ideological and moral forms of nihilism when he said of the philosophers whom he had earlier studied with such diligence that they *kept the truth imprisoned by their wickedness.*[3]

G. K. Chesterton famously said that small mistakes in doctrine lead to huge blunders in human happiness. The nihilism with which we are concerned is the result of an anthropological blunder the terminal incoherence of which has been nowhere better summarized than by the opinion of United States Supreme Court Justice Anthony Kennedy in his 1992 Planned Parenthood v. Casey decision: "At the heart of liberty is the right to define one's own concept of existence, of meaning, of the universe, and of the mystery of human life." That so many today find this statement unproblematic is a symptom of how a soft form of nihilism has triumphed in our time. According to this doctrine, nothing

---

3   Augustine, *De Trinitate*, I, 13, n. 19.

must be allowed to thwart the self-will of the sovereign self. Maureen Mullarkey provides the apt summation: "Decomposition of the cultural ecosystem that sustains our civil society has roots in Kennedy's precept. And the nihilism it epitomizes."[4] René Girard concurs: "No one takes the trouble to reflect uncompromisingly about the enigma of a historical situation that is without precedent: the death of all cultures."[5]

Extending the themes of our earlier book — *God's Gamble: The Gravitational Power of Crucified Love* — we want to argue here that what Christianity has done to cultures seriously exposed to it, and by extension to culture itself, it has also done to human subjectivity. It has revealed beneath and beyond the discourse of self and autonomy the mystery of the person as such. Like the other blessings we have enjoyed by virtue of living in a culture under Christian influence, many today experience degrees of interiority and social solidarity without realizing how indebted to Christianity they are for these blessings, or that these blessings will not long survive the waning of the faith that made them possible.

The reader might be reminded that the root meaning of the word apocalypse in our title is to reveal, uncover, or disclose. Thanks to the use made of this word by John of Patmos in the work that became the last book of the Bible, today it carries the implication of the end of history itself. That implication is only apropos to our explorations in the sense that the crisis of sovereign selfhood seems to be entering its final stages. More pertinent to the argument we are making is the literal translation of the Greek *apocalypsis*: to unveil or reveal. We want to argue that the experiment in psychological and social autonomy that is coterminous with modernity has failed because it was at odds with anthropological reality. In a roundabout and idiosyncratic way, we will inspect this failure before turning to the remarkable resources Christianity makes available for facing and rectifying this crisis.

The concept of the person, wrote Joseph Cardinal Ratzinger, "grew in the first place out of the interplay between human thought and the data of Christian faith,"[6] entering thereby into the intellectual history

---

4 Maureen Mullarkey, "Marginalia on Dobbs and Roe," *Studio Matters*, July 4, 2022.
5 René Girard, *Things Hidden Since the Foundation of the World*, trans. Stephen Bann and Michael Metteer (Stanford: Stanford University Press, 1987), 441.
6 Joseph Cardinal Ratzinger, "Concerning the Notion of Person in Theology," *Joseph Ratzinger in Communio*, Vol. 2: *Anthropology and Culture*, ed. David L. Schindler and Nicholas J. Healy (Grand Rapids: Eerdmans, 2013), 103.

of those cultures fortunate enough to have fallen under Christian influence. In bringing about this theological revolution, the theologians of the patristic age laid the foundation for a revolution in human self-understanding which has languished for lack of adequate anthropological elaboration. It is surely the special responsibility and unique privilege of the twenty-first-century Church to try to give a more adequate account of the mystery of which she is the custodian.

Arguably anxious about the issue with which we will be dealing, the distinguished French sociologist, Marcel Mauss, published his last essay in 1938 on the difference between the self and the person. In it he wrote:

> It is Christians who have made a metaphysical entity of the "moral person" (*personne morale*), after they became aware of its religious power. Our own notion of the human person is still basically the Christian one.[7]

As distinctive as was the mystery of personhood that came to light in Christian thought, however, intimations of it can be found in the Old Testament, most strikingly in the prophets. Pope Benedict XVI observed, as the word is used in the Old Testament, the category of prophet is "something totally specific and unique, in contrast to the surrounding religious world, something that Israel alone has in this particular form."[8] The renowned Old Testament scholar Gerhard von Rad captured this when he wrote of the prophets:

> These men became individuals, *persons*. They could say "I" in a way never before heard in Israel. At the same time, it has become apparent that the "I" of which these men were allowed to become conscious was very different from our present-day concept of personality.[9]

As for the "present-day concept of personality," it now largely consists of anything anyone might decide about himself. As recently as 1967, when the German edition of von Rad's book on the Old Testament prophets appeared, even the "present-day" concept of personality retained at least the aura of objective reality and anthropological

---

[7] Marcel Mauss, "A category of the human mind: the notion of the person; the notion of the self," in *The Category of the Person*, ed. Michael Carrithers, Steven Collins, Stevens Lukes (Cambridge: Cambridge University Press, 1985), 19.
[8] Benedict XVI, *Jesus of Nazareth: From the Baptism in the Jordan to the Transfiguration*, trans. Adrian J. Walker (New York: Doubleday, 2007), 1.
[9] Gerhard von Rad, *The Message of the Prophets* (New York: Harper & Row, 1965), 146. Emphasis added.

coherence. As for the disappearance of a shared understanding of the person, the observation of von Rad's German contemporary Romano Guardini is most apposite.

> Personality *is* essential to man. This truth becomes clear, however, and can be affirmed only under the guidance of Revelation, which related man to a living, personal God, which makes him a son of God, which teaches the ordering of his Providence. When man fails to ground his personal perfection in Divine Revelation, he still retains an awareness of the individual as a rounded, dignified and creative human being. He can have no consciousness, however, of the real person who is the absolute ground of each man, an absolute ground superior to every psychological or cultural advantage or achievement. *The knowledge of what it means to be a person is inextricably bound up with the Faith of Christianity. An affirmation and a cultivation of the personal can endure for a time perhaps after Faith has been extinguished, but gradually they too will be lost.*[10]

As we shall see in the later chapters of this book, the word *person* entered the vocabulary of Western culture only after Christian theologians, in speaking of the three Persons of the Trinity, gave the word *persona* a philosophical profundity never before associated with it. In bringing about this theological revolution, the Church fathers of the fourth and fifth centuries laid the groundwork for a radical reassessment of human subjectivity which has yet to be fully appreciated and which it may now be the special responsibility of twenty-first-century Christian thought to reconnoiter.

The British social anthropologist Alfred Radcliffe-Brown (1881 – 1955) saw the rough outlines of the issue that we want to explore:

> If you tell me that an individual and a person are after all really the same thing, I would remind you of the Christian creed. God is three persons, but to say that he is three individuals is to be guilty of a heresy for which men have been put to death. Yet the failure to distinguish individual and person is not merely a heresy in religion: it is worse than that; it is a source of confusion in science.[11]

---

10 Romano Guardini, *The End of the Modern World*, trans. Joseph Theman and Herbert Burke (Wilmington, DE: ISI Books, 1998), 98 – 99. Emphasis added.
11 Alfred Radcliffe-Brown, "On Social Structure," in *Structure and Function in Primitive Society* (London: Cohen and West, 1940), 194.

We may quibble with the eminent anthropologist about the relative dangers of religious heresy and scientific confusion. Inasmuch as we are awash in both in this time of trial, however, we might welcome an alliance of all those who have recognized these perils from their own fields of interest. The point is that Christ has altered man's psychological circumstances as much as he has altered man's cultural and historical situation. In both cases man's freedom is called into play in a far greater way than was the case prior to the Christian revelation. This increased freedom has come with its obvious corollary: a heightening of the perils associated with the misuse of that freedom.

"The revelation of the person," writes Paul Evdokimov, "is *the* event of Christianity," and human desire is simply "the inborn nostalgia to become a 'person'."[12] If this is so, then there is no more urgent question than the one Kenneth Schmitz asks. "Can such a call to spiritual personhood be made today in such a way that it might be heard?"[13] This book is an effort to answer that question in the affirmative. The key will be to show how anthropologically sound is the uniquely Christian understanding of personhood, and the work of René Girard can play a significant and salutary role in bringing this to light.

In place of a formal introduction to Girard's work, we will simply allude to its most familiar features and leave to subsequent pages of this book the task of drawing out its subtler implications. Suffice it at this point to say that in the eyes of this writer and of many of those familiar with it, Girard's work represents an indispensable anthropological resource for meeting the cultural and spiritual challenges facing us today, not least the challenge posed by the shockingly rapid de-Christianization of Western culture.

Perhaps not surprisingly, the scriptures that served to Christianize cultures continue to offer the most cogent analysis of the price that would have to be paid for their cultural repudiation. This price is nowhere more clearly stated than in this salient passage in John's Gospel:

> I am the vine, you are the branches. He who abides in me, and I in him, he it is that bears much fruit, for apart from me you can do nothing. If a man does not abide in me, he is cast forth as a branch and withers; and the branches are gathered, thrown into the fire and burned. (Jn 15:5–6)

---

12 Paul Evdokimov, *The Sacrament of Love* (Crestwood, NY: St. Vladimir's Seminary Press, 1985), 53.
13 Kenneth L. Schmitz, "The Geography of the Human Person," *Communio* 13 (Spring 1986): 203, 204.

Again, the "nothing" of which Christ spoke is today the nihilism that is the final phase of the sterile form of the putatively autonomous self and its exaltation of the will. That this willfulness should prove in the end to be withered branches finds an echo in the warning of John the Baptist: "His winnowing fork is in his hand, to clear his threshing floor, and to gather the wheat into his granary, but the chaff he will burn with unquenchable fire" (Lk 3:17; Mt 3:12). The withered branches of Jesus's discourse and the chaff of which the Baptist spoke have their contemporary analogue in what Henri de Lubac called "the waning of ontological density" and what Gabriel Marcel termed the loss of our "ontological moorings." The Scriptural treatment of chaff is instructive: it will either be scattered to the wind or gathered and burned in a fire. These outcomes could be both conflated and transposed into an anthropological key by saying that the alternative to the kind of genuine solidarity that Christ offers is social alienation fitfully — and all too temporarily — relieved by the fire and faux solidarity of collective animosity and mob violence. For just as the gospel throws down a radical challenge to conventional forms of cultural life, so it challenges with equal audacity the conventional forms of human subjectivity, calling familiar psychological adaptations into question and revealing a startling new form, namely the *person* properly understood with all its specific Christian meaning and theological overtones.

Glenn Olsen has observed that "the liberal self, replicating as it does a social order from which the idea of a common good and any hierarchy of public goods has been largely evacuated, is intrinsically disordered and dysfunctional."[14] It is this same symbiosis of self and social order to which the authors of *Gaudium et spes* alluded in insisting that "the progress of the human person and the advance of society itself hinge on one another" (§ 25). This reciprocal relationship between the human person and human society means that distresses in one of these spheres will be accompanied by distresses in the other and that whatever their short-term practical advantages, attempts to remedy distresses in one sphere which take for granted the erroneous presuppositions in the other sphere will exacerbate and prolong the crisis common to them both. As we have moved from the cosmological to the anthropological age, argued Balthasar, a change has taken place in mankind's religious topography, the principal consequence of which is that "men can no longer love each other without God."[15]

---

14 Glenn W. Olsen, "The Role of Religion in the Twenty-first Century," *Communio* 2 (Summer 2004): 303.
15 Hans Urs von Balthasar, *The God Question and Modern Man* (New York: Seabury Press, 1967), 143.

THE APOCALYPSE OF THE SOVEREIGN SELF

The burden of our exploration will be to argue for a Christocentric recovery of the mystery of the person. If in so arguing, attention is focused on the mature expression of this mystery, that is in no way to suggest any affinity with or sympathy for those who would attribute human status only to humans who have acquired this or that level of functionality — an unconscionable and ethically monstrous position. No one would argue that a four-year-old has taken full possession of the talents which, with time, he will develop and express. Similarly, a child one moment after conception, though a biological human person of inestimable worth, will only much later have an opportunity to fulfill the promise implicit in his personhood. There is, however, another debate about the person that deserves our attention, and that is the debate as to what it is about personhood that Christ reveals and that without Christ the world is incapable of recognizing. That is the question we will be exploring in the later chapters of this book.

It is a lot easier to turn a deaf ear and a blind eye to Christ and His Church than it is to fashion a post-Christian alternative to them. The latter task, in fact, is impossible. As Malcolm Muggeridge famously pointed out, the choice before us today is Christ or nothing. Both formerly Christian cultures and those individuals shaped by the overarching Christian tenor of the cultures in which they live will remain — in subtle but indelible ways — Christ-haunted. The entry into history of Christ and his Church represents a watershed which demands a decision for or against, and those who reject it often sometimes understand the inevitability of that choice better than do Christians.

Of the revelation on Golgotha, Balthasar has insisted: "From this point on, true, deliberate atheism becomes possible for the first time, since, prior to this, without a genuine concept of God, there could be no true atheism."[16]

> What then if man, no longer accustomed to taking his standard from the cosmos (now emptied of the divine), refuses to take it from Christ? This is post-Christian man, who cannot return to the pre-Christian fluidity that once existed between man and the cosmos but who, in passing through Christianity, has grown used to the heightening of his creaturely rhythms and

---

16 Hans Urs von Balthasar, *Love Alone is Credible*, trans. D. C. Schindler (San Francisco: Ignatius Press, 2004), 91–92.

wants to hold on to them as if they are his personal hallmark, a gift that now belongs to him entirely. This will be the general characteristic of the post-Christian era, however manifold and contradictory its concrete expressions may be.[17]

It has become increasingly obvious that the myth of autonomous individuality flies in the face of anthropological and psychological reality, but once the West had made protecting the rights of the individual the engine of its historical reforms and reconfigured all its institutions accordingly, it was understandably in no mood to quibble over the psychological plausibility of what had become its moral lodestar and organizing principle. After all, Western culture parleyed its solicitude for the rights of the individual into some of the most impressive moral and political reforms in history. It takes a lot more than mere misinterpretation to destroy the historical power of the revelation which the myth of individuality misinterprets. Overlooking the psychological naïveté of the premise that produced these historical marvels would have seemed a tolerable price to pay for their political utility. But, like the national debt, the price to be paid for this anthropological miscalculation compounds rapidly and falls most heavily on subsequent generations, and today's youth are now visibly staggering under the burden of it.

Sooner or later, the social and psychological invalidity of the individualist myth was bound to lead to problems. As soon as everyone became an "individual," and every social grievance was challenged as an infringement on the individual's rights, the moral force once marshaled to protect the rights of the individual lost its clarity. As Simone Weil put it during the dark years of war, Nazi concentration camps, and the aerial bombardment of cities: "The notion of rights, which was launched into the world in 1789, has proved unable, because of its intrinsic inadequacy, to fulfil the role assigned to it."[18] Not only did the notion of rights present no formidable barrier to the campaigns of mass slaughter that were rippling through the modern world, but the notion was problematic even at the level of ordinary human relations. We can expect only a paltry form of justice, Weil argued, from a justice system as dependent as ours is on the need to "agitate for our rights."[19]

---

17 Hans Urs von Balthasar, *Theo-Drama: Theological Dramatic Theory*, Vol. II, *Dramatis Personae: Man in God*, trans. Graham Harrison (San Francisco: Ignatius Press, 1990), 417.
18 Simone Weil, "Human Personality," *The Simone Weil Reader*, ed. George A. Panichas (New York: David McKay, 1981), 314.
19 Ibid., 315.

The "rights rhetoric," according to Tracey Rowland, "is ideological. Its objective is to secure a social consensus in circumstances where there is no commonly accepted moral tradition by construing all human relations in contractual terms."[20] The Catholic philosopher Alasdair MacIntyre concurs: "The dominant contemporary idiom and rhetoric of rights cannot serve genuinely rational purposes, and we ought not to conduct our moral and political arguments in terms derived from that idiom and rhetoric."[21]

The Christians who wrote the United Nations Declaration on Human Rights and the Christians who enthusiastically adopted it could hardly have foreseen that they were embracing by default a jurisprudence of "rights" that would one day be used to enforce "rights" like "reproductive rights" — a paper-thin euphemism for the "right" to kill children in the womb — or a myriad of other purported "rights" deeply antithetical to the moral tradition for which the rights discourse seemed at first to be the closest secular approximation.

Hans Urs von Balthasar has argued, correctly in our view, that "all ages after Jesus will be marked (perhaps increasingly) by a Yes or No to him."[22] We live at a moment when this alternative stands before us in all its starkness and promise. The words of Jesus in Luke's Gospel have lost none of their concrete pertinence.

> And when he drew near and saw the city he wept over it, saying, "Would that even today you knew the things that make for peace! But now they are hidden from your eyes. For the days shall come upon you, when your enemies will cast up a bank about you and surround you, and hem you in on every side, and dash you to the ground, you and your children within you, and they will not leave one stone upon another in you; because you did not know the time of your visitation." (Lk 19:41–44)

To better appreciate the challenge we face, we turn now to a series of parables by which we hope to bring to light the underlying spiritual crisis of our age.

---

20 Tracey Rowland, *Culture and the Thomist Tradition: After Vatican II* (New York: Rutledge, 2003), 63.
21 Alasdair MacIntyre, "Community, Law, and the Idiom and Rhetoric of Rights," *Listening*, XXVI, 2 (1991): 96–110, quoted in Rowland, *Culture and the Thomist Tradition*, 148.
22 Hans Urs von Balthasar, *Theo-Drama: Theological Dramatic Theory*, Vol. I, *Prologomena*, trans. Graham Harrison (San Francisco: Ignatius Press, 1988), 30.

2 Mediation:
"IT WAS LIKE AN EXPLOSION WENT OFF"

> Consider the masses of young people electrified by this famous singer or by that film actor. If one reflects on this it all testifies to man's invincible urge to find in this world some being, some reality to which he can devote himself body and soul in an attitude of adoration, admiration, self-renunciation and service.
> — Henri de Lubac[1]

> There is such a thing as "natural faith" whose logic issues from the esteem we accord to the "dignity" of the person speaking, and our desire to "model" ourselves on this person in trust.
> — Aidan Nichols, O.P.[2]

BOB DYLAN IS ARGUABLY ONE OF THE MOST innovative and enigmatic popular musicians of the last half-century. And yet his creativity has never been premised on his putative rejection of inspiring role models, quite the opposite. Dylan has happily acknowledged his debt to predecessors, not least country music, blues, and gospel composers and artists. This reverence for, and deference to, admired models and predecessors was clearly in evidence in Dylan's acceptance lecture upon receiving the 2016 Nobel Prize for Literature. He began his lecture with these words:

> If I was to go back to the dawning of it all, I guess I'd have to start with Buddy Holly. Buddy died when I was about eighteen and he was twenty-two. From the moment I first heard him,

---

1 Henri de Lubac, *A Brief Catechesis on Nature and Grace*, trans. Br. Richard Arnandez, F.S.D. (San Francisco: Ignatius Press, 1984), 296.
2 Nichols, *The Word Has Been Abroad*, 21.

I felt akin. I felt related, like he was an older brother. I even thought I resembled him.... He was the archetype. Everything I wasn't and wanted to be. I saw him only but once, and that was a few days before he was gone. I had to travel a hundred miles to get to see him play, and I wasn't disappointed.... He was powerful and electrifying and had a commanding presence. I was only six feet away. He was mesmerizing. I watched his face, his hands, the way he tapped his foot, his big black glasses, the eyes behind the glasses, the way he held his guitar, the way he stood, his neat suit. Everything about him. He looked older than twenty-two. Something about him seemed permanent, and *he filled me with conviction*. Then, out of the blue, the most uncanny thing happened. *He looked me right straight dead in the eye, and he transmitted something. Something I didn't know what. And it gave me the chills.*

I think it was a day or two after that that his plane went down. And somebody — somebody I'd never seen before — handed me a Leadbelly record with the song "Cottonfields" on it. And that record changed my life right then and there. Transported me into a world I'd never known. It was like an explosion went off. *Like I'd been walking in darkness and all of the sudden the darkness was illuminated. It was like somebody laid hands on me.* I must have played that record a hundred times.[3]

There are two striking things about Dylan's description of the conversion he underwent in Buddy Holly's presence. "He filled me with conviction," Dylan relates. "He looked me right straight dead in the eye, and he transmitted something. Something I didn't know what. And it gave me the chills." The palpably religious tone of these words was echoed in Dylan's account of listening to the Leadbelly album: "It was like an explosion went off. Like I'd been walking in darkness and all of the sudden the darkness was illuminated. It was like somebody laid hands on me." The biblical tenor of this account is no accident. Dylan's subsequent career has made it clear that he has been a grateful inheritor of the Jewish and Christian tradition.

Dylan began his account of his life with a reference to an extraordinary moment when his own calling was awakened. The encounter he described was one about which we might say that a longing was awakened. When we speak of longing, what do we mean? And why do we use

---

3 Bob Dylan, 2016 Nobel Lecture in Literature. Emphasis added.

that word for it? If we stop to savor the word, we soon find ourselves wondering about one of the truly most distinctly human experiences. Most of us will immediately recognize the difference between what we mean when speaking of *desire* and what we mean when speaking of *longing*, even though we may be at a loss to explain the difference. If René Girard taught us that desire is mimetic, Hans Urs von Balthasar has made a similar argument with respect to that deeper and richer form of desire we call longing.

> What is a person without a life-form, that is to say, without a form which he has chosen for his life, a form into which and through which to pour out his life, so that his life becomes the soul of the form and the form becomes the expression of his soul? For this is no extraneous form, but rather so intimate a one that it is greatly rewarding to identify oneself with it. Nor is it a forcibly imposed form, rather one which has been bestowed from within and has been freely chosen. Nor, finally, is it an arbitrary form, rather that uniquely personal one which constitutes the very law of the individual. Whoever shatters this form by ignoring it is unworthy of the beauty of Being, and he will be banished from the splendor of solid reality as one who has not passed the test. Thus, while physically he remains alive, such a person decays to expressionlessness and sterility, is like the dry wood which is gathered in the Gospel for burning. But if man is to live in an original form, that form has first to be sighted. One must possess a spiritual eye capable of perceiving the forms of existence with awe.[4]

Such a life-form, Balthasar declares, is neither extraneous nor externally imposed; it is both "bestowed from within" and "freely chosen." It is "uniquely personal." Even more germane to our theme is his insistence that if one is to live an original form, "that form has first to be sighted." When a corona of mystery and meaning surrounds the figure who has awakened a longing in another, something distinctively religious occurs, however confused, misdirected, and even evanescent the experience might be. As Balthasar notes:

> ... the natural man, if he has not already been artificially corrupted, does have a sense of awe in the face of the hidden mystery of being, in face of the ultimate origin and destiny

---

4 Balthasar, *The Glory of the Lord*, Vol. 1: *Seeing the Form*, 24.

of the world, of matter, of life, of evolution, of the fate of the individual and of humanity. Every religion, from the most primitive to the most sophisticated, lives essentially on this awe.[5]

In retrospect, Dylan's encounter with Buddy Holly seems to have been an initial moment in the unfolding of his unique personal vocation. His subsequent career, as those who have followed it well know, has taken many twists and turns. But it was when Dylan was in his late thirties that one of the most remarkable and unexpected turns occurred, causing something of a stir among his most loyal fans. It was the release of Dylan's 1979 album *Slow Train*, and specifically Dylan's song "Gotta Serve Somebody," the first lines of which are:

> You may be an ambassador to England or France
> You may like to gamble, you might like to dance
> You may be the heavyweight champion of the world
> You may be a socialite with a long string of pearls
>
> But you're gonna have to serve somebody, yes
> Indeed you're gonna have to serve somebody
> Well, it may be the devil or it may be the Lord
> But you're gonna have to serve somebody.

Dylan here performed an important service by suggesting that ultimately our lives will be lived in service.[6] It is the brevity of each life and the opacity of our self-understanding that prevent us from recognizing the truth Dylan was trying to honor. Nor should we pass over the fact that in this song Dylan enumerated only two options — the devil and the Lord — with the innuendo that this is what constituted the real drama and eschatological meaning of the choice. As one might expect, such a choice would have observable consequences in the life of the one who made it. As K. V. Turley observed, the choice Dylan was making would soon manifest itself in his demeanor and artistic expression.

> Whereas, before 1979, there was a slow-burn rage at injustice and lies, after his conversion that rage is filtered through the lens of the Gospel. Previously, Dylan had come across as something of an Old Testament prophet, pointing out what was wrong

---

[5] Hans Urs von Balthasar, *Elucidations*, trans. John Riches (San Francisco: Ignatius Press, 1998), 39.
[6] As we will see in future chapters, the word *performed* makes its own contribution to the mystery we are exploring.

in society; post-conversion, he had encountered the Messiah: then Dylan was not so much pointing out what was wrong as pointing to the only Person who could make things right.[7]

As these words are being written, the journey of Bob Dylan continues, and few dare predict what surprises might await Dylan and his loyal fans. We have chosen to begin our reflections with his encounter with Buddy Holly because his emphasis on its biographical importance exemplifies the mystery we will be exploring in the pages to follow, namely the trans-mission of a mission and its importance in the formation of the human person.

Thérèse of Lisieux (1873–1897) was a Carmelite nun who was canonized in 1925 and — remarkably, given her youth, cloistered life, and early death — declared a Doctor of the Church by John Paul II in 1997. One could hardly find someone whose life experience differed more from that of Bob Dylan. In one respect, however, the onsets of their respective vocations are comparable even though this first stirring of a spiritual awakening in the young French girl occurred in her infancy. Near the end of her short life, she was asked by her Carmelite Prioress Mother Agnes — who was, in fact, Thérèse's older sister Pauline — to write what would become the *Story of a Soul*, a spiritual classic. In it she wrote:

> I was very proud of my two sisters, but the one who was my ideal from childhood was Pauline. When I was beginning to talk, Mama would ask me: "What are you thinking about?" and I would answer invariably: "Pauline!" Another time, I was moving my little finger over the windowpanes and I said: "I'm writing Pauline!"
>
> I had often heard it said that surely Pauline would become a religious, and without knowing too much about what it meant I thought: "I too will become a religious." This is one of my first memories and I haven't changed my resolution since then! It was through you, dear Mother, that Jesus chose to espouse me to himself. You were not with me then, but already a bond was formed between our souls. You were my ideal; I wanted to be like you, and it was your example that drew me toward the Spouse of Virgins at the age of two.[8]

---

7   K.V. Turley, "'Gotta Serve Somebody' — Kanye West and Bob Dylan," *National Catholic Register*, Nov. 19, 2019.
8   *Story of a Soul: The Autobiography of Saint Thérèse of Lisieux*, trans. John Clarke, O.C.D. (Washington, DC: ICS Publications, 1996), 20.

This devotion to her sister was deepened when Pauline became Mother Superior of her convent. She would later write: "O Mother, it was especially since the blessed day of your election that I have flown in the ways of love. On that day Pauline became my living Jesus."[9] Again, we see the powerful role that a mediator plays in awakening a sense of purpose, a vocation. In a much later chapter, we will return to Thérèse and to another mediator in her life, one no less germane to our exposition.

We turn for the moment to a fictional depiction of the awakening of a longing, in this case one that is both wildly improbable and nonetheless insightful. It is "Parker's Back," a short story by the self-described Hillbilly Thomist, Flannery O'Connor. It is a story so rich in insight that we might dwell on it at greater length, but we must limit our reflection to a few details. The eponymous main character of the story, O. E. Parker, is a typically O'Connoresque figure: sullen, defiant, ignorant, and shiftless. In other words, a sinner like the rest of us. Of whom O'Connor writes:

> His mother wept over what was becoming of him. One night she dragged him off to a revival with her, not telling him where they were going. When he saw the big lighted church, he jerked out of her grasp and ran. The next day he lied about his age and joined the navy.[10]

As so predictably happens, the flight from what is perceived as the narrow constraints of Christianity prefaces a supine submission to another, less reliable, and far more circumscribed existence. Under the circumstances, the navy was hardly the worst choice Parker could have made, but the aptness of the choice was largely vitiated by the fact that he made it in order to avoid a brush with Christianity.

O'Connor's fictional O. E. Parker is of interest to us inasmuch as he had an experience not unlike the one that Bob Dylan had when Buddy Holly looked him "right straight dead in the eye" and that young Thérèse had when she thought: "I too will become a religious." In Parker's case, however, the encounter was entirely burlesque. It happened quite at random when at the age of fourteen he saw the tattooed man at the county fair.

---

9   Ibid., 174.
10 Flannery O'Connor, *The Complete Stories* (New York: Farrar, Straus and Giroux, 1973), 513.

> Except for his loins which were girded with a panther hide, the man's skin was patterned in what seemed from Parker's distance — he was near the back of the tent, standing on a bench — a single intricate design of brilliant color. The man, who was small and sturdy, moved about on the platform, flexing his muscles so that the arabesque of men and beasts and flowers on his skin appeared to have a subtle motion of its own. Parker was filled with emotion, lifted up as some people are when the flag passes.[11]

At roughly the age when Catholic adolescents receive the sacrament of Confirmation and young Jews receive their Bar Mitzva, young Parker experienced his conversion quite haphazardly. With irony and humor O'Connor captured something of what happened to Bob Dylan at the Buddy Holly performance, very much including the religious tonality of the experience. Something about Buddy Holly "seemed permanent, and *he filled me with conviction.*" Parker "was filled with emotion, lifted up as some people are when the flag passes." These are palpably religious experiences, albeit inchoate ones. Until he saw the man at the fair, it did not enter Parker's head "that there was anything out of the ordinary about the fact that he existed."[12]

O'Connor deftly notes that Parker's epiphany occurred when he caught a glimpse of the tattooed man while standing on a bench near the back of the tent. From his distance, the farrago of tattoos "seemed a single intricate design of brilliant color." The tattooed man became Parker's living inspiration: "He had his first tattoo some time after — the eagle perched on the cannon. It was done by a local artist. It hurt very little, just enough to make it appear to Parker to be worth doing."[13]

That the tattoo was made more meaningful by the fact that it hurt, albeit very little, is an allusion to the intertwining of meaning and sacrifice typical of O'Connor.

In a world in flux, the acquisition of a tattoo constitutes something of an irrevocable decision, but in Parker's case the satisfaction he felt was short lived. He returned to the tattooist to get another tattoo, and then another and another. Not only did he fill up more spaces on his skin with tattoos, but the themes he chose as advertisements for himself evolved toward incoherence.

---

11   Ibid., 512–13.
12   Ibid., 513.
13   Ibid.

> He had stopped having lifeless ones like anchors and crossed rifles. He had a tiger and a panther on each shoulder, a cobra coiled about a torch on his chest, hawks on his thighs, Elizabeth II and Philip over where his stomach and liver were respectively. He did not care much what the subject was so long as it was colorful; on his abdomen he had a few obscenities but only because that seemed the proper place for them.[14]

Parker returned again and again to the tattooist to light up his body with insignias chosen quite at random. In time, the appeal of each image would wear off and he would return to the tattooist for another one.

> Parker would be satisfied with each tattoo about a month, then something about it that had attracted him would wear off. Whenever a decent-sized mirror was available, he would get in front of it and study his overall look. The effect was not of one intricate arabesque of colors but of something haphazard and botched. A huge dissatisfaction would come over him and he would go off and find another tattooist and have another space filled up.[15]

O'Connor has here depicted the crisis of the sovereign self more insightfully than most of those who are ostensibly more qualified to do so. Ultimately of course, O. E. Parker's effort to lash all the psychological fragments of his existence together and make a raft out of them failed. His furious attempt to avoid self-disintegration by covering his body with one logo after another was having the effect of accelerating his psychological dissolution. For O'Connor, the incoherent assemblage of tattoos that covered Parker's body was symbolic of a spiritual disorder, one which in due course we will scrutinize under the rubric of hysteria, or better still: hysterical multiphrenia. Meanwhile, not even our Hillbilly Thomist could have predicted what has occurred in the half-century since this story was published, namely an overwhelming explosion of compulsive tattooing. Nor was this the only instance of O'Connor's prescience.

> His dissatisfaction, from being chronic and latent, had suddenly become acute and raged in him. It was as if the panther and the lion and the serpents and the eagles and the hawks had penetrated his skin and lived inside him in a raging warfare.[16]

---

14   Ibid., 514.
15   Ibid.
16   Ibid.

Mediation

The incipient religious awakening the tattooed man at the county fair had aroused failed to turn Parker's eyes upward, but now, his psychological integrity imperiled, he sought solace in another tattoo. O'Connor endowed her sullen and prideful protagonist with just that dollop of groping good sense to return to the tattooist one last time, determined to get a tattoo on the one available space — his back. This time, it had to be a tattoo of God. O'Connor's playfulness is on display in the exchange between Parker and the tattooist.

> "Let me see the book you got with all the pictures of God in it," Parker said breathlessly. "The religious one." . . .
> "Who are you interested in?" he said, "saints, angels, Christs or what?"
> "God," Parker said.
> "Father, Son or Spirit?"
> "Just God," Parker said impatiently. "Christ. I don't care. Just so it's God."[17]

Earlier in the story, O'Connor noted that the pain involved in his tattoos hurt "just enough to make it appear to Parker to be worth doing." This dim recognition of the self-sacrificial nature of the human vocation would reappear on his final visit to the tattoo artist. The tattooist handed him a book of religious images, recommending the "up-to-date ones" in the back of the book — "The Good Shepherd, Forbid Them Not, The Smiling Jesus, Jesus the Physician's Friend" — but Parker flipped frantically to the front of the book until he was arrested by "the haloed head of a flat stern Byzantine Christ with all-demanding eyes." The tattooist warned him: "That'll cost you plenty."

"Choice always involves choosing a model," writes René Girard, "and true freedom lies in the basic choice between a human or a divine model."[18] This perfectly valid insight can be further elucidated by distinguishing between a model and a mediator, a distinction that parallels that between an idol and an icon. A model can be imitated; indeed that is what the term means. A mediator, on the contrary, directs the desire he has awakened toward another, more spiritually efficacious, object of fascination. But of course, these forms of mimetic influence are not exclusive, far from it. It is often the case that one is attracted to

---

17 Ibid., 521 22.
18 René Girard, *Deceit, Desire, and the Novel*, trans. Yvonne Freccero (Baltimore: Johns Hopkins University Press, 1965), 83; 58.

a model for sundry reasons, whether superficial or more worthy, only to discover over time that what fascinates is less the distinctive features of the model and more the transcendent orientation that is the secret source of the fascination the model has aroused. At the point when the imitator becomes less interested in his model than in the source of the model's exemplarity, he has stumbled upon the mystery we are here exploring.

Few are awakened to the attraction of a divine model without the influence of an intermediate human mediator. Without the influence of his mother and her Christian faith, the fictional O. E. Parker's attraction to Christ would have lacked narrative plausibility. O'Connor was perceptive enough to have known that, which is why her brief mention of his mother's failed attempt to get him to church is so essential to her story. Parker would hardly have sought to relieve his fractured soul the way he did had not his mother and her Christian faith prepared him for it.

3 A Mimetic Anthropology

> It would be lamentable if sociology became an alibi for an era of religious indifference or short-sighted pragmatism, if it sought to be a substitute for philosophical research and meditation on the Gospel, if it were to transform itself in the hands of the faithful into an instrument for the profanation and finally the destruction of the faith.
>
> — Henri de Lubac[1]

> Alone of his generation of literary scholars, Girard bore within him the conviction that Western civilization, however much it owes to the intellectual and political foundations laid by Athens and Rome, is first of all the product of Jerusalem, of Judeo-Christian history.
>
> — Eric Gans[2]

RENÉ GIRARD, FORMER CHAIR OF FRENCH CUL-ture and Civilization at Stanford University, died in 2015, leaving behind an incomparable contribution to the social sciences generally and to Christian self-understanding specifically. We have tried previously to harvest some of the fruits of his work, first in *Violence Unveiled: Humanity at the Crossroads*[3] published in 1995, and in 2016, *God's Gamble: The Gravitational Power of Crucified Love*.[4] The present book calls on Girardian thought for yet another purpose, namely that of reckoning with what we are calling the apocalypse of the sovereign self. For the mimetic nature of human subjectivity which Girard explicated so

---

1 Henri de Lubac, *Paradoxes of Faith*, trans. Paule Simon and Sadie Kreilkamp (San Francisco: Ignatius Press, 1987), 123–24.
2 Eric Gans, "Originary phenomenology, naïve and hypothetical," *Chronicles of Love and Resentment* (blog), May 14, 2022.
3 Gil Bailie, *Violence Unveiled: Humanity at the Crossroads* (New York: Crossroad, 1995).
4 Gil Bailie, *God's Gamble: The Gravitational Power of Crucified Love* (Kettering, OH: Angelico Press, 2016).

lucidly throws light on a cultural, spiritual, and psychological situation that has become so endemic today that it tends to elude detection. His insights into the mimetic nature of human subjectivity will be useful in assessing the looming crisis of nihilism now threatening to engulf the once-Christian West.

René Girard, with whom this writer had a decades-long friendship, was led by the force of his own research from what de Lubac called a "basic attitude of real sympathy" to a simple, unaffected return to the Catholic faith of his youth. A personal anecdote (one of many) might serve to capture the simplicity and artlessness of Girard's religious faith. On a flight with this writer to an interview in Los Angeles many years ago, René passed the time by taking from his pocket a very small and very well-worn copy of the New Testament, from which he read with obvious intensity. Both the frayed pages of the text and the casual manner with which René consulted it suggested long familiarity.

Girard's cultural insights begin with an anthropologically convincing explanation of how the mimesis of desire sets in motion ever more vertiginous cycles of envy, jealousy, rivalry, and violence. He shows how, prior to the gradual compromising of this system by the Judeo-Christian revelation, conventional cultures were able to emerge from the ever-recurring crises to which mimetic entanglements lead by virtue of yet another form of mimesis which, for the purpose of the present exploration, we might call "social hysteria," and which we will analyze in later chapters. These social crises gave rise to the first rudimentary forms of social cohesion at the expense of the hapless victim on whom the incipient community's aggregate animosities were eventually offloaded, in scenes structurally identical to the one on Golgotha — which revealed both the truth about our fallen condition and the reason why God chose to redeem us by dying on a cross.

The Swiss cultural theorist, Denis de Rougemont, fairly anticipated the essence of Girard's later work in one of his letters, and a passage from it merits a lengthy quotation:

> The individual appears to me as the being that tears itself away from the dark sacredness, from the terror of the tribe, and profanes the taboos on the basis of antisocial Reason. It appears to me a necessary, preliminary stage for the appearance of the person. But if one remains at this preliminary stage, then one receives nothing more than anarchy, the social vacuum. There are then two possibilities: either artificially reconstruct the

sacred (racism or communism of the state) or accept an always urgent *vocation* that distinguishes the human being and binds him at the same time to his neighbor and founds the church. Only in such a community does the person exist truly. Person, act, vocation become for me virtually synonymous. The act is concrete obedience to a transcendent vocation: vocation brings forth the person in the *individuum*. Hence this new definition: the *individuum* is the natural man; the person is the new creature, as Paul understands it.[5]

"It is increasingly more evident," wrote the French philosopher and playwright Gabriel Marcel, "that intersubjectivity is the cornerstone of a concrete ontology."[6] To which one would have to add that this cornerstone was the stone rejected by the founding architects of modern social science. With his mimetic anthropology, Girard returns the cornerstone of intersubjectivity to its proper place, inviting us to recover forms of personhood of which both the Old and New Testaments give us a glimpse.

What follows is an interwoven montage of highly anecdotal snapshots of the postmodern self and its besetting distresses, including brief allusions to the roles played inadvertently by Augustine and more dubiously and culpably by Descartes, Rousseau, Freud, and their progeny and concluding with a reference or two to the contemporary effort to put the best face on the resulting crisis. In each of the chapters we will try to tease out one of the facets of the overall problem: the apocalypse of the sovereign self. The antecedents of this crisis have been rehearsed by many analysts more qualified than this writer. The purpose of this review of the older roots and contemporary consequences of our psycho-spiritual predicament is not excoriation but exemplification: to show a persistent antipathy, on one hand, toward evidence of the mimetic nature of human subjectivity and, on the other, the radical newness of the mystery of the person that the Christian revelation brought into view. We will begin by proffering evidence of the role of mimesis in human affairs, on which René Girard finally performed the long-awaited reconnaissance. The "originality" of Girard's thought paradoxically depended on his genius

---

[5] Quoted in Hans Urs von Balthasar, "On the Concept of Person," *Communio* (Spring 1986): 25.
[6] Gabriel Marcel, *The Mystery of Being*, Volume II, *Faith and Reality*, trans. René Hague (Lanham: University Press of America, 2011), 170.

for recognizing the antecedents of his approach in the work of his distinguished predecessors, whose mimetic intuitions, though occasionally noted, were largely left unremarked due to intellectual conventions and habits of thought of their subsequent interpreters.

"Talk to me of originality and I will turn on you with rage," wrote William Butler Yeats. Had Yeats lived before 1776, however, his rage might well have lain dormant, for it was only at that late date that the word originality came into popular usage. That "originality" enters English usage at the end of the eighteenth century, coincident with both the American and French Revolutions, is surely worthy of note. As is the fact that the word *individual* appeared at the same time. The need to be original is both one of the most telling signs of an existing mimetic crisis and the favored ruse for obscuring it. Whereas the run of the mill scramble for originality is often embarrassing and comical, the same competition among intellectuals can be for what appear to be real stakes: professional prestige. In 1996 René Girard told his interviewer:

> ... the way in which we intellectuals seek to differentiate ourselves from one another by ceaselessly inventing pseudo-differences, revolts that are even more radical than the ones that came before, leads to avant-garde fashions that are ever more sheep-like, ever more repetitive. In a hundred years, the imperative of originality at all costs has killed creativity.[7]

In due course, we will turn to the radically new understanding of the person that Christianity made possible, which we will reconnoiter and, as best we can, present as a challenge to reigning notions of human subjectivity and propose as an alternative to the deepening crisis that those notions have brought upon us.

In what immediately follows, however, we will bring Girard's insights to bear on a few literary, historical, and journalistic works, beginning with Arthur Miller's *Death of a Salesman*. In this play — appearing exactly in the middle of the twentieth century — Miller touches on a whole range of distresses on which Girard would throw so much light a generation later. The playwright has left us a literary treasure trove enabling us to tease out issues which we will explore in subsequent chapters.

---

7 Cynthia L. Haven, ed., *Conversations with René Girard: Prophet of Envy* (London: Bloomsbury Publishing, 2021), 75.

4 Willy Loman:
"THE MAN'S EXHAUSTED"

> De-Christianization drains all the drama out of the events of this world, which now become no more than the earthly course of events that unfolds in a less earnest, less anxious, and more natural way — or at least so it seemed at first.... The elimination of the world Beyond meant that its opposite, this world, lost much of its potency as well. The century of the Enlightenment was not just spiritually impoverished, then. It was also poor in inner-worldly sensuousness, hence superficial in the strictest sense of the word.
>
> — Erich Auerbach[1]

ARTHUR MILLER'S PLAY CAPTURES OUR CURRENT predicament at an earlier stage, and it limns its future trajectory with remarkable anthropological acuity. Far from compromising the value of Miller's most famous play, the fact that he knew nothing and could have known nothing of Girard's subsequent work and that he was something of a formulaic dramatist makes this play even more suitable for our purposes. Once we have applied the anthropological insights of René Girard in the relatively straightforward but nonetheless illuminating case that Miller's play provides, we will be in position to think more deeply about the nature, history, and evolution of the contemporary *self*, after which we will try to bring out by way of contrast the distinctively Christian understanding of the *person*.

In choosing to begin with a well-known and popular American drama, we are following Girard's own conviction that literary works are often much more insightful about social and psychosocial dynamics than are the works of social scientists and clinicians. By professional necessity,

---

1 Erich Auerbach, *Time, History, and Literature*, ed. James I. Porter, trans. Jane O. Newman (Princeton University Press, 2014), 274–75.

social scientists work in guilds. They are therefore more vulnerable than the more solitary writers of fiction to being swayed by the mimetic power of theories and intellectual fashions. Not only do literary artists work outside of such guilds, but they are forced by the nature of their work to give a believable account of social relations. Thus, they have often painted more accurate portraits of the spiritual and psychological exigencies of the late-modern or postmodern self. The psychological verisimilitude of these fictional works is directly proportional to the author's attentiveness to the role of mimesis in human affairs, or so Girard would argue.

In a subsequent chapter, we will note how those undergoing the loss of "ontological density" will often attempt to compensate for the loss by attracting the attention of others — social notoriety supplying a facsimile of ontological substantiality. Miller recognizes the ultimate vacuity of this makeshift psychological reassurance in one short comment at the end of the play, at Willy's funeral. Willy's next-door neighbor and only friend says to Willy's son, Biff:

> Willy was a salesman. And for a salesman, there's no rock bottom to the life. He don't put a bolt to a nut, he don't tell you the law or give you medicine. He's a man way out there in the blue, riding on a smile and a shoeshine. And when they start not smiling back — that's an earthquake. And then you get yourself a couple of spots on your hat, and you're finished.[2]

The protagonist of Arthur Miller's play is "a man way out there in the blue, riding on a smile and a shoeshine." In reality Willy is a hapless and aging salesman wearied by a life-long effort to maintain some sense of the meaning and value of his life. The play leaves no doubt that Willy's spiritual crisis began with the absence of a model. The single most salient fact about him is somewhat casually alluded to in the play: his fatherlessness. "Dad left when I was such a baby," Willy tells the ghostly apparition of his self-made brother Ben, "and I never had a chance to talk to him and I still feel — kind of temporary about myself."[3] Feeling kind of temporary about oneself is cognate with the diminution of "ontological density" mentioned earlier. Willy admits to feeling temporary about himself in the same sentence in which he laments the absence of a father in his life. And at a moment in his youth when Willy obviously felt that his lack of a model was having

---

2   Arthur Miller, *Death of a Salesman* (New York: Penguin Books, 1998), 111.
3   Ibid., 40.

destabilizing effects that could no longer be ignored, he prepared to remedy the situation by going in search of the father by whom he and his family had been abandoned. The longing of a young person for parental figures who can serve as primary mimetic models can as easily give rise to romanticism as it did in Willy's case. He found respectable adjectives for the father who had abandoned him. He imagined him to have been an adventurous and self-reliant man, and he decided to go in search of him. Just then, however, another model happened to cross his path. Almost completely at random, Willy found a guiding star. Here's how he describes his conversion:

> Oh, yeah, my father lived many years in Alaska. He was an adventurous man. We've got quite a little streak of selfreliance in our family. I thought I'd go out with my older brother and try to locate him, and maybe settle in the North with the old man. And I was almost decided to go, when I met a salesman in the Parker House. His name was Dave Singleman. And he was eighty-four years old, and he'd drummed merchandise in thirty-one states. And old Dave, he'd go up to his room, y'understand, put on his green velvet slippers — I'll never forget — and pick up his phone and call the buyers, and without ever leaving his room, at the age of eighty-four, he made his living. And when I saw that, I realized that selling was the greatest career a man could want. 'Cause what could be more satisfying than to be able to go, at the age of eighty-four, into twenty or thirty cities, and pick up a phone, and be remembered and loved and helped by so many different people? Do you know? when he died — and by the way he died the death of a salesman, in his green velvet slippers in the smoker of the New York, New Haven and Hartford, going into Boston — when he died, hundreds of salesmen and buyers were at his funeral.[4]

The pathos of Willy's life is summed up and foreshadowed in this passage. Willy's tragedy was that longing for a father figure, bereft of a model, and desperately in need of one, he just happened to notice Dave Singleman, whose name fairly defines him as an individual in the late-modern sense of the term: a self-made man.

It is worth noting that Willy's paean to Dave Singleman, the man who was "remembered and loved and helped by so many different people," reaches its climax with a reference to his funeral, attended by so

---

4   Ibid., 60–61.

many admirers from among his business associates. How will one be remembered and by whom and for how long? We are all tempted by what Ernest Becker famously exposed as the false eschatology of human remembrance: a worldly immortality project. Percy Bysshe Shelley put paid to that account of worldly renown in his famous poem about the fallen monument to the thirteenth-century Egyptian ruler Ozymandias.

What attracted Willy to Dave Singleman was that others found him admirable. What Willy longed for was the admiration of others. Typically modern, Willy Loman hoped to parley the admiration of others into a source of ontological substantiation, thereby giving weight to his otherwise tenuous existence. Miller recounts the results of Willy's gamble with considerable psychological perceptiveness.

Willy's fatherlessness and his conversion to Dave Singleman lie in the past. Miller's play begins many years later, and in its first scene Willy's loving wife, Linda, says of Willy that "a terrible thing is happening to him.... The man is exhausted."[5] Willy had been coaxed into thinking if only he could achieve Dave Singleman's popularity, he might one day slip into a pair of green velvet slippers and get some rest. Augustine's contention that our hearts are restless until they rest in God would have been an apt epigraph to Miller's play. As would Catherine Pickstock's reference to the "inevitable erasure of the subject through its very over-assertion."[6] "The soul," writes Romano Guardini in the same vein, "needs that spiritual relaxation in which the convulsions of the will are stilled, the restlessness of struggle quietened, and the shrieking of desire silenced."[7]

A shopworn liberal trope regards traditions, especially moral and patriarchal ones, as antithetical to individuality. In fact, these traditions constrain or bracket the impulses and appetites, and in doing so they provide the scaffolding thanks to which one acquires the self-discipline indispensable to moral maturity and social responsibility. The modern self is undergoing what Eric Gans calls a "prolonged post-romantic agony,"[8] some of the more agonizing features of which we will now trace, beginning with Arthur Miller's depiction of the next generation of the Loman family.

---

5   Ibid., 40.
6   Catherine Pickstock, *After Writing: On the Liturgical Consummation of Philosophy* (Oxford: Blackwell Publishers, 1998), 199.
7   Romano Guardini, *The Spirit of the Liturgy* (New York: Herder & Herder, 1998), 93.
8   Eric Gans, "René and the Romantic Model of Self-Centralization," *Studies in Romanticism*, Vol. 22, No. 3 (Fall 1983): 434–35.

5 Hap and Biff Loman

> "I've had twenty or thirty different kinds of jobs since I left home before the war, and it always turns out the same. I just realized it lately.... I'm mixed up very bad. Maybe I oughta get married. Maybe I oughta get stuck into something. Maybe that's my trouble. I'm like a boy."[1]

BY TURNING DAVE SINGLEMAN INTO AN IDOL, A guiding star whom Willy never came to doubt, the elder Loman at least avoided the spiritual degradation into which his sons, suffering from a more elusive fatherlessness, would sink in the next generation. Willy's older son, Biff, is lost and he knows it. He says, "I don't know— what I'm supposed to *want*." Can we tolerate the idea that we may be made in such a way that there is something that we are *supposed to want*? Can we even use the plural pronoun in speaking this way? Can what each of us wants—at the deepest level—be what all our fellow humans want? With due attention to the unique vocation to which each of us may be called, is there a *human vocation*? The question Biff asks is more profound than at first it might seem. Biff wants to know what he is *supposed* to want. How oddly ironic that question seems to us today. We believe that we want what we want, and we want that simply because we want it. Well, yes, we admit that most of what we want are those experiences and those things that we have seen others wanting or enjoying. But still, in being attracted to what we see others having or wanting, we exercise just that degree of volition that convinces us that we are operating autonomously.

Miller was no Homer or Shakespeare, but he deserves credit for bringing to light the role of mimesis in both social and psychological life. Indeed, in his depiction of the next generation of the Loman family, Miller has given us a snapshot of two of the chief symptoms of the mimetic crisis. Biff Loman has lost all desire, while Happy Loman has managed to keep his desire intense enough to justify in the eyes of others

---

1 Miller, *Death of a Salesman*, 12.

the nickname Miller has given him. Like Willy prior to his encounter with Dave Singleman, Biff has yet to fall under the influence of a model.

> BIFF (*with rising agitation*): Hap, I've had twenty or thirty different kinds of jobs since I left home before the war, and it always turns out the same. I just realized it lately.... I'm mixed up very bad. Maybe I oughta get married. Maybe I oughta get stuck into something. Maybe that's my trouble. I'm like a boy. I'm not married, I'm not in business, I just — I'm like a boy. Are you content, Hap? You're a success, aren't you? Are you content?
>
> HAPPY: Hell, no!... (*moving about with energy, expressiveness*) All I can do now is wait for the merchandise manager to die. And suppose I get to be merchandise manager? He's a good friend of mine, and he just built a terrific estate on Long Island. And he lived there about two months and sold it, and now he's building another one. He can't enjoy it once it's finished. And I know that's just what I would do. I don't know what the hell I'm workin' for.... But then, it's what I always wanted. My own apartment, a car, and plenty of women. And still, goddammit, I'm lonely.[2]

Happy has solved his problem by wanting what his professional rivals want. He is trying to climb to the top over those above him on the professional ladder, whom he both envies and despises. Happy has avoided the existential crisis from which Biff is suffering by playing the game of mimetic rivalry and turning its intoxicating social imperatives into a substitute for a coherent direction in his life. "As soon as the subject who desires recognizes the role of imitation in his desire," writes René Girard, "he has to renounce either this desire or his pride."[3] That Hap Loman wants what the man above him on the corporate ladder wants can be taken as proof that he "recognizes the role of imitation in his desire," but he has renounced neither his desire nor his pride. Indeed, each has been enflamed by the knowledge of how empty is the game he is playing.

After quoting Louis Ferrero's comment, "Passion is the change of address of a force awakened by Christianity and oriented toward God," Girard writes:

> Denial of God does not eliminate transcendency but diverts it from the *au-delà* (the hereafter) to the *en-deçà* (the here and

---

2 Ibid., 12.
3 Girard, *Deceit, Desire, and the Novel*, 272.

now). The imitation of Christ becomes the imitation of one's neighbor. The surge of pride breaks against the humanity of the mediator, and the result of this conflict is hatred.[4]

This citation from very early in Girard's writing career reveals a thinker for whom the human predicament had been decisively altered by the Incarnation, death, and Resurrection of Christ and by the historical presence of Christianity thereafter. This is no small thing to observe, for it shows that the crisis Girard spent his life trying to comprehend was inextricably linked to Christianity and more specifically to the futile but nonetheless dangerous and increasingly disastrous attempt to abandon it with impunity. "Men boast of having discarded their old superstitions," writes Girard, "but they are gradually sinking into an underworld ruled by illusions which become increasingly obvious."[5]

Hap Loman is one of these. His recognition of the emptiness of the mimetic contest has enflamed his passion for victory all the more. Hap has played the game reasonably well, but he is finding its rewards uninteresting at exactly the rate at which he is attaining them. Happy can see both the superficiality of his model's life and the ridiculousness of his emulation of him. In other words, he is unable to ward off, as Willy managed to do, the recognition of the emptiness of the life of mimetic desire. As Hap shows, however, this recognition by itself will not necessarily lead to a renunciation of desire and its phantasms. The mimetic reflexes are so powerful that even though Happy knows that his model's desire is chimerical, he nevertheless mimics it. With a little of his father's gift for breezy self-delusion, he just manages to keep the knowledge of his own self-denigrating slavishness from rising fully to consciousness.

Happy is unable to resist the mimetic allure of his business superior for whom he has only contempt. This is what Ulysses in Shakespeare's *Troilus and Cressida* calls "pale and bloodless emulation" (Act I, scene 3), to which we will return below. Compared to Happy, his father is a nineteenth-century man. Hap Loman's spiritual disaster consists precisely in the fact that his mimetic fascination has become entirely rivalistic. The one thing he finds repugnant is discipleship, and under the circumstances he cannot be faulted for that. He is perfectly typical. The instant anything remotely suggesting a master-disciple relationship is constellated, the putatively autonomous self begins to prepare a *coup d'état*. Happy's rivalrous passions threaten to override the social norms

---

4 Ibid., 59.
5 Ibid., 61–62.

and conventions that ordinarily keep it within bounds. Of his professional superiors Happy says:

> Sometimes I want to just rip my clothes off in the middle of the store and outbox that goddamn merchandise manager. I mean I can outbox, outrun, and outlift anybody in that store, and I have to take orders from these common, petty sons-of-bitches till I can't stand it any more.[6]

This passage marvelously points out the utter insignificance of the desired object in the world of mimetic desire and the inexorable way rivalrous mimesis drifts toward violence. Having earlier declared that the merchandise manager was "a good friend of mine," he now wants to rip his clothes off and "outbox, outrun, and outlift" these "common, petty sons-of-bitches." That these two sentiments occur in quick succession suggests that the latter one is not a repudiation of the former one. Rather, Hap both envies and despises his model. In his characters Willy Loman and his son Happy, Arthur Miller captured the difference between what Girard calls *external* and *internal* mediation.

Girard used the words model and mediator more or less as synonyms, distinguishing between internal and external models or mediators. For him, external models were those whose superior position in a stable social hierarchy prevented or discouraged the imitator from a lower social strata from becoming the model's rival. As we shall see, that distinction is immensely important. For our purposes, however, we will use the word *model* for a figure who awakens a mundane desire, a desire for what the model desires or possesses — whether an object or a social distinction. We will use the word *mediation* or *mediator* for a figure who awakens a desire — a longing — distinguished by the religious corona that accompanies the awakening: Dylan's "it gave me the chills.... It was like somebody laid hands on me," or Thérèse of Lisieux's "On that day Pauline became my living Jesus." Balthasar argues that we are creatures whose "very existence seems to be a latent prayer."[7] Thus, a mediator — as we are using the term — refers to a particular kind of model, one by whom the latent prayer at the core of one's being is coaxed out of its latency and becomes salient.

In contrast, what Girard calls an external mediator — a member of a royal family for instance — is sufficiently inaccessible to those of

---

6 Miller, *Death of a Salesman*, 12.
7 Hans Urs von Balthasar, *Prayer*, trans. Graham Harrison (San Francisco: Ignatius Press, 1986), 44.

humbler social status for the latter to be tempted to contest the model for this or that royal prerogative. To the extent that a royal awakens a desire in a commoner, it might be a desire to conduct himself with some measure of the dignity that — from his distance — appears to be exemplified by the members of the royal family. Were he to desire to overthrow the royal family or level it out of spite, then he would be in an internal rivalry, with all the perils that involves for both the imitator and those proximate enough to his mimetic passions to be drawn into them.

The *ultimate* external mediation with which we are concerned is one in which a mediator reorients the model's attention toward a transcendent mystery. Notwithstanding religious or metaphysical claims on which this redirection of religious longing is based, the social efficacy of such a transcendent object of attention is manifold. It is precisely this form of mediation which takes the pressure off the social world by directing the deepest longing of the human heart upward, so to speak, thereby preventing this longing from surcharging mundane affairs with passions incompatible with social harmony.

For example, Girard explodes the seemingly commonsensical idea that the assault on established cultural norms or received moral standards occurs when those norms and standards have become onerous and antithetical to liberty properly understood. On the contrary, writes Girard:

> Social norms and restraints exist for the purpose of suppressing and moderating mimetic rivalry. The revolutionary spirit arises in an already half-disintegrated social order, one in which these norms and restraints are being relaxed and mimetic rivalries are very much on the increase.[8]

The distinction between external and internal mediation is indispensable. As long as the model inhabits a social station that is both above and beyond that to which the imitator might aspire, the imitator will be less likely to fall into a rivalrous relationship with his model. As the mimetic crisis deepens, however, and the last vestiges of even the most beneficial hierarchies are gradually leveled, the model-imitator relationship will tend to collapse into a model-rival one. Willy's undying admiration for Dave Singleman will be replaced by Hap Loman's glowering contempt for the man whom he both envies and imitates.

---

8   René Girard, *Resurrection from the Underground*, ed. and trans. James G. Williams (East Lansing: Michigan State University Press, 2012), 85.

THE APOCALYPSE OF THE SOVEREIGN SELF

Girard rescued from neglect the New Testament Greek word *skandalon* — which is often translated as "stumbling block" or "offense" — insisting on its value in understanding otherwise elusive social phenomena. The English word scandal comes much closer to how the Greek term should be understood. To be scandalized in this sense is to fall under the mimetic power of another in a negative way. One is scandalized when one's social independence is compromised by a fascinating figure with whom one has become mimetically entangled. There are two prevalent ways of eluding the mimetic influence of one who poses a threat to one's ontological integrity. The enthralled subject can enact a performance of some kind aimed at dramatizing his autonomy vis-à-vis the model under whose spell he feels himself falling. Or he can retreat into social hibernation in an effort to insulate himself from the mimetic fascination threatening his autonomy. As we will see below, each of these reactions represents an incipient form of hysteria.

Biff asks the obvious question: If Hap knows that the merchandise manager is an unhappy man, an unworthy model for emulation, why is he so determined to follow his example? Because, Hap replies, "when he walks into the store the waves part in front of him. That's fifty-two thousand dollars a year coming through the revolving door, and I got more in my pinky finger than he's got in his head." A casual reader might mistake this for some actual interest in something tangible, namely a handsome salary. Not so. Hap says, "I gotta show some of those pompous, selfimportant executives over there that Hap Loman can make the grade. I want to walk into the store the way he walks in."[9] Hap has chosen to compensate for the waning of his "ontological density" by competing with his professional superiors, but the prize for which he is competing is not the ostensible material advantages his rival enjoys. Rather it is the attention of others; social centrality — being known by others — a pale worldly facsimile of the experience of being known and loved by God.

Willy's desire was to be like Dave Singleman and to be "remembered and loved and helped by so many different people." What Hap desires is simply to be envied, pure and simple. What Willy admires, Hap envies. Hap is perfectly aware of how empty and unfulfilling his model's life is and how ridiculous it is for him to follow his example. Nonetheless, he cannot resist. If there is a situation in which the emptiness of a life of desire is about to declare itself, this is it. The forces opposed to that

---

9   Miller, *Death of a Salesman*, 13.

revelation, on the other hand, are considerable. For the Willy and Hap Lomans of the world are legion. Their desires drive the dynamos of our social and economic system, and increasingly the empty but more or less socially benign desires of Willy Loman are being supplanted by Hap's socially disruptive ones.

The root of the phenomenon we call "materialism," for instance, may be an exaggerated focus on desirable *objects*, the function of which is to distract us from the mounting evidence indicating that these desires are awakened and intensified by the desires of others. Materialism's focus on objects may be akin to the focus on the ball in team sports: it obscures the fact that the real source of the fascination is mimetic rivalry and not the inherent desirability of the object. This is even more the case when the desires in play are surcharged with sexual appetite. One is not surprised, therefore, to find that just when the vacuity of Hap's mimetic rivalry becomes obvious the conversation turns to women. At a point roughly corresponding to this in our cultural history, Freud invented psychoanalysis, turning attention away from the mimetic complications from which his patients were quite obviously suffering and toward a more titillating alternative. We will return to this matter below.

Desires that are fundamentally mimetic can be cast in sexual terms or made to serve what appear to be sexual ends, thereby camouflaging their mimetic nature for a little while longer. Speaking listlessly about his easy sexual exploits, Hap Loman says:

> ... take those two we had tonight. Now weren't they gorgeous creatures?... I get that any time I want, Biff. Whenever I feel disgusted. The only trouble is, it gets like bowling or something. I just keep knockin' them over and it doesn't mean anything.[10]

Hap's life is tracing the journey from romanticism to nihilism. The just quoted passage looks to be about the half-way point. At this point in his descent, Hap's philandering can be rescued from the tedium and revulsion that threatens to expose it only by framing his sexual exploits vis-à-vis a mimetic rival. Hap needs another's desire to awaken and intensify his own. He tells Biff:

> You're gonna call me a bastard when I tell you this. That girl Charlotte I was with tonight is engaged to be married in five weeks... the guy's in line for the vice presidency of the store.

---

10   Ibid., 14.

> I don't know what gets into me, maybe I just have an over-developed sense of competition or something, but I went and ruined her, and furthermore I can't get rid of her. And he's the third executive I've done that to.[11]

"He's the third executive I've done that to." Could it be more revealing than that!? Hap is talking about a sexual affair with a woman whom he purports to have desired, but he talks of his sexual liaison as though it were occurring entirely between himself and an executive with whom he is in professional competition. This fascination with his rival is eroticism bending under the power of mimesis toward the homoerotic. Hap Loman's eroticism was completely determined by a male rival, whose professional status was far more the object of his attention than was the woman who was but a pawn in his elaborate plan to take his rival down and to "walk into the store the way he walks in."

How much longer will we be able to convince ourselves that the sexual carnival underway in our world has genuine sexual ardor as its source? With each passing day, the evidence grows that the sexual promiscuity that is so pervasive in our world is a symptom of an underlying and much more destabilizing form of *psychological promiscuity*. It is the kind of psychological instability that occurs in a world where our models are rivals and our rivals models. Mistaking this problem for a sexual one and assuming that disease and pregnancy are its only perils, we are preparing our young people for lives of regret compared with which the laments of the forlorn Loman family will seem almost charming.

It is important to point out that the problem we are exploring is a perennial one, however large it looms in our culture today. We pause, therefore, to avail ourselves of Shakespeare's incomparable insight into this problem. The setting for his *Troilus and Cressida* is the Trojan war. The war itself was fought over Helen, who was married to the Spartan Menelaus but was seduced and carried off by Paris, the son of Priam, the Trojan king. Homer's *Iliad* is the story of the ensuing war between a coalition of Greek forces and the Trojans who had taken Helen. The *Iliad* begins with a rivalry within the Greek camp that mirrors the one for which the war itself was being fought: a rivalry between Agamemnon, the commander of the Greek forces, and his subordinate, the greatest

---

11   Ibid.

Greek warrior, Achilles. A beautiful slave woman awarded to Achilles for his valor was subsequently claimed by Agamemnon, pitting the titular leader of the Greek expedition against its incomparable champion.

Like the conflict between Hap Loman and the merchandise manager, the conflict between Agamemnon and Achilles as well as the one between the Greeks and the Trojans had little to do with its ostensible object: in both cases a beautiful woman. In each case what was at stake was the honor and prestige of the two men — and the two armies — competing for a woman made desirable precisely by that rivalry. In other words, as Homer makes perfectly clear, the conflict was purely mimetic. It was metaphysical. As such, it was capable of destroying the social order. But the unsurpassable analysis of the cultural dangers of such a situation was put into the mouth of Ulysses [Odysseus] by Shakespeare in *Troilus and Cressida*. The bard of Avon brilliantly analyzes the story told by the blind bard of Ionia.

The salient passage is the warning Ulysses gives his fellow Greeks about how catastrophic the consequences of the internal rivalry within the Greek camp can be. What the bard knows is that the utility of socially tolerable hierarchies will ever be threatened by mimetic rivalries so intense that the social stratifications that function to bracket the controversies give way, allowing conflict to break out across hierarchical boundaries, with potential catastrophic consequences. This, of course, is what was happening in the relationship between Hap Loman and his immediate superior. The danger of this collapse of social stratifications is what Shakespeare's Ulysses has in mind when he warns of the complete breakdown of solidarity within the Greek camp. The term that Shakespeare uses for hierarchies is *degree*, by which he means the social stratifications that function like firewalls, keeping mimetic rivalry in each social stratum from spilling over and infecting the wider society.

> Take but degree away, untune that string,
> And hark what discord follows. Each thing meets
> In mere oppugnancy. The bounded waters
> Should lift their bosoms higher than the shores
> And make a sop of all this solid globe;
> Strength should be lord of imbecility,
> And the rude son should strike his father dead...
> And this neglection of degree it is
> That by a pace goes backward with a purpose
> It hath to climb. The general's disdained

> By him one step below, he by the next,
> That next by him beneath; so every step,
> Exampled by the first pace that is sick
> Of his superior, grows to an envious fever
> Of pale and bloodless emulation...[12]

Hap Loman's goal — walking into the store the way the merchandise manager walks in — will by a pace go backward with a purpose it hath to climb. Pierpaolo Antonello and João Cezar de Castro Rocha express this same insight in the introduction to their extended interview with René Girard:

> The gradual erosion of every *dharma*, of every rigid social hierarchy and division based on sacral norms, has plunged the modern individual into mimetic social flux, deep into ever more extreme oscillations of desire and resentment mobilized by the increasing democratization of societies.[13]

We will return below to an analysis of the anthropological role of hierarchy in cultural life, but nothing we might add will improve on this soliloquy by Ulysses.

---

12 William Shakespeare, *Troilus and Cressida*, Act I, scene 3.
13 René Girard, *Evolution and Conversion: Dialogues on the Origins of Culture*, ed. Pierpaolo Antonello and João Cezar de Castro Rocha (London: T & T Clark, 2007), 13.

6 Pale and Bloodless Emulation

> Both modernism and postmodernism are helpless when confronted with the intensification of mimetic desire that necessarily accompanies the dissolving of all prohibitions.
> — René Girard[1]

THE PREDICAMENT OF ARTHUR MILLER'S BIFF Loman serves as a segue to Virginia Woolf's literary exposition of the apocalypse of the sovereign self. In 1931, when Woolf's experimental novel *The Waves* was published, a critic commented on Woolf's technique for elucidating her characters. In response, Woolf wrote in her diary that what the critic didn't notice about the characters in *The Waves* is that there weren't any. The characters in this novel are as caught up in mimetic intrigues as O. E. Parker and Hap Loman. Each attempts to shore up a semblance of ontological substantiality as best he can, but all — or perhaps all but one — fail in the end. Inasmuch as Woolf was brilliantly reconnoitering the spiritual landscape of late-modern Western culture, the novel in which she masterfully does so merits our attention.

Notwithstanding her psychological struggles and inner anguish, Woolf was a brilliant woman and a gifted writer. She cannot be said to have distinguished herself as a social or cultural analyst, but she was both observant and brutally honest, and she has left us immensely helpful evidence of the spiritual crisis in the midst of which we are living. Her novel, *The Waves*, consists of a tangled skein of stream of consciousness monologues by characters whose lives interweave from very early childhood until late in life.

Late in the novel, its chief protagonist, Bernard, admits: "I need an audience. That is my downfall.... To be myself (I note) I need the illumination of other people's eyes, and therefore cannot be entirely sure

---

[1] René Girard, *Anorexia and Mimetic Desire*, trans. Mark Anspach (East Lansing, MI: Michigan State University Press, 2013), 13.

what is myself."[2] Here we have an instance of what is both a perennial and an especially modern attempt to shore up one's ontological deficit by attracting the admiring — and in extreme cases even the contemptuous or condemnatory — attention of others. Balthasar has provided an exquisite commentary on the "downfall" of which Bernard complains:

> The world situation today shows clearly enough that whoever discards this Christian or at least biblical view must in one way or another find in a personless collectivism or individualism (which converge upon one another) his downfall.[3]

Woolf is no less withering when she turns her analytical searchlight on the women who seek sustenance in social notoriety. In an internal dialogue with the reader, Jinny, momentarily enjoying her hard-earned but precarious social centrality and teetering on the edge of hysteria, says:

> The stones of a necklace lie cold on my throat. My feet feel the pinch of shoes.... I am arrayed, I am prepared. This is the momentary pause; the dark moment. The fiddlers have lifted their bows.... I glance, I peep, I powder. All is exact, prepared. My hair is swept in one curve. My lips are precisely red. I am ready now to join men and women on the stairs, my peers. I pass them, exposed to their gaze, as they to mine. Like lightning we look but do not soften or show signs of recognition. Our bodies communicate. This is my calling. This is my world.[4]

Jinny is a coquette. She is made to feel real only when under the astonished glances of others. Sin, Sebastian Moore once wryly remarked, is seeing myself through other people's eyes. That is Jinny's sin, as it was Hap Loman's. Who of us is entirely innocent of it? One of Jinny's less socially successful classmates, Rhoda, is a young woman without a model. Her anguish is much like that of Biff Loman. "I have no end in view, she says; 'there is no single scent, no single body for me to follow. And I have no face.'"[5]

> Other people have faces; Susan and Jinny have faces; they are here. Their world is the real world.... See now with what extraordinary certainty Jinny pulls on her stockings, simply to play tennis. That I admire. But I like Susan's way better, for she

---

2 Virginia Woolf, *The Waves* (San Diego: Harcourt Brace Jovanovich, 1978), 115, 116.
3 Balthasar, "On the Concept of the Person," 25.
4 Woolf, *The Waves*, 101.
5 Ibid., 130.

is more resolute, and less ambitious of distinction than Jinny.
Both despise me for copying what they do.[6]

Rhoda admires Susan more than Jinny. Why? Because Susan is less ambitious of distinction than Jinny. Rhoda has entered the next room of the mimetic labyrinth. She realizes that other players in the game despise her "for copying what they do." Woolf's genius shines forth in her depiction of the girls and women in the novel, perhaps for obvious reasons. The novel's principal protagonist, however, is Bernard, with whom the novelist appears to have chiefly identified. Several of the novel's characters appear to be modeled on the members of the famous Bloomsbury Group, which included Virginia Woolf and her husband Leonard. The *Waves* character Bernard seems to have been the author's representative in the novel. He is a man who fancies himself an aspiring writer but whose copious literary efforts have produced only a shapeless mass of fragments. From his time at boarding school and beyond, he fancied himself a writer, filling notebooks with fragments to be used for the novels he never seemed able to produce. Late in the novel, Bernard, in a mood of reverie, sensing it to be a propitious moment for a sagacious literary figure like himself to muse thoughtfully on the meaning of his life, feigns an avuncular tone: "Now to explain to you the meaning of my life," he says. As he readies himself to tell the story of his own life, however, he rambles:

> But in order to make you understand, to give you my life, I must tell you a story — and there are so many, and so many — stories of childhood, stories of school, love, marriage, death, and so on; and none of them are true. Yet like children we tell each other stories, and to decorate them we make up these ridiculous, flamboyant, beautiful phrases. How tired I am of stories, how tired I am of phrases.[7]

We live today in a world where the word truth has been largely replaced by the word narrative. It is as though we are ashamed to use a word that is as stern and serious as truth. It is not just that truth seems too demanding a concept. The very word offends. Anything that is true puts lies and delusions and half-truths to shame. So like Bernard, we tell stories. We call them *narratives*, of which there are an unlimited number. And none of them are true not because one or another of them

---

6   Ibid., 43.
7   Ibid., 238.

might not be factually accurate but because these narratives are offered precisely in order to make truth a synonym for opinion.

When her main character acknowledges that none of the stories he has penned are true, Woolf is obviously referring to something that is of great personal interest to her as a novelist. Like her protagonist, she is wondering aloud about certain perils storytellers face, not least those who experiment with the literary fashion according to which the traditional architecture of narration is deconstructed in favor of an episodic cluster of more or less disconnected and inconclusive fragments, the literary signature of postmodernity. Bernard is awash in narratives and in the verbal and grammatical spare parts out of which they are constructed, but from none of his ridiculous, flamboyant, and beautiful phrases can he fashion a reliable story.

Speaking symbolically, we can say that the stories in Bernard's notebooks are untrue because Bernard cannot see how they might fit into a larger story, a story, say, of progress, or liberation, or evolution, or any of modernity's other flamboyant half-truths and wan hopes. Virginia Woolf lived at a time when the naïve liberationist Grand Narrative, that had functioned as modern liberalism's leitmotif, was fraying around the edges. For Bernard and for the world he personifies such stories about the meaning of history and the reasons for hope had begun to fall like so many drops into a sea of disenchantment. He dares not let himself believe in such a story for fear he will be disappointed once again and be ridiculed by his peers for having been gullible enough to believe it in the first place.

Without some sense of an overarching story, Bernard the storyteller cannot tell a story about his own existence. All the individual stories that might have become episodes in a larger story have no meaning. "None of them are true." "Of story, of design," Bernard says, "I do not see a trace."[8] What is lacking, as the older Bernard recognizes, is design. For a story to be true in the enigmatic sense in which Bernard uses that term, it must have a pattern; it must be a variation on a theme; it must be situated within a larger story.

When Bernard says of the stories with which he has filled his notebooks that "none of them are true," he makes such a blanket statement that we can scarcely conclude that the veracity these stories lack is due to mere factual inaccuracy. In the case of what Bernard later tells us are thousands of stories, so sweeping a statement about their untruth

---

8 Ibid., 239.

would hardly be justified by reference to their fictional nature. Bernard seems to know without having to reflect on their veracity that none of them are true. His stories are metaphorical novels, and the untruth of novels — which is no doubt what concerns Virginia Woolf — rests on something other than their facticity. To say, for instance, that *The Brothers Karamazov* is untrue is to use an impoverished notion of truth. Obviously, Virginia Woolf is pondering the fate of her own literary craft and even perhaps trying to rescue it from an act of evasion, about which she has become apprehensive. It would not be the first time Woolf explored the nature of the novelistic craft and its relation to truth. "If truth is not to be found on the shelves of the British Museum," she wrote in an essay fittingly entitled *A Room of One's Own*, "where, I asked myself, picking up a notebook and a pencil, is truth?"[9]

Just as one must go to the chapel scene to fully understand Shakespeare's Hamlet, the key to the enigma that Bernard represents is a scene that takes place at the boarding school chapel during Bernard's youth. Whereas Hamlet was made fatherless by the treachery of his uncle Claudius, Bernard and his classmate Neville participate in the cultural patricide from the dire consequences of which their cultural heirs continue to suffer.

Reminiscing years later about the tedium he felt during the obligatory chapel services, Bernard recalls how he and two of his classmates reacted to the headmaster's orations: "I did not hate him like Neville, or revere him like Louis. I took notes as we sat together in chapel... the Doctor booming, about immortality... I made notes for stories."[10] Thus Bernard finds relief from the headmaster's stentorian but otherwise moribund rendition of the Christian story by making up stories of his own.

With conspicuous autobiographical innuendoes, Virginia Woolf acknowledges that her novel's would-be novelist has turned to storytelling precisely in order to evade the story that was told and retold from the pulpit at the chapel of his boarding school. By contrast, Louis — a character almost surely based on T. S. Eliot, for whose Christian conversion Woolf seems to have had an intense fascination — relished the chapel services. Even as Woolf gently mocks Louis and by implication Eliot, she evinces a certain envy of his faith and the psychological poise it provides:

---

9   Ibid., 32–33.
10 Ibid., 242.

> "Now we march, two by two," said Louis, "orderly, processional, into chapel. I like the dimness that falls as we enter the sacred building. I like the orderly progress. We file in; we seat ourselves. We put off our distinctions as we enter. I like it now, when, lurching slightly, but only from his momentum, Dr Crane mounts the pulpit and reads the lesson from a Bible spread on the back of the brass eagle. I rejoice; my heart expands in his bulk, in his authority."[11]

In these few words, Woolf has captured a spirit of reverence and respect with such perspicacity that the passage pulsates with the author's longing for such things, even as she has felt the need to mock them. Louis welcomes the opportunity that the chapel provides for putting off the very distinctions which are the primary concern of the social melodrama taking place outside the chapel. Nonetheless, the character who expresses these sentiments, Louis, is no less threatened by the mimetic forcefield of his classmates. Doubtless the solace he feels during chapel services provides respite from these otherwise constant threats to his spiritual and psychological composure. He seems cognizant enough of his predicament to find comfort in the chapel where he is reminded of being a man with a heritage, grateful for its sustenance and accepting of its demands. Such a figure stands out, as did Eliot among Woolf's friends, in a world of forgetfulness. Of the headmaster, now in his role as chaplain, Louis muses:

> Now all is laid by his authority, his crucifix, and I feel come over me the sense of the earth under me, and my roots going down and down till they wrap themselves round some hardness at the centre. I recover my continuity, as he reads, I become a figure in the procession, a spoke in the huge wheel that turning, at last erects me, here and now.[12]

To Woolf's credit, she has aptly captured the experience of sensing oneself to be the grateful inheritor of a time-tested tradition by participating in a liturgical drama — even one as sacramentally attenuated as the one that took place in the boarding school chapel. For here Louis was able to feel himself in continuity with an ancient tradition. Nonetheless, she is equally insightful when she reminds her readers that Louis was alone in this, and that most of the boys in the chapel were bored or offended by the headmaster's oration.

---

11   Ibid., 34.
12   Ibid., 35.

It perhaps bears mentioning that the chapel service was centered no longer on the altar but on the pulpit and on the part-time cleric reading from it, now shorn of the sacerdotal status by which both the authority and the reliability of his pre-Reformation predecessors were sustained. Half a millennium ago, a large swath of Western culture gambled on the hope that this liturgical adaptation had the bandwidth, so to speak, to pour a living religious tradition into the lives of those in attendance. In Woolf's tableau, the reaction of two of the boys in attendance is a literary augury of the challenges now facing Christianity in a liturgically and sacramentally depleted Western culture.

In contrast to Louis's chapel experience, his classmate, Neville, had quite another reaction. While Louis was rejoicing at the opportunity that the chapel ritual provides to set aside social distinctions and experience himself as the fortunate inheritor of a tradition, Neville was having a more modern experience.

> "The brute menaces my liberty," said Neville, "when he prays. Unwarmed by imagination, his words fall cold on my head like paving-stones, while the gilt cross heaves on his waistcoat. The words of authority are corrupted by those who speak them. I gibe and mock at this sad religion."[13]

It is doubtless the case that words of authority are routinely corrupted by those who speak them. Those spokesmen are, after all, fallen creatures. The point, however, is that perhaps the most important role of authority is to designate that which is worthy of emulation. For Neville and his kin, what offends their narrow understanding of liberty is not the headmaster's dry and lifeless sermons. It is when the headmaster *prays* that Neville feels his liberty assaulted. Whereupon Woolf shows herself to be both insightful and brilliant in her literary execution. No sooner has Neville renounced the chaplain-at-prayer and everything for which he stands as an insult to the schoolboy's vaunted liberty than he turns an idolatrous glance toward one of his classmates — the most athletic, physically attractive, and least mentally gifted one, Percival.

> "Now I will lean sideways as if to scratch my thigh. So I shall see Percival. There he sits, upright among the smaller fry. He breathes through his straight nose rather heavily. His blue, and oddly inexpressive eyes, are fixed with pagan indifference upon the pillar opposite.... He sees nothing; he hears nothing.

---

13 Ibid.

He is remote from us all in a pagan universe. But look — he flicks his hands to the back of his neck. For such gestures one falls hopelessly in love for a lifetime. Dalton, Jones, Edgar and Bateman flick their hands to the back of their necks likewise. But they do not succeed."[14]

The eyes of the schoolboys were invited to look *up* — literally and metaphorically — to the headmaster-chaplain and to do so not because he was a gifted expositor of biblical verses or a homilist of distinction — he was, rather, something of a windbag — but because he represented something far greater and more worthy of attention than himself. Neville's response is a perfect parable of the crisis of the post-Christian West. Unwittingly invoking the Donatist heresy, Neville conflates the all-too-human messenger and the incomparable message to which he gave mediocre witness. He proudly refused to look *up* to the representative of a venerable tradition — clay vessel though he surely was. Having, so to speak, lowered his gaze, he immediately glanced horizontally in search of an object worthy of his desire. His glance fell upon the most physically impressive and mentally lethargic of his classmates, awakening in Neville a palpably homoerotic fascination.[15] Nor was he alone. Other classmates found Percival equally fascinating, less for homoerotic reasons than for Percival's athletic prowess and not least because of his apparent imperviousness to the mimetic influence of his classmates, so thoroughly was he preoccupied with the mimetic competition of the many sports at which he excelled.

Percival is the quintessential natural man, the athlete who lives and moves and has his being far below the level at which the aerial displays and dogfights of his classmates were taking place. His effect on others is precisely comparable to the effect of "the noble savage" on the European elite from the eighteenth century and beyond. His contemporaries stand speechlessly before what appears to be his immunity to the mimetic intrigue with which they are compulsively engaged. He is too lethargic — except on the cricket pitch or rugby field — to pick up on mimetic suggestions. In a remark that applies to Woolf's Neville, Girard has written: "The individual who is spiritually too limited to respond to

---

14 Ibid., 35–36.
15 Girard writes that "the fascination with the rival of the same sex will always give an impression of 'latent homosexuality,' especially if the observer does not understand the mechanism of the rivalry." René Girard, "The Underground Critic," *To Double Business Bound* (Baltimore: Johns Hopkins University Press, 1978), 52.

our advances enjoys, in his relationships with everybody, an autonomy which inevitably appears *divine* to the victim of metaphysical desire."[16]

Compared to his mimetically entangled classmates, Percival appears to be in a pagan universe all his own. As Neville observed on another occasion: "Percival lying heavy among us. His curious guffaw seems to sanction our laughter. But now he has rolled himself over in the long grass. He is, I think, chewing a stalk between his teeth. He feels bored; I too feel bored."[17] To those caught up in a mimetic maelstrom, boredom — if skillfully *performed* — gives one the appearance of being immune to the otherwise psychologically disorienting gravitational forces at work. We will return to the affectation of boredom, of being "remote from us all in a pagan universe," when we explore below the phenomenon of the dandy.

It is highly significant that Bernard's thoughts return to this scene at a critical moment in his life. He recalls one of the periods of restless ennui following the collapse of one of his many passing illusions. Seeking a diversion, he decides to go to Rome in his effort to alleviate his gnawing emptiness. *Rome*, mind you. Sure enough, Bernard soon finds himself sitting in a Roman piazza "like a convalescent," watching dreamily as a parade of Catholic priests passes by. Whereupon Woolf puts into his mouth the key to his existential plight, giving us one of twentieth-century literature's greatest summary descriptions of the spirit of our age. It appears in the lines immediately preceding Bernard's lament about never having found the one true story.

> In these dilemmas the devout consult those violet-sashed and sensual-looking gentry who are trooping past me. But for ourselves, we resent teachers. Let a man get up and say, "Behold, this is the truth," and instantly I perceive a sandy cat filching a piece of fish in the background. Look, you have forgotten the cat, I say. So Neville, at school, in the dim chapel, raged at the sight of the doctor's crucifix. I, who am always distracted... at once make up a story and so obliterate the angles of the crucifix. I have made up thousands of stories; I have filled innumerable notebooks with phrases to be used when I have found the one true story, the one story to which all these phrases refer. But I have never yet found that story.[18]

---

16 Girard, *Deceit, Desire, and the Novel*, 283.
17 Ibid., 38.
18 Ibid., 187.

Bernard's literary problem is indistinguishable from his spiritual problem, and Virginia Woolf has laid his spiritual problem bare. Languishing without direction or aspiration "like a convalescent," he watches as Catholic priests parade by in their long black cassocks. "In these dilemmas," he says, "the devout consult those violet-sashed and sensual-looking gentry who are trooping past me." "In these dilemmas," these gentry are consulted by those who face the question of meaning, not because these cassocked ecclesiastics are particularly wise or possessed of philosophical acumen, but because they represent a tradition that has for two thousand years encouraged the asking of that question and supplied the wherewithal for answering it. Bernard is in precisely the predicament of those countless people who have found their bearings by turning to that tradition. Bernard, whose stories were written in order to obliterate the angles of the crucifix, does not consult the representatives of the faith that the crucifix symbolizes, and he tells us precisely why: "for ourselves, we resent teachers." "Modern humanism," writes Henri de Lubac, "is built upon resentment and begins with a choice."[19]

The real meaning of Bernard's boarding school reminiscence, however, turns on the word "so" twice repeated. After revealing that the very existence of the kind of truth-claim the headmaster was trying to convey was enough to provoke resentment in Bernard and his classmates, Bernard says: "*So* Neville... raged at the sight of the doctor's crucifix" while Bernard, distracted as usual, makes up yet another story and *so* obliterates the angles of the crucifix. The word "so" directly links Neville's rage and Bernard's literary profligacy to the resentment felt by those who have declared their emancipation from any and all truths. Here is the heart of the matter: facts can be established by observation, science, and mathematics, but truth does not exist without the virtue of truthfulness. And Bernard, who bemoans the untruthfulness of his literary output, has produced that output, not in service to truth, but precisely in order to avoid a truth. The truth-claim, the one against which the whole ideological system has marshaled its forces, is the truth-claim represented by the crucifix. In order to counter this truth-claim, something like a literary slaughter of the innocents is required. To annul this truth while not revealing that it is specifically this truth which is being targeted for annihilation, all truth-claims must be ruled out of order. The heart and soul of secular relativism's contempt for

---

19 Henri de Lubac, *The Drama of Atheist Humanism* (San Francisco: Ignatius Press, 1995), 25.

"metanarratives" — and the worm of Western self-loathing to which it eventually gives birth — here stands revealed. Bernard's literary efforts are driven not by a quest for truth, nor even by a serious literary aspiration, but by a determination to evade a truth-claim the validity of which he refuses to adjudicate. The purpose of his stories is the elimination of one story, precisely the story which Christianity proclaims to be the one true story wherein can be found both the truth about God and the truth about man — the "meta-narrative" Rosetta stone for all substantive theological and anthropological thought.

It is important to recognize that the antipathy that Bernard and Neville feel toward the crucifix is not something peculiar to them due to their particular personality traits. Rather, this antipathy is something that characterizes the age in which we live. "The power of a word ought to be at its height when the said word is authoritative, when it is a commanding word," writes the French historian Rémi Brague. Ours, however, is an age suffused with a spirit that recoils from the authoritative word. Nor should we deduce from this that we live in an age of clear and critical thinking. Quite the contrary. The democratic age — the age of the *demos*, the Greek word for the masses — is distinguished by the fickleness of fashion, in intellectual matters as in others, driven not by rationality but by mimeticism. Of such an age, Brague asks:

> Can we still experience a word of this sort?... Does not speech today show us a much different face? That, for example of open discussion, which takes place within our democratic societies? The first condition for that speech is the rejection of any authority that would claim to emanate from somewhere outside the democratic space.... Any discourse that claims authority because of its origin is, as such, deeply suspect, soon to be disqualified. This means that the divine word, precisely as divine, has no place in the modern world.[20]

The beloved mentor and professor of literature and classics John Senior aptly describes how the spirit of the late modern age mitigates against one of the essential features of pedagogy which just happens to be an indispensable ingredient in the transmission of Christian faith as well. Senior writes:

---

20 Rémi Brague, *On the God of the Christians (and on One or Two Others)*, trans. Paul Seaton (South Bend, IN: St. Augustine Press, 2013), 79–80.

> The student who comes to his teacher and subject primed with what the modern university praises as the virtue of "critical intelligence," ruined by the shallow skepticism of Hume and Kant before he even starts, rejecting a priori anything which will not stand some superficial dialectical and arbitrary test to tickle his curiosity — such a student may acquire the technology of science and the humanities but he will never experience the reason for either. Such a critical intelligence, whatever its use in the marketplace, is prophylactic of the beautiful, the good and the true.[21]

Professor Senior's academic heirs would probably be happy to find students who were ruined by something as intellectually weighty as "the shallow skepticism of Hume and Kant." By comparison, a great many university students today wander in a world of virtue-signaling, political slogans, and momentarily fashionable clichés. Learning in the truly classical sense, writes Senior, requires that the student "become assimilated to the spiritual, intellectual and moral model of the teacher."[22] It is hard to imagine a prospect more repugnant to contemporary pedagogy, but it is one that finds solid confirmation in the widespread appreciation for the value of good models, in the Catholic practice of the veneration of saints, and in René Girard's anthropology of mimetic desire. Virginia Woolf's Bernard, of course, has been thoroughly disabused of the attitude requisite to the fruitful experience of these blessings. In point of fact, he and his classmate Neville recoiled from the admittedly less than ideal catechetical efforts of their boarding school's headmaster. Not only does Bernard resent teachers, he has begun to feel the gravitational attraction of the nihilist abyss. "What *delights* me," he acknowledges, "is the confusion, the height, the indifference and the fury. Great clouds always changing, and movement; something sulphurous and sinister."[23]

Quite obviously the reason Bernard does not turn to the Christian religious tradition — represented as though in neon by the Catholic priests trooping by — is not because he has subjected its truth-claims to scrutiny and found them wanting, but rather precisely because this hopelessly ancient tradition continues to have the temerity to make such claims in the first place. It is not the dubiousness of a Christian

---

[21] John Senior, *The Restoration of Christian Culture* (Norfolk, VA: IHS Press, 2008), 94.
[22] Woolf, *The Waves*, 95.
[23] Ibid., 239. Emphasis added.

truth-claim for which Bernard and his spiritual kin feel revulsion; it is the *existence* of it. It is the very fact that a truth-claim has been made. "Let a man get up and say, 'Behold, this is the truth,' and instantly I perceive a sandy cat filching a piece of fish in the background. Look, you have forgotten the cat, I say."

The spirit of our age will never be more succinctly revealed than it is in this passage. Let someone make a truth-claim, of the sort that Christians must make if the word Christian is not to lose its meaning, and those like Bernard imbued with that passive-aggressive, resentful, postmodern spirit will instantly glance around for something — *anything!* — to which they can plausibly point as an exception, something to which the claim does not apply, for it is precisely the universality of the claim that arouses the resentment. For to acknowledge a universal and objective truth is to face the necessity of assessing the claim with a mind open to its possible validity and a willingness, if that should prove to be the case, to adjust one's life accordingly.

Whether the fictional Bernard and Neville were aware of it or not, their literary creator was at least intuitively aware that they were participating in what René Girard has called "the Kafkaesque rejection of all meaning" which is nothing less, Girard argued, than the "panic-stricken refusal to glance, even furtively, in the only direction where meaning could still be found, [a refusal that] dominates our intellectual life."[24] So "panic-stricken" was Bernard's refusal to glance even furtively in the direction toward which the headmaster and the passing Catholic priests were trying to coax his attention, he was ready to resort if necessary to a cat filching a piece of fish.

No self-respecting person would counter a truth-claim by alluding to something as utterly arbitrary and accidental as a cat which in the rush to voice objection to the truth-claim one just happens to have seen stealing a piece of fish. No, one would refute such claims with philosophically or theologically or scientifically respectable arguments. However, Virginia Woolf knew from her experience among the group of writers and assorted intellectuals that constituted the Bloomsbury group that these more respectable arguments camouflage — often even from those who advance them — the real animus that drives them. The greater the intellectual urbanity of the counterclaim, the less apparent will it be that it is driven by resentment. By substituting a philosophically absurd counterargument

---

24   René Girard, *Things Hidden Since the Foundation of the World* (Stanford: Stanford University Press, 1987), 261.

in place of an intellectually reputable one, Virginia Woolf has revealed the often-unconscious motive that drives even the intellectually credible ones, namely resentment toward any and all truth-claims to which moral deference might legitimately be due. But is it really an antipathy for any and all truth-claims? It declares itself thus, but again Virginia Woolf lifts the veil. She allows any readers so inclined to recognize the underlying antipathy for Christianity that has caused Bernard and Neville to rebel against the very story that serves as the anthropological key for understanding the human drama and deciphering the postmodern malaise. It is that Golgothan crater at the center of history, of which we have spoken, that inflection of sacrificial love toward which everything before and after is ordered and by which it is properly understood.

To obliterate the angles of the crucifix is not only to deprive oneself of the Christian truth-seeking impulse that has transformed the world but also to surrender the key to understanding the looming crisis whose deeper meaning it is now our moral obligation to assess. For, as René Girard has himself argued, the Passion story at the heart of the Christian New Testament — against which Neville raged and which Bernard tried to obliterate by making up thousands of stories — is the key to both the human predicament generally and to the crisis of our age specifically. Without that story, "the most basic phenomena of human culture will remain misunderstood and unresolved."[25]

Where Miller depicted the pathos and banality of his main character, in *The Waves* Woolf more deftly reveals the spiritual anguish of the character with whom she most identifies. Near the end of the novel Bernard strolls by Saint Paul's Cathedral in London. What follows seems a reprise of the long-ago scene in Rome when Bernard refused to consult the passing priests out of resentment. At this point, the resentment he felt toward those still capable of proclaiming truth has subsided, but the shrugging reflex that accompanied it has become incorrigible. Musing about how his old classmate Louis might have felt at the steps of Saint Paul's, the world-weary Bernard acknowledges the cathedral to be a "brooding hen with its spread wings from whose shelter run omnibuses and streams of men and women at the rush hour."

> I thought how Louis would mount those steps in his neat suit with his cane in his hand and his angular, rather detached gait. With his Australian accent ("My father, a banker at Brisbane")

---

25 René Girard, *Violence and the Sacred*, trans. Patrick Gregory (Baltimore: Johns Hopkins University Press, 1977), 276.

> he would come, I thought, with greater respect to these old ceremonies than I do, who have heard the same lullabies for a thousand years.[26]

Whereupon Woolf pens one of the genuinely touching passages in her brilliant but forlorn novelistic reconnaissance. Bernard describes the scene and his response to it.

> My wandering and inquisitive eye then shows me an awe-stricken child; a shuffling pensioner; or the obeisance of tired shop-girls burdened with heaven knows what strife in their poor thin breasts come to solace themselves in the rush hour. I stray and look and wander and sometimes, rather furtively, try to rise on the shaft of somebody else's prayer into the dome, out, beyond, wherever they go. But then like the lost and wailing dove, I find myself failing, fluttering, descending and perching upon some curious gargoyle, some battered nose or absurd tombstone...[27]

Here is a man for whom the Church is an old and all-too familiar building and nothing more. He pities and mocks those "tired shop-girls"—amused by how they turn to prayer to solace their "poor thin breasts"—and he shows how poor and thin his own heart is. And yet, almost instinctively he tries to rise, like a lost and wailing dove, on the prayers of one of these little ones, only to flutter and descend upon some gargoyle. This is more than literary genius: it is pure prophetic poetry.

Woolf's novel is gargoylesque in just the sense of this exquisite passage. It both mocks and longs for what the cathedral represents and for what her friend T. S. Eliot found there. The author's fascination throughout the novel with Louis and his faith is countered by the gargoyles glaring down on those at prayer below, awaiting a pagan renaissance. But then, suddenly and remarkably, the descending dove gives even the gargoyle a place in the story. Which is what the cathedral architects did in the High Middle Ages. And in a very real sense it is what Virginia Woolf has done in this novel which can be read in two ways: as a devastating gargoylesque depiction of the human predicament in early twentieth-century Western culture or as a muffled cry of longing by one of the era's most perceptive and most imperiled literary artists.

---

26   Woolf, *The Waves*, 281.
27   Ibid., 282.

7 "None of Them Are True"

> But in order to make you understand, to give you my life, I must tell you a story — and there are so many, and so many — stories of childhood, stories of school, love, marriage, death, and so on; and none of them are true.
> — Virginia Woolf[1]

> When we write novels...we are reactivating a way of seeing that was inaugurated by the New Testament authors. Merely to take seriously the small, personal mysteries of everyday life, as novels do, is in some sense to adopt a Catholic Christian view on reality.
> — Trevor Cribben Merrill[2]

RENÉ GIRARD ONCE OBSERVED THAT WE ARE IN a world today "where truly novelistic works are perhaps no longer possible."[3] In 1993 the cultural historian, Charlene Spretnak, provided an explanation:

> During a recent visit with a professor of British literature at my *alma mater*, a Jesuit University, he lamented the fact that many students today have difficulty grasping the thematic structure of Victorian novels because they are nearly ignorant of the basic concepts of Christianity. He has to explain metaphors of the fall, grace, redemption, and so forth before he can teach the classic literature![4]

Two cultural characteristics dominate in our day: nostalgia and nihilism, often commingled and each highly romanticized by its aficionados.

---

1   Woolf, *The Waves*, 238.
2   Trevor Cribben Merrill, *The Situation of the Catholic Novelist* (Milwaukee: Wiseblood Books, 2021), 26.
3   Girard, "Underground Critic," 60, n1.
4   Charlene Spretnak, *States of Grace* (San Francisco: Harper, 1993), 3, quoted in Aidan Nichols, O.P., *Christendom Awake: On Re-energizing the Church in Culture* (Grand Rapids, MI: Eerdmans, 1999), 41.

Both testify to the spiritual wasteland in which we increasingly live. Of the two, nostalgia seems at least to have the virtue of preserving a longing for meaning and truth and the community of those who are grateful for such things. One thinks of the wistfulness of many of the otherwise brilliant poems of T. S. Eliot as well as Matthew Arnold's famous lines in "Dover Beach" wherein the poet manages to weave together strands of romantic nostalgia and melancholy nihilism.

> The Sea of Faith
> Was once, too, at the full, and round earth's shore
> Lay like the folds of a bright girdle furled.
> But now I only hear
> Its melancholy, long, withdrawing roar,
> Retreating, to the breath
> Of the night-wind, down the vast edges drear
> And naked shingles of the world.[5]

As René Girard argued in his first widely read book, the intrigues of mimetic desire are exploited in romantic novels and exposed for what they are in what Girard called "Romanesque" literature, the great novels. In romantic literature, the protagonist struggles to liberate himself from cultural hierarchies, confident that it is traditional social structures that threaten his freedom and happiness. In the Romanesque novel, the "metaphors of the fall, grace, redemption, and so forth" convey a moral seriousness which the liberationist tropes of romantic novels can only satirize or deride. In these "Romanesque" novels the protagonist is obliged to negotiate the tension between desire and the moral and social constraints that serve to both constrain it and bring it to maturity.

Great novelists can no longer simply exploit the mimetic dynamic that animates their characters and electrifies the otherwise humdrum people and plots of their novels. They must become ever more explicit about the mimetic dynamic, and they can only do so at the expense of the "romantic" appeal of their novels. Only when the mimetic dynamic of the novel remains recessive and eludes both the writer and the reader, can the former enjoy the literary advantages and the latter the liberationist titillation of the work. At the same time, as the wider mimetic crisis further compromises the social structures against which the protagonist of earlier novels struggled, the novelist must scour the landscape

---

5   Matthew Arnold, "Dover Beach," *The Poetical Works of Matthew Arnold* (London: Forgotten Books, 2018), 212.

or mindscape for ever more elusive constraints or use his literary gifts and anthropological ingenuity to expose the underlying operation of mimetic desire, thereby producing a work that is revelatory and, if the author is sufficiently gifted and sufficiently honest, perhaps a true work of art. The novelist will, therefore, either become complicit in the larger culture's exploitation of mimetic desire or join forces with the entire biblical tradition in revealing the truth about the drama of human affairs.

Even as the spirit of antinomian individualism has swept away moral and social constraints essential to both a well-ordered life and the political freedom it makes possible, here and there one finds evidence of a hunger for a restoration of a morally and socially ordered world. One indirect piece of evidence for this is the debate that has been going on for decades about what José Ortega y Gasset called the decline of the novel and Walter Benjamin called the crisis of the novel. There is little doubt that the novel is the quintessential literary genre of the modern age, and its fate is likely to throw light on the curious exigencies of modernity so aptly symbolized by the inability to imagine its sequel implicit in the term post-modern. Walker Percy called attention to "the peculiar diagnostic role of the novel in this [twentieth] century."[6]

> The hero or anti-hero of the contemporary novel hardly qualifies under any... mental-health canons — emotional maturity, autonomy, and so forth. Indeed, he, and more recently she, is more often than not a solitary, disenchanted person who is radically estranged from his or her society, who has generally rejected the goals of his family and his peers, and whose encounters with other people, friendships and love affairs, are regularly attended by misunderstandings, misperceptions, breakdowns in communication, aggressions, and withdrawals, all occurring in a general climate of deflated meaning. People in novels meet, talk, make love, and go their separate ways without noticeable joy or sorrow. Indeed, the main emotion one encounters in contemporary fiction is a sense of unreality, a grayness and flatness, a diminished sense of significance. Relations between people take the form of silences, misunderstandings, impersonal sexual encounters.[7]

More recently, Joseph Bottum has weighed in on the question of the novel's demise. "For almost three hundred years," Bottum writes, "the

---

6   Walker Percy, *Sign-Posts in a Strange Land*, ed. Patrick Samway (New York: Farrar, Straus and Giroux, 1991), 147.
7   Ibid., 142.

novel was a major art form, perhaps the major art form, of the modern world — the device by which, more than any other, we tried to explain ourselves to ourselves."[8] The novel, Bottum quite plausibly claims, was the art form that "gave us a fascination with the interior self, its emotions and its reasonings, greater and more insistent than anything the world had ever known before."[9]

> The decline of the novel's prestige reflects and confirms a genuine cultural crisis. This is not just the old crisis of the self, but a new crisis born of the culture's increasing failure of intellectual nerve and terminal doubt about its own progress.[10]

The fate of the novel is a matter beyond the competence of this writer, but he is persuaded that the reflections on this subject by the distinguished historian John Lukacs (1924-2019) are worthy of attention. Lukacs was concerned with "historical consciousness" for decades, and his insights into this subject are fascinating and germane to the present theme. He observed the relative eclipse of the novel by books of history and biography. By his reckoning, during the second half of the twentieth century there was a great increase in popular interest in books of history, an interest which apparently shows no signs of diminishing. This shift may not be as dramatic as it first appears, however, at least according to Lukacs's assessment of the novel: "Every novel is a historical novel, in one way or another."[11] That is just another way of saying that the novel is a distinctly modern genre which recounts some feature of the modern storyline — whether with glee or ennui. That storyline is the victory of freedom narrowly understood as an ever-wider latitude given to human desires at the expense of social or moral constraints. Every novel is a historical novel inasmuch as the genre itself is situated within what is regarded — by the modern mentality — as the very nature of history itself, namely the ever-expanding freedom of individual choices ever less inconvenienced by social or moral conventions at odds with the desires of the individual.

In Lukacs's telling, history books had begun to outsell novels. The History Channel had become famously popular. Documentaries and "docudramas" were drawing sizeable audiences. Something was afoot, as

---

8   Joseph Bottum, *The Decline of the Novel* (South Bend, IN: St. Augustine's Press, 2019), 1.
9   Ibid., 3.
10 Ibid., 5.
11 John Lukacs, *The Future of History* (New Haven: Yale University Press, 2011), 120.

Lukacs insists: "The historical appetites of many Americans have become unprecedented and considerable."[12] In an age as volatile and wrenching as ours, it would be easy to dismiss this interest as nostalgia. There may be some truth to that assessment, but if so, it only begs the question about why this is so. "Tell me what you see vanishing," wrote the poet W. S. Merwin, "and I will tell you who you are." Lukacs is helpful: "The original Greek phrase '*nostos algos*' meant a longing not for a certain time but for a certain home."[13] Whatever else such a home might be, it would be an ordered world in the context of which one's own life has a recognizable and worthwhile place, and nostalgia of this sort could be symptomatic only of how predictably the experience of being comfortably at home has eluded the inhabitants of the modern democratic age.

The reason Lukacs gives for the relative decline of the novel vis-à-vis works of history and biography may also help explain the experience of dislocation so common in our time. The fascination the novel held for readers throughout the modern period may have depended on social structures which were gradually being eroded by the simplistic egalitarian imperative into which the principle of Christian universal brotherhood was degenerating. The decline in the popularity of the novel especially vis-à-vis works of history and biography may be due, Lukacs muses, to the "almost complete disappearance of classes."

> For the standard subjects of the novel involved always, in some way or another, the relationships of the inner lives of persons with the external structure of society. But large portions of this scaffolding of society have now been dismantled or have simply disappeared, a development corresponding to the relative formlessness of the democratic texture of history.[14]

Louis Sass seems to concur. For Sass, subjectivism — what we have called the *sovereign self* — tends to "efface the very distinctions on which it depends, thereby bringing on states of confusion and fusion that, at their limit, can cause subjectivity itself to dissolve."[15]

The novelistic convention according to which the protagonist struggles against social structures and moral conventions becomes less and less compelling in a world where these structures have lost their force

---

12   Ibid., 64.
13   Ibid., 68.
14   Ibid., 126.
15   Louis A. Sass, *Madness and Modernism: Insanity in the Light of Modern Art, Literature, and Thought* (New York: Basic Books, 1992), 301.

and the real problem people face is the anonymity and alienation of hyper-individualism and the howling winds of cultural aimlessness. Lukacs quotes the Nobel prize-winning British novelist V. S. Naipaul: "A literature can grow only out of a strong framework of social conventions," adding: "This dissolution of classes, society, etc., led many a novelist in the twentieth century to contemplate increasingly an individual's relationship with himself. This awareness of self-consciousness reflects the crisis of the novel, as it involves the consciousness of the narrator."[16]

For his part, the English novelist and journalist appositely named Will Self published an article in the May 7, 2014, edition of *The Guardian* in which he lamented: "How do you think it feels to have dedicated your entire adult life to an art form only to see the bloody thing dying before your eyes?" Though Self, mistakenly in our view, attributes much of the decline of the novel to the recent move from print to digital forms of reading, in doing so he recognizes what seems to us to be more central to its demise, namely the lamentable fact that "the web and the internet have created a permanent Now." However apparently at odds with this assessment is that of the French writer and filmmaker Alain Robbe-Grillet, on closer examination they complement each other. Robbe-Grillet complains that the novel has been unable to move beyond its nineteenth-century structures. The *standard* novel could not move beyond these structures for they served as the foil for the novelist, the key to the liberationist struggle the novel chronicled. In contrast to the *standard* novel, it was the great novels that led René Girard to his important exposition of the role of mimesis in human affairs. He was subsequently to question whether the genre to which he devoted so much careful attention would continue to play a role in intellectual and cultural life.

> However much my work is fundamentally based on the study of the great novels and the description of an experience of which they provide a privileged form, this subject now seems to me to be outmoded. I do not much concern myself with the novel. It no longer seems to me to embody the meaning of an era of which it nevertheless announces all the dangers.[17]

Meanwhile, the limited success of the experimental novel, usually written by those most enamored of the increasing formlessness of the democratic age, may indicate that Lukacs was right about the link between

---

16 Ibid.
17 René Girard, "The Future of the Novel," *Contagion: Journal of Violence, Mimesis, and Culture*, Vol. 19 (2012): 1.

the success of the novel and a set of social structures sufficiently constraining of human desire to force these fickle and mimetically aroused desires to deepen and mature and become the stuff not of romantic melodrama but of real drama. Like tennis without the net, the novel without a sufficiently rigorous moral and social infrastructure loses both its fascination for the reader and its claim to moral seriousness.

As for the comparative success of works of history vis-à-vis the contemporary novel, we might turn to a 2019 article by Susanna Hoffman arrestingly entitled: "While Americans Gobble Up History Books, Colleges Shut Down History Departments." Writes Hoffman:

> Americans have a hunger to understand, explore, and connect with their history. Richly sourced, intellectually demanding accounts of the country's defining moments and characters do more than break through the noise. Indeed, historians are probably the scholars most celebrated outside the confines of the academy.[18]

Writing in 2001, Wilfred M. McClay touched on the reason why the public's appetite was primarily for the work of historians operating by and large outside the academy.

> For a small but increasing number of our academic historians, the principal point of studying the past is to demonstrate that all our inherited institutions, beliefs, conventions, and normative values are arbitrary — "social constructions in the service of power" and therefore without legitimacy or authority. For them, history is useful not because it tells us about the things that made us who we are, but because it releases us from the power of those very things, and thereby confers the promise of boundless possibility. All that has been constructed can presumably be dismantled and reconstructed, and all contemporary customs and usages, being *merely* historical, can be cancelled.[19]

McClay's prescience was remarkable inasmuch as he wrote this comment two decades before the "cancel culture" became a widely recognized fact of American political, academic, and intellectual life. Outside the academy, however, the reading public today is no less eager for serious books of history, not because of a hunger for historiographic detail, but

---

18 Susanna Hoffman, "While Americans Gobble Up History Books, Colleges Shut Down History Departments," *The Federalist*, June 19, 2019.
19 Wilfred M. McClay, "Clio's Makeshift Laboratory," *First Things*, March 2001.

because of a longing for some sense of the larger drama in the midst of which they live.

We conclude the foregoing with the observations of the Irish writer Michael Kirke who has called attention to an area of novelistic craft which continues to bear fruit: the "Catholic novel."

> This is not just a genre in which Catholicism is the subject chosen by the authors. It is literature in which the authors, for good or for ill, cannot escape from the Catholic faith — or the culture of that faith and the condition of that culture in the time and place in which they may live. The authors may be practicing Catholics, doubt-filled Catholics, or lapsed Catholics.
>
> What we see in this genre of fiction is a trace in the soul of the author. It is a trace which enables a writer to tell something of the story of their faith, their vision of what it is to be human — and to be divine. Joyce did this, rebelling against much, but not all, of it; Waugh did it — exuberantly; Greene did it with some kind of a twist all his own. Some did it with a grim preoccupation with our sinfulness, others did it rejoicing more in our redemption.[20]

---

20   Michael Kirke, "Faith and the novel in a secular age," *Mercatornet*, August 18, 2020.

8 A Small Mistake in Doctrine

> Here it is enough to notice that if some small mistake were made in doctrine, huge blunders might be made in human happiness.
> — G. K. Chesterton[1]

> In two men and in two philosophies, the modern era with its mechanistic undertones and artistic overtones dominates us all. Let us speak of them, so that we don't remain addicted to them. Let us speak of Descartes and Nietzsche.
> René Descartes' mother died shortly after childbirth; when Friedrich Nietzsche was five years old, his father had a fatal accident. These two events — here, the disappearance of a mother; there, of a father — embody the beginning and the end of the modern era. These events created a one-generational time, a time without ancestors and without heirs.
> — Eugen Rosenstock-Huessy[2]

IF ROSENSTOCK-HUESSY IS RIGHT, THEN MODERNITY was, in a manner of speaking, fathered by a motherless Frenchman and euthanized by a fatherless German. If René Descartes (1596–1650) was literally motherless from an early age, he was neither spiritually fatherless nor wanting for intellectual legatees. Even though we are beginning *in medias res* with the French mathematician-turned-philosopher René Descartes, brief mention must be made of the theological and philosophical influences to which he was responding.

During one of the most creative periods of the Middle Ages several currents of theological and philosophical thought clashed and mutually

---

1   G. K. Chesterton, *Orthodoxy* (Nashville: Sam Torode Book Arts, 2008), 96.
2   Eugen Rosenstock-Huessy, *In the Cross of Reality*, Vol. I: *The Hegemony of Spaces*, trans. Jürgen Lawrenz (New York: Transaction Publishers, 2017), 281.

stimulated one another. In terms of their influence on René Descartes, chief among these was the thought of the Franciscan friar, William of Ockham (1285–1347). Ockham radicalized the thinking of an earlier Franciscan, Dun Scotus (c. 1265–1308), the Subtle Doctor. For many, Scotus represents the beginning of the modern age. At a public audience in July 2010, Benedict XVI, with characteristic economy, gave this summary:

> Dun Scotus has developed a point to which modernity is very sensitive. It is the topic of freedom and its relationship with the will and with the intellect. The author underlines freedom as a fundamental quality of the will, introducing an approach that lays greater emphasis on the will. Unfortunately, in later authors, this line of thinking turned into a voluntarism, in contrast to the so-called Augustinian and Thomist intellectualism.[3]

Chief among those "later authors" who transposed the divine freedom into a voluntarism reminiscent of the inscrutable will of Allah in Islam, was William of Ockham. Against the metaphysicians of his time, Ockham disparaged the idea that philosophical acumen was capable of knowing the mind of God, for any such knowledge would infringe on the divine will by presuming to know it in advance. God was absolutely free, ultimately and theoretically free even to demand of his creatures something they might regard as morally repugnant or intellectually inconsistent. Aidan Nichols, O. P. sums up the issue nicely, quoting Balthasar.

> Once the original Franciscan image of God as a love beyond all knowledge is married with the Scotist theology it readily turns into that of a potentially fearful monster, for a God of sheerest freedom could in principle "posit and demand what is contrary."[4]

God was free to change His mind — from moment to moment for reasons inaccessible to man. What might be the divine will at one moment could be its opposite at another. However unlikely Ockham believed such an alteration of God's will might be, he nonetheless insisted that it could not be ruled out. This was of course a shocking statement, a blunt instrument, so to speak, that Ockham used in his effort to break up what he regarded as the overly rationalistic logjam of his age. Since obeying God's will was the key to both moral rectitude in this life and

---

3 Benedict XVI, *Great Christian Thinkers: From the Early Church through the Middle Ages* (Minneapolis: Fortress Press, 2011), 304.
4 Nichols, *The Word Has Been Abroad*, 147.

happiness in the next, this radical view of divine freedom had sweeping and very unsettling consequences. It set the stage for both the Protestant and Cartesian reformations. As Michael Allen Gillespie put the matter:

> Contrary to Nietzsche's account, nihilism is not the result of the death of God but the consequence of the birth or rebirth of a different kind of God, an omnipotent God of will who calls into question all of reason and nature and thus overturns all eternal standards of truth and justice, and good and evil. This idea of God came to prominence in the fourteenth century and shattered the medieval synthesis of philosophy and theology, catapulting man into a new way of thinking and being, a *via moderna* essentially at odds with the *via antiqua*. This new way was in turn the foundation for modernity as the realm of human self-assertion. Nihilism thus has its roots in... the late medieval conception of an omnipotent God [that] inspired and informed a new conception of man and nature that gave precedence to will over reason and freedom over necessity and order.[5]

It is one of the ironies of history that just as the great flowering of theological and philosophical thought inspired by Latin Christianity's rediscovery of Aristotle was made possible by Islam's preservation of portions of the Aristotelian corpus, Ockham protested the excessive intellectualism of the scholastic enterprise by approximating the doctrine of divine inscrutability adopted two centuries earlier by the Islamic scholar Al-Ghazali. But the consequences in each cultural context were quite different. In the Islamic world a theological nominalism posited a God who was in no way constrained by mankind's moral or material considerations. In the West, on the other hand, an anthropological nominalism arose. "If there are no real universals," writes Gillespie of the Ockhamist revolution, "every being must be radically individual."[6]

If Descartes was among those thrown into metaphysical uncertainty by nominalism, his misgivings about the received wisdom of his culture were not so sweeping as to eliminate the influence of one of his most prominent forefathers, Saint Augustine. From the great Bishop of Hippo Descartes learned to turn inward and to place more trust in what he

---

[5] Michael Allen Gillespie, *Nihilism Before Nietzsche* (Chicago: University of Chicago Press, 1995), xii–xiii.
[6] Ibid., 22.

found there than in whatever might have come to him by way of his spiritual, cultural, or intellectual inheritance. This attitude hardly does justice to the vast legacy of the great bishop of Hippo, but it seems to be what Descartes found most congenial to his intellectual predilections.

Materially motherless by unhappy circumstance, Descartes, the mathematician, rendered himself culturally and spiritually fatherless on principle. He foreswore any external influence and determined to rely only on his own mental calculations. In doing so, he left his intellectual heirs a poisoned patrimony, one that was lethal to tradition and the transgenerational concord which it safeguards.

If Descartes attempted the impossible — to be free of influence — his own influence on subsequent generations was such that we cannot afford to overlook what were the resources on which he drew, for they are part of the story of the sovereign self that is today in such a spiritual and existential crisis. "Augustine," writes Robert Solomon, "described his 'inner' self quite thoroughly, even capping his analysis with the precocious Cartesian insight, 'I think *ergo* I am.'"[7] As the Orthodox theologian John Zizioulas has noted:

> Most of us today, when we say "person" mean an *individual*. This goes back to Augustine, and especially to Boethius in the fifth century CE, who defined the person as an individual nature endowed with rationality and consciousness. Throughout the entire history of Western thought, the equation of person with the thinking individual has led to a culture in which the thinking individual has become the highest concept in anthropology.[8]

For several years, Augustine was a follower of the Manicheans, a Gnostic and strictly dualistic sect, but a mind and heart like Augustine's could not long be housed in such narrow confines. Augustine's eventual conversion to Christianity was "mediated" by the inspirational example of two men: Saint Ambrose, bishop of Milan, and Saint Paul, the former by virtue of his personal sanctity and the eloquence of his preaching and the latter by the power of one passage from his Letter to the Romans, to which Augustine was providentially drawn in the midst of a spiritual crisis. In the year 386, he heard a child singing, "Pick it up and read, pick it up and read," and he took it to be a message from God. He opened a

---

7   Robert Solomon, *Continental Philosophy since 1750: The Rise and Fall of the Self* (Oxford: Oxford University Press, 1988), 5.
8   John D. Zizioulas, *Communion and Otherness*, ed. Paul McPartlan (New York: T & T Clark, 2009), 168.

volume of Pauline epistles at random and read: "... not in reveling and drunkenness, not in debauchery and licentiousness, not in quarreling and jealousy. But, put on the Lord Jesus Christ, and make no provision for the flesh, to gratify its desires" (Rom 13:13 – 14).

The future bishop of Hippo and one of the greatest minds and most impassioned hearts of the early Church was baptized by Ambrose during the Easter Vigil April 24, 387. It might be said, however, that Paul's "make no provision for the flesh" — valid as it is — did not exactly serve to inoculate Augustine against the Neoplatonic excesses of his earlier period. And it was this aspect of the Augustinian legacy that seems to have left its mark on Descartes. As Jeffery Stout has written:

> Descartes can now be located squarely within the Platonic-Augustinian tradition. Indeed, it was this tradition which supplied most of the concepts and images he used in his attempt to transcend all tradition. Once the unacknowledged debt is recognized, it should no longer be surprising that the attempt did not succeed.[9]

Irenaeus's foundational repudiation of Gnosticism in the second century dealt a blow to Neoplatonic interpretations of Christianity, but the struggle to extricate Christian thought from Gnostic and Neoplatonic influences would trouble the Church for centuries. According to Hans Urs von Balthasar, "the spiritualistic temptation in the purer form of the platonic and neoplatonic myths take control of Christian theology and it will require long and confusing struggles before the poison that had crept into Christian thought could be eliminated."[10] Indeed, one of the places where Neoplatonism burrowed into Christian thought in the post-Irenaean period was the thought of Augustine. Notwithstanding Augustine's immense and indispensable contribution to Christianity's historical self-understanding, the Neoplatonism on which the bishop of Hippo still partly drew led his intellectual and spiritual heirs into theological imprecisions the implications of which could hardly have been foreseen. "At the time of his conversion in Milan," writes Balthasar "Augustine was assiduously practicing Neoplatonic self-absorption."[11] "The story of Augustine's intellectual development does not begin with

---

9 Jeffery Stout, *The Flight from Authority: Religion, Morality, and the Quest for Autonomy* (Notre Dame, IN: University of Notre Dame Press, 1981), 68 – 69.
10 Hans Urs von Balthasar, *The von Balthasar Reader*, eds. Medard Kehland and Werner Loser (New York: Crossroad Herder, 1997), 383.
11 Balthasar, *Prayer*, 261.

Platonism and end with Christianity," writes Phillip Cary. On the contrary, Augustine's is "a distinctive brand of Christian Platonism in the making."[12]

As always, there are nuances and paradoxes. Henri de Lubac addressed the issue of Augustine's Neoplatonism more sympathetically: "We can only marvel at the assimilative power of Christian life as manifested in [Augustine's] attitude, and conclude with Mgr. Régis Jolivet that by means of Augustine's comments on Plato 'it was not Augustine who became a neo-Platonist, but Plato who became a Christian.'"[13] De Lubac cites another equally sympathetic philosopher, Etienne Borne: "Christian Platonism is a historical fact; but this demanded of St. Augustine a confrontation and a combat like that between Jacob and the angel, from which one of the protagonists, philosophy, emerged limping and bearing the traces of its lucky defeat."[14]

Whatever the lingering effects of Augustinian Christian Platonism, Joseph Cardinal Ratzinger was surely right when he insisted that Augustine's doctrine of the Trinity was "one of the most momentous developments of the Western Church. In fundamental ways it influenced both the concept of the Church and the understanding of the person."[15] The fact, revealed in scripture — Genesis 1:27 — that we are made in the likeness of our Creator, suggested to Augustine's creative mind that traces of our Trinitarian birthmark could be found, and he undertook the task of locating these traces. He brought to that task Neoplatonic habits of thought which predisposed him to search for evidence of man's Trinitarian godlikeness by turning inward. He famously proposed that the watermark of man's Trinitarian provenance was to be found in his memory, will, and intellect. This inward turn, according to the then-Cardinal Ratzinger, obscured the deeper anthropological implications of the revelation of the Divine Trinity.

> Augustine explicitly transposed this theological affirmation into anthropology by attempting to understand the human person as an image of the Trinity in terms of this idea of God. *Unfortunately, however, he committed a decisive mistake here*.... In his interpretation, he projected the divine persons into the interior life of the human person and affirmed that intra-psychic

---

12 Phillip Cary, *Augustine's Invention of the Inner Self: The Legacy of a Christian Platonist* (Oxford: Oxford University Press, 2000), 35.
13 Henri de Lubac, S.J., *The Mystery of the Supernatural*, trans. Rosemary Sheed (New York: Crossroad Publishing, 1988), 225.
14 Ibid., 226.
15 Ratzinger, "Concerning the Notion of Person in Theology," 117–18.

processes correspond to these persons.... As a result, the trinitarian concept of the person was no longer transferred to the human person in all its immediate impact.[16]

By transposing the Divine Persons into intra-psychic categories, Augustine seriously compromised what is surely the most essential, radical, and counter-intuitive element in Trinitarian theology, namely, the divine mystery whose human analogue Girard explored under the rubric of "interdividuality."

As noted above and as we will explore further below, the very word person found its way into popular usage thanks to the efforts of theologians trying to account for the greatest of all mysteries, the Divine Trinity. As Cardinal Ratzinger lamented, so elusive was the mystery that Augustine was trying to explicate that the confusions gave rise to a number of the early Christological heresies, many of which were "attempts at locating the concept of the person at some place in the psychic inventory."[17] As a result: "The contribution of Christian faith to the whole of human thought is not realized; it remains at first detached from it as a theological exception, although it is precisely the *meaning* of this new element to call into question the *whole* of human thought and to set it on a new course."[18]

A line stretches from Augustine's inward turn to Descartes' effort to arrive at certainty by trying to isolate himself from history, tradition, and human companionship. By Balthasar's reckoning, however, the line from Augustine to Descartes intersected with the Protestant rejection of the Aristotelian realism on which the older tradition had relied.

> Luther had deposed (Aristotelian) reason in order to make room for faith. But in the meantime, the reason that Luther rejected acquired a Cartesian structure.... Being thus limited, reason had nothing more to do with religion and so it became what the young Karl Barth called an "idol factory," and to that extent an adversary of genuine faith.[19]

For Augustine, the inward turn was a turn toward another, toward God. Augustine was the one who conceived the very idea of Christianity as a *civitas*, the City of God, a thriving, embattled community. For

---

16   Ibid., 111. Emphasis added.
17   Ibid., 112.
18   Ibid., 113.
19   Balthasar, *Love Alone Is Credible*, 35.

Descartes, however, the inward turn was a turn away from community, a liberation that required an act of insulation from the influence of others, whether they be contemporaries or ancestors. His was a radical emancipation proclamation, the assertion of an epistemological principle that constituted an anthropological claim: that only by renouncing even the most venerable of one's fellows or fore-fellows would one's own thought have access to truth. This was one of the seeds from which has grown the poisonous fruit of sovereign selfhood: the triumph of the will and the twilight of resolve. This obviously constitutes a radical break with the larger Augustinian vision, but neither can the Bishop of Hippo be completely exonerated. As Jaroslav Pelikan has written:

> The fundamental reorientation of Western philosophy associated with the name of Descartes was likewise a species of Augustinianism, and the Cartesian "Cogito ergo sum" stands in a direct succession, through the scholastics, with Augustine's use of thought and doubt for the reality of the self and ultimately for the reality of God.[20]

"On the way from Plato to Descartes," writes Charles Taylor, "stands Augustine."[21] And this Augustinian legacy is nowhere more clearly manifested than it is in this passage from Augustine's *De Trinitate*.

> Yet who ever doubts that he himself lives, and remembers, and understands, and wills, and thinks, and knows, and judges? Seeing that even if he doubts, he lives; if he doubts, he remembers why he doubts; if he doubts, he understands that he doubts; if he doubts, he wishes to be certain; if he doubts, he thinks; if he doubts, he knows that he does not know; if he doubts, he judges that he ought not to assent rashly. Whosoever therefore doubts about anything else, ought not to doubt of all these things; which if they were not, he would not be able to doubt of anything.[22]

Descartes was an eager recipient of this Augustinian trope. For all his determination to avoid the mimetic influence of others, living and dead, Descartes embraced this feature of the tradition with open arms. "In his desire to portray his thought as originating *ab ovo*," writes Gillespie

---

20 Jaroslav Pelikan, *The Mystery of Continuity: Time and History, Memory and Eternity in the Thought of Saint Augustine* (Charlottesville: University Press of Virginia, 1986), 151.
21 Charles Taylor, *Sources of the Self: The Making of the Modern Identity* (Cambridge: Harvard University Press, 1989), 127.
22 Augustine, *De Trinitate*, Book X, Ch. 14.

of Descartes, "he goes to considerable lengths to conceal his sources."[23] To conceal one's "sources" is to disguise the mimetic influence of one's model, and the self-proclaimed originality of Descartes' epistemological revolution required an obfuscation of the unmistakable influence of the great African bishop. (The concealing of one's sources has become a conspicuous feature of the dramatized individualism that characterizes late-modern psychological stagecraft.)

Some have disavowed a causal link between Augustine's exploration of the inner self and the desperate Cartesian quest for certainty, which radically renounces any and all received wisdom or cultural inheritance. But most acknowledge that Augustine's inward turn was there for the taking, and it cannot be doubted that Descartes helped himself to it. Another defender of Augustine, who similarly acknowledges both a link and a hiatus between Augustinian inwardness and Cartesian self-sufficiency, is Charles Taylor. He writes:

> Plainly the whole Cartesian project owes a great deal to its Augustinian roots and the enhanced place this tradition gave to inwardness. But plainly also there has been a transposition of this tradition as well. Cartesian internalization has transmuted into something very different from its Augustinian source. For Augustine, the path inward was only a step on the way upward. Something similar remains in Descartes, who also proves the existence of God starting from the self-understanding of the thinking agent. But the spirit has been altered in a subtle but important way. Following Augustine's path, the thinker comes to sense more and more his lack of self-sufficiency, comes to see more and more that God acts within him. In contrast, for Descartes the whole point of the reflexive turn is to achieve a quite self-sufficient certainty.[24]

In redeploying Augustine's Neoplatonic adaptation, the Cartesian inward turn managed to forsake the one thing that kept the Augustinian one from becoming fatal to Christian thought. Whereas Augustine turned inward in order to find God, Descartes turned inward in search of a self-sufficient source of certainty, and — by extension — identity: "cogito ergo *sum*."

---

23   Gillespie, *Nihilism Before Nietzsche*, 29.
24   Taylor, *Sources of the Self*, 156–57.

9 Descartes:
THE QUEST FOR CERTAINTY

> Man will never cease to want to be enclosed within himself.
> — Henri de Lubac[1]

> Only with Descartes does philosophy become dependent on the scientific ideal of the rising natural sciences, thereby beginning its rift with theology. Only from this point onwards do philosophers become eager to experiment with the question of what reason can accomplish without the aid of revelation and what the possibilities are for a pure nature without grace.
> — Hans Urs von Balthasar[2]

IN BALTHASAR'S OPINION, DESCARTES ESSENTIALLY launched the modern age by basing the idea of the person on self-consciousness, and Kant's subsequent attempt "to save the dignity of the person could not halt this drift."[3]

A glance at the evidence that Descartes himself left us of his great moment of conversion will make it clear that it was motivated by his need to insulate himself from the mimetic influence of others. Alas, it was easier to renounce the mimetic influence of his predecessors than it was to actually elude that influence. Yet we can only marvel at how far the famous mathematician was willing to go to free himself from the thought of even his most illustrious predecessors. At the beginning of the *Third Meditation*, Descartes describes the precautions he had to take in order to avoid the taint of such influence. Living at the time (1628) in the Dutch Republic, he describes the physical surroundings which most suited his purpose: "The onset of winter held me up in quarters in which, finding no company to distract me, and having, fortunately,

---

1   De Lubac, *Mystery of the Supernatural*, xxxv.
2   Balthasar, *The Glory of the Lord*, Vol. 1: *Seeing the Form*, 72.
3   Balthasar, "On the Concept of the Person," 24.

no cares or passions to disturb me, I spent the whole day shut up in a room heated by an enclosed stove, where I had complete leisure to meditate on my own thoughts."4

Not only did the Cartesian turn involve the "Neoplatonic self-absorption" of which Balthasar complained, but the ghost of Ockham's inscrutable and rationally unpredictable God was in evidence as well; conspicuously so in his *First Meditation*, where Ockham's God has "gone native," taking the form, hypothetically at least, of the Gnostic demiurge haunting a material world incurably infected with its malignity. Descartes writes:

> I will suppose not a supremely good God, the source of all truth, but rather an evil genius, supremely powerful and clear, who has directed his entire effort at deceiving me. I will regard the heavens, the air, the earth, colors, shapes, sounds, and all external things as nothing but the bedeviling hoaxes of my dreams, with which he lays snares for my credulity. I will regard myself as not having hands, or eyes, or flesh, or blood, or any senses, but as nevertheless falsely believing that I possess all these things. I will remain resolute and steadfast in this meditation, and even if it is not within my power to know anything true, it certainly is within my power to take care resolutely to withhold my assent to what is false, lest this deceiver, however powerful, however clever he may be, have any effect on me.5

Here we have a malignant, seductive deity, conjuring an illusory world of "external things" whose wiles could be defeated only by the (metaphorical) elimination of the body — "hands, or eyes, or flesh, or blood, or any senses." This is an eccentric blend of that hermeneutics of suspicion later associated with Nietzsche, Marx, and Freud, with the Gnostic deprecation of the body and material reality.

In place of the senses with which our species has been endowed for the purpose of assessing concrete reality, Descartes proposed an all-purpose instrument: methodological doubt, distrustful of the human body and gullible with regard to that portion of the body which cogitates. Not only does this passage presage the reemergence of Christianity's oldest adversary, the ancient Gnostic disdain for the body — a condescension that can be expressed either in a repressive or a licentious way — but,

---

4 René Descartes, "*Discourse on Method*" *and* "*The Meditations*," trans. F. E. Sutcliffe (Harmondsworth: Penguin Books, 1968), 35.
5 René Descartes, *Meditations on First Philosophy*, Meditation I (Hackett Publishing, 1993), 16–17.

as we shall see below, it bears a likeness as well to forms of hysteria — hysterical blindness or hysterical paralysis — which were to attract the attention of late-nineteenth- and early twentieth-century psychiatric clinicians.

When Rosenstock-Huessy declared Descartes to be the inaugurating thinker of our one-generational age, we have reason to believe that he chose precisely the right metaphor. For, of all the mimetic influences that a committed originalist must foreswear, one of the greatest is that of one's cultural and familial patrimony. The irony, of course, is that those who think themselves thus emancipated, readily expect generations of their descendants to be the beneficiaries of their own putatively novel contributions.

Descartes' strategy of renouncing the influence of God and men may tell us more about the Cartesian revolution than the philosopher's elaborate justifications for it. It indicates where the problem lies for Descartes. It lies with other people. Not only is it others that Descartes fears will distract him, but it is the "cares" and "passions" others arouse in him that he must extinguish in order to think clearly. Sartre's "hell is other people" is still more than three centuries away, but Descartes has taken a step in that direction, not because he is a misanthropist, but because he has intuitively sensed how susceptible to mimetic forces we humans are and how imperceptibly influential these mimetic stimuli can be. At the heart of this search for *unmediated* knowledge is a wariness about the mimetic influence of others and a fear of the epistemological corruption such an influence might have. It is, of course, a legitimate fear, as the God who created humans that way certainly knew, but for which redemptive provisions had been made, whose literary treasure trove can be found in the Jewish and Christian scriptures.

One could as well live without oxygen as eliminate the mediating influence of others. Descartes' efforts to do so anticipate the desperate self-referentiality of the modern self and its ridiculous determination to experience its own ever-elusive authenticity. Descartes represents himself as ensconced for six days in an isolated Dutch garret, where he communes only with his own thoughts, but at length there seems more to wall out than just the physical presence of others, and he must take extreme measures to ensure that it is, in fact, *his own thoughts* on which he is meditating.

In the *Third Meditation*, Descartes' vigilance requires that he take leave of his body for fear that physicality might compromise his quest for certain knowledge as much as would received wisdom. "I will now close my eyes, I will plug my ears, I will turn aside all my senses... in this way, concerned only with myself, looking only at what is inside me, I will try, little by little, to know myself, and to become more familiar to myself."[6]

William Temple called Descartes' withdrawal into himself "the most disastrous moment in the history of Europe."[7] This revolution was no less consequential for the Christian faith that Descartes formally — if not always convincingly — professed. It had been clear to Thomas Aquinas, wrote Joseph Cardinal Ratzinger, "that we cannot know God except through the senses and that even our way of thinking about God is dependent on and mediated by sense perception. If this is so, it means that every introduction to the faith — catechesis, catechumenate — must be by means of experiences made possible by the senses."[8]

If the prodigal son "came to his senses" at the nadir of his effort to live only for himself, Descartes has chosen quite literally to "lose his senses" in the radical attempt to insulate himself against whatever might be the machinations of the imagined "evil genius" who threatened his intellectual self-sovereignty.[9] It is precisely the straightforward truth of lived reality that defies the ideological chimeras conjured up in order to prolong the myth of autonomous individuality. According to Bishop Robert Barron, Descartes "brought all claims to knowledge before the bar of the self-validating ego for adjudication."[10] The result was that "the lonely but unassailably secure Cartesian ego, standing amidst the ruins of culture, intelligence, and sense experience, emerged as the sure foundation of knowledge," leading inexorably to the world of moral anarchy that fairly defines contemporary culture. It is easy to recognize the Cartesian contribution to our present confusions in Rémi Brague's observation: "The ultimate goal of Enlightenment, was not the joy that one finds in what is, but the pleasure of the subject in not being duped."[11]

---

6 Descartes, *"Discourse on Method" and "The Meditations,"* 36.
7 William Temple, *Nature, Man and God* (London: Macmillan, 1940), 57.
8 Joseph Cardinal Ratzinger, *Principles of Catholic Theology*, trans. Sister Mary Frances McCarthy, S.N.D. (San Francisco: Ignatius Press, 1987), 344.
9 In the Greek text of the prodigal son story, the younger son comes to his *autos*. But at that time the word had none of the connotations the word *self* has acquired in the modern era.
10 Robert Barron, *The Priority of Christ: Toward a Postliberal Catholicism* (Grand Rapids: Baker Academic, 2007), 137.
11 Rémi Brague, *The Kingdom of Man: Genesis and Failure of the Modern Project*, trans. Paul Seaton (Notre Dame, IN: University of Notre Dame Press, 2018), 192.

Descartes

The notion of a "self" has its etymological roots in the Greek term *autos*, the source of our idea of "autonomy." *Autos* and its cognates strongly imply, in the words of Kenneth Schmitz, "an identity that preserves itself *against* others."[12] As Schmitz explains, "in order to preserve itself and retain that identity, such a self must at some point exclude others, or even repel them." The prevailing Western notion of "individuality" is rooted in the act of "dis-identification" by which the individual distinguishes himself from others. However beneficial such a notion of human subjectivity might have been in helping to extricate "individuals" from the always dangerous mechanisms of social contagion, the West's canonization of this notion of selfhood was anthropologically untenable. As Joseph Ratzinger pointed out:

> Man does not find salvation in a reflective finding of himself but in the being-taken-out-of-himself that goes beyond reflection — not in continuing to be himself, but in going out from himself. It means that the liberation of man consists in his being freed from himself and, in relinquishing himself, truly finding himself.... Man finds his center of gravity, not inside, but outside himself.[13]

René Descartes claimed to have found a source of certainty that would replace the confidence that the older Christian order had found in the scriptural, liturgical, and sacramental life of Christian experience. The philosopher Jeffery Stout succinctly summarizes the point we have here tried to make:

> For Descartes, as for Luther before him, what most matters in life is no longer played out in the dimensions of community and tradition. One discovers truth in the privacy of subjective illumination, and this truth is underlined by a kind of self-certifying certainty. Community, tradition, authority: these have all started to give way to the individual, his inwardness, his autonomy.[14]

While the emphasis on religious individualism of the Protestant movement bears on the genealogy of the crisis of subjectivity we are here sketching in outline, the line leading from Ockham to Descartes will

---

12 Kenneth L. Schmitz, "Selves and Persons: A Difference in Loves?" *Communio* 18 (Summer 1991): 185. Emphasis added.
13 Ratzinger, *Principles of Catholic Theology*, 171.
14 Stout, *Flight from Authority*, 49–50.

suffice to exemplify the quest for an epistemological certainty by turning inward and disavowing the influence of others. As Thomas Bertonneau pointed out, "the line from 'I think, therefore I am' to 'my truth' is perfectly straight and follows the direction of gravity."[15]

In due course, Ockham's theological voluntarism gave birth to an anthropological voluntarism, which devolved into what Cardinal Ratzinger called the dictatorship of relativism. Which begs the question: Christianity has again and again survived crushing oppression; will it survive an autonomous and anarchistic understanding of freedom? Of course it will, but at what cost? That remains to be seen. "What happens," writes the theologian John Betz, "when the classical understanding of freedom as the freedom to become virtuous and wise is forgotten and becomes utterly irrelevant to the great western mythos of freedom?"

> Then, with nothing left to aim at and no higher standard to ennoble it, freedom degrades into what Isaiah Berlin aptly termed "negative freedom" — a freedom, that is, merely of *non*-interference and *non*-coercion. It degrades, in other words, into the freedom of modern liberalism, the freedom of the marketplace, in short, into *American* freedom, which, seen historically, is the last form of freedom, and seen philosophically is the lowest kind of freedom: a freedom whose chief, if formally negative virtue is that it opens markets, ensures the free exchange of goods, and provides a safe space for individuals to do, pursue, and purchase whatever they think will make them happy.[16]

The spiritual consequences of this truncated notion of freedom were glimpsed by Descartes' older English contemporary, the poet John Donne (1572 – 1631):

> Tis all in pieces, all coherence gone,
> All just Supply, and all Relation;
> Prince, subject, father, son, are things forgot,
> For every man alone thinks he hath got
> To be a Phoenix, and that then can be
> None of that kind, of which he is, but he.[17]

---

15 Thomas F. Bertonneau, "Two Recent Anti-Modern Critiques — Thaddeus Kozinski & Daniel Schwindt," *The Orthosphere* (blog), June 5, 2021.
16 John Betz, "Freedom on Holiday: The Genealogy of a Cultural Revolution," *Church Life Journal*, Sept. 6, 2021.
17 Quoted from Donne's "An Anatomy of the World," in Douglas Farrow, *Theological Negotiations: Proposal in Soteriology and Anthropology* (Grand Rapids, MI: Baker

Under this regime, what we have called the human vocation ceases to be an ordination shared by all members of our spectacularly gifted and sin-shackled species. Rather each human is thought to be entirely self-defined and self-determined, without regard to our natural endowment and the moral standards that might conduce to its fulfillment. Thus, the indispensable task of each subject is to refuse to *be* subject. Under such an anthropological premise, social life completely breaks down, there being no shared assumptions about the meaning and purpose of life itself. So, as Douglas Farrow has noted: "The autonomy principle acts like an acid to dissolve what remains of the moral and cultural fabric of Christian civilization."[18] The radical autonomy thus enshrined will be socially imperiled by manifold influences — real or imagined — and require protection by the State. The task of ordering rebellious creatures who have renounced their more ennobling bonds will fall to an implacable Hobbesian Leviathan.

The widespread acceptance of sovereign individualism floods the market with the cacophonous assertion of rights which necessarily diminishes the moral weight of each of the assertions, even as it necessitates an ever more autocratic political regime to keep order. There is thus a symbiotic relationship between radical autonomy and autocratic political control. About the consequences of abandoning the Christian foundations of our civilization, Gillespie ominously observed: "The notion of absolute freedom that had its origin in the nominalist notion of God came to a monstrous crescendo in Stalin's terror."[19]

Meanwhile, Jeffery Stout draws out the implications for our time of Descartes' inward turn, paralleling as it does the Reformation rejection of the role of tradition:

> Descartes's quest for certainty was born... in a flight from authority. The crisis of authority made an absolutely radical break with the past seem necessary. Methodical doubt therefore sought complete transcendence of situation. It tried to make the inheritance of tradition irrelevant, to start over again from scratch, to escape history. But is this possible?[20]

What Jeffery Stout has to say about the legacy of the Protestant Reformation is true as well of Descartes' legacy:

Academic, 2018), 255, n7.
18 Farrow, *Theological Negotiations*, 188.
19 Gillespie, *Nihilism Before Nietzsche*, xx.
20 Stout, *Flight from Authority*, 67.

The Protestant appeal to the individual conscience and inner persuasion in effect produces yet another version of the problem of many authorities. But now we have far more authorities than before, for *every* man recognizes his own inner light. Every conscience constitutes a separate authority. We are left with no means to settle disagreements about matters of public importance. What started out as an appeal to the single authority of scriptural revelation now seems to recognize, implicitly at least, ten authorities in every pew. The potential for anarchy did not go unnoticed by the Catholic critics.[21]

Among those Catholic critics was René Girard, who observed: "Once we are deprived of transcendental guideposts, we must trust our subjective experience. Whether we like it or not, we are little Cartesian gods with no fixed reference and no certainty outside of ourselves."[22] We are, in the dire warning of John the Baptist, chaff that the winnowing fork will separate from the wheat, and which will thereafter become fuel for a conflagration of the sort that turned the twentieth century into a charnel house of blood and tears and which threatens to do so again in the twenty-first.

"Greek religion," argued James Collins, "experienced alternative excesses of puritanical formality and dionysiac carnality, especially in its later phases." To which Edward T. Oakes responded: "The same could be said of the career of Western metaphysics since Descartes."[23] And to which we would add: What are the "excesses of puritanical formality and dionysiac carnality" if not the salient symptoms of our own social hysterias: blind and unflinching adherence to even the most counterfactual ideologies, on one hand, and a form of dionysiac carnality shorn of its pagan lustfulness and openly contemptuous of the body, on the other?

---

21 Ibid., 44.
22 Girard, *Resurrection from the Underground*, 83.
23 Edward T. Oakes, *Pattern of Redemption: The Theology of Hans Urs von Balthasar* (New York: Continuum, 1994), 34.

10 Rousseau:
THE VIRTUOSO OF VANITY VICTIMHOOD

> That a man of their own kind, born in Europe, imbued with humility, alienated from the world, and possessed of a desire to do penance and then be saved, could no longer find a place in any Christian church and also failed to found a new one, and wrote not a single word about the sufferings of Christ, the Fall, or the Last Judgment, even in the midst of all of his outbursts of both hope and despair — this seems to me to be decisive for the changes that Europe underwent in the second half of the eighteenth century.
>
> — Erich Auerbach[1]

IT HAS BEEN ARGUED THAT NO MAN BEFORE AUGUStine had enough inner life to write an autobiography. The Swiss cultural historian Jacob Burckhardt claimed that individualism began in the Renaissance, but individualism both drew on the Augustinian tradition and betrayed it. "Autobiographies by pagans," writes the German philosopher Wilhelm Dilthey, "were not comparable with what Christians were able to do from St. Augustine to Rousseau."[2] Dilthey's choice of Augustine and Rousseau as the bookends of his reflections on the autobiographical genre provides the starting point for our brief analysis of the latter's moral, spiritual, and cultural legacy.

"Our hearts are restless until they rest in Thee." This often-quoted line from the opening passage of Augustine's *Confessions* fairly summarizes

---

1 Auerbach, *Time, History, and Literature*, 252.
2 Arnaldo Momigliano, "Quest for the person in Greek biography," in *The Category of the Person*, eds. Michael Carrithers, Steven Collins, and Stevens Lukes (Cambridge: Cambridge University Press, 1985), 84–85.

the Bishop of Hippo's theological anthropology. When, toward the end of the eighteenth century, Jean-Jacques Rousseau wrote another book entitled *The Confessions,* it presented to the world, not the God in whom Augustine finally found rest, but an immensely restless man desperately trying to appear as impervious to mimetic influence as Virginia Woolf's far less gifted Percival had been in the eyes of his more precocious classmates. Whereas the fictional Percival was too dull to play the mimetic game, Rousseau was, at least for a while, its unparalleled master. His *Confessions* begins with these lines:

> I have resolved on an enterprise which has *no precedent*, and which, once complete, will have *no imitator.* My purpose is to *display* to my kind a portrait in every way true to nature, and the man I shall portray will be *myself.* Simply myself. I know my own heart and understand my fellow man. But I am made unlike any one I have ever met; I will even venture to say that *I am like no one in the whole world.* I may be no better, but at least I am *different.*[3]

More than anyone else, it was Rousseau who popularized the romantic notion of the autonomous self-constituting self, the equivalent of the flat earth theory, that was to become the operating orthodoxy of the modern world. Rousseau, writes historian Paul Johnson, "prepared the blueprint for the principal delusions and follies of the twentieth century."[4] Nor did he perform this remarkable feat singlehandedly. Not only had Cartesian autonomy thoroughly saturated European thought in the century separating the two thinkers, but the air of the age was growing thick with the fumes of romantic individualism. Few inhaled those fumes as deeply as the great writer who claimed to have *no precedent* and *no imitator*, but who was obviously mimicking Augustine's *Confessions.*

Among those Leo Braudy called the "warlocks of individualism" were such men as Voltaire, Denis Diderot, David Hume, Samuel Johnson, Benjamin Franklin, and Thomas Jefferson. But, as Braudy declared, Jean-Jacques Rousseau "was the most singular of the singular."[5] Despite tendencies in the direction of exhibitionism that can be discerned in some of the other warlocks, Rousseau is distinguished by having been an admitted exhibitionist: a sexual exhibitionist as a youth and a literary one throughout his

---

3 Jean-Jacques Rousseau, *The Confessions,* trans. J. M. Cohen (London: Penguin, 1953), 17. Emphasis added.
4 Paul Johnson, *Intellectuals* (New York: Harper & Row, 1988), 26.
5 Leo Braudy, *The Frenzy of Renown: Fame and Its History* (New York: Oxford University Press, 1986), 371.

adult life. His early experiments in physical nakedness in Turin — where he exposed himself to women passersby — were followed by the wildly more successful moral nakedness that culminated in his *Confessions*. "This act of sexual confusion and passiveness," writes Paul Zweig, "reveals Rousseau in more ways than one."[6] Indeed, Rousseau's attempt to convince others of his insusceptibility to mimetic influence revealed to more discerning observers an acute susceptibility to such influence, requiring ever more dramatic, and ever more spiritually precarious, self-dramatizations.

In any competition with the other shamans of individualism for preeminence, Rousseau had an immense advantage. His writings were for a while banned in France and Geneva, and he was attacked and excoriated by many. There cannot be the slightest doubt that Rousseau's flamboyant claims to be a victim of intellectual, literary, and political persecution played an important role in making him "the most singular of the singular" individualists of his age. Nor can we account for the conflation of anathematized victim and celebrated individual without reference to the Passion of Christ and its monumental effect on its moral and spiritual beneficiaries. Again, in terms of the roles they have played in modern social history, the category of *individual* and the category of *victim* cannot be entirely distinguished. Therein, no doubt, lies some of the secret power of the myth of autonomous individuality.

Paul Zweig perceptively notes of Rousseau that "his persecution saved his sanity," and that his confessional works "convince us, and explain to us, with unexampled power, if not Rousseau's 'innocence,' then at least what he means by that innocence."[7] His innocence depended on his claim to be a victim. In retrospect, we can now see that Rousseau deserves the dubious distinction of being the person who discovered and popularized a piece of moral prestidigitation that now goes by the name of victimary thinking, a curiosity that floods a moral environment shaped by Christianity with so many claims to the solicitude that Christianity accords to victims that the moral system, overloaded with such claims, collapses in empathy fatigue and is easily overrun with countless Jean-Jacques Rousseau epigones elbowing one another for their moment in the sun — or, perhaps better, their moment as the Son.

The self that Rousseau discovered, Robert Solomon argued, "was discovered by a sociopath, free and alone with his self-aggrandizement,

---

6 Paul Zweig, *The Heresy of Self-Love* (New York: Basic Books, 1968), 145–46.
7 Ibid., 150–51.

but one who inspired some of the most spectacular and successful philosophy that the world has ever known."[8] "Rousseau," writes Douglas Farrow, "turned the older Renaissance quest for self-understanding in the direction of what we think of today as personal authenticity, though it may be more accurate to call it self-absorption."[9]

Inasmuch as Eugen Rosenstock-Huessy found the motherlessness of Descartes and the fatherlessness of Nietzsche a decisive fact in designating them as the beginning and end of the one-generational modern age, it is intriguing to note that Rousseau — a man deprived of both mother and father — appears almost exactly midway between Descartes and Nietzsche. His mother died of a postpartum infection nine days after he was born, which — no doubt accurately — he later described as the first of his misfortunes. His father abandoned him in childhood as he, in turn, abandoned each of his own five children.

Conveniently for his own strikingly irresponsible life, Jean-Jacques Rousseau believed in the natural goodness of humanity, attributing all malice and wickedness to the effect of society and culture on the otherwise spontaneous and inherently innocent person. For Rousseau, as for Descartes, the truth of things was to be found by looking inward. It is hardly an exaggeration to say that the legacy of both these towering figures is simply the modern world and, by extension, the postmodern one. When G. K. Chesterton was asked what was wrong with the Church, he replied: "I am." When Rousseau asked what was wrong with the world, he declared: civilization. The obvious moral conclusion to which this view of things leads is that the challenge facing humanity is not that of renouncing sin but that of changing the social order. Thus: modernity.

For Rousseau, sincerity — of which he claimed to be a rare paragon — carried moral weight all its own. An act was to be judged, not by either its inherent virtue or lack thereof, but simply by the honesty of the one who acknowledged having committed the act in question. An honest recognition of one's sins and crimes served — in and of itself — as absolution for them. Thus, for Rousseau, the public acknowledgement of sin, *sans* remorse or rectification, sufficed to exonerate the offender, all the more so if others found the acknowledged sins to be reprehensible, thereby allowing the accused to bemoan his excoriation by a heartless public and tapping into the subtle privileges attached to the victimary status in a culture under Christian influence.

---

8   Ibid, 2.
9   Farrow, *Theological Negotiations*, 180.

There is no better way of refuting the romantic notion of psychological autonomy than to read Rousseau's original promulgation of it with an eye to the role of mimesis in the life of its author. The contradiction between Rousseau's romantic theory of psychological self-sufficiency and the mimetic facts of his own life is nowhere more apparent than in his last book, *Reveries of the Solitary Walker*. In this series of reflections, Rousseau's self-proclaimed self-reliance stands in sharp contrast with the obvious fact that he was completely preoccupied with how others assessed his masquerade. He writes: "When I think of the way they have made themselves dependent on me in their attempt to make me dependent on them, I feel genuinely sorry for them."[10] "Under pressure from all sides," he later continues, "I remain upright because I cling to nothing and lean only on myself."[11]

Unable and unwilling to acknowledge his preoccupation with how he was seen by others, Rousseau accounts for his eccentric demeanor in ways that anticipate the psychological paradigms of a later era. It is, he says, "the ardor of *my character* that excites me and the *nonchalance* of my character that pacifies me."[12] Rousseau had to deflect the evidence of the mimetic entanglements that so preoccupied him without the benefit of Freud's notion of the unconscious, but he was living at a stage in the crisis when there was less of this evidence to be deflected, and he managed to deflect it reasonably well with a notion only slightly less metaphysical than Freud's, the idea of *character* subtly wedded to the little social performance he called *nonchalance*. It is perfectly clear, however, that these totemic terms did for Rousseau more or less what the notion of the unconscious did for psychoanalysis: they allowed him to treat the mimetic phenomena that could have undermined his basic premises as something intrapsychic, not social, in nature. By the time he wrote *Reveries*, however, it was clear that "character" was not up to its appointed task.

―――

As Peter France remarks, *Reveries* is "full of obsession with enemies and extravagant protestations of innocence, it breathes self-doubt, self-pity, and self-aggrandizement."[13]

---

10 Jean-Jacques Rousseau, *Reveries of the Solitary Walker*, trans. Peter France (London: Penguin, 1979), 100.
11 Ibid., 126.
12 Ibid., 134.
13 France, Introduction to *Reveries of the Solitary Walker*, 14.

> Again and again in the *Reveries* we come across the idea of the refuge, the stable resting-place; the old and anxious author seems to be reassuring himself (and us) that he has at last recovered or discovered the secure peace he longs for. And yet this very repetition and the eloquence with which he creates and conveys this sense of security alert us to the fragility of his construction.[14]

The *Reveries*, no less than his earlier *Confessions*, fairly mock the author's strident assertion of autonomy. He begins his *Reveries* this way:

> So now I am alone in the world, with no brother, neighbour or friend, nor any company left me but my own. The most sociable and loving of men has with one accord been cast out by all the rest. With all the ingenuity of hate they have sought out the cruelest torture for my sensitive soul, and have violently broken all the threads that bound me to them. I would have loved my fellow-men in spite of themselves. It was only by ceasing to be human that they could forfeit my affection.[15]

It was Nietzsche — precariously nearing the precipice of madness — who explicitly declared himself Christ's triumphant rival, but Rousseau can be said to have approached this same dizzying peak. In his case, a semblance of sanity, if not the emotional equilibrium commensurate with it, was made possible both by his confident assertion of innocence and by the presence of enemies, mockers, and naysayers — a combination that could only have appealed to onlookers under Christian influence and could only have been thought to be self-justifying to someone formed by a Christian culture.

The truth comes out. Speaking of his childhood, Rousseau insists: "My desires were so rarely excited and so rarely thwarted, that it never came into my head to have any. I could swear indeed that until I was put under a master, I did not so much as know what it was to want my own way."[16] This both restates and upends Saint Paul's seminal insight that "knowledge of sin comes through the Law" (Rm 3:20). For Rousseau it was the presence of a master — read: civilization — that was to blame for his towering pride saturated with resentment. Rousseau regarded man's natural state as solitary, an anthropological absurdity which found ready believers among those whose taste for anthropological absurdity was insatiable: utopians and misanthropes.

---

14 Ibid.
15 Rousseau, *Reveries of the Solitary Walker*, 27.
16 Rousseau, *The Confessions*, 22.

A passage in his novelistic treatise on education sums up one of Rousseau's most notorious anthropological absurdities:

> Every attachment is a sign of insufficiency: if each of us had no need of other people, we should scarcely think of uniting with them. Thus it is to our infirmity that we owe our fragile happiness. A truly happy being is a solitary being; only God enjoys absolute happiness, but which of us has any conception of it?[17]

Smarting from the scorn with which he sensed others looked on him, Rousseau wrote in *Reveries*:

> I have regained my peace and tranquility and lead a quiet and happy life in the midst of them, laughing at the incredible tortures my persecutors are constantly inflicting on themselves while I live in peace, busy with flowers, stamens and such childish things, and never giving them a moment's thought.[18]

This disavowal is perfectly contradictory. Not only did he give the slights he felt from his contemporaries much more than a moment's thought, he nursed them incessantly. They supplied the evidence he constantly needed to prove his social centrality. "In the *Reveries*," writes Jean-Michel Oughourlian, "it almost looks like Rousseau is doing field tests of Girardian psychopathology! The paranoiac has nothing but enemies. He is alone on earth, he is the perfect scapegoat, at least in his own eyes."[19]

A glaring example of Rousseau's self-absorption and paranoia appears in the introduction to Peter France's translation of Rousseau's *Reveries*:

> Believing himself encircled in an impenetrable conspiracy of silence and misrepresentation, he had attempted in vain to deposit the manuscript of the *Dialogues* on the high altar of Notre Dame, had then given copies of it to the philosopher Condillac and an English visitor, and finally, despairing of ever making his voice heard, had tried to hand out to passers-by a hand-written circular beginning:
>
> *To all Frenchmen who still love justice and truth.*
>
> People of France! Nation that was once kind and affectionate, what has become of you? Why have you changed towards an

---

17 France, Introduction to *Reveries of the Solitary Walker*, 21.
18 Rousseau, *Reveries of the Solitary Walker*, 125.
19 Jean-Michel Oughourlian, *The Mimetic Brain*, trans. Trevor Cribben Merrill (East Lansing: Michigan State University Press, 2016), 118.

unfortunate foreigner who is alone, at your mercy, without any support or defender...[20]

Descartes' anthropological miscalculation worked its way into the cultural presuppositions by way of its philosophical seductiveness, but Jean-Jacques Rousseau's subsequent contribution to anthropological absurdity passed much more directly into popular culture. Rousseau was the flamboyant self-declaration of the implausibility of Cartesian anthropology appearing as its quintessential triumph. If Descartes warded off the influence of others in order to purify his thinking, Rousseau did so in order to establish his own psychological authenticity. His most famous book, named after Augustine's most famous one, announces on its opening page the author's immunity to mimetic influence, the chief demonstration of this adamantine imperturbability being Rousseau's celebrated role as mimetic model imitated by others.

Rousseau was the first widely celebrated figure in Europe to discover the social power of self-deprecating self-referentiality, and surely the first to exploit this power so methodically. His claim to mimetic independence had a spellbinding effect on his contemporaries, too few of whom bothered to wonder why a man who claimed to be indifferent to the opinion of others would go to so much trouble to persuade others that this was the case.

Whereas Descartes was searching for epistemological certainty, a quest that led him to avoid mimetic influence and mistrust the testimony of his senses — a disposition Freud was later to find among his hysterical patients — Rousseau's attempt to immunize himself against mimetic influence led to recognizable episodes of hysterical excitation, for which Freud's patients were later to become famous.

The cultural environment in the latter half of eighteenth-century Europe, when Rousseau was asserting his imperviousness to the influence of others, was more credulous of this claim than is the world today. Thus, Rousseau was able to strike his pose of Olympian nonchalance without fear of a clinical diagnosis of hysteria. In retrospect, however, his psychophysical reactions to those who either attacked or ignored him could have served as one of Freud's case studies in hysteria. Seen in this light, the crypto-hysteria of Descartes, his effort to imagine himself to be without "hands, or eyes, or flesh, or blood, or any senses," presages Rousseau's actual experience of anatomical disturbance, which foreshadowed the symptoms Freud diagnosed as hysteria at the end of

---

20   France, Introduction to *Reveries of the Solitary Walker*, 9.

the nineteenth century. When Rousseau was made to feel the sting of social opprobrium, he was, he wrote, resigned to the "impossibility of repressing these first involuntary reactions."

> Whenever I am provoked, I allow my blood to boil and my senses to be possessed by anger and indignation; I give way to this first explosion of nature, which all my efforts could not prevent or impede. I merely try to stop it leading to any undesirable consequences. My eyes flash, my face flares up, my limbs tremble and palpitations choke me; these are all purely physical reactions and reasoning has no effect on them, but once nature has had its initial explosion one can become one's own master again and gradually regain control over one's senses; this is what I have tried to do, for a long time to no avail, but eventually with greater success.[21]

The late nineteenth-century clinicians with whom Freud collaborated, predisposed though they were to look for hysteria only in women, would have had little trouble diagnosing these physical and emotional convulsions as symptoms of the disorder. Rousseau managed, with considerable effort, to avoid playing the role of imitator by playing the role of the model. The more his spiritual heirs tried to follow his example, the more conscious they became of the nature of the game they were playing; the more they saw how the game was played, the less adroit they were at playing it with anything like Rousseau's deftness.

What Rousseau sought most of all was to be free from shame, which in his case was no small undertaking. To live without guilt and shame is to live a hollow and dishonest life. His strategy for eluding the shame which honesty would otherwise have obliged him to admit was to promote himself as a victim, nay, the victim par excellence. Central to this claim was an insistence on the utter uniqueness of his existence and a practiced disregard for what others thought. The world is now teeming with Rousseau's spiritual descendants, each hoping to avoid becoming an imitator by successfully playing the role of the model and becoming the object of others' attention — increasingly today by posing as a victim or the champion of victims.

Setting out to renounce imitation, Rousseau managed only to demonstrate beyond doubt its unavoidability. His claim to be disinterested in what others thought of him made him the most interesting man in France. It was only a matter of time before Ralph Waldo Emerson was bidding for the American franchise.

---

21   Rousseau, *Reveries of the Solitary Walker*, 134.

THE APOCALYPSE OF THE SOVEREIGN SELF

> Let me admonish you, first of all, to go alone; to refuse the good models, even those which are sacred in the imagination of men, and dare to love God without mediator or veil.... Imitation cannot go above its model. The imitator dooms himself to hopeless mediocrity.[22]

There is a degree of anthropological insight in Rousseau's analysis of envy, shame, and inequality — as there is in Freud's analysis of the Oedipal complex — but neither came to grips with their historical dimension. Both saw these pathologies as primordial and universal. They were right in the sense that these pathologies — what Girard called crises of undifferentiation — appear when the moral and cultural structures that function to prevent them are dissolved by fierce mimetic animosities.

The many serious flaws in Rousseau's anthropological premises notwithstanding, his influence lingers. One such influence became increasingly detectable over the last few decades. As we have said, Rousseau abandoned all five of his illegitimate children — packing them off to orphanages and fashioning philosophical rationalizations for what he had done. Of Rousseau, Paul Johnson writes:

> Many of those who had dealings with him — Hume, for instance, saw him as a child. They began by thinking of him as a harmless child, who could be managed, and discovered to their great cost they were dealing with a brilliant and savage delinquent. Since Rousseau felt (in some ways) as a child, it followed he could not bring up children of his own. Something had to take his place, and that something was the State, in the form of the orphanage.[23]

Of all the circumstances that foster moral maturation, meeting parental responsibilities is perhaps the most reliable. To abandon these responsibilities, whether with regard to children born or unborn, is an act of moral immaturity of which Rousseau is the epitome. The day before yesterday it might have been too early to tell whether this heartless feature of Rousseau's legacy would have lingering cultural consequence. That is no longer the case. Today millions of children are abandoned, less often to the orphanage, but to a shocking extent to medical professionals hired to dispose of children in the womb. In our

---

22 Delivered before the Senior Class in Divinity College, Cambridge, Sunday Evening, July 15, 1838.
23 Johnson, *Intellectuals*, 23.

culture today, the child's first nine months in the womb are statistically the most dangerous period in his entire life.

Less morally odious but nonetheless deeply problematic is the growing tendency of the State to preempt the responsibility that parents have for the moral and social formation of their children. Increasingly, and at an increasingly early age, state schools, social agencies, school boards, and so on are shaping the moral, social, and political outlook of the young. To the extent that this usurpation of the parental role succeeds, not only are the children robbed of their childhood, but parents and other adults are robbed of their agency and freedom. In a very real sense, Rousseau was the windsock for the howling storm that slammed into France in 1789. Paul Johnson writes:

> What began as a process of personal self-justification in a particular case — a series of hasty, ill thought-out excuses for behavior he must have known, initially, was unnatural — gradually evolved, as repetition and growing self-esteem hardened them into genuine convictions, into the proposition that education was the key to social and moral improvement and, this being so, it was the concern of the State. The State must form the minds of all, not only as children (as it had done to Rousseau's in the orphanage) but as adult citizens. By a curious chain of infamous moral logic, Rousseau's iniquity as a parent was linked to his ideological offspring, the future totalitarian state.[24]

In order to plausibly propose his anthropologically implausible vision, the extant cultural order would have to be completely overhauled, as Johnson notes:

> It was necessary to replace the existing society by something totally different and essentially egalitarian; but, this done, revolutionary disorder could not be permitted. The rich and the privileged, as the ordering force, would be replaced by the State, embodying the General Will, which all contracted to obey. Such obedience would become instinctive and voluntary since the State, by a systematic process of cultural engineering, would inculcate virtue in all. The State was the father, the *patrie*, and all its citizens were the children of the paternal orphanage.[25]

Until recently, this hauntingly totalitarian specter would have seemed

---

24 Ibid., 23.
25 Ibid., 24.

as bizarre as it was politically inconceivable to the average American. Again, that is no longer the case, which is another reason why our brief reflections on Rousseau's legacy seem in order. The State as a stern Father, or more recently as a coddling Mother *and* a stern Father, is cognate with the breakdown of the family as the central institution in cultural life. In other words, the more we behave like Jean-Jacques Rousseau, the more inexorably we move toward the totalitarian state, whose apparatchiks are made all the more dangerous by the conviction that they are acting in the best interest of those whose liberties they are suppressing.

Zhou Enlai, the Chinese foreign minister under the murderous Mao Zedong, was once asked what he thought were the consequences of the French Revolution. He famously responded: "It's too early to tell." It subsequently came to light that he understood the question to refer, not to the French Revolution, but to the French student revolts of 1968, which occurred a few years prior to his comment. The popularity of the original interpretation of the comment is itself quite telling. It presupposes that the French Revolution represents a historical inflection point, the ramifications of which are still with us. That this is so has recently become manifestly obvious. Indeed, as Hans Urs von Balthasar has opined, the French Revolution is "the intellectual locus of Christian anxiety" inasmuch as it is understood as "the collapse of the entire old world order before the advancing chaos of liberty... which, considered from the Christian perspective of openness to God can only be assessed as a diabolical counterfeit of truth."[26] Not only is Balthasar's "advancing chaos of liberty" cognate with what Pope Benedict called the dictatorship of relativism and his predecessor on the chair of Peter called the culture of death, but it brings into even sharper focus the paradox and irony of our present predicament.

When the intoxicating brew of romanticism, anthropological naïveté, and heartlessness that the Jacobins found in Rousseau was decanted into the imagination of the mobs in the streets, the result was almost unimaginable savagery. The hysteria of a gifted but emotionally and morally defective man helped to catapult the French nation into a spasm of political hysteria which presaged a series of similar upheavals in Europe in the nineteenth century, and in Russia, Germany, Spain, Cuba, China, Venezuela and elsewhere in the twentieth, the reappearance of which we have recently seen in the streets of major cities in the United States.

---

26 Hans Urs von Balthasar, *The Christian and Anxiety*, trans. Dennis D. Martin and Michael J. Miller, foreword by Yves Tourenne, O.F.M. (San Francisco: Ignatius Press, 2000), 111.

11 Nietzsche and the "Imitatio Christi"

> Nearly two centuries ago, Alexis de Tocqueville said that Americans are all Cartesian without ever having read Descartes. We might say something similar with respect to Nietzsche today: it is increasingly becoming the case that the Western mind is Nietzschean even if most people have never read a word of Nietzsche.
> — Matthew J. Ramage[1]

> The apostate has seen, and then denied what he has seen. Through and through, he remains branded by the image he rejects: with terrible power this image leaves its imprint on his whole existence, which blazes brilliantly in the fire of denial.
> — Hans Urs von Balthasar[2]

> We must be careful not to jettison any of the precious stellar material that the Nietzschean supernova throws out in all directions, on the faint-hearted or morally fastidious pretext that it is too hot to handle.
> — Giuseppe Fornari[3]

How many faithful Christians have seen the seriousness of Christianity as well as did the man who opposed it to the point of madness? Let us begin, therefore, by acknowledging that Nietzsche deserves our grudging respect for drawing out what was for him the most catastrophic effect of the Christian revelation. Like his contrast between Christ and Dionysus, this assessment has much truth in it. Perhaps the best way to summarize the charge that Nietzsche made against Christ and his Church is to quote a passage in

---

1 Matthew J. Ramage, *The Experiment of Faith* (Washington, DC: The Catholic University of America, 2020), 4.
2 Balthasar, *The Glory of the Lord*, Vol. 1: *Seeing the Form*, 524.
3 Giuseppe Fornari, *Dionysus, Christ, and the Death of God*, Vol. II (East Lansing: Michigan State University Press, 2021), 382.

Hans Urs von Balthasar's work which, without mentioning the German thinker, perfectly expresses Nietzsche's accusation against Christianity. It appears in the most unusual of Balthasar's many books, *Heart of the World*. In this passage, all the more compelling inasmuch as it sounds a very audible Girardian theme, the Swiss theologian puts Christ in the dock and arraigns him on charges of having crippled man by destroying his precious innocence and daring.

> You [Christ] will be guilty of the fact that men have lost their childlike faith in the gods and now, despairing with disillusionment in you, they pass over to a resolute godlessness. Do you see what you have caused with your redemption? You wanted to restore to the blind the light of their eyes, but now those who gained back their sight are doubly guilty. When they crucified you in the first instance, they did not know what they were doing; their sin resembled the native cruelty of a beast of prey: it was in their nature. But now they know what they do. You have drawn back the veil from the mystery of eternal love.... Now their sin becomes revolt against love. What used to be pardonable and excusable has, through you, become deadly and unforgivable.... Believe me, men would do better to keep to their nature and their instincts. The only thing you have accomplished is to give men a bad conscience.[4]

With this reference to a bad conscience, let us turn first to the Epistle to the Hebrews and then to Nietzsche's variation on it.

> If, after we have been given knowledge of the truth, we should deliberately commit any sins, then there is no longer any sacrifice for them. There will be left only the dread prospect of judgment and of the raging fire that is to burn rebels. (Heb 10:26-27)

The author of the Letter to the Hebrews here addresses this dire warning specifically to those who have been given knowledge of the truth, that is, Christians. But his warning pertains as well to those who have fallen under Christian influence, whether confessionally or culturally. The tortures of impenitence of which the Hebrews author warns befall those who deliberately commit sin after the Christian revelation has fatally exposed and crippled the old system for taking away sins by

---

4   Hans Urs von Balthasar, *Heart of the World*, trans. Erasmo S. Leiva (San Francisco: Ignatius Press, 1979), 112, 113.

sanctimoniously offloading them onto some hapless victim. By revealing — quintessentially on Golgotha — the truth about this most ancient of man's rituals, Christianity brought into view the moral problems that the old system swept away. As de Lubac observed, Nietzsche was a man "whom Minerva did not fail to visit occasionally."[5] To which Duane Armitage has provided the footnote:

> The seemingly innate instinct we have to side with the weak, to feel pity and compassion for the persecuted, for Nietzsche and Girard, is nothing more than the result of two thousand years of habituation — catechesis — in Christianity. That is, Nietzsche (and Girard) asks us to consider why we care for victims, have compassion for weakness, for poverty, and so on?[6]

The obvious difference between Girard and Nietzsche is that, while Girard is wary of its current misuse, he regarded this empathy for victims to be of crucial — pun intended — importance for our civilization, while for Nietzsche this empathy for victims had become indistinguishable from the incipient forms of virtue-signaling from which he recoiled in the Protestant Germany of his day.

Whether consciously or not, in the famous aphorism 125 of *Gay Science* (*Joyful Wisdom*), Nietzsche essentially paraphrased what the author of Hebrews had written about the Christian crippling of the sacrificial system for transferring the onus of sin onto surrogate victims. The madman tells his uncomprehending listeners that God is dead and that *we have killed him*.

> What did we do when we loosened this earth from its sun? Whither does it now move? Whither do we move? Away from all suns? Do we not dash on unceasingly? Backwards, sideways, forwards, in all directions? Is there still an above and below?... God is dead! God remains dead! And we have killed him! How shall we console ourselves, the most murderous of all murderers?... Who will wipe the blood from us? With what water could we cleanse ourselves? What lustrums, what sacred games shall we have to devise?[7]

---

5 Henri de Lubac, *Theology in History*, trans. Anne Englund Nash (San Francisco: Ignatius Press, 1996), 503.
6 Duane Armitage, *Philosophy's Violent Sacred* (East Lansing: Michigan State University Press, 2021), 98.
7 Friedrich Nietzsche, *Joyful Wisdom*, trans. Thomas Common (New York: Frederick Ungar Publishing, 1964), 168.

If the author of Hebrews says that there is no longer any sacrifice for sin and that, as a result, there will remain only "the dread prospect of judgment and of the raging fire that is to burn rebels," Nietzsche asks: "Who will wipe the blood from us? With what water could we cleanse ourselves?" What lustrums (*ritual absolutions*) and what sacred games (*religious rituals*) can be found that, after the Christian revelation, will exonerate those whose guilt stands revealed?

Near the end of the famous death of God aphorism, Nietzsche's madman acknowledged that he had come early and that the cultural and historical consequence of the murder of the Christian God was "still on its way." Later in aphorism 343, Nietzsche returns to the consequences of the death — the murder as he sees it — of the Christian God. Having previously noted that the consequences would only later become apparent:

> What must all collapse now that this belief [in the Christian God] had been undermined — because so much was built upon it, so much rested on it, and had become one with it: for example, our entire European morality. This lengthy, vast and uninterrupted process of crumbling, destruction, ruin and overthrow which is now imminent: who has realized it sufficiently to-day to have to stand up as the teacher and herald of such a tremendous logic of terror, as the prophet of a period of gloom and eclipse, the like of which has probably never taken place on earth before?[8]

If the author of Hebrews declares that once we have been given knowledge of the truth there is no longer any sacrifice for sin, Nietzsche's madman — thrown into a state of hysteria — bemoans the loss of any ritual absolution that might cleanse us from the criminal act of having killed God. Nietzsche is brilliant enough to realize the catastrophic consequences of "killing" the God Incarnate in Christ, and honest enough — at least in this passage — to declare it.

If this revelation was instantaneous for some — the centurion at the Crucifixion — and more gradual for others — Saul after witnessing the stoning of Stephen — it would gradually overtake those remotely touched by Christianity, depriving them of the moral satisfaction of occasionally offloading their sins onto the back of a socially execrated figure. Having exposed "things hidden since the foundation of the world,"

---

8   Ibid., 275.

the Christian revelation had the effect of driving unforgiven sins ever deeper into the hearts of the unrepentant, there to become "the raging fire that is to burn rebels." It is from this point of reference that we can best understand the resentment of which Nietzsche and Kierkegaard complained, and from which the former conspicuously suffered. The word Greek term translated here as "rebels" is *hupenantios*. It derives from *hupo*, meaning hyper, and *enantios*, the word from which we have the word antagonism. Thus, the *hupenantios* means hyper-antagonism, or a rebel without a cause.

In what could be regarded as a gloss on the above passage from Hebrews, René Girard writes: "The imitation of Christ becomes the imitation of one's neighbor. The surge of pride breaks against the humanity of the mediator, and the result of this conflict is hatred."[9] "When faith is lost, the victory falls to hatred," Balthasar observed in his analysis of the poetry of Reinhold Schneider, who had written of "the hatred of the one who has decided in full consciousness for damnation in order to torment for all eternity the one who had insulted him."[10] It is in this context that one can best understand how Girard saw Nietzsche's favored god, Dionysus: as the god of mania, the god of homicidal fury. So here we have the cluster of terms which touch on the cultural crisis coincident with the de-Christianization of a once Christianized culture: *hupenantios* (hyper-antagonism), hysteria, mania, "homicidal fury," all driven by a demonic spirit that is "sulphurous and sinister." To that can be added Giuseppe Fornari's conclusion that, whereas the ancient world was "mortgaged to Dionysian sacrifices," modernity is "darkness, aglitter with collectivist hysteria and the first global conflagration."[11]

What is more central to the issue at hand — the apocalypse of the sovereign self — for which Nietzsche's life is evidence, is that the nihilism that has its origin in the amoral and irrational god conduces to a conspicuous form of hysteria at the personal level. Jean-Jacques Rousseau's underlying psychological circumstance may have been limned by his namesake, the American historian G. S. Rousseau, who concluded that hysteria is a form of "nervous self-fashioning."[12] As we have noted, the intellectual provocateur from whose breathless prose the French

---

9   Girard, *Deceit, Desire, and the Novel*, 59.
10 Hans Urs von Balthasar, *Tragedy Under Grace: Reinhold Schneider on the Experience of the West*, trans. Brian McNeil, C.R.V. (San Francisco: Ignatius Press, 1997), 169.
11 Fornari, *Dionysus, Christ, and the Death of God*, Vol. II, 145.
12 G. S. Rousseau, "A Strange Pathology: Hysteria in the Early Modern World, 1500–1800," *Hysteria Beyond Freud* (University of California Press, 1993), 158ff.

Revolution inhaled its world-altering break with common sense and common decency began his *Confessions* with an assertion that fairly defines one prominent form of hysteria: "I am made unlike any one I have ever met; I will even venture to say that *I am like no one in the whole world. I may be no better, but at least I am different.*"[13] A hundred years later, in a letter written to Franz Oberbeck, an equally brilliant and equally self-absorbed iconoclast, Friedrich Nietzsche, sounded a distinctly similar note: "I do not know why this happens to fall just on my shoulders — but it is possible that I am *the first* to have an idea that will divide the history of humanity into two parts."[14] To whom could Nietzsche be comparing himself with that statement? Quite obviously the one from whose birth we chronicle time, dividing the two Testaments of the Bible and counting subsequent time from the birth of Christ. In the first paragraph of *Ecce Homo*, Nietzsche introduces himself with a swagger that might have come, word for word, from the pen of Jean-Jacques Rousseau:

> As it is my intention within a very short time to confront my fellow-men with the very greatest demand that has ever yet been made upon them, it seems to me above all necessary to declare here who and what I am. As a matter of fact, this ought to be pretty well known already, for I have not "held my tongue" about myself. But the disparity which obtains between the greatness of my task and the smallness of my contemporaries, is revealed by the fact that people have neither heard me nor yet seen me.... Under these circumstances, it is a duty — and one against which my customary reserve, and to a still greater degree the pride of my instincts, rebel — to say: *Listen! for I am such and such a person. For Heaven's sake do not confound me with anyone else!*[15]

When Nietzsche posits a stark contrast between the greatness of his task and *the smallness of his contemporaries*, we have every reason to conclude that what constitutes the deficiency of his contemporaries is their refusal to recognize the greatness of the one whom they have neither heard nor seen. This is a form of that "nervous self-fashioning" which G. S. Rousseau recognized as the essence of hysteria. That this self-fashioning in Nietzsche's case was palpably mimetic — that his preeminent model

---

13 Rousseau, *The Confessions*, 17. Emphasis added.
14 Quoted in de Lubac, *Drama of Atheistic Humanism*, 470, n. 5.
15 Friedrich Nietzsche, *Ecce Homo*, trans. Anthony M. Ludovici (N.p.: Digireads. com Publishing, 2009), 5.

Nietzsche and the "Imitatio Christi"

and cosmic rival was Christ — gave Nietzsche's hysteria a special power, albeit the very power to which he was to succumb in the end.

As Nietzsche vociferously claimed, the choice facing European civilization was between Dionysus and the Crucified. In fact, it is on that claim that his enduring greatness rests. At this point in time, it is easy to recognize that he was right about the choice facing humanity. His tragedy was that he made the wrong choice. Nietzsche chose Dionysus and went mad. Understood most charitably, he is a kind of self-immolated post-Christian martyr, whose life stands as a largely unheeded warning about the perils involved in trying to fashion a post-Christian god and a post-Christian culture, a fool's errand that leads in the end to an exaltation of hysteria as the distinguishing mark of the radically emancipated and deracinated individual.

And yet, Nietzsche remains an important part of the story we are sketching. For he shows that the flight from Christ, his revelation, and his Church leads to a raging and hysterical parody of all that is being rejected. As Susan Nieman, among countless others, has noted:

> Nietzsche spent a lifetime wondering which god to become. Many of his texts suggest Dionysus as the clear favorite. But why call his intellectual autobiography *Ecce Homo*, or write *Zarathustra* in the style of the Gospels, choked with allusions to the Sermon on the Mount?[16]

Writes André Gide:

> In the presence of the Gospel, Nietzsche's immediate and profound reaction was — it must be admitted — jealousy. It does not seem to me that Nietzsche's work can be really understood without allowing for that feeling. Nietzsche was jealous of Christ, jealous to the point of madness. In writing his *Zarathustra* Nietzsche was continually tormented with the desire to contradict the Gospel. Often he adopted the actual form of the Beatitudes in order to reverse them. He wrote *Anti-Christ* and, in his last work, *Ecce Homo*, set himself up as the victorious rival of him whose teaching he proposed to supplant.[17]

Nietzsche insisted that *Thus Spake Zarathustra* was "a fifth gospel" and, as Henri de Lubac observes:

---

16 Susan Nieman, *Evil in Modern Thought: An Alternative History of Philosophy* (Princeton: Princeton University Press, 2002), 218.
17 Quoted in de Lubac, *Drama of Atheistic Humanism*, 297.

> There is no doubt, moreover, that it must be understood, in the thought of Nietzsche, that this fifth gospel abolishes the preceding ones, the four Christian Gospels.... From this day on, Nietzsche, an inspired prophet, and more than just a prophet, to be sure, did not pass himself off any more as a mere critic and adversary of Christianity but as a rival and successor to Jesus.... Already he is aware of himself as the one who will be able to say of himself with obvious literal intent: *Ecce Homo*.[18]

Anticipating the slight-of-hand by which Freud managed to avoid confronting the mimetic problems from which his hysterical patients were more or less obviously suffering, Nietzsche's division between the Dionysian and the Apollonian served to endow the two principal forms of hysteria — the ostentatious and the lymphatic, the histrionic and the phlegmatic, the melodramatic and the robotic — with a pedigree as venerable as the one Freud and his collaborators would bestow on the disorder a few years later. In an interesting parallel to the bipolarity that Rousseau described as the alternation of *ardor* and *nonchalance*, David Healy, a professor of psychiatry, uses the terms *frenzy* and *stupor*. Nietzsche's variation on these alternating pairs was Dionysus and Apollo. And as the Freudian analyst Fritz Wittels noted: "Nietzsche's division into Dionysian and Apollonian, removes the reproach which adheres to the word hysterical."[19]

Indeed, clinical hysteria can be seen as a spontaneous ritual exorcism, by which the hysteric tries to protect his autonomy, either by a flamboyant act of self-dramatization, the desperate supernova of a dying star, or, on the contrary, by a retreat behind an Easter Island countenance of imperturbability. Each of these is an attempt to resist the gravitational lure of a more compelling personality, around which the subject might otherwise circle as a spellbound satellite — precisely as the young classmates in Woolf's novel were spellbound by Percival.

Keeping in mind Descartes' cramped garret, wherein he resolutely determined to ignore "the heavens, the air, the earth, colors, shapes, sounds, and all external things as nothing but the bedeviling hoaxes of my dreams," here is how Stefan Zweig described Nietzsche, huddled in his "small, narrow, modest, coldly furnished" room:

> ... innumerable notes, pages, writings, and proofs are piled up on the table, but no flower, no decoration, scarcely a book and

---

18 Ibid., 477.
19 Fritz Wittels, *Freud and His Times* (New York: Grosset & Dunlap, 1931), 238.

> rarely a letter... on a tray innumerable bottles and jars and potions... a frightful arsenal of poisons and drugs, yet the only helpers in the empty silence of this strange room in which he never rests except in brief and artificially conquered sleep. Wrapped in his overcoat and a woolen scarf (for the wretched stove smokes only and does not give warmth), his fingers freezing, his double glasses pressed close to the paper, his hurried hand writes for hours — words the dim eyes can hardly decipher. For hours he sits like this and writes until his eyes burn.[20]

There are many reasons for such a miserable existence, but the one that comes closest to the prime one is what Nietzsche has in common with Descartes: the determination to rely only on his own genius, to regard all but his most ancient predecessors as nothing more than his own failed precursors. How many young people today, taught from childhood to hold even their most illustrious predecessors as morally flawed and politically rapacious, post or tweet or text shopworn slogans to their social media "friends" or "followers," cryptic messages which constitute an ironclad case against the educational system that has reduced them to this unintentional self-abasement?

Jean-Jacques Rousseau's sub-clinical hysteria was on display in his insistence that his *Confessions*, notwithstanding that its title was borrowed so blatantly from Augustine, had no precedent and would have no imitator. His German counterpart in the nineteenth century showed no less a flare for self-adulation. Nietzsche's *Ecce Homo* is broken into four sections: "Why I Am So Wise," "Why I Am So Clever," "Why I Write Such Good Books," and "Why I Am a Destiny."

We know that Nietzsche used opium and other psychotropic drugs, in forms and dosages congruent with the scant nineteenth-century understanding of their toxicity. We cannot know how much these drugs might have played a role in his determination to be caught up into some ecstatic process and become its willing instrument. Whatever the causes, however, the experience itself was never more on display than in Nietzsche's description of his ecstasy in *Ecce Homo*. Reminiscent of Rousseau, Nietzsche declares:

> Has anyone at the end of the nineteenth century a clear idea of what poets of strong ages have called *inspiration*? If not, I will describe it.... A rapture whose tremendous tension occasionally

---

20 Quoted in *The Portable Nietzsche*, ed. and trans. Walter Kaufmann (New York: Viking Press, 1979), 104.

discharges itself in a flood of tears — now the pace quickens involuntarily, now it becomes slow; one is altogether beside oneself, with the distinct consciousness of subtle shudders and of one's skin creeping down to one's toes; a depth of happiness in which even what is most painful and gloomy does not seem something opposite but rather conditioned, provoked, a *necessary* color in such a superabundance of life.... Everything happens involuntarily in the highest degree but as in a gale of feeling of freedom, of absoluteness, of power, of divinity.... This is *my* experience of inspiration; I do not doubt that one has to go back thousands of years in order to find anyone who could say to me, "it is mine as well."[21]

One can hardly read Nietzsche's account of what he imagines to be the key to his inspiration without recalling Rousseau's depiction of his reaction to what he perceived as the social scorn of his contemporaries: "My eyes flash, my face flares up, my limbs tremble and palpitations choke me; these are all purely physical reactions and reasoning has no effect on them." In both cases, we have conspicuous symptoms of what late nineteenth- and early twentieth-century clinicians would dub hysteria. Henri de Lubac seems to have reached the same conclusion:

> [Nietzsche] can be driven passively, caught up in the enormous, despairing cyclical movement, but he can also share in the controlling power that thus moves the universe; he can suffer the iron law of universal determinism, but he can also freely be the law itself; he can love this fatality to the point of identification with it: "*Amor Fati. Ego Fatum.*"[22]

This secret lust for becoming the law itself, emerging from the bloody womb of violence and savagery, is the dark and terrifying reality that burst onto the scene at the French Revolution, and which thereafter has erupted time and again, unleashing horrendous violence. Girard saw with great perspicacity one of the most pernicious of Nietzsche's legacies, namely his "radicalizing the concern for victims in an anti-Christian manner."[23] "What only the great insight of a Nietzsche could formerly

---

21 Friedrich Nietzsche, "*On the Genealogy of Morals*" *and* "*Ecce Homo,*" trans. Walter Kaufmann (New York: Random House, 1967), 300–301.
22 Henri de Lubac, *Affrontements mystiques* (1950), quoted in Hans Urs von Balthasar, *The Theology of Henri de Lubac* (San Francisco: Ignatius Press, 1991), 50.
23 René Girard, *I See Satan Fall Like Lightning*, trans. James G. Williams (Maryknoll, NY: Orbis Books, 2001), 179.

perceive, now even a child can perceive. The current process of spiritual demagoguery and rhetorical overkill has transformed the concern for victims into a totalitarian command and a permanent inquisition."[24]

Few people are brazen enough and delirious enough to declare their superiority to Christ, but our world today is filled with people, mildly less delirious, who breezily declare their superiority to the moral sensibilities that Christ awakened. However ludicrous the comparison might seem, Nietzsche's preoccupation with Christ bears a likeness to Hap Loman's pathological preoccupation with the merchandise manager in Miller's *Death of a Salesman*. In each case, the imitator-rival is openly contemptuous of the figure whose preeminence he is nonetheless determined to acquire for himself. What Marie-Anne Cochet said of Nietzsche could be said of Miller's Hap Loman, namely that "Nietzsche identifies himself with those whom he fights as well as with those whom he admires," adding that this is not altogether surprising, "inasmuch as he only fights those whom he admires."[25] If that seems paradoxical, it is at the heart of René Girard's anthropological discoveries. Apropos of which de Lubac observes:

> Nietzsche will not stop being haunted, right to his last day, by the figure of Jesus. With respect to Jesus he passes alternatively between admiration and denigration, tenderness and sarcasm, which can be explained by a secret jealousy.... What comes first is an anxiousness to antagonize in the very act of imitation, through the need to play an analogous and superior role.... He cannot do other than take his own measure with reference to Jesus, and for his part he never stops looking at him surreptitiously out of the corner of his eye, so to speak. All of *Zarathustra* witnesses to this desire to imitate.[26]

De Lubac has given us a lapidary summary of Girard's anthropology of mimetic desire, precisely at the point where the imitator-turned-rival aspires to replace the model, the point at which the *antichrist* — or the anti-merchandise manager — comes into view, consumed by "an anxiousness to antagonize in the very act of imitation." Of course Rousseau, who explored every twist and turn of the mimetic labyrinth, was Nietzsche's predecessor in this, as is demonstrated by Rousseau's declaration previously quoted: "I could swear indeed that until I was put

---

24   Ibid., 178.
25   Quoted in de Lubac, *Drama of Atheistic Humanism*, 498, n84.
26   Ibid., 496–97.

under a master, I did not so much as know what it was to want my own way."[27] Here is a source of *ressentiment* of which Nietzsche hasn't taken account and from which he suffered. It's difficult to think of a way of accounting for it that would not have the effect of exposing Nietzsche's will-to-power as the archetypal symptom of, rather than the cure for, *ressentiment* — the resentment which has become a social epidemic in the twenty-first century, the resentment which Kierkegaard called the constituent principle of the modern age. As René Girard noted:

> Nietzsche shared with many intellectuals of his time and our own a passion for irresponsible rhetoric in the attempt to get one up on an opponent.... Since the Second World War a whole new intellectual wave has emerged, hostile to Nazism but more nihilist than ever, more than ever a tributary of Nietzsche.[28]

In a section of his *The Drama of Atheistic Humanism* most interestingly entitled "Nietzsche as Mystic," Henri de Lubac quotes from one of Nietzsche's letters:

> At times I tell myself that in essence I am leading one of the most dangerous of lives, for I am one of those machines that can *explode*. The intensity of my feelings makes me tremble and laugh at one and the same time. Several times already I have not been able to leave my room for the ridiculous reason that my eyes were inflamed.... And these were not tender tears of pitiful emotion, but tears of jubilation. At those times I sang and spoke stupid, foolish things, possessed as I was by a new vision that I am the first of men to know.[29]

This defiant and titanic act of hubris leads in the end, as Balthasar noted, to the grim determination to affirm the world as it is, in all its savagery, heartlessness, and concentration camps. "Let him attempt it and see whether he can retain his sanity."[30]

Had this brilliant and unstable man lived long enough to turn to Dr Sigmund Freud, there cannot be the slightest doubt that Freud would have treated him as a hysteric. Alas, Nietzsche finally went irreversibly mad a few years before Freud launched his career by examining and

---

27 Rousseau, *Confessions*, 22.
28 Girard, *I See Satan Fall Like Lightning*, 175.
29 Quoted in de Lubac, *Drama of Atheist Humanism*, 470.
30 Balthasar, *Elucidations*, 54, 55.

analyzing patients suffering from hysteria, of which there suddenly appeared so many. The point at which Nietzsche's final plunge into madness occurred, however, is itself instructive in a way that merits revisiting.

Nietzsche had long fulminated against the charity, mercy, and solicitude for victims — Christianity's transvaluation of all values — which he contemptuously dismissed as Christian pity or slave morality. His early enthusiasm for the nihilist philosopher Arthur Schopenhauer was complicated by Nietzsche's sharp rejection of the German philosopher's emphasis on compassion as the appropriate moral attitude in a meaningless world. For Nietzsche — whose father, a Lutheran pastor, died when he was five years old — this capitulation to the Kantian ethos of Protestant Christianity was anathema. Nietzsche was ever the champion of the *Übermensch*, the superman or over-man whom he insisted was destined to replace the gentler ethic of Christ. As we previously mentioned, in Nietzsche's defense it can be said that he was the first to speak contemptuously of what today is called "virtue-signaling." Unfortunately, he despised the virtue being signaled even more than the preening act of signaling it. Writes Giuseppe Fornari: "It becomes increasingly evident from the texts and testimonies that while insulting the cross, and because he insults it, Nietzsche is obsessed and absorbed by it to a point where he can no longer see himself apart from it but must ascend, or collapse, onto it."[31]

The collapse to which the obsession led occurred in Turin: the famous Turin horse event, long seen as the onset of Nietzsche's final fall into madness, from which he never recovered. The authenticity of the event is debated, but the account of it has survived in part because there seems something hauntingly congruent about it. Nietzsche's final plunge into the madness that was to last for the last ten years of his life began with an act that can be described only as a pitiable act of pity, an episode of sobbing hysteria by the champion of the unflinching *Übermensch*.

On January 3, 1889, on leaving the home of his hosts in Turin, Nietzsche saw the driver of a horse-drawn cart beating the collapsed horse. Suddenly overwhelmed, Nietzsche threw himself on the horse to shield it from the blows. Other strange disturbances followed until his Italian hosts were able to rescue him. The facts are disputed. But even if part or all of the story is apocryphal, its wide popularity among both Nietzsche's defenders and critics suggests an affinity between the man who philosophized with a hammer and the man whose final plunge

---

31 Fornari, *Dionysus, Christ, and the Death of God*, Vol. II, 390.

into madness occurred at the moment when he was overtaken by pity for a helpless victim of a boorish and unflinching *Übermensch*. At that moment, the man who had spent a life trying to acquire the animal innocence of a beast of prey was overcome with compassion precisely for an animal being preyed upon by a heartless man.

Henri de Lubac declared Nietzsche to be a mystic, only to insist that Nietzsche's mysticism was "a mysticism without God."[32] His mysticism was not, however, without Christ, albeit a Christ who — in Girardian terms — was the fiery philosopher's model-rival. Notwithstanding his erudition and raw genius, in Lubacian terms which we will address below, precisely because Nietzsche's mysticism was a mysticism without God, he was a mystic in the primitive state.

Our assessment of Nietzsche's legacy might indeed remain highly critical, even as the Turin horse episode allows us to hope that in the end Fredrich Nietzsche's heart was finally broken by the spontaneous empathy he felt for a beast of burden. To the extent that this was the case, we would concur with Giuseppe Fornari: "Nietzsche approaches the truth of Dionysus, and it turns out to be the truth of Christ."[33]

---

32   De Lubac, *Drama of Atheist Humanism*, 490.
33   Fornari, *Dionysus, Christ, and the Death of God*, Vol. II, 383.

12 Underground Man:
REBEL WITHOUT A CAUSE

> We do not know how to join in Dostoyevsky's laughter because we do not know how to laugh at ourselves. Today many people praise *Notes from the Underground* without any idea that they are unearthing a caricature of themselves written a century ago.
> — René Girard[1]

DOSTOEVSKY PUBLISHED NOTES FROM UNDER-*ground* in 1864, ten years before publishing his more definitive treatment of nihilism, *The Demons*. In what once would have seemed a wild exaggeration, however, the diagnosis of nihilism in the earlier work touches on all the most essential issues of concern to us here. In his foreword to René Girard's book on Dostoevsky, James Williams writes:

> Girard wonders whether Dostoevsky is neglected in our time because our age could be described as "underground" in the great Russian novelist's sense of the term. Popular culture and political life is *hysterically mimetic*, rife with mimetic rivalry and scandal, which lead to polar extremes of conflict and hostility. Thus it is distressing for us to see ourselves in the Dostoevskyan mirror. We have simply warmed-over nineteenth-century ideas concerning the autonomy of individuals and the rejection of ancient law and prohibition, while we become further and further enmeshed in the mimeticism that ironically diminishes our personal freedom and communal life.[2]

In the second half of the nineteenth century, Dostoevsky began diagnosing a spiritual malignancy that was at that moment giving birth to both political nihilism and psychoanalysis. This adumbration of the

---
1 Girard, *Deceit, Desire, and the Novel*, 262.
2 James G. Williams, in the foreword to Girard, *Resurrection from the Underground*, xi. Emphasis added.

current crisis was appearing, unnamed, in literary works and, variously misdiagnosed, in the social sciences. It was cognate with the rising tide of resentment which Nietzsche was blaming on Christians even as he was bottling and labeling it as a cure for what he perceived to be an essentially Christian disease. When a Dostoevsky and a Nietzsche agree on something like this one can confidently assume that their concern is well placed, however divergent their analyses might be. Virginia Woolf was hardly a match for either. As remarkable as was her literary prescience, her Russian and German predecessors had reconnoitered the problem more thoroughly than she and decades earlier. Nonetheless, in the opening lines of Dostoevsky's *Notes from Underground*, its glowering anti-hero puts his physical health at risk for the same reason that Virginia Woolf's Bernard refused to consult those who might have been the physicians of his troubled soul.

> I am a sick man... I am a spiteful man, I am an unpleasant man. I think my liver is diseased.... I refuse to treat it out of spite.... I am perfectly well aware that I cannot "get even" with the doctors by not consulting them. I know better than anyone that I thereby injure only myself and no one else. But still, if I don't treat it, it is out of spite. My liver is bad, well then — let it get even worse! [3]

The Underground Man would rather be consumed by a diseased liver than abandon a desire to "get even" with physicians whom he has never met and whose medical interventions he rejects out of spite. For, as the Underground Man further notes:

> One's very own free, unfettered desire, one's own whim, no matter how wild, one's own fantasy, even though sometimes roused to the point of madness — all this constitutes precisely that previously omitted, most advantageous advantage which isn't included under any classification and because of which all systems and theories are constantly smashed to smithereens. [4]

What the Underground Man fails to acknowledge, and what his literary creator knows so well, is that "one's very own free, unfettered desire" is entirely focused — not on the purported object of desire — but on everything and everyone he resents. It is the nihilistic itch to smash all systems and theories to smithereens that is the only altogether fleeting

---

[3] Fyodor Dostoevsky, *"Notes from Underground" and "The Grand Inquisitor,"* trans. Ralph E. Matlaw (New York: E. P. Dutton, 1960), 3.
[4] Ibid., 18.

satisfaction for a man suffering from this late stage of hysterical disintegration. He has become a *maniac*, a man succumbing to "homicidal fury." Virginia Woolf gave her readers a glimpse of it when her character Bernard lifted the veil on this spiritual predicament: "What *delights* me then is the confusion, the height, the indifference and the fury. Great clouds always changing, and movement; something sulphurous and sinister."[5] Dostoevsky's Underground Man gives us a closer look at this quintessentially late-modern despair masquerading as an aspiration for freedom from constraint.

> Shower upon [man] every earthly blessing, drown him in bliss so that nothing but bubbles would dance on the surface of his bliss, as on a sea; give him such economic prosperity that he would have nothing else to do but sleep, eat cakes and busy himself with ensuring the continuation of world history and even then man, out of sheer ingratitude, sheer libel, would play you some loathsome trick. He would even risk his cakes and would deliberately desire the most fatal rubbish, the most uneconomical absurdity, simply to introduce into all this positive rationality his fatal fantastic element.[6]

For the Underground Man, the sign of true vitality was the ability to take revenge with no hesitation, moral or otherwise. Those who can do so, he insisted, have a primary cause, and those who cannot suffer from the constant torment of resentment: an antipathy for which there is no legitimate outlet, neither revenge nor forgiveness. That is the Underground Man's condition: Christian charity and the ethic of forgiveness have crippled his ability to take revenge with no lingering pangs of conscience, as is clear from his rambling ruminations:

> How many times it has happened to me — well, for instance, to take offense at nothing, simply on purpose; and one knows oneself, of course, that one is offended at nothing, that one is pretending, but yet one brings oneself, at last, to the point of really being offended. All my life I have had an impulse to play such pranks, so that in the end, I could not control myself.... I said that a man revenges himself because he finds justice in it. Therefore he has found a primary cause, found a basis, to wit, justice. And so he is completely set at rest, and consequently

---

5 Woolf, *The Waves*, 239. Emphasis added.
6 Dostoevsky, *Notes from Underground*, 27.

he carries out his revenge calmly and successfully, as he is convinced that he is doing a just and honest thing. But, after all, I see no justice in it, I find no sort of virtue in it, either, and consequently if I attempt to revenge myself, it would only be out of spite.... But what can be done if I do not even have spite...? Again, in consequence of those accursed laws of consciousness, my spite is subject to chemical disintegration. You look into it, the object flies off into air, your reasons evaporate, the criminal is not to be found, the insult becomes fate rather than an insult, something like the toothache, for which there is no one to blame, and consequently there is only the same outlet left again — that is, to beat the wall as hard as you can.[7]

Since there was no one to blame, there was no cause — no plausible *accusation* — sufficiently compatible with justice to sanction vengeance. The Underground Man suffers this handicap precisely because he lives in a culture that has long been under Christian influence. It is not chemical disintegration that has deprived him of his righteous indignation; it is the fact that he inhabits a culture which has been taught that the splinter in the neighbor's eye cannot be used to obscure the plank in one's own.

We have noted the diagnostic pertinence of the comment by James Williams about how "hysterically mimetic" our cultural and political life can and will become if we persist in trying to forget our Christian patrimony. Perhaps the quintessential literary depiction of this mimetic hysteria is found in the tavern scene in *Notes from Underground*:

> One night as I was passing a tavern, I saw through a lighted window some gentlemen fighting with billiard cues, and saw one of them thrown out of the window.... I actually envied the gentleman thrown out of the window, and I envied him so much that I even went into the tavern and into the billiard-room. "Perhaps," I thought, "I'll have a fight, too, and they'll throw me out of the window." I was not drunk, but what is one to do — after all, *depression* will drive a man to such a pitch of *hysteria*.[8]

Here is where Nietzsche's assessment of Dostoevsky as the only reliable psychologist is substantiated. The Russian novelist has located the origin

---

7   Ibid., 15, 16.
8   Ibid., 42–43. In all three English translations of the novel we have consulted, the translator has chosen *hysteria* as the English equivalent of the Russian.

of hysteria in the loss of ontological substance and the maneuverings aimed at compensating for the loss by attracting the attention of others. Whereas Jean-Jacques Rousseau gave incessant expression to his status as an innocent victim, the Underground Man dropped the moral pretense. Irrespective of innocence or guilt, he envied the man who was able to attract enough scorn to enjoy a blessed moment of social centrality. The effort made to attract that attention was conspicuously *performative* in the superficial sense, to which we will later contrast the performative character of Christian existence.

Having come to the end of his rope, the Underground Man longed to be "sacrificed," thereby to discover or recover the mystery of his existence. To that extent, he was surely right. In the end, however, the stunt he contemplated was itself a parody of self-sacrificial Christian heroism: making such an obnoxious fool of himself that he would momentarily enjoy the ersatz luxury of being a universally despised victim, not a fool for Christ in the great Orthodox tradition, but a crude parody of Christ.

Since the attempt leads only to a further ontological depletion, the one desperate for the transfusion of *being* from the eyes of others can grow so desperate that it becomes immaterial whether the attention is adulatory or disdainful. About being run out of town on a rail, Abraham Lincoln is reputed to have wryly observed: "If it weren't for the honor of the thing, I'd just as soon it happened to someone else." What makes that remark so clever is manifold: the faux-ontology of social centrality — the ecstatic experience of being, like Shakespeare's Hamlet, "the observed of all observers" and the subtle recognition of the privilege that the victim enjoys in a world under Christian influence.

The Underground Man's crisis of insubstantiality was such that he no longer cared whether the attention of others was adulatory or contemptuous, just as long as he was able to compensate for the diminution of his "ontological density" by bathing in a fleeting moment of social centrality. On one occasion, for instance, the Underground Man invited himself to a reunion of former classmates, even though he despised them and they him. Once at the gathering, he began to perform the Rousseauesque autonomy play — the late modern and postmodern analogue for the medieval morality play.

> I tried my utmost to show them that I could do without them, and yet I purposely stomped with my boots, thumping with my heels. But it was all in vain. They paid no attention at all. I had the patience to walk up and down in front of them that way

from eight o'clock till eleven, in one and the same place, from the table to the stove and from the stove to the table. "I walk up and down to please myself and no one can prevent me."9

His attempts to show them that he didn't need them were all in vain, because they paid no attention to him. If he really didn't need them, he could have stayed at home. The mythology of autonomous individuality here stands revealed. This is the tipping point into that "pitch of hysteria" which Dostoevsky has both vividly exemplified and properly labeled, justifying Nietzsche's admiration for the Russian novelist, which was based largely on his reading of *Notes from Underground*. The Underground Man clings to one small victory:

> Once — only once — they turned toward me, just when Zverkov was talking about Shakespeare, and I suddenly gave a contemptuous laugh. I snorted in such an affected and nasty way that they all at once broke off their conversation, and silently and gravely for two minutes watched me walking up and down from the table to the stove, *paying no attention whatsoever to them*.[10]

This is what passes for victory, temporary as it is. Not fifteen minutes of fame, but two minutes of sneering curiosity. Virginia Woolf and Dostoevsky reveal how the cultural resources that made it possible for the modern, autonomous self to affect an effortless self-possession were vanishing. What was happening in their fiction was happening more elusively in the culture at large.

In *Notes from Underground*, Dostoevsky provides one of the most revealing and disturbing depictions of the late-modern spiritual and psychological crisis. The man he shows us is fiercely trying to extricate himself from the influence of others and doing so, ironically, by trying to attract the attention of those from whom he wants to be free. He needs, indeed he craves, the attention of those whom he both envies and resents. He is Jean-Jacques Rousseau at a later stage of the ontological diminution from which the latter suffered. We may recall Rousseau's effort to prove to others that he has no need of them by getting them to notice how disinterested he is in their opinion. Even more comically, Dostoevsky's Underground Man goes to absurd lengths to get others to notice that he doesn't care if they notice.

---

9   Ibid., 69–70.
10 Ibid., 70. Emphasis added.

By the mid-twentieth century, the Catholic theologian Henri de Lubac offered an assessment of this situation which can serve as a transition to our next topic:

> There are certain times when one sees springing up in every direction the symptoms of an evil which catches on like an epidemic — a collective neurasthenic crisis. To those who are afflicted by it, everything becomes matter for denigration, and this is not just a case of irony, quarrelsomeness or bitterness which are at all times a perpetual threat to a certain kind of temperament. Everything gets a bad construction put upon it, and knowledge of all kinds, even when accurate, only serves to intensify the evil. Half-digested new discoveries and clumsily used new techniques are all so many occasions for believing that the traditional foundations of things have become shaky. The spiritual life goes but limpingly — so much so that nothing is really seen in the light of it any more.[11]

The final stage of this nihilism justifies the use of that label. As Jonathan M. Smith has noted: "Radical and absolute evil crosses the hateful river and enters the stygian blackness where good things are destroyed *for no reason other than that they are good.*"[12]

---

11   Henri de Lubac, *The Splendor of the Church*, trans. Michael Mason (San Francisco: Ignatius Press, 1986), 288.
12   J.M. Smith, "An Enacted Curse with which He Damned the World," *Orthosphere* (blog), May 25, 2022.

13 The Freudian Interlude

> It is hardly news, by now, that psychoanalytic theory constituted a thoroughgoing inversion of Christian principles, with sexual gratification triumphant over virtuous sacrifice for heaven, and with the clinical interview serving as a mock confessional in which absolution could be granted without any need for repentance.
>
> — Frederick Crews [1]

> The therapeutic ritual, the encounter between a sick person and a clinician, is a powerful psychosocial event. Clinicians, particularly physicians, are our society's designated healers and their prestige, status, and authority help engender patients' trust and expectations of relief from suffering.
>
> — Alyson Clayton [2]

GAZING AT THE CROWDS AWAITING HIS ARRIVAL at the New York dock in 1909, Sigmund Freud is reported to have turned to Carl Jung and said: "They don't know it, but I'm bringing them the plague." If Virginia Woolf acknowledged something "sulphurous and sinister" in the delight her chief protagonist took in a world reeling into chaos, one could be forgiven for detecting something of the same fiendish delight in Freud's mordant remark: an envenomed amusement in pondering how much cultural disruption he was poised to unleash.

Freud's star has fallen, but there is a lingering legacy of the earlier Freudian triumph. It lasted long enough, and enjoyed enough respectability, to have provided intellectual incubation for the sexual revolution, which can be seen — and will increasingly be seen — as a plague.

---

[1] Frederick Crews, *Freud: The Making of an Illusion* (New York: Henry Holt, 2017), 630.
[2] Alison Clayton, "Gender-Affirming Treatment of Gender Dysphoria in Youth: A Perfect Storm Environment for the Placebo Effect — The Implications for Research and Clinical Practice," https://link.springer.com/article/10.1007/s10508-022-02472-8.

The Freudian Interlude

When Freud died in 1939, that revolution was still gestating, but signs of its later effect were at hand. "Whether he was a true scientist or not, Freud's place is secure if for no other reason than that he broke down ancient taboos and cleared the way for a new approach to the mind," the New York Times unsigned obituary rhapsodized, adding that he was "the most effective disturber of complacency in our time."[3]

In the opening gambit of his masterful survey of Sigmund Freud and his legacy, Samuel Bendeck Sotillos makes the following observation:

> Freud recognized the full scope of the corrosive impact of the Freudian doctrine on society and civilization: "psychoanalysis is regarded as 'inimical to culture' and has been put under a ban as a 'social danger.'" Freud in no uncertain terms was conscious of the nefarious and destructive implications of his theory that was cloaked in the dress of modern science, which would come to challenge the very foundations of Western civilization.[4]

Carroll Smith-Rosenberg declared that psychoanalysis is "the child of the hysterical woman."[5] It was with the publication of *Studies in Hysteria*, co-authored by Josef Breuer, that Freudian theory began to take shape. Writes Freud:

> What is the meaning of hysterical identification?... I shall be told that this is not more than the familiar hysterical imitation, the capacity of hysterics to imitate any symptoms in other people that may have struck their attention — sympathy, as it were, intensified to the point of reproduction.[6]

The man who thought his sexual theories were bringing the curtain down on religion was in fact cluttering his cutting room floor with penetrating observations that would one day contribute to the revitalization of the kind of Christocentric anthropology we are here trying to limn. Understood in its original sense as an affective communion, both

---

3 Nicholas Bakalar, "Freud, 1909," *The New York Times*, Oct. 10, 2011.
4 Samuel Bendeck Sotillos, *Dismantling Freud: Fake Therapy and the Psychoanalytic Worldview* (Brooklyn, NY: Angelico Press, 2020), 1.
5 Carrol Smith-Rosenberg, "The Hysterical Woman: Sex Roles and Role Conflict in Nineteenth-Century America," in *Disorderly Conduct: Visions of Gender in Victorian America* (New York: Knopf, 1985), 197, quoted in Mark S. Micale, *Approaching Hysteria: Disease and Its Interpretations* (Princeton, NJ: Princeton University Press, 1995), 3.
6 Sigmund Freud, *The Interpretation of Dreams*, trans. James Strachey (Basic Books, 2010), 139.

Christian discipleship and Christian subjectivity can be aptly summarized as "sympathy intensified to the point of reproduction," the classical expression of which is the *Imitatio Christi*.

Modern psychology was called into existence by a symptom of distress that amounts to the most explicit declaration of our imitative propensity that one can imagine: sympathy intensified to the point of reproduction — what René Girard calls *mimetic desire*. Girard was the first to provide an in-depth analysis of mimesis, but Freud was not the first to notice its role in hysteria. "At least since the late seventeenth century," writes Mark Micale, "medical observers have noted in hysteria an extraordinary, chameleon-like capacity to reflect the environment in which it develops."[7] Micale was quick to note that: "No disorder was more important for this historical development of Freud's thinking than hysteria.... Psychoanalysis, in essence began as a theory of hysteria."[8]

Like the Freudian theory of Oedipal conflict within the family, a widespread and low-level form of hysteria is a late modern condition, the implications of which were eluded by ascribing great antiquity to both these disorders. In one form or another, ancient cases can be found of each of these psycho-spiritual disorders. But the search for evidence of ancient instances of Oedipal conflict and hysteria was prompted by a sudden emergence in the nineteenth century of symptoms for which such a venerable pedigree proved professionally advantageous for the practitioners of a fledgling psychotherapeutic regime.

Modern psychology was born at the moment when symptoms of the mimetic crisis in the midst of which we are now living became acute enough and prevalent enough to justify the invention of a new discipline for managing the distresses, the presenting symptom of which was labeled *hysteria*. The very antiquity of this term, while lending scientific weight to the new discipline, fostered one of its most crippling misunderstandings. If the hysteria that Freud and his colleagues were treating was, as early researchers theorized, the most ancient of all psychopathologies, then the assumption central to Freud's later Oedipal theories was plausible, namely, that the contemporary distresses were manifestations of *perennial* pathologies, and that there was nothing fundamentally *historical* about them, nothing conspicuously "modern" or "Western." As Hans Urs von Balthasar noted, however, the phrase "modern neurosis" is "almost a tautology, inasmuch as there were, strictly

---

7 Micale, *Approaching Hysteria*, 112–13.
8 Ibid., 27.

speaking, no neuroses in the earlier, humane world (and hence no need for their poisonous antidote, psychotherapy)."[9]

"Mimetic phenomena have their own specific temporality or historicity," writes Girard, "and they must be read in a historical as well as in an anthropological key."[10] Once one recognizes the historicity of the contemporary cultural and spiritual crisis, however, and its cultural and chronological coordinates, elements of Freudian theory — such as the Oedipus complex — regain a degree of pertinence, inasmuch as they can be seen, not as the continuation of perennial sexual dramas, but as the social and psychological consequences of a widespread application of unsound anthropological assumptions, and as the sovereign self's first, faint de facto cry for help.

Jean-Michel Oughourlian sees the cultural and historical dimension of what Freud dubbed the Oedipal conflict: "We are thus witnessing the emergence of new phenomena that I have baptized diseases of desire, that is to say illnesses of relationship, in other words illnesses that are purely cultural and not natural, and that are linked to our modern, Western society."[11]

Turning interest away from the obvious mimetic features of these distresses and toward their supposed sexual origin was for Freud no easy task. Re-reading today passages in which he accomplished it, one senses how precarious this crucial Freudian maneuver really was, and how dependent its success was on the eager credulity of those intrigued by the sexual theories and sympathetic to what seemed the scientifically formidable challenge to religion. "It is on the subject of religion," writes Philip Rieff, "that the judicious clinician grows vehement and disputatious.... Freud's customary detachment fails him here. Confronting religion, psychoanalysis shows itself for what it is: the last great formulation of nineteenth century secularism."[12] Mark Micale makes the same point when he writes: "nineteenth-century commentators most often conceptualized [the diagnosis of hysteria] as a battle between science and religion."[13]

We are here concerned with the anthropological mistake that underlies the modern and postmodern notions of selfhood, and, more

---

9   Balthasar, *The Christian and Anxiety*, 36.
10 Girard, *Anorexia and Mimetic Desire*, 25.
11 Oughourlian, *The Mimetic Brain*, 160–61.
12 Philip Rieff, *Freud: The Mind of the Moralist* (Garden City, NJ: Doubleday, 1961), 281.
13 Micale, *Approaching Hysteria*, 34.

immediately, with what Freud, his predecessors, collaborators, and later explicators refused to confront fully, specifically as they were faced with so conspicuous an instance of it in the psychopathologies they labeled hysteria. Freud's now discredited sexual theories are of interest in this regard, for they served as decoys, diverting attention from the real issue that called out for further investigation.

Freud's attention to sexual symptoms can be defended to a degree, but not for the reasons he proposed. As societies slide into a mimetic crisis of the sort that is now engulfing the Western world, sexuality is predictably the first area of social life to become problematic. The power of the sexual drive, the deep longing for true intimacy, and the drama involved in competition for sexual partners combine to make it all but inevitable that in a crisis-ridden society — rife with envy, rivalry, and resentment — these aggravations will be especially exasperated in relationships where sexuality is in play. And so it is that — with the ascendance of the individualistic, secularized, and "social contract" sense of self in the West — sexual intimacy has tended to be instrumentalized and robbed of its sacramentality, and thereby deprived of the very source of its deepest emotional and spiritual satisfactions. The chief requirement of "social contract" sexuality is the prevention of its natural consequences: exchanging a sacramental self-donating intimacy for a sexuality of plumbing, pleasure, performance, and prevention.

Far from being a reaction to sexual prudery, therefore, the sexual revolution was an attempt to compensate for emotional disappointments that accompanied earlier stages of the revolution, as each subsequent generation entertained the chimerical hope that a loosening of moral restraint might unleash enough passion to make up for the loss of intimacy coincident with the moral laxity of the previous generation. The cure was the next stage of the disease. The result of this spiraling process has been a spiritual calamity rooted, not just in moral laxity, but in anthropological error, a catastrophe which continues unabated and whose most serious consequences are spiritual and cultural, not sexual. For these and other reasons, it is worthwhile to rummage through the dustbin of psychoanalytic history for clues to the contemporary evisceration of the sovereign secular self. There are treasures to be retrieved from the wreckage.

Freud gave a sexual interpretation to what were fundamentally mimetic complications. Where he recognized mimetic conflict — in the father-son rivalry — he interpreted it as an unconscious sexual rivalry for the mother, structuring his analysis around Sophocles's drama *Oedipus the King*, the story of a man fated to kill his father and marry his mother. Like his theory of the great antiquity of hysteria, the venerable status of Sophocles's play gave weight to Freud's claim to have discovered a *perennial* feature of the human drama. What he failed to notice was the *historical* character of the disorders and complications his patients exhibited.

By looking to Sophocles, Freud could theorize that this family drama was as perennial as he imagined hysteria to be in another context. Had he looked elsewhere, he might have found an anthropologically lucid key to the very problem he sought. Both Matthew and Luke recount a warning issued by Jesus regarding the breakdown of domestic harmony.

> "Do not think that I have come to bring peace on earth; I have not come to bring peace, but a sword. For I have come to set a man against his father, and a daughter against her mother, and a daughter-in-law against her mother-in-law; and a man's foes will be those of his own household." (Mt 10:34–36, see Lk 12:51–53)

Like many others, this passage contains an anthropological insight that Girard's work helps us bring into focus. Anticipating the gradual effect of the Golgothan and Easter events at the center of the gospel revelation, Jesus is warning his disciples that the revelation that his life, death, and Resurrection would bring about would slowly cripple the ancient system for restoring harmony to fractured communities, even domestic ones.

Recall that even families and clans have long and notoriously restored their inner cohesion by standing in opposition to other clans and families, as was the case with the paradigmatic clan rivalries: the Hatfields and the McCoys, the Capulets and the Montagues, the Guelphs and the Ghibellines. Any society exposed to the Golgothan Event would gradually lose its ability to revive domestic solidarity by transferring its internal animosities onto outside adversaries. Resort to such things would of course continue, for such reflexive primordial rituals are not easily overcome, but the efficacy of these ploys for restoring domestic harmony would diminish with each effort to exploit them, leaving internal tensions to fester.

Thus, what Freud saw — or thought he saw — in the Oedipal conflicts of his patients was not an ancient and perennial sexual drama between fathers and sons. To the extent that his analysis of the conflict was remotely plausible, it was not because what was taking place was a primordial sexual drama. He was seeing the fulfillment of the warning of Christ, namely: that animosities which once could be offloaded onto those outside the family circle were now eating away at the most intimate forms of social life.

Elaine Showalter touches on one of the subsequent developments that reinforces both the mimetic and the theatrical dimension of hysteria. "The theatrical subtext of hysteria was codified in 1987," she writes, "when the *Diagnostic and Statistical Manual of Mental Disorders* officially renamed what had previously been 'hysterical personality disorder' as 'histrionic personality disorder.'" Showalter goes on to quote the aforementioned *Manual*:

> The essential feature of this disorder is a pervasive pattern of excessive emotionality and attention-seeking, beginning by early adulthood.... People with this disorder constantly seek or demand reassurance, approval, or praise from others and are uncomfortable in situations in which they are not the center of attention. They characteristically display rapidly shifting and shallow expression of emotions.... These people are typically attractive and seductive, often to the point of looking flamboyant and acting inappropriately. They... are lively and dramatic and always drawing attention to themselves.[14]

Just as many organic disorders arise less from an invasive parasite, virus, or bacterium than from the body's immune response to these things, so too with hysteria. The symptoms of hysteria appear when the integrating power of the person suffering the symptoms — and the interdividual boundaries that make human social life possible — are relatively weak with respect to the mimetic power of others with whom the person comes into contact. Thus, hysteria can be likened to a heightened spiritual and psychological autoimmune response, a survival instinct deployed in the face of mimetic allurements instinctively felt to be ontologically threatening.

---

14 Quoted in Elaine Showalter, *Hystories: Hysterical Epidemics and Modern Media* (New York: Columbia University Press, 1997), 102.

The Freudian Interlude

The term hysteria comes from the Greek word for uterus and carries with it the long-discredited implication that hysteria is a female sexual disorder. Indeed, as Mark Micale has observed: "Freudian psychology in a real sense represents a second resexualization of the hysteria diagnosis."[15] On the other hand, mimetic passion, writes Mikkel Borch-Jacobsen, "can of course bear sexuality in its wake (especially in the form called homosexuality), but can by no means be reduced to sexuality."[16] Still under the sway of his sexualized theories, however, and thus still reinforcing the ancient world's feminization of hysteria, Freud was nonetheless an honest enough clinician to recognize the essential matter:

> The physician who has, in the same ward with other patients, a female patient suffering from a particular kind of twitching, is not surprised if one morning he learns that this peculiar hysterical affection has found imitators. He merely tells himself: The others have seen her, and have imitated her; this is psychic infection. — Yes, but psychic infection occurs somewhat in the following manner: As a rule, patients know more about one another than the physician knows about any one of them, and they are concerned about one another when the doctor's visit is over. One of them has an attack to-day: at once it is known to the rest that a letter from home, a recrudescence of lovesickness, or the like, is the cause. Their sympathy is aroused, and although it does not emerge into consciousness they form the following conclusion: "If it is possible to suffer such an attack from such a cause, I too may suffer this sort of an attack, for I have the same occasion for it."[17]

We recall Dostoevsky's Underground Man. Perhaps, he thought: "I'll have a fight, too, and they'll throw me out of the window." Confronted by such glaring indications of the mimetic character of hysteria, it would be difficult to defend Freud's powers of observation other than by reference to his most famous — and most intentionally mystifying — doctrine: the unconscious. "Freud's continual relegation of mimesis to a secondary position," writes Mikkel Borch-Jacobsen, is a *"deliberate*

---

15 Micale, *Approaching Hysteria*, 28.
16 Mikkel Borch-Jacobsen, *The Freudian Subject*, trans. Catherine Porter (Stanford, CA: Stanford University Press, 1988), 49.
17 Sigmund Freud, *The Basic Writings of Sigmund Freud*, ed. and trans. A. A. Brill (New York: Random House, 1938), 228.

gesture — the very gesture that had made a properly psychoanalytic interpretation of hysterical symptoms possible, thus creating the possibility of psychoanalysis itself."[18]

Psychologically speaking, the hysteric is someone who is especially vulnerable by reason of social, psychological, or personal circumstances to the mimetic influence of others and who finds such influence suffocating and intolerable. Hysteria is a kind of private exorcism ritual, involving typically either exaggerated histrionics or autistic or cataleptic unresponsiveness — each an effort to ward off or neutralize a mimetic influence which the subject experiences as ontologically threatening. A person risks being diagnosed as hysterical if his attempts to ward off mimetic influence and retain or assert his self-sufficiency are debilitating enough or flamboyant enough to attract the attention of clinicians. For the hysteric, the power of the mimetic model threatens to spiritually eviscerate the reluctant but vulnerable imitator. The latter has available essentially two strategies for resisting the spellbinding influence: autistic imperviousness or histrionic self-proclamation. In commenting on the work of historian Janet Oppenheim (1991), Micale touches on these two strategies:

> Two contradictory readings of the hysterical female, she finds, emerge from Victorian medical literature: the *willess hysteric*, who lacked the ability to control her emotional impulses and fell into childish and self-indulgent invalidism, and the *willful hysteric*, who insubordinately asserted her demands in the face of societal imperatives.[19]

These two basic strategies can be used alternately, as two researchers, unaware of the mimetic dynamic at work, nevertheless observed:

> Hysterics privately enact the battle between Carnival and Lent, a battle in which the anorexic figure of Lent — a figure represented as emaciated, old and female, a figure of humorless fasting and sexual abstinence — is invariably the victor.[20]

---

18   Borch-Jacobsen, *The Freudian Subject*, 49.
19   Micale, *Approaching Hysteria*, 104. Incidentally, the American Psychiatric Association defines histrionic personality disorder (HPD) as one that features extreme attention-seeking, usually in the form of a need for approval or flirtatious behavior. Doctors diagnose four times as many women with HPD as men, and it affects around three percent of the general population. Beyond certain symptoms, individuals with HPD will be able to function at a high level and remain successful socially, in school, and at work.
20   Peter Stallybrass and Allon White, *The Politics and Poetics of Transgression* (Ithaca, NY: Cornell University Press, 1986), 184.

What Stallybrass and White see as the hysteric's carnivalesque and penitential options represent what we have called the histrionic and catatonic strategies for escaping a mimetic invasion — a hostile takeover so to speak — due to the hysteric's relative ontological deficit vis-à-vis the model.

If the anorexic figure of Lent is victorious in the arena of her choosing — namely thinness competition, approximating the holocaust survivors or the starving poor — her opposite appears in the carnivalesque exhibitions of unbridled sexual exuberance and deviance, to which even young children are now routinely exposed. The "Lenten" form of hysteria invites professional intervention. Meanwhile, its Carnivalesque manifestation is so widespread as to elude clinical detection. Indeed, the least expression of moral discomfort with the Carnivalesque mockery of sexual modesty can damage one's social reputation and employment opportunities and bring down the wrath of the forces that today control the educational, corporate, entertainment, social media, and mainstream news media institutions. Thus does the abandonment of traditional norms quickly morph into the adamant enforcer of new ones deeply at odds with both common decency and anthropological reality.

Further evidence for recognizing hysteria as a mimetic disorder is the fact that the treatment Freud found most helpful was itself a mimetic stratagem: the subtle commandeering of the patient's consciousness by the physician's adroit manipulation of the encounter. Nor should we be surprised to find that the relief that hypnosis provided had only limited therapeutic efficacy, depending, as it did, on an extended relationship between the patient and the clinician. As Freud observed:

> The situation is the same as if the hypnotist had said to the subject: "Now concern yourself exclusively with my person; the rest of the world is quite uninteresting."...The hypnotist...makes the person upon whom he is experimenting sink into an activity in which the world is bound to seem uninteresting to him; but at the same time the subject is in reality unconsciously concentrating his whole attention upon the hypnotist, and is getting into an attitude of *rapport*, of transference on to him.[21]

---

21 Sigmund Freud, *Group Psychology and the Analysis of the Ego*, trans. James Strachey (New York: W. W. Norton, 1989), 74.

For the patient, the psychotherapist served to arrest the otherwise fickle mimetic fascination and anchor it in one place. Freudian transference gave the patient relief from whatever mimetic entanglements had given rise to the hysteric symptoms from which relief was being sought. The relationship with the therapist provides the patient with the ballast needed to retain a semblance of subjective authenticity.

Before we turn to Freud's description of therapeutic hypnosis at work, let us revisit a passage from Bob Dylan's Nobel Laureate lecture, which will prepare us to assess what Freud called the transference.

> He was powerful and electrifying and had a commanding presence. I was only six feet away. He was mesmerizing. I watched his face, his hands, the way he tapped his foot, his big black glasses, the eyes behind the glasses, the way he held his guitar, the way he stood, his neat suit. Everything about him. He looked older than twenty-two. Something about him seemed permanent, and *he filled me with conviction.* Then, out of the blue, the most uncanny thing happened. *He looked me right straight dead in the eye, and he transmitted something. Something I didn't know what. And it gave me the chills.*

Again, we call attention to the religious tone that Dylan obviously felt was entirely appropriate to his experience. However inchoately, Dylan's encounter with Buddy Holly awakened him to the fact that his life was not about himself. And that is the beginning of a religious awakening, the crowning glory of which was first declared by Saint Paul: " It is no longer I who live, but Christ who lives in me" (Gal 2:20).

With that in mind, here is how Freud describes the effect of therapeutic hypnosis:

> Let us recall that hypnosis has something *positively uncanny* about it; but the characteristic of uncanniness suggests something old and familiar that has undergone repression. Let us consider how hypnosis is induced. The hypnotist asserts that he is in possession of a mysterious power that robs the subject of his own will; or, which is the same thing, the subject believes it of him.... This mysterious power... must be the same power that is looked upon by primitive people as the source of taboo, the same that emanates from kings and chieftains and makes it dangerous to approach them (*mana*). The hypnotist, then, is supposed to be in possession of this power; and how does he manifest it? By telling the subject to look him in the eyes;

his most typical method of hypnotizing is by his look. But it is precisely the sight of the chieftain that is dangerous and unbearable for primitive people, just as later that of the Godhead is for mortals. Even Moses had to act as an intermediary between his people and Jehovah, since the people could not support the sight of God; and when he returned from the presence of God his face shone — some of the *mana* had been transferred on to him, just as happens with the intermediary among primitive peoples.[22]

"I felt related, like he was an older brother. I even thought I resembled him," Dylan told his Nobel audience. "He was the archetype. Everything I wasn't and wanted to be." How (asks Freud) does the hypnotic power of the therapist take hold of the patient? By "telling the subject to look him in the eyes," the effect of which is that the therapist becomes a god in the eyes of his patient.

Freud veered away from the huge mimetic implications of therapeutic hypnosis and embraced the sexual and Oedipal theories as an alternative. Nevertheless, the therapeutic successes, such as they were, remained dependent on the mimetic influence of the psychoanalyst operative in the transference. Writes Mikkel Borch-Jacobsen:

> Do we really know what psychoanalysis defined itself *against*, and why? Hypnotic suggestion had undoubtedly been relegated to the obscurity that bordered and preceded psychoanalysis. But precisely *as obscurity*: it had been rejected with no one the wiser as to exactly *what* had been rejected.... Hypnosis was abandoned... by virtue of a denial, a rejection, a suppressed hostility that was obscure, so to speak, to itself. Freud simply wished to hear nothing further on the subject of hypnosis.[23]

Admitting to a "feeling of muffled hostility" to what he called the "tyranny of suggestion," Freud nevertheless had to admit, as he put it, that "suggestion (or more correctly suggestibility) is actually an irreducible, primitive phenomenon, a fundamental fact in the mental life of man."[24] He grudgingly conceded that "the riddle of suggestion" would have to be investigated further. In doing so, however, he began with an assumption that decided the matter from the outset. "There is no doubt," he wrote, "that something exists *in* us which, when we become

---

22 Ibid., 73–74. Emphasis added.
23 Borch-Jacobsen, *The Freudian Subject*, 150.
24 Freud, *Group Psychology*, 27.

aware of signs of an emotion in someone else, tends to make us fall into the same emotion."[25] Like Descartes before him, Freud turned inward to escape from evidence of the mimetic realities of human existence, which he must have instinctively realized would leave his sexual theories in shambles.

What Freud called the "riddle of suggestion" is the truth about the mimetic nature of desire, which was beginning to break through the conceptual barriers built and repaired over centuries to keep it sequestered. But by assuming that symptoms of mimetic hyperactivity were due to something located *inside* the hysteric — in Cardinal Ratzinger's terms, something *in the psychic inventory* — Freud managed to turn away from the very mimetic reality that was declaring itself in his patients' symptoms. As Jean-Michel Oughourlian put it, "by hiding the Other *inside* the subject in the guise of the *unconscious*, Freud preserved and protected its autonomy."[26] Hysteria, hysterical identification, and suggestibility were all found to have fundamentally sexual origins. Childhood sexual trauma was their cause. Psychoanalysis was born, and the anthropological revelation with which we would eventually have to reckon was postponed for another hundred years. Freudian theory triumphed because, as Oughourlian puts it: "culture recognized in that new mythology the least harmful of disguises for the reality it wanted to keep hidden."[27]

If hysterics exhibited symptoms that they had reason to believe would attract the attention of therapists, it was no less the case that clinicians tended — consciously or unconsciously — to elicit those symptoms most likely to reinforce the prevailing assumptions about hysteria, for which they presumed to have found, if not a cure, at least a rather lucrative palliative. Elaine Showalter notes that many have begun to peel away the veil and peer critically into Freud's treatment of his hysteric patients:

> Freud pressured his patients to produce narratives congruent with his theories. In other words, Freud's patients were not molested by their fathers and did not fantasize about them. Instead, they fabricated stories along the lines of Freud's own hysterical hypotheses.... Their "memories" of abuse were responses to Freud's hints, suggestions, and persuasion.[28]

---

25 Ibid., 27.
26 Oughourlian, *The Puppet of Desire*, 151. Emphasis added.
27 Ibid., 159.
28 Showalter, *Hystories*, 41.

In a typically illuminating passage, David Goldman observed:

> Sigmund Freud was a dreadful physician but a brilliant salesman who understood all too well what the world wanted to buy. After two centuries of the Age of Reason, he grasped that a world that had given up its religion wanted permission to be irrational once again. The world wallowed in hysterical misery; he offered to replace it with ordinary unhappiness.... He might've been a snake-oil salesman, but he sold a potion to cure what ailed the world: disgust at life disenchanted. That explains why Freud's influence grows in inverse proportion to his credibility. The post-religious world is not in the market for clinical proof or historical consistency. What it wants is a palliative for the hysterical misery it derives from unrestricted sexual gratification and arbitrary self-invention.[29]

Goldman has provided a most apposite observation, reminding us that what a world which had given up religion wanted most was "permission to be irrational again," and that it wants this precisely as "a palliative for the hysterical misery it derives from unrestricted sexual gratification and arbitrary self-invention."

---

29 David Goldman, "The Prophet of Ordinary Unhappiness," *The Claremont Review of Books*, Vol. XVIII, no. 2 (Spring 2018).

14 A Chameleon-like Disorder

> There can be no doubt at all that a future theory of hysteria will go far beyond the narrow confines of psychiatry and neurology. The deeper we penetrate into the riddle of hysteria, the more its boundaries expand.
> — Carl Jung[1]

> So large are the apparent changes in the symptoms and frequency of hysteria and of mania at different times and in different cultures... that many intriguing questions are raised.
> — Simon Shorvon[2]

SIMON SHORVON REGARDS HYSTERIA AND MANIA as at least related disorders. Acknowledging the continuing fluidity of psychotherapeutic categories and terminology, we have found it more useful to speak of two manifestations of hysteria: the histrionic and the catatonic. Both Dostoevsky and René Girard explored the psycho-spiritual affliction which Dostoevsky referred to as *hysteria* and Girard associated with the oscillations of the *manic-depressive*. The reflections to follow will inquire into the more prevalent sub-clinical variations of these two faces of the disorder, each in its own way symptomatic, in our view, of the contemporary crisis—indeed the apocalypse—of the sovereign self.

There is hardly a more elusive psychopathology today than hysteria, no less in terms of its actual history than in its exotic symptomology. Indeed, today the word hysteria appears regularly in reference to both individual and collective agitations of a roughly contagious nature. We have political hysteria, sexual hysteria, environmental hysteria, social media hysteria, and so on, not to mention a vast array of individually

---

[1] Carl G. Jung, *Collected Works*, vol. 18 (Princeton, NJ: Princeton University Press, 1976), 369.
[2] Simon Shorvon, "Hysteria, mania and the commercial-political nature of psychiatric disease," *Brain: A Journal of Neurology*, Vol. 133, No. 5 (May 2010).

manifested behaviors for which the word seems an apt moniker. We are chiefly concerned with these broader and less psychiatrically defined forms of hysteria. We nonetheless think the word apt in the approach we are taking, not least because of the very interesting history of the term.

Mark Micale cites the work of Helen King, a British classicist who argued that, the claims of early psychiatrists notwithstanding, the term hysteria doesn't appear in the ancient sources.

> By the sixteenth century, she shows, something with the ontological status of a disease category and a descriptive profile discernibly similar to our own clinical picture of hysteria emerged. The term itself, King finds, emerged extremely late. King's researches in medical and etymological dictionaries reveal that the French adjective *hystérique* first appeared in 1568 and its English counterpart "hysterical" in 1615. ... *Hystérie*, the French noun for the disease, cannot be found before 1731. The first known usage of the English noun "hysteria," in a London medical journal, dates from 1801![3]

Inasmuch as the wide range of symptoms ascribed to hysteria derive from humanity's heightened mimeticism, it is only logical to expect to find evidence of these symptoms in ancient sources. But the suggestion that the adjective appeared in Europe only in the early modern era and attracted the attention of medical professionals only at the end of the eighteenth century begs the historical question. Is there something at work in the modern era that is favorable to the occurrence of hysterical symptoms? Helen King is not alone in suspecting that clinicians were too eager to ascribe great antiquity to the disorder, thereby enhancing — rather prematurely we might add — the professional status of the emerging psychiatric disciplines.

Some have challenged King's assessment, but what is not contested is what appears to be the sudden, sharp, and inexplicable decline of the disorder in the second half of the twentieth century. This lends some credibility to the argument that its widespread appearance has to do with the circumstances extant in the culture in which it appeared, namely Western culture during the centuries when it was undergoing its dechristianization — from the sixteenth to the twenty-first century. As Micale notes, "if hysteria is partly or primarily sociogenic, then we need to turn for an explanation to the surrounding historical environment."[4]

---

3   Micale, *Approaching Hysteria*, 43.
4   Ibid., 158.

THE APOCALYPSE OF THE SOVEREIGN SELF

No serious social scientist would deny that the modern era involved the "progressive" fading of the Christian watermark on Western culture, but what most have not noticed is the correlation between this gradual de-Christianization and social and psychological disturbances that, in our view, trend toward nihilism in a way that invites deeper reflection on the warning that Jesus gave to his own disciples: "Apart from me, you can do nothing (*nihil*)" (Jn 15:5). Writes Mark Micale: "If the received wisdom about classical hysteria is partly a latter-day positivist creation, and if the clinical syndrome can only be identified reliably beginning two and a half centuries ago, then is not the long diagnostic lineage on which these histories are predicated in danger?"[5]

Without jeopardy to the diagnostic precursors of the affliction, in our view the most fruitful approach to that affliction is one that recognizes its sudden emergence in the culture which was undergoing a process of de-Christianization.

Andrew Scull, professor of sociology and science studies at the University of California, San Diego, underscores the mimetic nature of hysteria:

> Hysteria is a pathological condition with a fascinating and tortuous medical and cultural history. If the malady seems to change its shape and its form over the centuries, who can be surprised? For here is a disorder that even those who insist on its reality concede is a chameleon-like disease that can mimic the symptoms of any other, and one that somehow seems to mold itself to the culture in which it appears.[6]

Chameleons, of course, adapt to their environment by changing color and blending in. This would be consistent with those manifestations of the disorder found on the lymphatic or phlegmatic end of the spectrum. In the nineteenth century, catatonia was thought to be a variant of hysteria, not without good reasons. In cases of manic or overly histrionic hysteria, which more readily come to the attention of clinicians, the response is not to blend in but to stand out. This is the case today among many of those who are suffering sub-clinical forms of hysteria, those, that is, who try to dramatize their uniqueness by imitating those who appear to be unique and then adding one or two affectations to the performance in an attempt to show that they are not imitating.

---

5 Ibid., 46.
6 Andrew Scull, *The Disturbing History of Hysteria* (New York: Oxford University Press, 2009), 6.

A Chameleon-like Disorder

Doctors Allan H. Ropper and Brian David Burrell point out that the Parisian hospital, the Salpêtrière, was ground zero for the launching of the study of hysteria. It was at the Salpêtrière that the most famous hysterical patient, Blanche Wittman, was treated by Jean-Martin Charcot.

> Throughout the 1880s, dancers, magicians' assistants, models, opera divas, and stage actresses traipsed over to the Salpêtrière to see the one person who embodied the fullest range of emotive performance on the Continent. When Sarah Bernhardt, the on-again, off-again darling of the European theater scene, wished to recapture her popularity upon her return to the Paris stage in 1881, she too headed to the Salpêtrière to see Blanche perform.[7]

The key to this rich observation, of course, is the word *perform*. Writes Andrew Scull:

> Jane Avril, the most famous dancer at the Moulin Rouge and a favorite model for Henri Toulouse-Lautrec, wrote a memoir of her eighteen-month stay in the hysteria ward at the Salpêtrière, among the "stars of hysteria," as she called them.
>
>> "There were those deranged girls whose ailments named Hysteria consisted, above all, in simulation of it.... How much trouble they used to go to in order to capture attention and gain stardom.... In my tiny brain, I was astonished every time to see how such eminent savants could be duped in that way, when I, as insignificant as I was, saw through the farces."[8]

The public fascination with both the physicians and patients of the Salpêtrière faded with the death of Jean-Martin Charcot. Ropper helps us see why.

> At the announcement of [Jean-Martin Charcot's] death, the Paris School he had founded ceased to exist. The theory of *la grande hystérie* was shelved... and most tellingly, Blanche Wittman [Charcot's most famous patient] never again had a hysterical attack.... At first diagnosed as epileptic, then as hysterical, then treated with hypnosis, electrotherapy, and massage by a team of physicians over a fifteen-year period, Blanche was finally cured by the departure of the only audience she cared about.[9]

---

7   Allan H. Ropper, MD, and Brian David Burrell, *How the Brain Lost Its Mind* (New York: Random House, 2019), 210.
8   Scull, *The Disturbing History*, 51–52.
9   Ibid., 51.

The Salpêtrière was where hysteria was both cured and cultivated. Discharge was arguably more likely to bring about the cure than was the cure to lead to discharge. "Perhaps the best proof that Salpêtrière hysteria was *une hystérie de culture* [a culture of hysteria], as Charcot's adversaries called it," writes Frederick Crews, "lies in the fact that patients who exited the hospital soon overcame their susceptibility to *grande hystérie*."[10] But what would happen if these freshly discharged patients found themselves in a world that was gradually becoming an unacknowledged version of both the Salpêtrière and the Paris School that purported to be treating the disorder, in other words, *une hystérie de culture?*

Clinicians retrieved their professional respectability by turning more and more to pharmacology, sacrificing the disorder on which their discipline had been founded. Once the physicians no longer accorded the disorder the respect it had once enjoyed, patients quickly abandoned it in favor of other symptoms more likely to warrant the attention of medical professionals. "By defining certain symptoms as illegitimate," suggests Edward Shorter, "a culture strongly encourages patients not to develop them or to risk being thought 'undeserving' individuals with no real medical problems. Accordingly, there is great pressure on the unconscious mind to produce only legitimate symptoms."[11] Herein lies the key to understanding the explosion over the last few decades of disorders listed in the *Diagnostic and Statistical Manual* (DSM).

Meanwhile, as Andrew Scull notes: "Hysteria and indeed the whole array of 'neurotic' disorders had been carved up and thrust out of sight."[12] The outlines of classical hysteria, Scull observes, survived under a few terms, prominent among them the histrionic personality type. And with that, we are back in the theater.

The antiquity of hysteria can be conceded without jeopardy to our premise: namely that — either in its clinically diagnosed or sub-clinical forms — hysteria is indicative of an ontological deficit, a condition now widespread in the post-Christian and increasingly deracinated West. Such a deficit is due not to a natural process, a psychological version of the second law of thermodynamics, but to the loss of that central but subtle factor that gave Western civilization its remarkable dynamism: its Christian ambience.

---

10   Crews, *Freud: The Making of an Illusion*, 174.
11   Edward Shorter, *From Paralysis to Fatigue* (New York: Free Press, 1992), x; quoted in Scull, *The Disturbing History*, 186–87.
12   Scull, *The Disturbing History*, 185.

Scull and others have stressed the role of the American Psychiatric Association's *Diagnostic and Statistical Manual* (DSM) in a burgeoning number of official psychiatric disorders, driven, as many see the matter, by the health insurance and pharmaceutical industries. We will leave these matters to others. Our concern is with whether and to what degree no small number of the psychiatric disorders of the last two centuries are related to mimetic disturbances. Beginning with Freud and his collaborators, modern psychopathology — and especially psychoanalysis — owed both its short-term success and its long-term failure to what Freud called "the tyranny of suggestion."

We have chosen to speak of the "catatonic" and "histrionic" forms that hysteria often takes. In extreme cases, the "catatonic" form involves what appears to be an anatomical impairment — a partial paralysis for example. Carl Jung reported a case in which the patient's hysterical symptom was deafness.

> One lady, who had completely lost her hearing because of an hysterical affection, often used to sing. Once, when she was singing, her doctor seated himself unobserved at the piano and softly accompanied her. In passing from one stanza to the next he made a sudden change of key, whereupon the patient, without noticing it, went on singing in the changed key. Thus she hears — and does not hear. The various forms of systematic blindness offer similar phenomena: a man suffering from total hysterical blindness recovered his power of sight in the course of treatment, but it was only partial at first and remained so for a long time. He could see everything with the exception of people's heads. He saw all the people around him without heads. Thus he sees — and does not see.[13]

René Descartes comes again to mind:

> I will regard the heavens, the air, the earth, colors, shapes, sounds, and all external things as nothing but the bedeviling hoaxes of my dreams, with which he lays snares for my credulity. I will regard myself as not having hands, or eyes, or flesh,

---

13 C. G. Jung, *The Collected Works of C. G. Jung*, Vol. 7: *Two Essays on Analytical Psychology* (Princeton, NJ: Princeton University Press, 1977), 11.

or blood, or any senses, but as nevertheless falsely believing that I possess all these things.[14]

Whomever the hysteric Jung treated might have been trying to shut out — to "cancel" — by remaining deaf, it was when she was able to sing *in concert* with her analyst's musical accompaniment that a path to recovery opened up. To be cured by accompanying her therapist is as important a metaphor for her cure as her hysterical deafness was for her underlying disorder. *Both* the deafness and the duet with her therapist involved *conversions*. The former is the conversion of anxiety into bodily symptoms, a purely reflexive pathological ritual of dis-identification. The latter is a conversion at least structurally parallel to the Christian understanding of the term, namely an incipient identification with a model, in rapport with whom the fractured self might begin to reconstitute and regain the latent or frittered away birthright of personhood.

Jean-Michel Oughourlian probed the pre-history of modern psychoanalysis much further back than did many. Oughourlian studied cases in archaic societies where symptoms consistent with hysteria were in evidence. His research showed that in these primitive societies, the cure for these distresses was possession. Hysteria seemed to be the dissociated person's attempt to renounce any mimetic influence and assert the priority and anteriority of his own desires, motivations, and self. He was cured of his delusional symptoms through the ritual possession by an "other" being — a god or tutelary creature of some kind — a being greater than himself. In the service of this "other," he found sanity again. The difference, Oughourlian observed, between possession and hypnotism was that in the former the "other" was a virtual other, a totemic sponsor, a god or spirit, and so on, whereas in hypnotism, the "other" was the hypnotist. The hypnotist was a priest-like figure in whose superior knowledge and wisdom the hysteric has placed his trust. "Identification is a mimetic therapy," Oughourlian has insisted, "in fact the mimetic therapy par excellence. Hysteria is a mimetic malady, the mimetic illness par excellence on every level."[15]

Whether in the acute form Freud treated at the turn of the twentieth century or in the milder but more chronic forms that are more prevalent today throughout Western culture, hysteria is a *spontaneous*

---

14 Descartes, *Meditations on First Philosophy*, Meditation I, 16–17.
15 Oughourlian, *The Puppet of Desire*, 180.

ritual dispossession. Oughourlian observed, however, that in primitive societies the cure for a person suffering from acute versions of this same pathology is a formal possession ritual. It was, and is, Oughourlian argues, rapport with another that is the therapeutic solution for the self in crisis. For two thousand years, Christianity has offered the supreme and unsurpassable cure for this malfunctioning of humanity's incomparable mimetic predisposition, the key to our destiny and the cause of so much of the scandal that blinds us to it.

As Simon Shorvon so aptly put the matter, the fluctuations of disease symptoms and labels "reveal as much about the post-lapsarian human condition" as they do about the churning nature of psychiatric fashion. For René Girard, "the hell of bi-polarity [is] the never-ending come-and-go of mimetic desire that makes us feel like we are everything when the 'god is near,' and like nothing when the god moves away." This understanding of bi-polarity in no way disputes the reality of the disorder. Indeed, it underscores it. For Girard, the greatness of the nineteenth-century German poet Hölderlin was that he struggled with bipolarity, giving poetic expression to its depths and heights. Girard's most lapidary remark on the poet and his struggles is illuminating.

> Despite the pressure he suffers from fashion and his friends, the poet feels the truth: Dionysus is violence and Christ is peace. I cannot think of a better way of putting what we are trying to say. It is said by a Christian whose rare utterances during the time of his retreat include the statement "I am precisely on the point of becoming Catholic." This anecdote interests me in that it provides an anthropological basis for Catholic *stability*, which is the only thing that can hold the world together after the shock of the Revelation.[16]

The burden of this book is to supply circumstantial evidence in support of the final sentence of Girard's lapidary comment. Pursuant to this task, we approach the question of hysteria, less on strictly psychiatric grounds, and more in terms consonant with Simon Shorvon's use of the term "post-lapsarian." Whether wittingly or not, the very term post-lapsarian has purchase on our attention only in light of the Fall story recounted in the Old Testament and the path of reconciliation set forth in the New. Thus, Shorvon's use of the term "post-lapsarian" is hardly

---

16 René Girard, *Battling to the End*, trans. Mary Baker (East Lansing, MI: Michigan State University Press, 2010), 130.

distinguishable from our emphasis on the "post-Christian" character of the culture in which sub-clinical forms of hysteria abound.

Our predicament is therefore paradoxical. Whatever the moral, social, and cultural tasks entailed, there is an anthropological one that necessarily converges with a theological one. For the subject of our inquiry is a creature made in the image and likeness of his Creator. Since what we know of the latter — the God in whose image and likeness we are made — we know less by inquiry and reflection than by revelation, in later chapters we will turn to the revelatory tradition that has been preserved and curated by Catholic Christianity for two millennia.

15 "I Keep My Countenance, I Remain Self-possessed"

> The affirmation of or mad search for one's identity proves first of all that one fears losing it, or has already lost it.
> — Jean-Luc Marion[1]

IN 1915, THE YOUNG T. S. ELIOT WROTE A PROSE poem entitled "Hysteria." Eliot shows how keenly he sensed the nature of the psychological crisis that was already brewing. As allusive and enigmatic as his references to this crisis are, taken together, they are superior to the psychoanalytic orthodoxy that was already solidifying at the time the poem was written. The speaker in the poem is in the presence of a woman who is exhibiting moderately mild symptoms of hysteria. In our view, however, it is not the woman's hysteria that is at stake. What's at stake is whether the speaker in the poem will be able to keep from catching a case of hysteria from a contagious carrier of it. Can he hang on to his autonomy in the presence of her hysterical display? He is struggling to avoid being mimetically swept up into the orbit of this woman's psychological gyrations. His very anxiety, as per Marion's quotation above, is symptomatic of his own ontological precariousness.

> As she laughed I was aware of becoming involved in her laughter and being part of it. . . . I was drawn in by short gasps, inhaled at each momentary recovery. . . I decided that if the shaking of her breasts could be stopped, some of the fragments of the afternoon might be collected, and I concentrated my attention with careful subtlety to this end.[2]

---

1 Jean-Luc Marion, *A Brief Apology for a Catholic Moment*, trans. Stephen E. Lewis (Chicago: University of Chicago Press, 2021), 84.
2 T. S. Eliot, *The Complete Poems and Plays 1909–1950* (New York: Harcourt, Brace & World, 1971), 19.

THE APOCALYPSE OF THE SOVEREIGN SELF

The speaker in Eliot's poem makes the same assumption that is implicit in the very term hysteria, namely, that hysteria arises from the surcharged power of female sexuality. Therefore, he tries to avoid succumbing to hysteria by striving to defuse its incidental sexual element. His miscalculation is more or less the defining mistake in modern Western social science: the tendency to overemphasize the sexual element whenever it appears in the human drama. The further removed from antiquity one is, or rather the further removed from the primordial social situation, the more likely it seems that the taboos which confine sexuality will be regarded as having primarily to do with sexuality. In fact, however, these taboos are aimed at constraining certain mimetic *affects* and their interpersonal *effects*, for fear of their inevitable catastrophic *social* repercussions.

Freudian psychoanalysis virtually institutionalized this typically modern preoccupation with sexuality. It is the natural extension of the historically questionable sociological cliché against which it took its stand: namely, Victorian repressed sexuality. Both the Victorian emphasis on the need to quarantine sexuality and the Freudian theory of the sexual basis of psychopathology make the same mistake that the speaker in Eliot's poem makes. In each instance, the recognition that a social and psychological disturbance includes a sexual element leads almost immediately to the easy and obvious conclusion that it is fundamentally a sexual phenomenon.

In accord with the spirit of his age, the speaker in Eliot's poem believes that the force he must resist in order to maintain his fragile psychological poise is the force of sexuality. His reflexive choice is a conservative one, as the choices of those more keenly aware of the abyss often are. Its purpose is conservative only in the sense that the speaker in this poem is trying to arrest a self-dissolution of which he has become anxious. He hopes against hope that if the shaking of the breasts can be stopped, he might be able to resist being drawn helplessly into the hysterical laughter. Take the speaker in this poem to a psychoanalyst circa the date of the poem and the predictable will occur. The concentration on the breasts will be seized upon, the fixation on the mother surmised and explored at length. Childhood memories will be pored over, like entrails or tea leaves, for clues to the problem. The latent rivalry with the father will eventually surface, and lengthy psychoanalysis will follow.

The fascination with the undulating breasts of the hysterical woman, despite being surcharged by sexuality, is no match for the mimetic power of social scandals, and it is interesting to note that Eliot subtly returned to this theme with his characteristic insight. The pertinent lines of Eliot's "Portrait of á Lady" are these:

> You will see me any morning in the park
> Reading the comics and the sporting page.
> Particularly I remark
> An English countess goes upon the stage.
> A Greek was murdered at a Polish dance,
> Another bank defaulter has confessed.
> I keep my countenance,
> I remain self-possessed
> Except when a street piano, mechanical and tired
> Reiterates some worn-out common song
> With the smell of hyacinths across the garden
> Recalling things that other people have desired....
> My self-possession flares up for a second;...
> I feel like one who smiles, and turning shall remark
> Suddenly, his expression in a glass.
> My self-possession gutters; we are really in the dark....
> I must borrow every changing shape
> To find expression... dance, dance
> Like a dancing bear,
> Cry like a parrot, chatter like an ape.[3]

The speaker in this poem, his fragile autonomy at stake, is determined to avoid the more sensational sections of the newspaper, restricting his reading to the inconsequential matters found in the sporting and comic pages, which were far less likely to *scandalize*, that is, to arouse mimetic fascination. The resolve to read only the comic and the sporting sections of the newspaper is part of a strategy for remaining self-possessed. The strategy nevertheless requires more self-control than he can muster. An English countess on a stage, a homicide at a Greek dance, a banking scandal, these are not to be found in the comic or sporting sections. The speaker seems incapable of even this minimal form of sustained self-discipline. He cannot resist the more titillating features of the news. Though it manifests itself in our day with more hysteria than resignation, it is precisely this sort of distractedness that characterizes so much of late modernity's everyday life. Imagine how

---

[3] T. S. Eliot, *Collected Poems 1909–1935* (New York: Harcourt, Brace & World, 1971), 10–11.

little resistance this fragile self could muster against these allurements now that they are presented with all the incredible power and ubiquity of social media sites and smartphones, which make the rumor mills of old seem bastions of solidity by comparison.

Despite the mimetically alluring episodes of human melodrama he is unable to resist, the speaker in Eliot's poem just manages to remain self-possessed, the ultimate goal of a disintegrating self. As psychologically tenuous as he is, with effort, he seems to have made it all the way through even the paper's more scandalizing sections with his self still more or less intact. He hardly has time to savor his little victory, however, before its gains are all lost. He hears the street piano play the worn-out common song and smells the hyacinths. In a trice, he muses on what "other people have desired" and finds himself succumbing to mimetic allurements in the most comedic way: crying like a parrot and chattering like an ape.

These stimuli manage to do what the newspaper scandals could not; they awaken in him a remembrance of things past, most notably: things that other people have desired. In response, he will either have to throw himself into ever more idiosyncratic forms of self-presentation in order to exorcize the other's influence or, in spite of this influence, to customize his imitation in such a way that it will elude detection. A quick glance will reveal the obvious: these two options are the same. What we are now in a position to see, and what was not visible from the psychoanalytical perspective, is that whether the self chooses to resist mimetic arousals or to be aroused by them while disclaiming any mimetic influence, the resulting behavior will be the same. Inasmuch as hysteria is a dramatic gesture meant to ward off a threatening and unwanted mimetic influence, the term applies to the speaker in "Portrait of a Lady," no less than to the speaker in the poem explicitly entitled "Hysteria."

In the fresh air and the shaft of sunlight Girard's mimetic proposal throws on the social scene, Victorian sexual reticence, the age of psychoanalysis, and the loudly touted sexual revolution are only slightly different versions of each other. They are a triptych devoted to the modern idol. Whatever the degree of sexual wariness in nineteenth-century society, underlying it was a fear of mimesis imprecisely understood and indiscriminately directed toward sexuality, the perennial arena of mimetic complications. The difference between the stuffy Victorian parlor and the relentlessly mandatory (though scrupulously "safe") sex of today may be simply that the Victorians could still find an occasional respite from it in the bedroom and the moderns cannot. For the latter, sex and boredom have embraced.

By making essentially the same miscalculation as the speaker in Eliot's poem, Freud and his movement bridged a gap between the age of unresponsive sex and the age of sexual irresponsibility, and made possible an alliance of sorts between them, an alliance that would never have occurred had it not been brokered by Freudian theory. Common to all three of these seemingly so disparate social phenomena is the tendency to overlook the central role of mimesis in social and psychological life in favor of a social arena that is inordinately vulnerable to mimetic disruptions, namely sexuality. Because they all share in the error of thinking in sexual rather than in mimetic terms about the human condition, they each contributed in their own special way to the sexual hysteria of our world.

Today, the signs of an apocalypse of the sovereign self are everywhere to be seen. The confusion in the psychological sciences, the singular lack of coherence among them, the modest record of therapeutic interventions, and the new interest along a broad front in mimetic facts long ignored by psychological science — all these things indicate that an anthropological reckoning is overdue.

16 "Bug Off and Look at Me"

> Despite philosophical fantasizing about self-sufficient individuals, human beings need a deep sense of belonging and the more they are individualized, the more they are eager to assimilate collective identities — even absurd ones — without realizing to what extent their self-proclaimed individual sovereignty is illusory.
>
> — Ryszard Legutko[1]

IN *THE WAVES*, WHAT MADE VIRGINIA WOOLF'S Percival the object of his classmates' fascination was his single-minded interest in athletic competition, to the exclusion of the far fiercer mimetic competition with which most of the other characters in the novel were preoccupied. In the eyes of his classmates, Percival's astonishing disinterest in the social drama gave him an aura of Olympian majesty. If Percival's disinterest in mimetic intrigue was genuine, his classmates, hungry for the social centrality he acquired honestly, learned to parade their putative social indifference in the same way that the Underground Man did when he tried his "utmost to show them that I could do without them." "Dalton, Jones, Edgar and Bateman flick their hands to the back of their necks likewise. But they do not succeed."

The dandy is a figure who has intuitively understood the attraction those entangled in mimetic intrigues have for anyone who seems immune to the mimetic maelstrom. In a sense, the dandy is a Rousseauian figure who feigns indifference to what others might think of him while remaining preoccupied with nothing else. He is Percival without the athletic prowess but with a keen sense of the mimetic effect he can have on others by appearing to be indifferent to their attention.

---

[1] Ryszard Legutko, *The Cunning of Freedom: Saving the Self in an Age of False Idols* (New York: Encounter Books, 2021), 152.

If anyone can be said to have taken Rousseau's ritual of self-presentation to its logical conclusions it was the French poet Baudelaire. His short, reckless, and self-absorbed life was epitomized by the determination to live the life of the "dandy," to remain at the center of social attention precisely by exhibiting absolutely no interest in others. If in the first lines of his *Confessions*, Rousseau wrote that his life was based on "no precedent," and that above all he was "different," Baudelaire would write to his mother in an irascible mood: "Understand one thing which you seem always to ignore, I am not made like other men."[2] Baudelaire discovered that the air of indifference the dandy labors to exude works like a social aphrodisiac on those around him, those suffering from a milder form of the "ontological sickness" whose advanced phase the dandy represents. The self he advertises as self-sufficient fascinates others precisely because of its eccentricity, but it is the attention of others and not the eccentricity required to attract it that keeps the dandy's helium-filled existence airborne. Reminiscent of the Underground Man who, snorting and stomping around the tavern, managed — for two whole minutes — to acquire the social centrality by which he sought to repair his ontological emaciation, the Baudelairean dandy mastered the art of paying no attention to those on whose attention his social singularity depended. In other words, for as long as the dandy can maintain the pretenses, he can relieve the symptoms of his ontological sickness by becoming the carrier of the disease and infecting others with it. In his book, *Madness and Modernism*, Louis A. Sass writes:

> Baudelaire was the first to crystallize a form of solitude that was virtually unthinkable before the nineteenth century: a profound, self-generated isolation so unaffected by the presence of others that it is likely to be felt most strongly amid a crowd. And he was the first major poet to revel in the self-imposed, self-glorifying alienation that was to become virtually *de rigueur* in the artistic avant-garde.[3]

"If ever a man was ill, in ways that had nothing to do with medicine," wrote Baudelaire, "that man is me."[4] At the end of his life, according to one commentator, Baudelaire was "unable to remember his name or recognize his face in a mirror."[5] The same observer concluded, however,

---

2 Zweig, *Heresy of Self-Love*, 222.
3 Sass, *Madness and Modernism*, 86.
4 Zweig, *Heresy of Self-Love*, 224.
5 Lillian Herlands Hornstein, ed., *The Reader's Companion to World Literature*, 2nd ed. (New York: New American Library, 1973), 53.

that Baudelaire had "recorded something that was happening to human nature as a whole."[6] No, not human nature, but the late modern and postmodern self. Sass cites the observation of the psychiatrist Ernst Kretschmer regarding the kind of indifference Baudelaire exhibited, namely disinterest "ostentatiously manifested."[7] Baudelaire died in 1867. His effort to float on the fascination he was able to evoke in others failed in the end. He came into the Catholic Church on his deathbed, suggesting that the inability to remember his name or recognize his face in a mirror had not impaired his capacity to respond to the love that passes understanding.

The "dandy" is an adept at the mimetic game who understands its operating principles well enough to exhibit a flare for blasé self-presentation, fully aware of how fascinating such a performance is for an audience of less savvy onlookers, whose minor role in the sociodrama is rewarded occasionally by recognition from the maestro. The quintessential dandy of the late twentieth century was Andy Warhol. He was the Percival of his time, not because he was as oblivious as Percival was to the mimetic intrigue, but rather because he was its preeminent virtuoso, its ringmaster. René Girard attributed the social success of the dandy's carefully dramatized indifference to the fact that it simulated the conquering of desire by Christian saints. In Warhol's case, this association was especially valid inasmuch as he remained deeply and reverently — if not always scrupulously — Catholic all his life. Girard writes.

> Nondesire once more becomes a privilege as it was for the wise man of old or the Christian saint. But the desiring subject recoils in terror before the idea of absolute renunciation. He looks for loopholes. He wants to create a personality in which the absence of desire has not been won with difficulty out of the anarchy of instincts and metaphysical passion. The somnambulist hero of American writers is the "solution" of this problem. Nondesire in this hero has nothing to do with the triumph of the mind over evil forces, nor with the self-discipline extolled by the great religions and higher humanisms. It makes one think rather of a numbing of the senses, of a total or partial loss of vital curiosity.[8]

One might liken such a faux-saint who carefully struts his imperviousness to temptation to René Descartes' "numbing of the senses" and his well-publicized delight in "finding no company to distract me, and

---

6 Ibid., 55.
7 Ibid.
8 Girard, *Deceit, Desire, and the Novel*, 272–73.

having, fortunately, no cares or passions to disturb me." Such nondesire, Girard insists, "has nothing in common with abstinence and sobriety."[9] While Descartes was straining not to be seduced by the vicissitudes of mimesis, the dandies of a later age were the studied avatars of seduction, compensating for an ontological deficit by attracting the gaping fascination of their social peers. Baudelaire provides the incomparable definition of the dandy: "The dandy has to be a lymphatic and cold man, who is sick and tired of everything and wants to make himself original. Indifference is the supreme virtue of the dandy.... *The dandy should feel the pleasure of astonishing and the proud satisfaction of never being astonished.*"[10]

"In the French poet's case," writes Louis A. Sass, "it is less a matter of fear or envy than of disdain, less of *Angst* than of *spleen* — the latter being Baudelaire's term for a new kind of emotion, a peculiar mix of disillusionment, irony, bitterness, and ennui that he invented as much as described."[11] No assessment of the present state of our formerly Christian civilization will succeed without addressing the strange new psychological condition to which Baudelaire first drew attention: spleen. This is finally what lies at the end of the road for the sovereign self. This is where it turns nihilistic and metamorphoses into a mood that is brazenly incompatible with civil discourse and moral seriousness.

As Robert Hughes analyzes it in 1982, Andy Warhol's prominence coincided with a social convolution in which "the press and television, in their pervasiveness, constructed a kind of parallel universe in which the hierarchical orders of American society... were replaced by the new tyranny of the 'interesting.'"

> To enter this turbulence, one might only need to be born — a fact noted by Warhol in his one lasting quip, "In the future, *everyone* will be famous for fifteen minutes." But to remain in it, to stay drenched in the glittering spray of promotional culture, one needed other qualities. One was an air of detachment; *the dandy must not look into the lens*. Another was an acute sense of nuance, an eye for the eddies and trends of fashion, which would regulate the other senses and appetites and so give detachment its point.[12]

---

9 Ibid., 273.
10 Quoted in Kelly Comfort, *European Aestheticism and Spanish American Modernismo: Artist Protagonists and the Philosophy of Art for Art's Sake* (London: Palgrave Macmillan, 2011), 117–18. Emphasis added.
11 Sass, *Madness and Modernism*, 86.
12 Robert Hughes, "The Rise of Andy Warhol," *The New York Review of Books Anthology 1963–93* (originally published February 1982). Emphasis added.

THE APOCALYPSE OF THE SOVEREIGN SELF

Diligent and frigid, Warhol had both an air of detachment and an acute sense of social nuance. Hughes describes those circling in the Andy Warhol orbit:

> They were all cultural space-debris, drifting fragments from a variety of Sixties subcultures (transvestite, drug, S&M, rock, Poor Little Rich, criminal, street, and all the permutations) orbiting in smeary ellipses around their unmoved mover.... If Warhol's "Superstars," as he called them, had possessed talent, discipline, or stamina, they would not have needed him. But then, he would not have needed them. They gave him his ghostly aura of power. If he withdrew his gaze, his carefully allotted permissions and recognitions, they would cease to exist.... In this way the Factory resembled a sect, a parody of Catholicism enacted (not accidentally) by people who were or had been Catholic.... In it, the rituals of dandyism could speed up to gibberish and show what they had become — a hunger for approval and forgiveness. These came in a familiar form, perhaps the only form American capitalism knows how to offer: publicity.

Having noted that many of Warhol's acolytes were or had been Catholic, Hughes came to understand that the "rituals of dandyism" were little more than "a hunger for approval and forgiveness."

If Warhol is the phlegmatic hysteric, wan, waif-like with the studied demeanor of a semi-autistic, Camille Paglia is his opposite: the full-blown theatrical hysteric. Each performed the role of the hysteric with exquisite aplomb. Her intellectual showmanship notwithstanding, Paglia enacted spiritual high wire feats that leave savvy onlookers holding their breath. The correlation with hysteria is conspicuous. In her book *Vamps and Tramps*, she writes of her own "meteoric rise" and says this of herself:

> I was a parallel phenomenon to businessman-turned-politician Ross Perot and radio personalities Rush Limbaugh and Howard Stern, with their gigantic nationwide following. We have widely different political views, but all four of us, with our raging egomania and volatile comic personae tending toward the loopy, helped restore free speech to America.[13]

If this is not enough to suggest the model-rival matrix of hysteria, here's what Paglia has to say about her *female* model-rival, the writer, Susan Sontag: "I am the Sontag of the '90s.... I'm her worst nightmare.... I've

---

[13] *The New York Times*, November 15, 1994, B2.

been chasing that bitch for 25 years, and I've finally passed her!" That this is intentional self-parody does not entirely remove the perils involved in such high wire performances. As clever and witty as were Paglia's jabs at Sontag, they masterfully illuminate the dynamics of hysteria that are rarely exhibited so candidly. Dismissing Sontag's writings as "bleak, boring, pedestrian, clumsy, wobbly and corny," Paglia anguishes over the apparent fact that Sontag has exhibited absolutely "no awareness that I had written any books or that she had even seen them, even through a telescope."[14]

"I feel I should use my name recognition for service, for art," Paglia said in 2015.[15] In a 2019 piece in the *City Journal*, Emily Esfahani Smith noted that Paglia rejected the academic preference for "a watered-down Marxism that sees the world in terms of society, politics, and economics — a materialistic philosophy that has no sense of the spiritual or sublime."[16]

"That's why they're in a terrible fever and so emotional," Paglia said. "There is a total vacuum in their view of life. They don't have religion any longer. Religion teaches you metaphysics. It shows you how to examine yourself and ask questions about your relationship with the universe." The Bible, she said, is "one of the greatest books ever written."[17]

If Baudelaire came into the Catholic Church on his deathbed, we are permitted to hope that other raging egomaniacs and volatile comic personae might likewise exhaust the faux substantiality of social centrality and, in the end, discover what George Santayana called "the old Roman road of tradition." Meanwhile, the ontological diminution is filtering down to the very young. Almost three decades ago, a harbinger of the coming crisis appeared in the pages of *The New York Times*. It was one of a series of articles focusing on people coping with the evisceration of the self in postmodern America. The article by Catherine S. Manegold focused on a twelve-year-old girl living in Brooklyn.

> Crystal wears two streaks of bright magenta in her hair. They hang, strands of Kool-Aid, down her loose, long strands of blonde like a seventh grader's twist of punk: Don't come too close. Don't mess with me. Don't tell me what to do. I'm not like you.
> At her Brooklyn public school, a kaleidoscope of teen-age rage, Crystal's teachers see a young girl with an attitude. They focus on

---

14   Jackie Jones, "More Paglia Essays to Offend and Entertain," *San Francisco Examiner-Chronicle* Sunday Book Review Section, October 23, 1994, 3.
15   Emily Esfahani Smith, "The Provocations of Camille Paglia," *City Journal*, Summer 2019.
16   Ibid.
17   Ibid.

her slouch, her Kool-Aid streaks, her grunge clothes and sullen anger and see all the signs of trouble. But those vivid slashes say the most, communicating a basic paradox of adolescence, the double-edged message: "bug off" and "LOOK AT ME."[18]

Here we have the quintessential expression of the Underground Man's performance in the tavern. Like so many cultural commentators, the *Times* reporter overlooked the cultural and historical dimensions of the suffering this girl was experiencing. As prevalent as it is in our present society, this child's "bug off" and "LOOK AT ME" attitude is not "a basic paradox of adolescence," and to dismiss it as such is to unwittingly join in the conspiracy of misrecognition. Nor should we dismiss her sad plight as something due to her personal and family circumstances, however much they may have contributed to her predicament. There are far too many people today, both older and even younger than this child, who suffer a similar psycho-social distress.

What is worthy of attention, however, is the characterization of this child's Brooklyn public school as "a kaleidoscope of teen-age rage." When there are countless social competitors seeking alleviation from their insubstantiality in more or less the same sulking way, the whole tenor of the social order becomes one of a sullen and potentially explosive "kaleidoscope of (nihilistic) rage," which, alas, is no longer confined to adolescent school children.

Bearing in mind the mystical attraction that the exquisitely lymphatic Warhol had for those caught in his orbit, as well as the attraction Percival exerted on his classmates due to his "blue, and oddly inexpressive eyes" that were "fixed with pagan indifference upon the pillar" in front of him, we conclude these reflections with John Horvat's comment about the 2019 *Time Magazine* Person of the Year.

> There is also an element of mystery and mysticism in her presentation. Unfortunately, she suffers from Asperger's Syndrome, which impairs her emotional expression, making it cold, mysterious, and disconnected. Thus, everything about her tragically defies the standard definition of what might be expected of this child seemingly without a childhood.... The media have been quick to capitalize on ascribing to her mystical persona special powers, not unlike that of a prophetess or oracle.[19]

---

18 Catherine S. Manegold, "To Crystal, 12, School Serves No Purpose," *The New York Times*, April 8, 1993.
19 John Hovat, "Why Greta Thunberg Should Be *Time*'s 'Person of the Year,'" *The Imaginative Conservative*, December 17, 2019.

17 The Illness of Our Age

> The illness of our age is hysteria. One encounters it everywhere. Everywhere one rubs elbows with it.... It is not only enclosed within the gray walls of the Salpêtrière, this singular neurosis with its astonishing effects; it travels the streets and the world.[1]

SO OBSERVED JULES CLARETIE, THE FRENCH LITerary figure and director of the Théâtre Français in 1881. If the director of the Théâtre Français might be expected to have been disproportionally exposed to hysteria, his contemporary, the French writer Guy de Maupassant, perhaps a century ahead of the historical situation to which his comment might be more widely applicable declared in 1882 that "we are all hysterics."[2] A few decades later, the Swiss philosopher Max Picard offered a similar—if a decidedly more ominous—assessment. "In this world *the* sickness is hysteria.... In this world no one is so happy as the hysterical person, no sick person so little desires to be robbed of his sickness as he does."[3]

But then: the oddest thing about the epidemic of hysteria which accompanied and occasioned the birth of psychoanalysis, and which was quickly determined to be one of the oldest psychological distresses — dating back four thousand years — is that in the latter half of the twentieth century it appears to have vanished, to the astonishment of almost everyone. Writes Mark Micale:

> Ironically, the most consequential development in the history of hysteria during the twentieth century has been the dramatic and mysterious decline in the incidence of the disorder. A more or less unbroken textual record of hysteria runs from the ancient Greeks to Freud. Yet in recent generations, a drastic diminution of the rate of occurrence of hysterical neurosis has

---

1 Quoted in Micale, *Approaching Hysteria*, 216.
2 Ibid., 216.
3 Max Picard, *The Flight from God*, trans. Marianne Kuschnitzky and J. M. Cameron (Washington, DC: Regnery Gateway, 1989), 75.

taken place.... After twenty centuries of medical history, this extraordinary disease is for all intents and purposes disappearing from sight today. Nobody knows why.[4]

But did it disappear? Or did clinical forms of hysteria dissolve into a sea of sub-clinical ones? Freud likened "anxiety" — that most familiar of psychological symptoms — "to an individually acquired hysterical attack."[5] And the physician, novelist, and careful observer of social and psychological developments, Walker Percy, announced categorically: "This is the age of anxiety because this is the age of the loss of the self."[6] Clearly, susceptibility to hysteria varies from person to person, but epidemics — whether of clinical hysteria in individuals or low-grade chronic forms of hysteria affecting larger swaths of the population — continue to occur. In fact, these things have become such a familiar feature of today's popular culture that they are widely regarded as normative.

When Fritz Wittels wrote in 1931 that the "seizures of gross hysteria... have to-day disappeared from the amphitheaters of the clinic," little did he suspect that these clinically recognizable forms of hysteria might be replaced by more elusive and ubiquitous forms operating in a much more spacious social amphitheater. Indeed, today it seems these low-level, sub-clinical forms of hysterical dis-identification take the form of assertions of autonomy and individuality so flamboyantly and desperately asserted that the assertion becomes a self-parody.

Whereas infectious diseases are spread by germs or viruses, infectious epidemics of hysteria, writes Elaine Showalter, "spread by stories circulated through self-help books, articles in newspapers and magazines, TV talk shows and series, films, the Internet, and even literary criticism."[7] It is by following suggestions such as this that the rare and acute psychiatric incidences of hysteria in Victorian times and the milder, more chronic and more widespread manifestations of it today can be linked. And it is in light of that linkage that the comment made in the Britannica's summary piece on hysteria is itself so "hysterical" in the comedic sense of the term. After stating that hysteria occurs mostly among unsophisticated and less intelligent people, the author of this piece writes, "The incidence of hysteria appears to have been diminishing over the years

---

4 Micale, *Approaching Hysteria*, 29.
5 Sigmund Freud, *New Introductory Lectures on Psychoanalysis*, trans. James Strachey (New York: W.W. Norton, 1964), 81.
6 Percy, *Sign-Posts in a Strange Land*, 254.
7 Showalter, *Hystories*, 5.

in many areas of the world, probably because of cultural factors such as increasing psychological sophistication, diminishing sexual prudery and inhibition, and a less authoritarian family structure." We invite the reader to decide whether someone who is that blithely optimistic about the social consequences of the diminution of sexual inhibition, and that dismissive of what is pejoratively characterized as authoritarian family structure, possesses sufficient "psychological sophistication" to warrant credulity.

The evidence contradicting this assessment was abundant enough when it was originally published, but today it is overwhelmingly so. The diminution of chastity and sexual continence and the almost complete elimination of anything faintly resembling the "authoritarian family structure" has coincided with an explosion of sub-clinical manifestations of hysteria — in personal habits as well as in political and ideological affairs. Writing of one of the earlier social hysterias, David Goldman notes:

> Child-abuse hysteria has abated, but the public is still consumed by witch hunts against micro-aggressions, triggering, sexual harassment, and so forth. To remedy the dysfunctional sexual life of millennials, the abysmally low college graduation rate of minority men, and other perceived ills, whole universities have been transformed into controlled therapeutic environments, subjecting every aspect of life to inquisitorial control.[8]

Just as a new scientific discipline had to emerge in order to treat the increasing number of psychological distresses and disorders, so a comparably venerable institution, the university, has lately been retrofitted for the purpose of alleviating the stress experienced by students emotionally traumatized by even the rarest exposure to ideas at odds with the bromides and platitudes of secular progressivism. In the unlikely event that such ideas manage to be voiced on today's campus, an outbreak of howling hysteria predictably ensues, quickly affecting both students and professors.

> Political correctness is a generalization of Freudian theory; it presumes that the waking consciousness of women as well as ethnic, racial, and sexual minorities consists of a minefield of traumatic memories. Public policy must prevent the triggering of these minds. Public institutions, starting with universities, must be converted into the functional equivalent of psychiatric hospitals and all communications censored to minimize trauma.[9]

---

8 Goldman, "Prophet of Ordinary Unhappiness."
9 Ibid.

Inasmuch as Freud's oedipal theory placed the libidinal sexual drive — stripped of the grace of self-gift with which Christianity had labored to restore its splendor — at the center of his anti-religious anthropology, it is not altogether surprising that it was in the area of sexual morality — and the intact family that sexual continence undergirds — that the crisis of contemporary subjectivity would first appear. "Without hysteria," writes David Healy, Professor of Psychiatry at McMaster University Canada, "it is unlikely we would have had Freud and all the changes to modern and Western sensibility that he brought about."[10]

> Their political skill lay in pushing forward the boundaries of science while at the same time persuading a variety of political masters that their new discoveries were consistent with traditional values and with the maintenance of order in society. This new knowledge was no less dangerous if not contained within a moral framework than twentieth-century nuclear knowledge would later be.[11]

Today these systems of public discourse have themselves become vectors of contagious hysteria. Showalter notes that "patients learn about diseases from the media, unconsciously develop the symptoms, and then attract media attention in an endless cycle."[12] The last two sentences of Mark Micale's study of hysteria are these:

> Almost assuredly, the corpus of texts that compose the new hysteria studies, including the present one, reflect other "deep structures" of our age too, but we are too close to the spectacle to perceive these meanings. At best, we can only record the phenomenon as accurately as possible and speculate dimly on its larger implications — leaving these to be discovered, perhaps, by some enterprising historian of the late twenty-first century.[13]

Micale's extraordinarily fine book was published in 1995, and in it he made no references to René Girard. Nor is there any indication that the author had come into contact with the Girardian corpus. This lacuna gives Micale's discussion of the mimetic dimension of hysteria even greater weight, as he arrived at those insights solely on the basis of the data. Because its standing as "a demonstrable physical or mental

---

10 David Healy, *Mania: A Short History of Bipolar Disorder*, Johns Hopkins Biography of Disease Series (Baltimore: Johns Hopkins University Press, 2008), 17.
11 Ibid., 31.
12 Showalter, *Hystories*, 6.
13 Micale, *Approaching Hysteria*, 294.

disease is so uncertain," Micale writes, "hysteria may not be a 'real' disease at all."[14] He notes that the "neurologically oriented theorists in the nineteenth century characterized hysteria as 'neuromimetic.' To them, it was the masquerading malady that assumed its very identity by taking on the form of other diseases."[15]

As Stallybrass and White note, the declining incidence of clinical hysteria was accompanied by the rise of various and sundry "bohemian" social fashions whose marginality and carnivalesque features were roughly parallel to those experienced individually and psychopathologically by hysterics.[16] "Anorexia and bulimia," writes Elaine Showalter, "are examples of modern hysterical epidemics."[17] The fashionable disorder in the mid-1990s was eating disorders.

The disorder at this moment is neither gastronomic nor strictly speaking concupiscent; it is gender fluidity, and it is to date the most demonstrably absurd manifestation of fashionable hysteria, surpassed only by the insane and terrifying transhuman project, about which we will speak below. More candid researchers, such as J. Michael Bailey and Abigail Shrier, have not hesitated to speak of the transgender craze as a social hysteria. Shrier cites Bailey: "Dr. Bailey believes that for these teenage girls gender dysphoria is a hysteria much like multiple personality disorder, another historical example of disturbed young women convincing themselves they possess an ailment and then manifesting the symptoms."[18]

The intensification of mimetic rivalry, wrote René Girard, "necessarily accompanies the dissolving of all prohibitions."[19] Of course, the behaviors that the prohibitions proscribed do not thereby become wholesome. Their exemption from moral scrutiny, when that exemption is not absolute, requires that unhealthy behaviors and the ethical confusions they foster be addressed in ways that explicitly preclude moral judgment. In a breathtaking extension of Freud's intellectual sanctioning of the sexual revolution, latter day variations of that revolution have found respite from moral scrutiny in the American Psychiatric Association's *Diagnostic and Statistical Manual*. John Lawrence Hill concisely summarizes the state of that transformation circa the mid-1990s.

---

14   Ibid., 181.
15   Ibid., 182.
16   Stallybrass and White, *The Politics and Poetics of Transgression*, 188.
17   Showalter, *Hystories*, 20.
18   Abigail Shrier, *Irreversible Damage: The Transgender Craze Seducing Our Daughters* (Washington, DC: Regnery, 2020), 133.
19   Girard, *Anorexia and Mimetic Desire*, 14.

Every traditional vice now has an entry in the psychiatrist's Diagnostic and Statistical Manual of Mental Disorders — from compulsive overeating to antisocial disorder to an ever-metastasizing plethora of sexual dysfunctions, including exhibitionism, pedophilia, transvestic fetishism, and sexual sadism disorder. Each of these conditions is believed to operate outside the direct control of the acting person. In the last half century at least forty new defenses have crept into the annals of criminal law, including battered woman syndrome, battered child syndrome, adopted child syndrome, the black rage defense, computer addiction syndrome, distant father syndrome, the mob-mentality defense, parental alienation syndrome, patient-therapist sex syndrome, the "pornography made me do it" defense, postpartum and premenstrual stress syndromes, ritual abuse syndrome (used by members of satanic cults), the steroid defense, the Twinkie defense, and urban survivor syndrome. These are just a representative sample. This breathtaking expansion of criminal defenses constitutes the slow working out of the deterministic hypothesis in modern criminal law.[20]

This is simply the institutionalization of Jean-Jacques Rousseau's moral ruse for blaming civilization and robbing citizens of their agency, the responsibility that those vulnerable to these disorders might have for avoiding them. If, however, the tendency is to redefine "traditional vice" as a disorder for which those exhibiting the disorder bear little or no responsibility, the opposite is not true. Those who might have once been held morally or legally accountable for such behaviors now accuse those who have the temerity to hold to the tradition that regards these behaviors as morally or legally reprehensible as heartless, censorious pharisees. The love-the-sinner-hate-the-sin principle is roundly mocked by people who are so lacking in Christian moral experience that they find the principle laughable on the face of it. "A generation ago one could speak of America as a therapeutic society," writes David Goldman. "Today we resemble a gigantic asylum."[21]

Earlier in our reflections on Virginia Woolf's novel *The Waves*, we noted the fluid form of subjectivity experienced by the principal protagonist Bernard, who at one point declared: "I am not one and simple, but complex and many.... They do not understand that I have to effect different transitions; have to cover the entrances and exits of several

---

20 John Lawrence Hill, *After Natural Law* (San Francisco: Ignatius Press, 2016), 197.
21 Goldman, "Prophet of Ordinary Unhappiness."

different men who alternatively act their parts as Bernard."[22] Near the end of the novel there appear the first faint signs of what are the most startling consequences of the mimetic crisis: the indistinguishability of the sexes. The world-weary and wistful Bernard muses, "this is not one life; nor do I always know if I am man or woman, Bernard or Neville, Louis, Susan, Jinny or Rhoda — so strange is the contact of one with another."[23] Woolf gives her reader access to Bernard's interior musings:

> ...we are slipping away. Little bits of ourselves are crumbling.... I cannot keep myself together.... But what is odd is that I still clasp the return half of my ticket to Waterloo firmly between the fingers of my right hand, even now, even sleeping.[24]

Woolf's protagonist is suffering a version of the disintegration Flannery O'Connor's O. E. Parker experienced when he felt as though "the panther and the lion and the serpents and the eagles and the hawks had penetrated his skin and lived inside him in a raging warfare." While Parker was tenuously sustained by the trace left on his soul by his mother's Christian faith, Woolf's main character had only his return ticket to the central railway station in London on which to rely. (Woolf was surely cognizant of the metaphorical implications of the word Waterloo as she was of how incommensurate it was as insurance against Bernard's ontological dissolution.) She sees Bernard approaching that point of no return, the advanced stage of the mimetic crisis, at which he can no longer tell if he is a man or woman.

In the space of a very few years, an astonishing number of people have come to believe — or pretend to believe — that sexual differences are neither definitive nor stable. Gender is thought to be subject to alteration at the whim of the individual, contradicting thereby one of the few legitimate instances of "settled science" and obliging those adhering to biological and anthropological reality to curtsy before the most nonsensical idol of the age. The speed with which these cavalier abdications of anthropological commonsense have occurred is but one of the indications that they will be recognized in hindsight as social hysterias.

Western civilization, writes Jane Robbins, is "now gripped by a cultural cyclone" that is slamming into culture "with a totalitarian force."

> Transgenderism has shaken the foundations of all we know to be true. Scientific knowledge is rejected and medical practice

---

22 Woolf, *The Waves*, 76.
23 Ibid., 281.
24 Ibid., 235.

co-opted in service of a new "reality"—that "gender" is independent of sex, that males and females of any age, even young children, are entitled to their own transgender self-identification based only on their feelings, and that literally every individual and every segment of society must bow to their chosen identity at risk of losing reputation, livelihood, and even freedom itself.[25]

As of this writing, the American Medical Association has urged states to remove from birth certificates any reference to the child's sex on the grounds that such a designation can be properly determined, not by indisputable anatomical data, but solely by a subsequent decision of the child or adult. Similarly ridiculous is the apology issued by a professor of medicine at the University of California for the offense of using the term "pregnant women" to refer to pregnant women; "pregnant people" being the required nomenclature. To his credit, René Descartes abandoned his senses in the interest of a self-certainty. His heirs today are losing their senses out of slavish and craven deference to the most undeniable nonsense of the age. The eschatological ramifications of this betrayal of anatomical reality are brought out by Hans Urs von Balthasar's insistence that our sexual binary "makes its effects felt in all the corners of the spirit. Even in eternal life, where there will no longer be sexual procreation, a man who dies, a woman who dies, will not lose sexual identity or exchange it for something else."[26]

Mary Eberstadt notes that "ten countries now allow for identification as something other than male and female, and that a growing number of states and other authorities leave gender identity in various forms to personal say-so."[27]

> Anyone who has ever heard a coyote in the desert, separated at night from its pack, knows the sound. The otherwise unexplained hysteria of today's identity politics is nothing more, or less, than just that: the collective human howl of our time, sent up by inescapably communal creatures trying desperately to identify their own.[28]

---

25 Jane Robbins, "The Cracks in the Edifice of Transgender Totalitarianism," *Public Discourse: The Journal of the Witherspoon Institute*, July 13, 2019.
26 Hans Urs von Balthasar, *Epilogue*, trans. Edward T. Oakes, S.J. (San Francisco: Ignatius Press, 2004), 100.
27 Mary Eberstadt, *Primal Screams: How the Sexual Revolution Created Identity Politics* (West Conshohocken, PA: Templeton Press, 2019), Kindle edition §496.
28 Eberstadt, *Primal Screams*, Kindle edition §1538.

18 Multiphrenia

> I will not take part in the cheerful masquerade today, once again so much in vogue, where one ties on this or that store-bought or self-designed definition of human being, today this one, tomorrow that.
> — Hans Urs von Balthasar[1]

> The liquid narcissism saturating the developed world means that a person is expected to flow from one identity to another, with only consumerist desire as the guide.
> — Angela Franks[2]

> We can also predict that when the fascinated being reaches the paroxysmal stage of his sickness he will be completely incapable of maintaining his original pose and will constantly change roles.
> — René Girard[3]

D R PAUL MCHUGH, THE DISTINGUISHED PROFESsor of psychiatry at Johns Hopkins School of Medicine, saw journalist Flora Rhea Schreiber's *Sybil*—written in collaboration with the Manhattan psychiatrist Cornelia Wilbur and first published in 1973—as exemplifying the phenomenon of hysteria, both in its individual and social manifestation. Apropos of the latter form of hysteria, the back cover of the 2009 edition of *Sybil* blared *Time Magazine*'s enthusiastic endorsement: "Spellbinding." In retrospect, the magazine's characterization may be more apt than even the book's publisher and reviewers realized. Indeed, the publisher's blurb on the back cover of the book—self-serving though it was—suggests how apposite its subtitle was:

> More amazing than any work of fiction, yet true in every word, it swept to the top of the bestseller lists and riveted the

---

[1] Balthasar, *The von Balthasar Reader*, 64.
[2] Angela Franks, "Fluidity: Man, the Triune God, and the Eucharistic Christ," *Communio*, No. 46 (Fall–Winter 2019): 590.
[3] Girard, *Deceit, Desire, and the Novel*, 266.

consciousness of the world. As an Emmy Award-winning film starring Sally Field, it captured the home screens of an entire nation and has endured as the most electrifying TV movie ever made. It's the story of a survivor of terrifying childhood abuse, victim of sudden and mystifying blackouts, and the first case of multiple personality ever to be psychoanalyzed. You're about to meet Sybil — and the sixteen selves to whom she played host, *both women and men*, each with a different personality, speech pattern, and even personal appearance. You'll experience the strangeness and fascination of one woman's rare affliction — and travel with her on her long, ultimately triumphant journey back to wholeness.[4]

After the 2020 – 2022 COVID-19 pandemic, we are more keenly conscious of the problem of contagious pathogens. At a slightly less conscious level, many have a rudimentary awareness of comparable contagions of a psycho-social nature spread by infectious agents of a mimetic sort. Both the book that "riveted the consciousness of the world," and the *Time Magazine* encomium for it, spawned a multiple-personality-disorder craze. The latter's mention that the personalities manifested in the subject were both male and female tends to corroborate what Mark Micale suspected, namely that the theme of the androgyne and the image of the hysterical writer as "man-woman" was opportune to the romantic fascination with "exposing, exploring, and extending the androgynous element in their own natures, their psychological bisexuality."[5] Writes Paul McHugh:

> In their book, the collaborating authors proposed that this "disintegration" of Sybil's mind into several personalities was the result of her "repressing" the memory of sexual abuse she suffered at the hands of her mother in childhood. Although the abuse was never confirmed, the book and the television movie made from it ignited the MPD [*Multiple Personality Disorder*] craze.[6]

The diagnosis of *Multiple Personality Disorder* was disputed by other specialists consulted, notably by Dr David Spiegel, who declared the patient to be suffering from hysteria. Spiegel noted that the book and

---

[4] Emphasis added.
[5] Micale, *Approaching Hysteria*, 250.
[6] Paul R. McHugh, *Try to Remember: Psychiatry's Clash Over Meaning, Memory, and Mind* (New York: Dana Press, 2008), 151.

Multiphrenia

the film made from it started "a whole new cult, a whole new wave of hysteria restated in a new way... basically it's a hysterical response to hysteria."[7]

As we saw in an earlier chapter, Freud recognized early in his observations of those exhibiting hysterical symptoms, "the capacity of hysterics to imitate any symptoms in other people that may have struck their attention." He recognized not only the psychological instability that this trait involved but the extreme fluidity of symptoms likely to be exhibited by those bombarded by multiple mimetic influences. Without an overarching, paradigmatic, "external" mediator, the mimetic phenomenon can careen wildly and erratically. One recalls the insight of the French philosopher Rémi Brague:

> In my country, and in other ones, too, like Spain, when a cab is for hire and looking for a customer, it has a flag of sorts on which is written "free." For many of our contemporaries, the model of what "being free" means is the way in which this cab is "free." This means that it is empty, that it doesn't go to any particular place, and can be taken over and hired by anybody who can pay.[8]

What justifies the adjective in the phrase "sovereign self" is the self's entirely unencumbered license to become whatever it might wish to be, notwithstanding any moral, cultural, social, or biological facts. To be free in this sense is to be profoundly impoverished, deprived of the heritage, commitments, human bonds, and unique circumstances which condition human life and enrich it.

The very attempt to survey and catalogue the magical, shape-shifting world of a full-blown mimetic crisis runs the risk of appearing to be yet another instance of it. As we have done heretofore, we turn to a few literary adumbrations of this crisis. For instance: whether consciously or not, in the above quotation Rémi Brague adopted the same metaphor on which T. S. Eliot relied in his own poetic allusion to the selfsame postmodern predicament. At the end of a day structured by responsibilities to one's employer, one enjoys a few hours of relative freedom.

---

7 Quoted in McHugh, *Try to Remember*, 152.
8 Rémi Brague, *Curing Mad Truths (Catholic Ideas for a Secular World)* (Notre Dame, IN: University of Notre Dame Press, 2019), 59.

THE APOCALYPSE OF THE SOVEREIGN SELF

> At the violet hour, when the eyes and back
> Turn upward from the desk, when the human engine waits
> Like a taxi throbbing waiting...⁹

So fickle is the deracinated self today and so evanescent are the models on which it more or less unconsciously relies that once the routine tasks it has contracted to perform come to an end for the day, the search begins for another scent to follow, another example to imitate, another opportunity to perform the pantomime of autonomy.

Jean-Michel Oughourlian concurs, noting that the self is "filled with and saturated by otherness throughout its history and constituted as a patchwork of all integrated others."¹⁰ There is in Oughourlian's basically sound insight an inner tension captured by the words *patchwork* and *integrated*. He is doubtless correct that each of us owes a debt to the countless people who have touched our lives. Therein is the patchwork. Ordering that patchwork into a coherent unity requires a touchstone, a polestar, an ordering principle of some kind. In the first instance, parents provide the child with such a touchstone, which connects Willy Loman's lament that his father left when he was just a child with the fact that he still felt kind of temporary about himself.

Be that as it may, it is worth recalling that the honor due to one's forebearers is subordinate to the devotion to God. To change metaphors, the role of parental figures — to which we will return later — is that of the Big Dipper, which serves to direct the uplifted eyes of the stargazer to the Polestar of a rightly ordered life. It is the core reality of Christian faith to see Christ as the divine, divinely chosen, and unsurpassable Mediator, in relation to whom all other ancillary influences can be assessed and given their proper place in a well-ordered life.¹¹ Absent the gravitational field of that Master Mediator, the quest for authenticity becomes both fickle and feverish. We see all of this foreshadowed in Luke's Gospel:

> When the unclean spirit has gone out of a man, he passes through waterless places seeking rest; and finding none he says, "I will return to my house from which I came." And when he comes he finds it swept and put in order. Then he goes and brings seven other spirits more evil than himself, and they

---

9   T. S. Eliot, *The Waste Land*.
10 Oughourlian, *The Mimetic Brain*, 187.
11 Again, the cover image of this book was chosen for its depiction of the relationship between the intermediate models and the ultimate One.

Multiphrenia

enter and dwell there; and the last state of that man becomes worse than the first. (Lk 11: 24–26)

Our ineradicable mimetic nature has grown famished because of the simultaneous emergence of the myth of autonomous individuality, which considers imitation beneath the dignity of the sovereign individual, and the technologies that present us with an ever-swirling aggregation of enticing models. The opportunity for mimetic fascination has grown exponentially as the claim of autonomy grows both shrill and more unconvincing.

In an inner monologue in Virginia Woolf's novel *The Waves*, Neville analyzes his classmate, Bernard:

> Once you were Tolstoi's young man; now you are Byron's young man; perhaps you will be Meredith's young man; then you will visit Paris in the Easter vacation and come back wearing a black tie, some detestable Frenchman whom nobody has ever heard of.[12]

Bernard acknowledges the validity of Neville's assessment in his own inner monologue: "I am Bernard; I am Byron; I am this, that and the other."[13] And near the end of the novel Bernard casts a glance back over his life:

> I changed and changed; was Hamlet, was Shelley, was the hero, whose name I now forget, of a novel by Dostoevsky; was for a whole term, incredibly, Napoleon; but was Byron chiefly. For many weeks at a time it was my part to stride into rooms and fling gloves and coat on the back of chairs, scowling slightly. I was always going to the bookcase for another sip of the divine specific.[14]

A page or two of Byron, Bernard hopes, will work on him like a tuning fork. As Woolf knows quite well, the hero whose name Bernard has forgotten is surely the antihero in *Notes from Underground* whose name doesn't appear in Dostoevsky's novel. Woolf seems to know from personal experience that at the end of the journey marked by Hamlet, Shelley, Byron, and Napoleon, Bernard will find himself in the Dostoevskyan underground.

---

12   Woolf, *The Waves*, 87.
13   Ibid., 89.
14   Ibid., 249.

THE APOCALYPSE OF THE SOVEREIGN SELF

In *The Saturated Self: Dilemmas of Identity in Contemporary Life*, Kenneth Gergen captured the spiritual and psychological predicament in which many — especially the young — are today living. Remarkably, Gergen's many valuable insights notwithstanding, the predicament he describes was made all the more distressing by his effort to remain sanguine in the face of it. Like several of the thinkers we have discussed, Gergen provides an inestimable service by insightfully surveying social and psychological phenomena, the terminal phases of which he has nevertheless understood inadequately. The lived experience of the postmodern self, Gergen seems happy to announce, is *multiphrenia*.

Like so many postmodern apologists, Professor Gergen — having diagnosed a self-dissolution occasioned by the attenuation of an anthropology rooted in the Judeo-Christian tradition — must try as best he can to celebrate the wreckage he so impressively surveys. Now perfectly unencumbered by the modern quest for what de Lubac termed "static sincerity," postmodern man accommodates to his life as a de-centered "social chameleon," taking bits and pieces at random from the incessant parade of mimetic models to which he is exposed, all in the putative effort to be true to himself. "If one's identity is properly managed, the rewards can be substantial," Gergen strains to assure his readers: "the devotion of one's intimates, happy children, professional success, the achievement of community goals, personal popularity, and so on." All this is possible, he imagines, "if one avoids looking back to locate a true and enduring self, and simply acts to full potential in the moment at hand."[15]

At this point in our explorations, it hardly needs pointing out that what Freud diagnosed as hysteria and what Gergen characterizes as multiphrenia are species of the same predicament. On this point the Russian philosopher Nicholas Berdyaev was prescient: "Inner division wears away personality, and this division can be overcome only by making a choice, by selecting a definite object for one's love.... Debauchery means the absolute inability to choose from among many attractions."[16]

The Russian philosopher is echoed by the Polish poet Czesław Miłosz who offers a more sobering assessment of what Gergen calls multiphrenia, one more in sync with Jesus's reference to the seven demons more wicked than the one expelled:

---

15   Kenneth J. Gergen, *The Saturated Self* (New York: Basic Books, 1991), 150.
16   Nicholas Berdyaev, *Dostoevsky* (New York: New American Library, 1974), 125.

Multiphrenia

> What reasonable man would like to be a city of demons,
> who behave as if they were at home, speak in many tongues....
> The purpose of poetry is to remind us
> how difficult it is to remain just one person,
> for our house is open, there are no keys to the doors,
> and invisible guests come in and out at will.[17]

Professor Gergen has recognized better than most the features of human anthropology that many find convenient to ignore, and he has seen the contemporary spiritual, psychological, and cultural crisis with great insight. Not least when he writes:

> There is an important sense in which each of us is a metaphor for those with whom we come in contact. They provide the images of what it is to be an authentic person, and as we incorporate others' modes of being — their mannerisms, their styles — we become their surrogates, metaphors of their reality.[18]

This is undoubtedly so. What is more problematic and elusive, however, is how this can be done without compromising the subject's ontological and psychological integrity.

The fully saturated self, Gergen insists, is an accomplishment. It begins, he argues, with the populating of the self by multiple influences. The subsequent achievement of social saturation leads eventually to a multiphrenic condition and the "vertigo of unlimited multiplicity." "Both the populating of the self and the multiphrenic condition are significant preludes to postmodern consciousness."[19] That every achievement seems but a prelude to yet another one need not be taken as evidence of the value of what is eventually achieved. The notion that a series of steps, each just unsatisfying enough to be abandoned as a mere "milestone" but not so obviously wrong-headed as to provoke an about-face, will lead in the end to full satisfaction may seem a wan hope on which to gamble one's fulfillment. But it happens to be the animating principle of contemporary liberalism.

As for points of stability in this endless flux, Gergen turns to a columnist in the *Washington Post*.

---

17   Czesław Miłosz, "Ars Poetica?" from *The Collected Poems: 1931–1987*. Copyright © 1988 by Czesław Miłosz Royalties, Inc. Used by permission of HarperCollins Publishers.
18   Gergen, *The Saturated Self*, 223.
19   Ibid., 49.

> The columnist Cynthia Heimel argues that because celebrity figures are known by so many people, they serve as forms of social glue, allowing people from different points of society to converse with each other, to share feelings, and essentially to carry on informal relations. "Celebrities," she proposes, "are our common frames of reference, celebrity loathing and revilement crosses all cultural boundaries."[20]

It warrants mention that there was a time in Western culture when the figure who served as a form of "social glue, allowing people from different points of society to converse with each other, to share feelings, and essentially to carry on informal relations," was Christ. Heimel may not have noticed that, but she has stumbled upon one of the consequences of replacing Christ with a series of celebrities, namely that, in due course, the social glue will take the form of "celebrity loathing and revilement." Again, René Girard's opus is a massive explication of this the final stage of a mimetic crisis, at which point the idol becomes the scapegoat.[21]

Heimel goes on to say, "Celebrities are not our community elders, they are our community." And this touches on the collapse of social hierarchies in the aftermath of which no paragons of moral virtue, civic pride, honorable conduct, and nobility — no "elders" — are allowed to grace the public square, much less exert a serious claim on the public imagination of subsequent generations. A celebrity culture is an anti-culture inasmuch as those figures who attract social attention come and go with such frequency that in due course what is left of the genuine social cohesion inevitably dissipates, leaving the celebrities at the unenviable center of a spiritually and morally exhausted society's attention. In his defense, it must be said that Kenneth Gergen cannot be accused of deception. His honesty is bracing:

> We are not dealing here with doubts regarding claims about the truth of human character, but with the full-scale abandonment of the concept of objective truth. The argument is not that our descriptions of the self are objectively shaky, but that the very attempt to render accurate understanding is itself bankrupt.[22]

---

20 Ibid., 56.
21 We have explored this theme in *God's Gamble: The Gravitational Power of Crucified Love*.
22 Gergen, *The Saturated Self*, 82.

Multiphrenia

There is a great deal of gibberish in Gergen's book, much of it one suspects *de rigueur* at Swarthmore College in the last decades of the last century. For instance:

> As one casts out to sea in the contemporary world, modernist moorings are slowly left behind. It becomes increasingly difficult to recall precisely to what core essence one must remain true. The ideal of authenticity frays about the edges; the meaning of sincerity slowly lapses into indeterminacy. And with this sea change, the guilt of self-violation also recedes. As the guilt and sense of superficiality recede from view, one is simultaneously readied for the emergence of a pastiche personality. The pastiche personality is a social chameleon, constantly borrowing bits and pieces of identity from whatever sources are available and constructing them as useful or desirable in a given situation.[23]

Gergen is intelligent enough to realize and honest enough to acknowledge the cultural consequences of the multiphrenia he so masterfully surveys. Having dismissed truth as a sufficiently stable category, he helps explain a very troubling feature of both our political and journalistic cultures in recent years. "With postmodernism the distinction between truth and falsity lapses into indeterminacy," he writes. "The existence of lying in society is thus not an outcome of individual depravity, but of pluralistic social worlds."[24] These social worlds are held precariously intact by whatever *narrative* their advocates manage to make plausible — the word *narrative* having largely replaced the word *truth* in our public discourse. Writes Gergen:

> The initial stages of this consciousness result in a sense of the self as a social con artist, manipulating images to achieve ends. As the category of "real self" continues to recede from view, however, one acquires a pastiche-like personality. Coherence and contradiction cease to matter as one takes pleasure in the expanded possibilities of being in a socially saturated world. Finally, as the distinction between the real and the contrived, style and substance, is eroded, the concept of the individual self ceases to be intelligible.[25]

---

23 Ibid., 150.
24 Ibid., 169.
25 Ibid., 170.

THE APOCALYPSE OF THE SOVEREIGN SELF

Writing at the dawn of the Internet age before the technologies of saturation achieved anything like their present scope, Gergen managed to update the situation which both Rémi Brague and T. S. Eliot found analogous to the weary office worker soliciting an empty, waiting taxi.

> Not only do the technologies of social saturation fashion "the individual without character," but at the same time, they furnish *invitations to incoherence*. In a humdrum moment, the Vancouver tax accountant can pick up the phone and rekindle a relationship in St. Louis, within less than an hour the restless engineer can drive to a singles bar thirty miles away; on a tedious Friday a New Jersey executive can decide to fly to Tortola for the weekend.... In the final analysis, we find technology and life-style operating in a state of symbiotic interdependence.[26]

Since these words were written, the symbiotic interdependence of technology and life-style has mushroomed beyond what could have been imagined three decades ago. Gergen's reprise of the Karl Marx lullaby was surely intentional. Whereas Marx imagined a world in which one could fish in the morning, hunt in the afternoon, rear cattle in the evening, and do critical theory at night, Gergen composes a tribute to "techno-personal systems." A glance at how the Marxist dream has become a nightmare everywhere it has been tried might make one wary of putting too much faith in Gergen's endorsement of its direct descendant. Thirty years on in any case, the veterans are returning. The romance is over. The daily ruses for exorcising these "humdrum moments" become themselves humdrum. But from a professorship at Swarthmore in 1991, it seemed promising. We close Professor Gergen's insightful book with a sense of gratitude and sadness. Indeed, there are hints here and there that the author himself was haunted by such misgivings, however heroically he struggled to keep the tone of his prose basically upbeat.

> Many are dismayed by the current state of events. It is painful to find the old rituals of relationship — deep and enduring friendships, committed intimacy, and the nuclear family — coming apart at the "seems." Continuity is replaced by contingency, unity by fragmentation, and authenticity by artfulness. Yet there is no obvious means of return at hand.[27]

---

26 Ibid., 173.
27 Ibid., 181.

Multiphrenia

That's a nice touch: coming apart at the "seems," as if what appeared to be the relatively greater coherence of an earlier age only seemed to be so, flattering those who see only the fallen condition while remaining blind to the traditions and institutions that served to ennoble and sanctify the lives of fallen creatures. "Truth as a correspondence between word and world lapses into nonsense," writes Gergen triumphantly. "Terms such as *sham* and *pretense* in their traditional sense simply don't apply."[28] Whatever the shortcomings of this shrugging surrender of human agency to the incoherent flux of the postmodern world, Gergen focuses only on the benefits as he sees them:

> With the spread of postmodern consciousness, we see the demise of personal definition, reason, authority, commitment, trust, the sense of authenticity, sincerity, belief in leadership, depth of feeling, and faith in progress. In their stead, an open slate emerges on which persons may inscribe, erase, and rewrite their identities as the ever-shifting, ever-expanding, and incoherent network of relationships invites and permits.[29]

A man who doubts the benefits of a shared culture and the lively exchange in a marketplace of ideas comes at last to dismiss truth as nothing more than a "totalizing discourse" carefully disguised as the ardent enemy of such things.

> Totalizing discourses have a final deficit. Not only do such systems truncate, oppress, and obliterate alternative forms of social life; they also set the stage for schism. To be convinced of the "truth" of a discourse is to find the alternatives foolish or fatuous — to slander or silence the outside. Warring camps are developed that speak only to themselves, and that seek means of destroying others' credibility and influence (and life), all with an abiding sense of righteousness.[30]

This, of course, is the most platitudinous of contemporary objections to truth or the search for it. The opposite is the case. If the reasoned adjudication of truth claims involves lively debate, once that time-honored process is set aside, "hark what discord follows, each thing meets in mere oppugnancy," as Shakespeare warns. The sliver of truth in Professor Gergen's view is that truth and the claims made for it can, indeed, set

---

28 Ibid., 187.
29 Ibid., 228.
30 Ibid., 252.

the stage for conflict and even schism, but the cure Professor Gergen has proposed is simply schism as a way of life, a radical and permanent flux in which the search for truth has become passé.

Another of the prejudices current circa the publication of Gergen's book was that "totalizing discourses" were inherently traditional ones. Three decades on, something like the opposite is conspicuously the case. As of the writing of this book, those holding traditional views are routinely silenced by those who rose to power — in educational, entertainment, journalistic, and corporate institutions — in the years since Gergen's book was published. The latter decline to put their chosen *narratives* to the test in competition with other truth-claims. Rather they anathematize the voices of tradition and moral common sense as oppressive and offensive.

Writing three years after Gergen's book was published, the psychiatrist Robert Jay Lifton picked up on Gergen's theme. He began his exploration of the contemporary predicament of the self with these jauntily cheerful words:

> We are becoming fluid and many-sided. Without quite realizing it, we have been evolving a sense of self appropriate to the restlessness and flux of our time. This mode of being differs radically from that of the past, and enables us to engage in continuous exploration and personal experiment. I have named it the "protean self" after Proteus, the Greek sea god of many forms.[31]

Which raises a question: If we can assume that today's university students are the demographic cadre most likely to have undergone a transition into the protean self, how do we explain that they are on average far less open to points of view other than or contrary to those which they have been badgered into espousing by those who have shaped their moral and intellectual horizon?

The extreme fluidity of the protean self is reflected in the official website of the University of California, once one of the most respected educational institutions in the world. As of this writing, it lists sixty-six approved terms for expressing one's chosen identity, the great majority of which are terms defining one's preferred gender or sexual identity. In testimony to the extreme fluidity of such definitions, the website

---

31 Robert Jay Lifton, *The Protean Self: Human Resilience in an Age of Fragmentation* (New York: Basic Books, 1993), 1.

prominently and cravenly acknowledges the date of the survey and guardedly declares:

> These terms were last updated in May 2019. For the most complete definitions, we encourage you to compare what you find here with information from other sources as language in our communities is often an evolving process, and there may be regional differences. Please be aware that these terms may be defined with outdated language or concepts.[32]

This is what Justice Anthony Kennedy's opinion in the Planned Parenthood v. Casey Supreme Court case looks like today in the fluid world of what was once called, without irony, higher education. So craven were the university bureaucrats who sanctioned this absurdity that they felt obliged to append an apology for overlooking any novel sexual identity that might not have been listed, providing an email address for anyone who might want to add a different identity to the officially approved list.

Such voluminous lists of sexual orientations and novel pronouns may seem either tragic or laughable to some, but the lunacy comes with serious perils. George Orwell warned that those who allow themselves to be badgered into verbally conceding that $2 + 2 = 5$ would soon thereafter be required to repeat equally nonsensical but far more soul-crushing political slogans. Voltaire's often quoted quip is ominously apropos: "Those who can make you believe absurdities can make you commit atrocities." Let us conclude by again recognizing the penetrating insight that animates Kenneth Gergen's analysis, but which, in our opinion, he seriously leaves unexamined. By way of gratitude for Gergen's many insights, let us offer a complementary assessment by Joseph Ratzinger:

> We receive our lives each day from without, from others who are not ourselves yet relate to us in some way. Man's self is not contained only within himself but exists almost even more so outside himself. He lives in those whom he loves, in those on whom his life depends, and in those for whom he lives. Man is relational, and his life, his very self, only exists by way of relationship. I, by myself, am not "I" at all, but am so only in relation to a "Thou," and it is the "Thou" that makes me myself.[33]

---

32 https://campusclimate.berkeley.edu/students/ejce/geneq/resources/lgbtq-resources/definition-terms.
33 Joseph Cardinal Ratzinger (Benedict XVI), *The Divine Project: Reflections on Creation and Church*, trans. Chase Faucheux (San Francisco: Ignatius Press, 2022), 103.

19 From Transgender to Transhuman

> Those who despise the past never seem to suspect that far worse excesses are now going on right under their noses, on a scale unprecedented, no doubt, since the beginning of human history.
> — René Girard[1]

> I would say that in some ways I change my gender as often as I change my hairstyle.
> — Martine Rothblatt[2]

> The media and social media may also foster these effects and contribute to the dissemination of symptoms and illness throughout the general population.
> — Alyson Clayton[3]

THE MORPHING OF IDEOLOGICAL QUESTS INTO ever more radical, irrational, and anthropologically reckless forms continues today on a broad front. Though each of these secular creeds tends to be even less constrained by reality than its predecessor, each shares aspects we found in the ideologies we have heretofore explored: Descartes' uncoupling of the mind and the body, Freud's resexualization of hysteria and the sexual revolution for which it provided the original intellectual rationalization, Rousseauesque exploitation of the moral privilege of the victim which Christianity had made possible, the Underground Man's lust to kick over any surviving traces of moral decorum, and David Gergen's multiphrenia. All these impulses can be seen in the truly absurd twin ideologies that have arisen over the last two or three decades: transgenderism and transhumanism. These movements embody (pun intended) virtually every anthropological heresy

---

1 Girard, *Anorexia and Mimetic Desire*, 35.
2 Martine Rothblatt, May 18, 2015 TED interview.
3 Clayton, "Gender-Affirming Treatment of Gender Dysphoria in Youth."

that Christianity has both brought to light and vigorously disputed, gnosticism chief among them.

"The transhumanist push towards a reimagining of the human, humanity, and our shared future," writes Libby Emmons, "is a primary component of three growing cultural trends: artificial intelligence, human augmentation, and the transgender phenomenon."[4] Transhumanism, she writes, "holds that humans must harness technological advancements to take an active, intelligent role in our own evolution and the evolution of our species." Based strictly on the avowals of its proponents, the transgender and transhumanist projects are unabashedly both Promethean and Gnostic. In the Nietzschean lexicon, each, most explicitly with the transhuman project, aspires to bring about the overman or superman, the *Übermensch*. Like his literary creator, the *Übermensch* is filled with pride and driven by a fiendish impulse to kick over the traces of any preexisting moral or civil order. He is both hysterical and nihilistic. Writes Anne Hendershott:

> Most faithful Catholics have viewed the burgeoning transgender industry as encouraging a misguided belief that individuals — including even pre-school children — can change their God-given identity. However, the truth is that this rejection of human nature and natural law has opened not only the door to gender construction, it has also opened an even darker door to an emerging multi-billion dollar transhuman industry. And that industry is led by some of the wealthiest and most brilliant tech trailblazers. It is an industry that promises us that not only can we choose our own gender, but we can also choose to live forever as transhuman persons — with full citizenship rights — in a new and "perfect" body that will be created for us.[5]

As Hendershott reports, one of the most influential driving forces behind the transhumanist movement, and the living embodiment of its link to its transgender harbinger, is Martine Rothblatt, who "chose to undergo radical sex-reassignment surgery in 2014." Rothblatt, whom the *New York Magazine* honored as "the highest paid female CEO in America," is now devoted to achieving transhuman immortality. In his 1995, *Apartheid of Sex*, he wrote that he had come to realize that "21st century

---

[4] Libby Emmons, "The Transhumanism Revolution: Oppression Disguised as Liberation," *Quillette*, August 11, 2018.
[5] Anne Hendershott, "From Transgender to Transhuman," *Catholic World Report*, February 2, 2021.

software made it technologically possible to separate our minds from our bodies," the recrudescence of the Cartesian reflex. As Hendershott notes, this epiphany led to the renaming of his book, which now carries the title: *From Transgender to Transhuman*.

In a 2015 TED interview, Rothblatt touted the ostensible benefits of both gender-fluidity and transhumanism. Seeing even the most dangerous extremes of the sexual revolution through the lens of the civil rights movement, he was able to wax rhapsodic about the liberated world he saw on the horizon:

> People could choose whatever gender they want if they weren't forced by society into categories of either male or female the way South Africa used to force people into categories of black or white.... I would say that in some ways I change my gender as often as I change my hairstyle.

Later in the interview Rothblatt turned to the related case of transhumanism:

> What we're working on is creating a situation where people can create a mind-file, and a mind-file is the collection of the mannerisms, personality recollection, feelings, beliefs about truth and values, everything we pour today into Google, Amazon, into Facebook, all this information stored there.... We'll be able in the next couple of decades — once software is able to recapitulate consciousness — be able to revive the consciousness which is immanent in our mind-file... billions of people will be able to develop mind-clones of themselves that will have their own life on the web.

Thus, the Gnosticism latent in the Cartesian proposition flowers in all its spectacular garishness — perhaps the most explicit and compelling admission to date of the apocalypse of the sovereign self. That intellectually gifted and extremely wealthy people could look forward to such a world is ironclad evidence of the spiritual crisis in the midst of which we now live.

The transhuman project has made great strides since then. Some very astute cultural observers see this rush toward the transhuman point of no return as the greatest challenge facing humanity in the years ahead. That these savants focus so much attention on transhumanism, when there are so many forces competing for the distinction of being the preeminent peril of our age, should awaken us from the assumption that something this obviously preposterous could not possibly become reality. Even less would most of us expect that it might become a dystopian reality by the mid-twenty-first century.

The journalist Joe Allen has written a number of articles on artificial intelligence. Though we know little about this "strange new world," we find Allen's work valuable. He writes, for instance, of one of the pioneers of the AI revolution, Max Hodak. According to Allen, Hodak "looks forward to an era when AI-powered electrodes connect the brain directly to the Metaverse." Allen quotes Hodak:

> "It could just be a computer screen that looks as solid as any ever has, and it's just floating in front of you," he says. "When your eyes are open, you would see the world of atoms. When you close your eyes, you see the world of bits." Hodak thinks that in a generation, children will be "baffled when we tell them that there used to be just nothing there when we closed our eyes."
>
> "Transhumanism is the issue of our age," Allen writes, "and it doesn't matter if old folks reject it as a disgusting abomination. The kids will love it, blissfully indifferent to the perils."[6]

To take but one detail: imagine what the world would be like for someone who could not find refuge from it by closing his eyes. Blessed solitude would vanish, to be replaced by an inescapable loneliness relieved only by drugs or artificially released endorphins.

In a 2019 paper published by *The Royal Society of London*, entitled "iHuman: Blurring lines between mind and machine," the authors can hardly contain their enthusiasm:

> Linking human brains to computers using the power of artificial intelligence could enable people to merge the decision-making capacity and emotional intelligence of humans with the big data processing power of computers, creating a new and collaborative form of intelligence. People could become telepathic to some degree, able to converse not only without speaking but without words — through access to each others' thoughts at a conceptual level. Not only thoughts, but experiences, could be communicated from brain to brain.[7]

---

6   Joe Allen, "Chipped Hands, Chipped Heads — The Dark Future of Bio-Implants," *Salvo Magazine*, December 16, 2021.
7   Quoted in Allen, "Chipped Hands, Chipped Heads."

What could possibly go wrong? One wonders: What has gone wrong in the lives of those who imagine such a future to be desirable? Joe Allen provides an apt overview:

> These devices can potentially manipulate the brain itself, controlling mood, thought patterns, or behavior. Most importantly, the people at the forefront of this endeavor are openly stating that their healing potential is just a steppingstone to an enhanced Human 2.0.... The materialist philosophy underpinning this work sees the human soul as mere neurological phenomena. Dreams and visions arise from flowing electrons and magnetic bonds. From that perspective, a brain-computer interface connects the soul to the digital realm.[8]

Neither in the religious nor in the political realm is resignation a morally acceptable option. Rather we should find resolve in how our predecessors faced the challenges of their time. As Henri de Lubac reminds us, a living faith "gets its food from poisons and proceeds by dint of obstacles."[9] We begin in the chapter to follow by recognizing how much hunger and longing there is at the heart of what appears to be so desperate and so pitiable. The raw intelligence of many of the transgender and transhuman enthusiasts notwithstanding, one can most charitably think of them, in de Lubac's cogent phrase, as mystics in the primitive state.

---

8 Ibid.
9 De Lubac, *Paradoxes of Faith*, 28.

20 "Potential Mystics or Mystics in the Primitive State"

> Every religious man, who has not the knowledge of Christ... is on the look-out.
> — John Henry Newman[1]

> We are often told that our problems are due to our inability to shake off our religious tradition, but this is not true. They are rooted in the debacle of that tradition, which is necessarily followed by the reappearance in modern garb of more ancient and ferocious divinities rooted in the mimetic process.
> — René Girard[2]

O F THE "VERY SPECIAL GROUP OF PEOPLE—THE 261 holy women officially recognized by the Roman Catholic church as saints, blessed, venerables, or servants of God who lived between 1200 and the present on the Italian peninsula... more than half displayed clear signs of anorexia." So writes Rudolph M. Bell in his 1985 *Holy Anorexia*, a valuable study that is nonetheless handicapped by Bell's adherence to the prevailing analytical reflexes at the time. These reflexes are conspicuous in Bell's treatment of two of the most well-known religious women of the thirteenth and fourteenth centuries respectively:

> The holy anorexia of Clare of Assisi or Catherine of Siena was, in its time, both holy and anorexic, a positive expression of self by a woman in response to the world that attempted to dominate her. With the Reformation, however, female religious autonomy came to be seen [by the Catholic Church] as heretical or as the work of the devil. Since the Church was passing

---

1 John Henry Newman, *The Heart of Newman, A Synthesis Arranged by Erich Przywara*, S.J. (San Francisco: Ignatius Press, 2010), 27.
2 Girard, *Anorexia and Mimetic Desire*, 18.

judgment upon proposed saints, something less negative was bound to emerge, and it did in the model of the suffering holy female, immobilized and racked by pain. However, while male prelates found this acceptable as proof of saintliness, holy women came to do so less frequently, turning instead to good works. Ultimately even male authority conceded that illness was not saintly, and so holy anorexia disappeared as an inspired mode of religious self-assertion.[3]

There is much here to unpack, not least the anachronistic reliance on the language of sexual liberation operative at the time, and the concomitant designation of anorexia as a "mode of religious self-assertion." Without conceding the validity of these preconceptions, we can recognize in them the hint of something we addressed in our discussion of Sigmund Freud's writings on hysteria, namely the role played by the attending authority — whether ecclesial or psychiatric — in fostering either the persistence or attenuation of the symptoms of the "disorder" in question. For, as Bell notes, the incidence of anorexia fell off sharply as the religious authorities ceased to valorize these "holy anorexics."

But there is a great deal more in Bell's book that is worthy of our attention, much of it tucked away in the epilogue written subsequently by William N. Davis, Executive Director at the time of the Cornell Center for the Study of Anorexia and Bulimia. Davis acknowledges the similarities between the mystics of an earlier age and the anorexics with whom Bell conflated them. Both the "holy anorexics" and those caught up in the anorexia craze of the 1980s can be "characterized by an unwillingness to eat, but one is driven by the desire to be holy and the other by the desire to be thin."[4] Both, Davis writes, "represent ideal states of being in the cultural milieus under consideration."[5] He thereupon draws out the mimetic dimension operating in both cases:

> According to Bell, female holiness in particular received a great impetus with the appearance of Clare of Assisi and Catherine of Siena. Women were presented with specific models of holiness toward which they could aspire. Struggling to live up to them could provide new and enhanced experiences of self-esteem.

---

3 Rudolph M. Bell, *Holy Anorexia* (Chicago: University of Chicago Press, 1985), 178–79.
4 Ibid., 181.
5 Ibid., 181–82.

> Similarly, in contemporary western culture thinness is constantly extolled as the feminine ideal. Adolescent females are literally deluged with cultural messages that place enormous value upon the ability to get slim and to stay slim.[6]

To reduce the religious ardor of Clare and Catherine to efforts to enhance "self-esteem" is as facile as it is untenable. What is valuable here, however, has pertinence for any number of the crazes of the last few decades, perhaps not least the single greatest manifestation of the apocalypse of the sovereign self: the bisexual and, even more astonishingly, the transgender movements, each saturated with gnostic preconceptions. "The point is," writes Davis, "both holy anorectics and those today express a powerful urge to feel deeply, intensely, and consistently connected in a way that is beyond the abilities of most human relationships."[7]

> Rudolph Bell emphasizes that saintly anorectics had to do battle with the Catholic male clergy in order to attain their desired state of holiness. Again and again there is mention made of the saints' need to resist tradition and to conquer or overcome patriarchal authority. Implied are male-female power struggles and ultimate triumph of feminine will. Several points are worth noting here. In the first place, the gender struggles that no doubt occurred do not appear to have been of primary importance for the holy anorectics. Bell comments that "even among these holy anorexics there is no reason to suggest that they intended in a careful and planned way to appropriate male prerogatives."[8]

Indeed, René Girard lends credence to Davis's suggestion by emphasizing the mimetic dimension of eating disorders. Not only are eating disorders, including anorexia, mimetically determined, but, according to Girard, they manifest a "sacrificial competition." In a culture under Christian influence, which regards sacrifice as ennobling, competition can be expected to arise between those striving to live self-sacrificial lives, notwithstanding the less ennobling competition for preeminence in this area. As Girard argues: "The problem is not that these eating disorders are too complex for our current systems of interpretation — which

---

6   Ibid., 182.
7   Ibid., 183.
8   Ibid., 183–84.

would make our explicators salivate with delight. The problem is that they are too simple, too readily intelligible."[9]

Human nature being what is it, there is no reason to contest Davis's observation: "When, finally, female saints came to be recognized in terms of their capacity to do good works, the phenomenon of holy anorexia largely disappeared. Self-starvation lost its appeal for Catholic women when it became irrelevant as a means to gain the highly valued state of holiness."[10]

Far from impugning the motives of medieval mystics, reducing their fasting to "sacrificial competition," the point to be taken from Girard's analysis is that the anorexic craze that was so conspicuous two or three decades ago — and the even more astonishing hyper-mimetic "sexual orientation" and transgender-fluid spectacle of the moment — have a religious dimension. For as long as those "identifying" with one or another of these fashions are socially celebrated for doing so, and momentarily relieved thereby of an ontological precariousness of which they are vaguely aware, this cascade of increasingly absurd trends will continue. For a while, at least. In the end, all these evanescent fashions will dissolve into a sea of regret, remorse, and lucrative litigation. Inasmuch as these crazes provide their adherents with the status of victims, no explanation will suffice if it fails to recognize how much these social epidemics depend on the empathy for victims awakened and instantiated by the Judeo-Christian tradition.

"There is great irony," Girard writes, "in the fact that the modern process of stamping out religion produces countless caricatures of it."[11] For, he argues, "There can be rivalries of renunciation rather than acquisition, of deprivation rather than of enjoyment."[12] Evidence suggesting that every sustained rejection of religion gives rise to a new religion is everywhere to be found in our world today. What Girard said several decades ago about anorexia and other eating disorders applies even more obviously to many of today's mimetic contagions.

> Our eating disorders are not continuous with our religion. They originate in the neopaganism of our time, in the cult of the body, in the Dionysiac mystique of Nietzsche, the first of our great dieters, by the way. They are caused by the destruction of

---

9   Girard, *Anorexia and Mimetic Desire*, 5.
10 Bell, *Holy Anorexia*, 190.
11 Girard, *Anorexia and Mimetic Desire*, 18.
12 Ibid., 23.

the family and other safeguards against the forces of mimetic fragmentation and competition, unleashed by the end of prohibitions.[13]

"The crisis stage is reached," writes Girard, "when competition feeds exclusively upon itself, forgetting it initial objects. Anorexic women are not interested in men at all; not unlike these men, they compete among themselves, for the sake of competition itself."[14]

What René Girard said of Dostoevsky's *The Possessed* could as well be said of sundry incidences of "sacrificial competition." "There is not one element of this distorted mysticism which does not have its luminous counterpart in Christian truth."[15] Inasmuch as this remark touches on the distorted mysticism of a distinctively nihilistic kind, it stands as testimony to the observation — previously cited — that ultimately the choice is between Christ and nothing, nothing manifested in nihilism of one sort or another.

Nor can we overlook the hysterical dimension of such "sacrificial competition." One reputed expert on hysteria at the Salpêtrière hospital where Freud and his mentor Jean Martin Charcot collaborated, Henri Legrand du Saulle, anticipated the argument in *Holy Anorexia*. Du Saulle contended that Catholic female mystics, including Joan of Arc, Catherine of Siena, Teresa of Avila, and Marie Alacoque, were hysterics. Freud's closest collaborator Joseph Breuer thought of Teresa of Avila as the patron saint of hysterics. It is easy to see in this chink in the scientific façade an animus against Christian and especially Catholic sensibilities. But Breuer's hypothesis also calls attention to a convergence of mystical and hysterical phenomena to which Henri de Lubac alluded when he spoke of how important it is to reach out to the "potential mystics, or *mystics in the primitive state*."[16] For mystics may very well have a gift for mimesis that makes it easier for them, on one hand, to enter into an identification with Christ (becoming the mystic), and on the other, to be pulled this way and that by the unwelcome mimetic effect of those in their environment (becoming the hysteric).

Indeed, under the right circumstances, those spiritually gifted with a heightened mimetic endowment that might otherwise make them vulnerable to some form of hysterical identification may find themselves

---

13   Ibid., 18.
14   Ibid., 28.
15   Girard, Deceit, *Desire and the Novel*, 61.
16   Quoted in Balthasar, *The Theology of Henri de Lubac*, 101.

drawn to the eremitical life, a life which both minimizes the danger of hysterical complications and fosters the conditions for a spiritual union with Christ, to which they may be especially predisposed. In fact, de Lubac's concern for "potential mystics, or mystics in the primitive state" provides the bridge which allows us to see the linkage between the *imitatio Christi* of the mystic and the bewildering hyper-mimeticism of the hysteric.

Those whom de Lubac called mystics in the primitive state have something of Saint Paul's gift of spiritual interior communion, but their lives have not prepared them for coping with the very experience for which they are most inwardly disposed. They lack either the psychological and spiritual ballast or the ecclesial and sacramental resources conducive to the fulfillment of their unique vocation. Nor were the mystics and saints who experienced something of Saint Paul's "I live, now no longer I, but Christ lives in me" spared the bewilderment that was not infrequently a facet of their lived experience.

———

In an article in *The New Encyclopædia Britannica*, Professor Paul Murry Kendall wrote of the origins of autobiography. Professor Kendall notes first that few forerunners of this genre are to be found in antiquity and that Saint Augustine's *Confessions*, written in the fifth century, belongs to a "special category." Augustine aside for the moment, Professor Kendall takes up the origin of autobiography in the strict sense. He writes:

> Speaking generally, then, it can be said that autobiography begins with the Renaissance in the 15th century; and, surprisingly enough, the first example was written not in Italy but in England by a woman entirely untouched by the "new learning" or literature. In her old age Margery Kempe, the sobbing mystic, or hysteric, of Lynn in Norfolk, dictated an account of her bustling, far-faring life, which, however concerned with religious experience, racily reveals her somewhat abrasive personality and the impact she made upon her fellows. This is done in a series of scenes, mainly developed by dialogue. Though calling herself, in abject humility, "the creature," Margery knew, and has effectively transmitted the proof, that she was a remarkable person.[17]

Kendall sharpens our curiosity by casually conflating "sobbing mystic" and "hysteric," while noting how Margery Kempe "racily reveals her

---

17 *The New Encyclopædia Britannica* (1984), Vol. II, 1010.

somewhat abrasive personality." Was it, we have reason to ask, Margery Kempe's "sobbing mysticism" or her "hysteria" that led her to become, at least in Professor Kendall's assessment, the first unmistakable autobiographer? Therein lies an exceedingly fascinating question. The distinction between hysteria and Christian mysticism has not always been perfectly clear. Both the hysteric and the mystic have what Jean-Michel Oughourlian calls a "virtual partner."[18] Each falls more easily under the influence of others or an Other. It was, we are to suppose, Kempe's mysticism that lies behind her concern "with religious experience," while Kendall's diagnosis of hysteria is traceable to how Kempe "racily reveals her somewhat abrasive personality and the impact she made upon her fellows." The degree to which Kempe's hysterical affliction undermined the mystery to which she might otherwise have given witness is arguably true as well of Rousseau and Nietzsche, each of whom issued what might be called the hysteric's *cri de coeur*:

> I am like no one in the whole world. I may be no better, but at least I am different.[19]

> Hear me! For I am such and such a person. Above all, do not mistake me for someone else.[20]

At least in one sense, mimetic desire is metaphysical; it cannot and will not be satisfied forever by mere mortal models. In those with genuine mystical dispositions, this transcendent ordination exposes the imitator — more than in those with less hunger for transcendence — to idolatry with regard to his fascinating models and to nihilism when these models disappoint.

Our claim that the Event of Christ altered both mankind's cultural-historical and personal-psychological predicament, and that the attempt on the part of those whose circumstances were thus altered to fashion a post-Christian alternative are doomed to failure, finds confirmation in the thought of Henri de Lubac:

> One who gives way to the temptations of a false spiritualization and wants to shake off the Church as a burdensome yoke or set her aside as a cumbersome intermediary will soon find himself embracing the void, or end up by worshipping false gods. If a man begins by using her as his support, and then comes to

---

18 Oughourlian, *The Puppet of Desire*, 80.
19 Rousseau, *Confessions*, 17.
20 Nietzsche, "*On the Genealogy of Morals*" *and* "*Ecce Homo*," 217. Italics in original.

believe that he can go beyond her, he will be nothing more than a mystic run off the rails.[21]

How many of the most obviously troubled mavens of political and ideological fanaticism today might be mystics who have been run off the rails by circumstances both personal and cultural? We earlier spoke of the Old Testament prophets who knew themselves to be articulating in word and deed Another's will. Thought by their detractors to be the betrayers of their religious and cultural heritage, these strange figures were in fact the socially pugnacious agents of its restoration. The ambivalence that has forever surrounded such persons is due to the fact that it is not always easy to distinguish between the mystic and the hysteric. False prophets abound, and in their desperate attempts to conjure a mystical aura they behave hysterically. But both hysterics and mystics undergo a kind of self-dissolution; each seems in the process of losing his psyche, but one — the mystic — discovers the paradoxical mystery of personhood, while the hysteric is thrown helter-skelter into a cycle of mimetic intrigues.

The other or others with whom the hysteric is enthralled threaten his fragile autonomy. The Other for the mystic is God, or for the Christian mystic, the incarnate face of God's love. In an inchoate way the Hebrew prophet, and in a more explicit way the Christian mystic, surrenders his strictly *autonomous* self. He loses his life in order to find it. The mystic has the subjective experience that his life is not his own, that something has been given him to do or say or be. He feels a call or a charge of some kind to which he strives to respond. The fact that the specific nature of this mandate is often excruciatingly vague does not prevent the one on whom the charge is laid from feeling that only he, only one with his gifts and shortcomings, situated precisely in his social circumstance, can fulfill the calling that is uniquely his. This accounts for the occasionally bristling self-confidence of the genuine mystic and the anxious self-assertion of the hysteric.

The genuine mystic is *sui generis*, paradoxically so inasmuch as he assents to reprise in his own life the ancestral traditions for which he is a restorative agent. Like Margery Kempe, he often realizes this. The fateful question is how will he eventually account for his uniqueness? If he accounts for his uniqueness in terms of his relatedness to that which is being articulated in him and through him, the *Logos* for whom he

---

21   De Lubac, *The Splendor of the Church*, 204, 205.

strives to serve as a conduit, then he takes the step toward becoming a *person* in the fullest sense of the term. He crosses the threshold into the world for which the mystics have left testimony. To be a person is to be a disciple, an agent, a spokesman, a herald, an ambassador, a person on a mission — however modest and indetectable by others — with which he is so identified that no account of his existence that fails to reckon with his mission will do justice to his life. If he accounts for his uniqueness in terms of whatever distinction might be found to exist between his life and that of others in the social order, then he barters away the real gift of the personal in favor of becoming a "personality." He moves into the world of experience for which hysteria is the ultimate expression. A hysteric is a disciple who is appalled by his own mimicry — often enough because his discipleship is so capricious and vacillating that he becomes a "leaky cistern that holds no water" (Jer 2:13).

21 Sylvia Plath:
"A MIMICKING NOTHINGNESS"

> Hell... may be understood not as a state imposed from the outside, but as a state we have nurtured and brought to completion in ourselves.
> — Giorgio Buccellati[1]

> The world situation today shows clearly enough that whoever discards this Christian or at least biblical view (in theology or philosophy) must in one way or another find in a personless collectivism or individualism (which converge on one another) his downfall.
> — Hans Urs von Balthasar[2]

> Sylvia Plath was a person of many masks, both in her personal life and in her writings. Some were camouflage cliché facades, defensive mechanisms, involuntary. And some were deliberate poses, attempts to find the keys to one style or another. These were the visible faces of her lesser selves, her false or provisional selves, the minor roles of her inner drama.
> — Ted Hughes (Plath's husband)[3]

THE POET SYLVIA PLATH WAS A WOUNDED, GIFTED, troubled, and complex person. She occasionally wrote penetrating and powerful poetry. She suffered from a psychological precariousness which made her vulnerable to the mimetic influences to which she was drawn and from which she recoiled. She didn't live long enough to be tutored in multiphrenia by Professor Gergen, but she was, as her husband was to note, "a person of many masks." Two passages in her journals provide a backdrop for a later passage—the one most pertinent to our explorations.

---

1 Giorgio Buccellati, *Landscapes of the Beyond* (Malibu: Chervo, 1992), 30.
2 Balthasar, "On the Concept of Person," 25.
3 Sylvia Plath, *The Journals of Sylvia Plath* (New York: Random House, 1998), xii.

> I was getting worried about becoming too happily stodgily practical: instead of studying Locke, for instance, or writing — I go make an apple pie, or study *The Joy of Cooking*, reading it like a rare novel. Whoa, I said to myself. You will escape into domesticity & stifle yourself by falling headfirst into a bowl of cookie batter.[4]

Both Plath's literary ambition and the lure of a domesticity she feared would hinder it are detectable in another journal entry:

> Last night: finished *The Waves*, which disturbed.... But then the hair-raising fineness of the last 50 pages: Bernard's summary, an essay on life, on the problem: the deadness of a being to whom nothing can happen.... I underlined & underlined: reread that. I shall do better than she. *No children until I have done it.*[5]

Clearly, Virginia Woolf was for Plath both a model and a rival, as was the merchandise manager for Miller's fictional Hap Loman and many others to whom we have referred. This model-rival nexus is fostered in situations where the aspiration of the mediator of one's desire has no genuinely transcendent orientation. A merely mundane aspiration can prompt an admirer to strive for worldly achievements that can and often are fruitful in their own way. But in the end these aspirations cannot nourish the soul. This difference can be seen by comparing Thérèse of Lisieux's desire to follow the example of her older sister — who had entered the Carmelite order as a cloistered nun — and Plath's desire to surpass a model whose literary achievements she both admired and envied. Even as Plath envied Woolf's literary accomplishments, she had to admit how much her own writing depended on the inspiration Woolf provided. "Virginia Woolf helps," she wrote, "Her novels make mine possible."[6]

Plath was a gifted woman who — like Virginia Woolf — gave an account of her predicament that belies the cheery optimism of Professor Gergen's encomium to multiphrenia. In a few heart-wrenching lines, she shows us what the apocalypse of the sovereign self looks like and feels like. "I am afraid," she wrote, "I am not solid, but hollow."

> I feel behind my eyes a numb, paralyzed cavern, a pit of hell, a mimicking nothingness.... I do not know who I am, where I am going — and I am the one who has to decide the answers

---

4 Ibid., 152.
5 Ibid., 164. Italics in original.
6 Ibid., 168.

to these hideous questions. I long for a noble escape from freedom — I am weak, tired, in revolt from the strong constructive humanitarian faith which presupposes a healthy, active intellect and will. There is nowhere to go — not home, where I would blubber and cry, a grotesque fool, into my mother's skirts — not to men, where I want more than ever now their stern, final, paternal directive — not to church, which is liberal, free — no, I turn wearily to the totalitarian dictatorship where I am absolved of all personal responsibility and can sacrifice myself in a "splurge of altruism" on the altar of the Cause with a capital "C."[7]

Herein lies a clue to an unanalyzed link between the psychological, spiritual, and ontological distresses of the twentieth and twenty-first centuries and the passionate political ideologies contemporary with them, ideologies that have laid waste the world in a "splurge of altruism," sacrificing hundreds of millions of people "on the altar of the Cause with a capital 'C'." This agonizing passage is an echo of Mary Eberstadt's metaphor of the howling coyote in the desert, "the collective human howl of our time." It is symptomatic of what we are calling the apocalypse of the sovereign self. And yet, pride of place belongs to Sylvia Plath's heart-rending cry, for it consists of a sweeping catalogue of both the deprivations suffered in the late stages of the sovereign self's spiritual emaciation and a deep longing for what had been forsaken along the way.

As we argued at length in *God's Gamble,* Christ is the Incarnation of the *Logos,* the summoning Word, the living *Clue* to the mystery of human longing, summoning each of us into the very mystery of our unique existence. "Christ himself," writes Balthasar, "becomes the norm that dwells in a new way within his followers without their ever being able to control it."[8] Those who have been exposed to this summons may renounce it, but they will nonetheless remain Christ-haunted, even as they have surrendered the resources that would allow them to see their predicament clearly. Such a one hungers for he knows not what. And if he has had a brush with Christianity — even one that is only culturally mediated — he hungers all the more as his connection with Christianity becomes more attenuated. He finally finds himself in the midst of "the

---

7 Ibid., 60–61.
8 Balthasar, *Epilogue,* 76.

frantic muddle of human incomprehension and the moral savagery that is its dismal outcome."[9]

The splurge of altruism that absolves one of all personal responsibility is the source of the world's greatest crimes. It is what the Underground Man longed for when he complained that he could no longer find any justification for the rage which threatened to consume him. Both at the individual and collective level, there is a link between ontological diminution and the nihilistic appetite for destruction. If recent social developments have not sufficiently confirmed this link between the deracinated self and the maddened mob, Sylvia Plath's longing for a cause with a capital "C" makes it perfectly explicit.

Like Woolf's Bernard, Plath returns metaphorically to the bookshelf. Her ontological moorings slipping away, she turns again to her model-rival: "Why did Virginia Woolf commit suicide?"[10] At the depth of her anguish, Plath cried out: "God, where is the integrating force going to come from?"[11] That is the question this book asks: Where is the integrating force going to come from? "God" as little more than an expletive does not exhaust the depths of Plath's cry for divine succor. It is akin in its own way to O. E. Parker shouting at the tattoo artist: "'Just God,' Parker said impatiently. 'Christ. I don't care. Just so it's God.'"

"Potential mystics, or mystics in the primitive state," said Henri de Lubac, "are scattered in the world. These, above all, are the ones who must be reached."[12] As it happened, it fell to the poet Richard Wilbur to try to reach Sylvia Plath, who certainly deserves to be counted among those to whom de Lubac referred. In his 1953 poem "Cottage Street," Wilbur leaves moving testimony to the task he was asked to perform. His account of his inadequacy for that task is a moving testimony to the predicament faced by those who try to give succor to those de Lubac described as "mystics in the primitive state."

> The visit seems already strained and long.
> Each in his turn, we tell her our desires.
> It is my office to exemplify
> The published poet in his happiness,
> Thus cheering Sylvia, who has wished to die;
> But half-ashamed, and impotent to bless,

---

9 Fornari, *Dionysus, Christ, and the Death of God*, Vol. II, 301.
10 Plath, *The Journals of Sylvia Plath*, 62.
11 Ibid., 60.
12 Quoted in Balthasar, *The Theology of Henri de Lubac*, 101.

> I am a stupid life-guard who has found,
> Swept to his shallows by the tide, a girl
> Who, far from shore, has been immensely drowned,
> And stares through water now with eyes of pearl.
> How large is her refusal; and how slight
> The genteel chat whereby we recommend
> Life, of a summer afternoon, despite
> The brewing dusk which hints that it may end.[13]

At the age of thirty, Plath took her own life. The task of being a Virgil to a lost soul is indeed a daunting one, and no one can be blamed for failing in the effort. But Wilbur has left us a poignant summary of the task. Alas, his was not to be a Virgilian role, but that of Orpheus, sent to the underworld to rescue a lost Eurydice by giving the lost poet an example of "the published poet in his happiness." His task was to be a lifeline by which Plath might have had her poetic vocation restored and returned to the land of the living. Wilbur's Catholic sensibility prepared him for the task he was asked to perform, the sensibility that informed the poetry for which he is justly admired.

The Underground Man envied the man who could take his revenge with a sense of justice, a man, that is, who acts in service to a "Cause with a capital 'C'." But finding no justice for the resentment by which he was consumed, he was left only to beat the wall as hard as he could. The literary depictions of "potential mystics or mystics in the primitive state" are grim enough, as are the true-life stories of spiritual desperation, but there are historical instances that are even more shocking.

Joseph Goebbels was raised in a devout Catholic home, and his parents had reason to believe that he would enter the seminary and become a priest. He apparently considered that possibility. As the *New York Times* reviewer of Ralf Georg Reuth's biography *Goebbels* notes, Goebbels had a club foot, and he therefore had "ample acquaintance with the power of stigmatization." Not unlike the Underground Man, Goebbels had been an outsider in his youth. On one occasion he nursed his grievances by composing a "fragment of a drama" in a school notebook. "I ... want to be able to hate.... Oh, I can hate, and I don't want to forget how. Oh, how wonderful it is to be able to hate."[14]

---

13   Richard Wilbur, "Cottage Street, 1953," *Collected Poems 1943–2004* (Orlando: Harcourt, 2004), 143.
14   Ralf Georg Reuth, *Goebbels*, trans. Krishna Winston (New York: Harcourt Brace & Co., 1993), 31.

There have been times and places in history in which being able to hate was as easy as falling off a log, but Goebbels had a substantial encounter with Christianity both in his childhood home and in the Germany of his youth. His notebook strongly suggests that great effort was needed if he was to outwardly vent the hate that threatened to consume him.

Years after this ominous entry in his school notebook, with the German army in retreat, Goebbels had Berlin painted with the slogan: "Hatred our duty — revenge our virtue," an act of swaggering and defiant nihilism that has its literary prefiguration in the Underground Man's impotent rage. Recall the warning issued by the author of the Letter to the Hebrews. Once given "knowledge of the truth," there is no longer any sacrifice for sin, and the torment of unforgiven sin will lead in the end to "the raging fire that is to burn rebels" (Heb 10:26 – 27).

Goebbels, like Dostoevsky's Underground Man, envies the man who can take revenge without qualms and whose inability to do so was cognate with Nietzsche's laments that no new god had emerged in two thousand years. Hitler was Goebbels's new god, and his shrill and murderous effort to revive hatred was a doomed attack on the Judeo-Christian deconstruction of sacrificial violence that has been working in the background of our cultural life for two millennia, crippling the god-making machinery and making it harder and harder to insulate hate from the pangs of conscience and remorse that are the forerunners of contrition, repentance, and grace. Inasmuch as once-Christian cultures continue to repudiate the religious tradition that provided these blessings, more and more people will instinctively try to suppress — or shamelessly exploit — the ethic that is the key to Christianity's cultural blessings. They will ravage the world with causes with "a capital 'C'," each serving to unleash the load of resentment that burdens the hearts of unforgiven people.

In his foreword to her *Journals*, Ted Hughes comments on Plath's "impulse to apprentice herself to various masters" and the "fever of uncertainty and self-doubt" by which she was haunted.

> In spite of the care she devoted to each thing she wrote, as soon as she finished, she cast it behind her with something like contempt, sometimes with rage. Such things were not what she wanted at all. But what did she want? In a different culture, perhaps, she would have been happier. There was something about her reminiscent of what one reads of Islamic fanatic

lovers of God — a craving to strip away everything from some ultimate intensity, some communion with spirit, or with reality, or simply with intensity itself. She showed something violent in this, something very primitive, perhaps very female, a readiness, even a need, to sacrifice everything to the new birth. With her, this was vividly formulated at every level of her being. The negative phase of it, logically, is suicide.[15]

A vast chorus of Christian theologians have variously attested to what John Ruysbroek called man's "deiformity."

> It is the obscure feeling that there exists in each of us, even the greatest sinner, a hidden room where no one but God can enter in, "that sacred point in us that says *Pater noster*," as Paul Claudel says magnificently... that cannot hide from love. It is the intuition of a Georges Bernanos at the threshold of death, noting in his diary that "sin makes us live on the surface of ourselves" and that even when we offend God, "we never cease entirely to desire what He desires in the depths of the sanctuary of our soul."[16]

In de Lubac's felicitous formulation, Sylvia Plath can be seen as a mystic in the primitive state. "God," she cried, "where is the integrating force going to come from?" Douglas Farrow offers an appropriate response to that cry for help:

> All live and move and have their being in God. All are made to feel after God, and the word of God goes out wordlessly to the entire creation, inviting every creature to return God's call in the manner appropriate to it.... Words of grace and peace require a response. When they do not get one, or the response is hostile, the word returns to him who sent it (Matt. 10:11–15), leaving no mark of protection on the lintel of the house or town to which it came.[17]

---

15   Plath, *The Journals of Sylvia Plath*, xi–xii.
16   De Lubac, *Theology in History*, 143.
17   Farrow, *1 & 2 Thessalonians*, Brazos Theological Commentary on the Bible (Grand Rapids, MI: Brazos Press, 2020), 172.

22 The Prodigal Son

One might even advance the paradox that the full realization of what sin is does not exist in the *sinful* Christian, however lucid he may be, but only in the *repentant* Christian.
— Henri de Lubac[1]

The organ with which man perceives the truth is the conscience, and the form in which he receives it is the confession of sin.
— Hans Urs von Balthasar[2]

There is a floor. There is a level beneath which men and women cannot sink in the name of autonomy without crashing through to a pit.
— Mary Eberstadt[3]

AS WE TURN OUR ATTENTION FROM THE WRECKage caused by tragically flawed anthropological premises to the requisites for a restoration of human dignity and decency, we will begin with a short reflection on the Prodigal Son story in the Gospel of Luke. The story could as well be called the parable of the jealous son or the parable of the merciful and generous father. For our purposes, however, we want to attend to the conversion of the ungrateful and self-regarding younger son.

> And he said, "There was a man who had two sons; and the younger of them said to his father, 'Father, give me the share of property that falls to me.' And he divided his living between them." (Lk 15:11–12)

The Greek word for the "property" that the younger son demands is *ousia* — an important term in Greek philosophy and a word that played a prominent role in the Trinitarian debates of the fourth and fifth centuries.

---

1 De Lubac, *A Brief Catechesis on Nature and Grace*, 131.
2 Balthasar, *Tragedy Under Grace*, 133.
3 Mary Eberstadt, "What the Nurses Knew," *National Review*, August 1, 2022.

THE APOCALYPSE OF THE SOVEREIGN SELF

The word is derived from the past participial form of *eimi*, the verb *to be*, and the Latin Vulgate translated the word as *substantia*, a synonym for "being." Our translation tells us that the father divided his "living" between the two sons. The Greek word here translated as "living" is the Greek *bios*, which simply means life. The prodigal son wants to have his life to do with as he pleases, unencumbered by any responsibilities to others that it might otherwise entail. These etymological facts help us think about the modern, and especially the postmodern, spiritual predicament, one that is most aptly characterized, as we have repeatedly said, by what Henri de Lubac calls the loss of "ontological density." Along with Gabriel Marcel we are concerned with a situation in which "the more the *ego* attempts to assert for itself a central or autocratic position in the economy of consciousness, the more the density of being is *attenuated*."[4]

The prodigal son wants to have his inheritance to do with as he will. He wants to have his inheritance, not as an inheritance which he holds in trust for those to whom he will in turn bequeath it, but as something over which he will have complete control, without either gratitude for its source or solicitude for those for whom he is the temporary custodian. Understood in this way, the prodigal son's assertion of independence and autonomy has been a distinguishing characteristic of the age of autonomous selfhood. Commenting on the parable, Jean-Luc Marion observes:

> The son requests that he no longer have to request, or rather, that he no longer have to receive the *ousia*. He asks that he no longer... have to receive the *ousia* as a gift. He asks to possess it, dispose of it, enjoy it without passing through the gift and the reception of the gift. The son wants to owe nothing to his father, and above all not to owe him a gift; he asks to have a father no longer — the *ousia* without the father or the gift.[5]

The parable runs quickly to its dénouement:

> Not many days later, the younger son gathered all he had and took his journey into a far country, and there he squandered his property in loose living. And when he had spent everything, a great famine arose in that country, and he began to be in want. So he went and joined himself to one of the citizens of

---

4 Marcel, *The Mystery of Being*, 16.
5 Jean-Luc Marion, *God Without Being* (Chicago: University of Chicago Press, 1995), 97.

The Prodigal Son

that country, who sent him into his fields to feed swine. And he would gladly have fed on the pods that the swine ate; and no one gave him anything. (Lk 15:13–16)

No small number of our contemporaries identify with the prodigal son's demand for self-sovereignty, and an increasing number of them are slowly awakening to find themselves inhabiting "a far country" — no longer sustained by the networks of affiliation, on which their very declaration of autonomy secretly drew its strength. The squandering and dissolution of the younger son's *ousia*, his loss of ontological ballast, was not simply the result of his moral laxity. It is rather the working out of the son's initial choice: his disgruntled refusal to receive his inheritance as a gift and accept the responsibility for passing it on to his heirs. In other words, his is the act of *non serviam*, the essence of Lucifer's rebellion in Milton's *Paradise Lost*. The younger son has severed the thread linking him to both his ancestors and his heirs.

> But when he came to himself he said, "How many of my father's hired servants have bread enough and to spare, but I perish here with hunger! I will arise and go to my father, and I will say to him, 'Father, I have sinned against heaven and before you; I am no longer worthy to be called your son; treat me as one of your hired servants.'" And he arose and came to his father. But while he was yet at a distance, his father saw him and had compassion, and ran and embraced him and kissed him. (Lk 15:17–20)

In verse 13, the Greek term for "himself" is *heauton*, a cognate of *autos*, self, but the phrase in which this Greek term appears has often been translated: "he came to his senses." This colloquial English phrase captures how we might best understand the meaning of the text. Apropos of which is Balthasar's observation: "life on a dunghill can belatedly bring some people to their senses."[6] To say that the prodigal son *came to his senses* is to notice how in doing so he retraces the path chosen by René Descartes who, in his desperate and crypto-Gnostic quest for certainty, *abandoned his senses* by declaring: "I will regard myself as not having hands, or eyes, or flesh, or blood, or any senses, but as nevertheless falsely believing that I possess all these things."[7]

The prodigal son's extrication from the trap of autonomy begins when he calls to mind his father. In recalling his father, he is recalled

---

6   Hans Urs von Balthasar, *New Elucidations* (San Francisco: Ignatius Press, 1986), 295.
7   Descartes, *Meditations on First Philosophy*, Meditation I, 16–17.

by him. He recollects the bonds of family and culture. In the midst of his degradation, he arguably recognizes his father for the first time, not as the patriarch of his family or clan, but as father. In so doing, he regains his sense of personal responsibility — his ability to respond in love — and simultaneously his moral reckoning concerning the folly of his adventure in sovereign selfhood. "I will arise and go to my father, and I will say to him," he says. He begins to recover his own voice as he prepares to apologize to his father for his misadventure in radical autonomy. His absent father thereby becomes present to him. His self-absorption prevented him from being present to his father even when he was in his physical proximity. Now — even while still in the "far country" — he feels his father's presence as if for the first time.

If the sustaining mystery of familial bonds eludes sensory detection, the stench and squalor of a pigsty does not, especially not for a Jew of Jesus's time for whom swine were regarded as vile and contaminated. The prodigal son's plunge into alienation reaches its nadir when out of desperation he sinks to feeding swine. "No one gave him anything" (Lk 15:16). What is dissolute about the prodigal son's existence is not his moral depravity, though that is certainly among its likely consequences. He was as oblivious as his postmodern heirs to the fact that the waning of his ontological density correlated directly with the success of his efforts to live an autonomous existence. He has, so to speak, bartered away his ability to *be a person* in exchange for the dubious luxury of *functioning as a self*.

Like the prodigal son, no small number of the inhabitants of the post-Christian secular world have gradually lost their senses. The loss of senses in our age has occurred in the name of freeing us from the ostensible burden of moral and indeed anthropological constraints — precisely the "constraints" which alone can discipline our passions and awaken us to our true calling. Since the chief source of those constraining and ennobling principles in the cultural history of the West has been Christianity generally and Catholic Christianity in particular, it is hardly surprising that the cultural renunciation of those moral and anthropological constraints involved the repudiation of the Christian patrimony. But as Romano Guardini rather ominously observed:

> As unbelievers deny [the Christian] Revelation more decisively, as they put their denial into more consistent practice, it will become the more evident what it really means to be a Christian. At the same time, the unbeliever will emerge from the fogs of

secularism. He will cease to reap benefit from the values and forces developed by the very Revelation he denies. He must learn to exist honestly without Christ and without the God revealed through him; he will have to learn to experience what this honesty means. Nietzsche has already warned us that the non-Christian of the modern world had no realization of what it truly meant to be without Christ. The last decades [the 1930s and 1940s] have suggested what life without Christ really is. The last decades were only the beginning.[8]

The freedom of Christ was not *autonomous*; it was *obediential*. It was what in the Letter of James is called the perfect law, the law of liberty (Jas 1:25). Christ was unsurpassably free because his will was ever attuned — at one with — the will of the Father. His inexplicable freedom was the freedom of obedience. In our world as in his, this form of freedom is virtually unintelligible. At the burning heart of every Christian vocation is the call to live in that freedom, and to do so as an act of gratitude for one's life and for the sake of others. Writes Hans Urs von Balthasar:

> Sin alone gives man the mentality of the private individual, because it deprives him (Latin: *privatus*) of the spirit of communion and of the will to selfless communication. In contrast, the more purely a man receives God's grace, the more obvious is his readiness not to keep it for himself, his readiness to let everyone participate in it.[9]

We are endowed and we are called. Our endowments sometimes suit the call we have been given and sometimes they do not, but in either case the endowments and the call are objectively independent of our will and desire. Any tension between our endowments and our vocation must be worked out with all the creativity we can summon for the task. Indeed, the essence of the spiritual life is the harmonization of our will and desire to the facts of our endowment and the contours of our call — our vocation.

Like the prodigal son, we humans have long been culturally predisposed to regard the path we take in life to be entirely subject to our decision. It is only recently that this same presumption has been applied to our natural endowment. It is perhaps quintessentially apropos of

---

8   Guardini, *The End of the Modern World*, 124.
9   Hans Urs von Balthasar and Joseph Cardinal Ratzinger, *Mary: The Church at the Source*, trans. Adrian Walker (San Francisco: Ignatius Press, 2005), 110.

our present predicament that many now think that even their sexual endowment depends on their sovereign will. Those who feel similarly about their intellectual endowment, say, or their athletic endowment, may still be thought quite delusional, but these latter claims are no less absurd than is the former one.

There is today a widespread withering of the form of subjectivity which, like the supernova that accompanies the dying of a star, glowed so luminously for the Enlightenment rationalists and Romantic individualists. "It looks as if the self," writes Robert Solomon, "which had been raised to transcendental then cosmic status has now disintegrated into nothingness."[10] Willy Loman told the ghost of his older brother: "I still feel — kind of temporary about myself."[11] Sylvia Plath wrote: "I feel behind my eyes a numb, paralyzed cavern, a pit of hell, a *mimicking nothingness*.... I do not know who I am, where I am going."[12]

Christ, the author of the Prodigal Son parable, has said: "Apart from me, you can do nothing" (Jn 15:5). If this shockingly categorical statement applies especially to those who have *known Christ* confessionally, it applies more generally to those whose knowledge of Christ has been culturally mediated. Those who intentionally separate themselves from whatever exposure to Christianity they may have enjoyed will for a while draw energy from the very faith they reject. Their attack on that faith will connect them to it, albeit antagonistically. The exhilaration of a post-Christian existence will survive for as long as it is able to draw energy from its antipathy for the faith. When that thin thread snaps, they will discover the truth of the "Christ or nothing" option of which we have repeatedly spoken.

In most cases this renunciation of Christ and the Christian patrimony will pose as forward-looking progress. Nonetheless, it will be culturally and spiritually retrogressive, regardless of how technologically proficient it might be. The post-Christian world will return to pre-Christian patterns except that those sufficiently touched by Christianity will remain morally lucid enough to feel the loss and to hunger for a sufficiently reconstituting alternative. As a deracinated society grows increasingly fractious the social conglomerate will grope toward some semblance of solidarity in the oldest and most reprehensible way: by uniting against a scapegoat or a socially vulnerable or ideologically execrated race, class,

---

10 Solomon, *Continental Philosophy Since 1750*, 128.
11 Miller, *Death of a Salesman*, 51.
12 Plath, *The Journals of Sylvia Plath*, 60. Emphasis added.

or social subset. Without jeopardy to any of the other applications of the vine and branches discourse in John's Gospel, the situation just sketched is consonant with Jesus's earlier quoted warning: "Whoever does not abide in me is thrown away like a branch and withers; such branches are gathered, thrown into the fire, and burned" (Jn 15:6).

The relationship between the withering — the diminishing of ontological density — and the violent conflagrations that have characterized our age is one to which we may only now be awakening but one which this text written at the end of the first century perceives with uncanny perspicacity. Pedro Morandé, Dean of the Faculty of Social Sciences at the Catholic University of Chile in Santiago, provides a late-twentieth-century explication of the Johannine insight:

> Since satisfactory answers [to the question of the meaning of human existence] have not been found apart from Christ, there is an attempt today to cancel the questions or at least to rob them of their dramatic quality. We are living in a time marked by nihilism. But it is no longer the same nihilism as in the first half of the [twentieth] century. The earlier nihilism was ideological and programmatic. Following Nietzsche, it aimed to fill the vacuum left by the abandonment of personal and social morality with the will to power; it desired to return to "the birth of tragedy," to challenge the Lord of history by declaring him dead and dispensable. Its purpose was to overturn the calculating, everyday morality of the bourgeoisie through the dramatic éclat of *the hero, who has no model other than his own action and will*. The nihilism at the basis of the totalitarian ideologies disguised itself as an enthralling optimism, as the conquest of new goals. It could proclaim, as in Spain, "Long live death!" and appear on various stages of the world as the ideology of "the great march," the great leap forward. This was true in the economic no less than in the political field, in science no less than in the vanguard of culture. Its last death-rattle was urban warfare, terrorism, the intoxication of violence merely for violence's sake.[13]

In 1996 when these words were written, it seemed to this wise and perspicacious Chilean that urban warfare, terrorism, and the intoxication

---

13 Pedro Morandé, "The relevance of the message of *Gaudium et Spes* today: The Church's mission in the midst of epochal changes and new challenges," *Communio*, Vol. XXIII, no. 1 (Spring 1996): 145. Emphasis added.

of violence for its own sake constituted the death-rattle of a spent force. Today, alas, the air is filled with expressions of precisely this terminal form of nihilism. In commenting on the historical relevance of the Second Vatican Council document *Gaudium et Spes* — Joy and Hope — Morandé calls attention to what is both surprising and quite explicable in Christian terms, namely "the extremely deceptive and paradoxical fact that concern for the enforcement of human rights can exist in a highly nihilistic and self-destructive context."[14] When the fulfillment of even the most absurd and impossible desires is accorded the status of a universal human right, we have entered precisely the nihilistic and self-destructive world of which Morandé spoke. As Jean-Luc Marion has written:

> Nihilism extends its empire over us, all the more silently and powerfully as it shuts us up in ourselves, closes us in on ourselves alone and never shows itself as such. We imagine that we possess the universe, when in fact we ourselves construct our prison, voluntary slaves, willed slaves, slaves of the will to will — and we glorify ourselves by celebrating our autonomy![15]

Those who casually assumed that the moral order that arose in Judeo-Christian cultures could be sustained without this tradition are discovering otherwise. Those who considered the dismantling of that religious foundation a price worth paying for moral license in this or that area of life are watching the entire moral architecture collapse into "urban warfare, terrorism, the intoxication of violence merely for violence's sake." In the face of this dark prognosis, we must be reminded that we have an alternate option, one that is aptly limned by Hans Urs von Balthasar:

> Indeed, from the Christian point of view, the world is no longer an anonymous collection of individuals; for in proportion as the light of heaven penetrates through Christ and the Church into the darkness of the world, so *it visibly gives personality to the whole human community*. Each man encountering this light receives a *call* and a *commission*; to him is given the task of living for others, and he becomes one of those who have begun to grasp the meaning of communion and sharing. We are back once more to the parable of the leaven. The dough that is as yet unleavened is a shapeless mass of private existences that, because they are under the dominion of the powers of this

---

14   Ibid., 148.
15   Marion, *Brief Apology for a Catholic Moment*, 65–66.

The Prodigal Son

world, are pushed together into a collective lump. The leavening promises two things that cannot be seen in isolation: on the one hand, a release from merely private existence in order that men may become fully individual, and on the other hand, a release from collective existence for the sake of a genuine communion and sharing.[16]

Balthasar has captured with splendid economy the twin paradoxes most pertinent to our present historical and spiritual predicament: a release from merely *private* existence that, paradoxically, leads to a genuinely *personal* existence, and a release from *collective* existence that, paradoxically, leads to the experience of *communion*. Elsewhere Balthasar warned of the self who "did not turn its inquiry totally away from itself and to the Word of God, but applied this word as a longed-for remedy to its own dreadful situation."[17]

At the moment of his conversion, the prodigal son turned his heart toward his father and his people — those with whom his true mission was waiting to be carried out. To his utter amazement, his father was eager to the point of patriarchal foolishness to embrace him and welcome him home. Jean-Luc Marion has argued that we cannot liberate ourselves from self-will by suppressing or anesthetizing the will. There is, Marion argues, only one path out of the twisting labyrinth of self-will. We can only escape from that trap by willing something *other* than what we will. "Father, if *you* are willing, remove this chalice from me; nevertheless not my will, but *yours*, be done" (Lk 22:42). "He alone tears himself from nihilism," writes Marion, who, in imitating Christ, succeeds, not just in setting aside his own will, but in willing "a *different* will... to will differently, to will the only other will, that of the Father."[18]

---

16 Hans Urs von Balthasar, *Engagement with God*, trans. John Halliburton (San Francisco: Ignatius Press, 2008), 35. Emphasis added.
17 Hans Urs von Balthasar, *Convergences: To the Source of Christian Mystery*, trans. E. A. Nelson (San Francisco: Ignatius Press, 1983), 38.
18 Marion, *Brief Apology for a Catholic Moment*, 65.

23 The Absolute Opposite of All Hysteria

> With the coming of Christ man's existence took on an earnestness which classical antiquity never knew simply because it had no way of knowing it. The earnestness did not spring from human maturity; it sprang from the call which each person received from God through Christ. With this call the person opened his eyes, he was awakened for the first time in his life.
> — Romano Guardini[1]

> The concept of person, as well as the idea that stands behind this concept, is a product of Christian theology. In other words, it grew in the first place out of the interplay between human thought and the data of Christian faith and so entered intellectual history.
> — Joseph Cardinal Ratzinger[2]

> The individual exists for society, but the society exists for the person.
> — Jacques Maritain

IT SHOULD NOT BE SURPRISING TO LEARN THAT THE uniqueness of the "Christ Event" left those whose lives had been altered by exposure to that event at a loss for a vocabulary capable of doing justice to their experience and to the experience of those of their predecessors in the faith, whose testimony was unimpeachable. This is borne out by the heated controversies in the first centuries of Christianity over which words and phrases were adequate to the task of proclaiming the truth of Christ, most especially when it came to the Trinitarian relations. The truths that constitute the central teachings of the Christian faith are revealed truths, which is to say truths which could not have been

---

1   Guardini, *The End of the Modern World*, 125.
2   Ratzinger, "Concerning the Notion of Person in Theology," 439.

acquired by any epistemology other than that of faith itself. Henri de Lubac quotes the Reformed theologian Gabriel Widmer:

> The prophets uttered the Word: Jesus incarnated it. Still, God did not provide them with any heavenly language, syntax, or grammar; to express themselves they had to strain their ingenuity to twist borrowed words and phrases. Thus, as soon as it appeared in Palestine, the theology of biblical revelation was as halting as Jacob after his struggle with the angel. It suffered from a disproportion between what it was supposed to announce on behalf of God and the means at its disposal for saying something to men.[3]

The challenge for the early Fathers of the Church was to fashion the linguistic resources capable of accounting for the mystery of the Trinity without thereby jeopardizing its unfathomability. Analogously, the mystery of the human person remains regardless of how precise or useful might be the linguistic or analytical tools we employ in our probing of that mystery. For instance, we have relied on the anthropological insights of René Girard, but we would be unfaithful to both Girard's contributions and to his Catholic faith were we to use his insights reductively and in a clumsy way. For both the divine and the human mystery — entirely interrelated as they are — stand in need of revelation if we are to approach their essence. That revelation now exists in its full and final form. And yet, as it was for the Christians of the early centuries of the Christian era, the task of finding ever more illuminating and evangelically efficacious ways of accounting for faith in Christ — always within the theological framework of our patristic forebearers — falls on each generation. If the ardors of that task seem formidable, it is wise to recognize, as Giuseppe Fornari has done, that the textual and historical complications call for "one of two things... either supreme interpretive skill or a simple and humble faith — two extremes that are not so far apart as our intellectualism might think."[4] As for the combined power of simple faith and serious inquiry among the first Christians, the Protestant theologian B. B. Warfield noted:

> This linguistic revolution, which, as regards its essential elements, was achieved in the course of a few generations, is the most eloquent witness to the spiritual revolution effected by Christianity

---

3 Quoted in Henri de Lubac, *The Christian Faith: An Essay on the Structure of the Apostles' Creed*, trans. Richard Arnandez, F.S.C. (San Francisco: Ignatius Press, 1986), 267.
4 Fornari, *Dionysus, Christ, and the Death of God*, Vol. II, 245.

in the ancient world. No other sect, no other oriental religion, ever occasioned such a profound linguistic differentiation.[5]

The scriptural prehistory of this revelation in Israel, indispensable to its initial intelligibility, did not provide adequate conceptual or terminological resources for codifying and bearing witness to the ramifications of the life, death, and Resurrection of Christ. Neither the linguistic resources of Judaism nor that of Greek metaphysics were capable of accounting for the Trinitarian theology that came into view with Christ. These resources were gradually acquired thanks to the labors of the early Fathers of the Church. The fruits of these labors depended on the recognition that the Event of Christ represented a decisive inflection point in human history. In his extended research on Origen of Alexandria (184 – 253), Henri de Lubac wrote that "Origen... stresses the impact of the coming of Christ and of the gift of the Spirit — already evoked by Paul — which divide history into a before and an after."[6] Apropos of which, Douglas Farrow writes:

> For the incarnation of the eternal God as Israel's Messiah is an unprecedented affirmation of time that gives new significance to "before" and "after," distinguishing and separating them quite decisively for the benefit of theology, history, hermeneutics, psychology, literature, music, and so forth — even for cosmology and natural science. "Before" and "after" begin to matter after the incarnation in a way they did not matter before.[7]

Perhaps the most startling claim in Farrow's remarkably bold assessment is his assertion that the event of the Incarnation represented an alteration in *human psychology*, a break between the "before" and "after." For, in fact, the word "person" assumed its prominence in the vocabulary of Western culture only after Christian theologians, in speaking of the three Persons of the Trinity, gave the word *persona* a philosophical profundity never before associated with it. *Hypostasis* was the Greek word for "substance," with the implication suggested by the compound English word *sub-stance*. The *hypostasis* stood *under* and stood *for* something other than itself. The use of the term posed problems in the fourth and fifth centuries, when, in general parlance, the term was used as a synonym for a concrete individual. The connotation of standing *under* and standing *for* something other than the individual receded or was lost.

---

5   De Lubac, *The Christian Faith*, 267.
6   De Lubac, *Theology in History*, 144.
7   Farrow, *1 & 2 Thessalonians*, 27.

The Absolute Opposite of All Hysteria

For centuries, the mystery of the person as embedded in Trinitarian and Christological thought — mystifying as it was even there — was regarded as revelatory only of the Persons of the Trinity and of the unique Person of Christ. Unfortunately, according to then-Cardinal Joseph Ratzinger, the Church Fathers considered Christ to be a "simply unique ontological exception, which must be treated as such."[8] Thus the anthropological implications of the Incarnation and the subsequent patristic revolution were not fully explored. And it is these intimations that we are trying to draw out, for they are indispensable to following up on Douglas Farrow's emphasis on the psychological ramifications of the before and after demarcation effected by Christ.

To put this issue in perspective, Cardinal Ratzinger redeploys a metaphor used in another context by Teilhard de Chardin: the discovery of radium. "How could one understand the new element?" Teilhard asks: "As an anomaly, an aberrant form of matter?... As a curiosity or as the beginning for a new physics?" Had radium been considered an aberration — an "ontological exception" so to speak — modern physics would not have developed, and Cardinal Ratzinger makes an analogous point about the true construal of personhood as revealed by the Person of Christ. For many of the Church Fathers, however, and their theological heirs down into our own time, Jesus remained an "ontological exception" whose uniquely Other-constituted form of personhood appeared to have little or no bearing on the circumstances and spiritual predicament of fallen humanity.

It was from the theological workshops where Christian thought was struggling to find a vocabulary with which to express both the Christian revelation and the lived experience of those whose lives had been altered by that revelation that the word *person* acquired its status. Benedict XVI drew special attention to the contribution of one of the early Church's most brilliant protagonists.

> Tertullian shaped Latin into a theological language and with an ingenious, almost incredible assurance was able to set down in writing a theological terminology that later centuries could not surpass, because at the first attempt it coined permanently valid formulas for Christian thought. So it was Tertullian who

---

8 Ratzinger, "Concerning the Notion of Person in Theology," 449.

also established for the West its formula for presenting the Christian idea of the Divinity: God is *"una substantia — tres personae,"* one Being in three Persons. At this point the word "person" enters intellectual history for the first time with its full import. Several centuries passed before this statement could be intellectually assimilated and mastered, so that it was no longer merely a statement but really became an insight into the mystery, which it taught Christians to apprehend somehow, if not fully to comprehend.[9]

The future pope marveled at the boldness of the Tertullian formulation, amazed at how the second century Carthaginian seemed to have done so with an "almost somnambulistic assurance."[10] Somnambulance is not always a reliable guide, and it may have contributed to Tertullian's later drift into heterodoxy, but this was after he had left an indelible mark on Trinitarian thought and challenged Christian posterity to recognize the Christian ordination of the human person, which it is the burden of this book to defend. Be that as it may, to be guided by the hand of providence is to experience an "almost somnambulistic assurance," and it was this providential guidance that brought the word person into prominence not only in Christian theological thought but in the discourse of those cultures that had the great good fortune to fall under Christian influence.

As we noted earlier, the Greek word for the "property" that the prodigal son demands to have on his own terms is *ousia*, a word derived from the verb *to be*, and which was translated in the Latin Vulgate as *substantia*, a synonym for "being." The First Council of Nicaea (325) affirmed that the Father, Son, and Holy Spirit are of the same essence, the same substance: *homo-ousious* in Greek. The Council refuted the alternate formulation that the Son and the Father were of a similar essence or substance, *homoiousious* in Greek. The two Greek words were distinguished by the letter *i* in the pre-Nicaean formulation and its elimination by the council Fathers. In the Greek alphabet, the letter *i* is pronounced *iota*, and this controversy is the source of the English idiom that something might not differ one *iota* from something else.

Alas, the christological difference between *homoousious* and *homoiousious* is immense. Was the Son of the same Divine Nature as the Father or was he only similar? The orthodox doctrine was both shaped and

---

9   Benedict XVI, *Dogma and Preaching* (San Francisco: Ignatius Press, 2011), 182.
10 Ibid.

defined by this controversy which concluded in the principle that the Trinity consisted in "one *ousia* and three *hypostaseis*" — one being and three persons. Thus, the term *"ousia"* characterized what is common, such as goodness and divinity, while the *hypostasis* characterized the particularity — the personhood — of the Father, Son and Holy Spirit. The Trinity was three *persons* in one *divine essence*. Thus, the concept of the person found its anchor in the linguistic workshop of early Christianity. It was born of the paradoxes that Christ brought into the world, paradoxes which would thereafter — even into our own time — continue to play a role in breaking up the mental and spiritual logjams that plague the fallen world. Writes Orthodox theologian John Zizioulas: "The history of the disputes which broke out on this great theme... includes a philosophical landmark, a revolution in Greek philosophy. This revolution is expressed historically through an identification: *the identification of the 'hypostasis' with the 'person.'*"[11]

The word *prosopon* came with its own history, one so hidden and revelatory that Tertullian's somnambulance might rather be regarded as the work of the Holy Spirit. The word referred to the role the actor played on stage. When the term was adopted for theological use in exploring the mystery of the Trinity, the connotation of a role was decisively rejected. The idea of God changing roles from Father to Son to Spirit was a heresy that would have suffocated Christianity in its cradle. However, as the term moved beyond the theological arena in which it came to prominence and took its place in man's ongoing inquiry into his own mystery, its theatrical provenance came to the fore. This was especially the case as the term was transposed from Greek into the Latin *persona*.

Not only did the linguistic ramifications of the patristic formulations alter subsequent theological and anthropological thought, but they serve as also the lens through which to peer into the most ancient experience of our species. For, like so many cultural institutions, the theater has its most ancient origin in ritual sacrifice. Such ancient rituals reenacted the drama that had climaxed in the very social solidarity which the subsequent rituals existed to revive. The key to that revival was the cathartic experience of the ritual onlookers as their aggregate animosities were offloaded on to a tragic figure, their experience of catharsis coinciding with the victim's actual or dramatized immolation. Thus was the social harmony and the associated

---

11 John Zizioulas, *Being as Communion* (Crestwood, NY: St. Vladimir's Seminary Press, 1997), 36.

psychological poise of its members secretly indebted to the execrated victim.

Very early in the proto-cultural history of our species, our ancestors became sufficiently aware of the efficacy of this ritual offloading of animosity onto a surrogate victim to invest enormous energy in its regular ritual reenactment. With the acquisition of greater sacerdotal and dramaturgical competence, the role that the ancient sacrificial rituals played in cultural life evolved in the direction of tragic theater. To the extent that these performances were able to climax in the experience of catharsis, they played the same role as had the blood sacrifices of an earlier period. Indeed, the link between these ancient ritual immolations and theatrical productions is still quite conspicuous, even though the Golgothan revelation has gradually crippled their ability to achieve the cathartic dénouement or cement the social solidarity, which was their chief purpose in the ancient world.

These rituals required a liturgical performer to *speak through a mask* the actor wore on stage. These masks, it is important to note, served more to amplify the actor's voice than to represent features of the face, the audibility of the actor's oration being more essential to the dramatic experience of the audience than the features of his mask might have been. A vestige of the ancient preeminence of the auditory over the visual is found in the word we use to refer to the beneficiaries of theatrical performances — audience — which of course derives from the Latin word for listening: *audientia*.

The most remote origin of the concept of the person appears to be associated with the ancient Etruscan venerations of the goddess Persephone. The Etruscan word for the mask — *phersu* — was derived from the goddess's name. The Etruscans influenced Roman theater, and the Romans in adopting the Etruscan term for the mask fused it with a homonymous Latin verb for "speaking through" — the verb: *personare*, to "re-sound" — the noun form of which is *persona*. Thus, the term *persona* was derived from the word for the actor's mask, the primary purpose of which was the amplification of the putative voice of the character being portrayed. Eventually the term was used to refer to anyone playing a role whether on stage or in social life. Writes Giuseppe Fornari:

> The mask... is not merely a means, an effective agent, or a factor serving to hide a preexisting identity, but an element that acts to *produce identity*. Hence the first identity was the identity of the mask, and it explains why the Greek and Latin for mask, πρόσωπον or *persona*, came to indicate a person

as we understand the word. The mask, then, corresponds to the face of mediation put on by everyone to derive a personal identity, both *personata* ("impersoned") and im-personating; lasting just as long as the rite lasted, it was nevertheless the only true identity.[12]

John Zizioulas posed the question, how and why did the identification of the mask with the person occur? "What connection does the actor's mask have with the human person?"[13] Zizioulas concluded: "It is precisely in the theater that man strives to become a 'person.'"[14] In "speaking through" the mask of another, the actor dispossesses himself of his "own self" in order to re-present the voice of the actor whose spirit he strives to make palpable. "I live, now no longer I, but... Persephone or Creon or Iphigenia lives (temporarily) in me." In a similar way, Christ "comes alive" in us because he sends the Holy Spirit into our hearts. The Holy Spirit pierces our armor and animates us, ennobling our lives and *casting* us according to our gifts and circumstances into the theodrama of revelation, repentance, and conversion. "Christology," writes Zizioulas, "emerges as the only way of fulfilling the human drive to personhood."[15] Henri de Lubac concurs: "Christ completes the revelation to man himself. By taking possession of man, by seizing hold of him and by penetrating to the very depths of his being Christ makes man go deep down within himself, there to discover in a flash regions hitherto unsuspected."[16]

The point was reached, writes Joseph Cardinal Ratzinger, at which "there is a transition from the doctrine of God into Christology and into anthropology."[17] This is the moment when, in the words of Giuseppe Fornari, we all become "actors and interpreters of the truth" and whatever our response is, it "can only confirm the truth, whether it be to accept or reject it."[18] In other words, Christ is not simply a model whom Christian try to follow. His gift is mediated to us by the Spirit. Thanks to that mediation, whatever degree of Christlikeness we might achieve will remain entirely unique to us.

---

12   Giuseppe Fornari, *Dionysus, Christ, and the Death of God*, Vol. I (East Lansing: Michigan State University Press, 2021), 387. Emphasis added.
13   Zizioulas, *Being as Communion*, 31.
14   Ibid., 32.
15   Ibid., 108–9.
16   Henri de Lubac, *Catholicism: Christ and the Common Destiny of Man*, trans. Lancelot Sheppard and Sister Elizabeth Englund (San Francisco: Ignatius Press, 1988), 339.
17   Ratzinger, "Concerning the Notion of Person in Theology," 109.
18   Fornari, *Dionysus, Christ, and the Death of God*, Vol. II, 359.

THE APOCALYPSE OF THE SOVEREIGN SELF

It is clear from the New Testament and completely shocking to moderns, even Christian ones, that the specifically Christian phenomenon of the person depends precisely upon the dynamic that Jean-Michel Oughourlian terms *possession*. We might suggest that *mediation* is perhaps a more salutary term than possession, but Oughourlian's account of the underlying mystery remains completely valid: "By giving himself over," he writes, "the possessed gains himself; by letting himself become another, he preserves himself; by yielding himself, he discovers himself; by submitting, he becomes healed." Alas, as Balthasar, anticipating John Zizioulas, pointed out: "What the actor on the stage ultimately cannot find, and what the created human being, without God, cannot find either, that is, the role with which he can and must completely identify himself, becomes a reality in Christian theo-drama."[19] We return again to Paul's incomparable summation: "I live, now no longer I, but Christ lives in me" (Gal 2:20).

To enact the drama of Christ in the unique circumstances of one's own life is both to enter the mystery of Christ and bear witness to that mystery, playing one's role in the drama of salvation. Quoting the French philosopher and playwright Gabriel Marcel, Balthasar observes:

> One can ask "whether the actor does not possess quite unique opportunities of grace, whether there is not something in his existence that can somehow attract God's favor. There is a word of scripture that, in its secondary meaning, can be applied to him: 'Ye are not your own.' He can only find himself if he is prepared to lose himself. Thus, pursuing his vocation, he can provide us, through his unusual life, with a metaphor of human life as it aims toward its supernatural goal."[20]

As the observation of the Austrian playwright Hermann Bahr brings out, the experience of the actor is analogous to that of the patient in psychotherapy.

> During the transformation [the actor is] seized and wrenched from himself, is at the same time in control of the power that overwhelms him — this is *the absolute opposite of all hysteria*.

---

19 Hans Urs von Balthasar, *Theo-Drama: Theological Dramatic Theory*, Vol. III: *Dramatis Personae: Persons in Christ*, trans. Graham Harrison (San Francisco: Ignatius Press, 1992), 533.
20 Gabriel Marcel, "Réflexions sur les exigences d'un théâtre chrétien," in *La vie intellectuelle*, March 25, 1937, quoted in Hans Urs von Balthasar, *Theo-Drama: Theological Dramatic Theory*, I: *Prologomena* (San Francisco: Ignatius Press, 1988), 10n.

[The actor] presents us directly with the ultimate mystery of human nature: i.e., that, when we have entirely overcome ourselves and totally ceased being ourselves, we then find our true selves and begin for the first time to be ourselves. The hysteria of the inexperienced actor leads directly to metaphysics.[21]

We live today in a world where a great many of us have become "inexperienced actors" in Bahr's sense of the phrase. The inexperience of a thespian consists of a failure to understand either the drama into which he has been inserted or the role which it has fallen to him to perform. To compensate, he resorts to histrionics, which, like hysteria, calls undo attention to the personality of the performer, eclipsing the *dramatis persona* whom it was his professional responsibility to make vivid. Nonetheless, as a result of his mask, writes Zizioulas, even the naïve actor acquires "a certain taste of freedom, a certain specific 'hypostasis,' a certain identity." As a result of his mask, such an actor "has become a person, albeit for a brief period, and has learned what it is to exist as a free, unique and unrepeatable entity."[22]

Given what we have called the religious corona that can surround a mimetic attraction to a model that the imitator finds especially compelling, what, if any, might be the religious or metaphysical implications of our mimetic disposition? To put the matter in its starkest terms: Do we humans not only have an extraordinary mimetic predisposition, but is that predisposition transcendentally weighted toward models who awaken in their imitators a distinctively religious acuity? Moreover, and this is the crux of the matter with which this book is grappling: Are we members of the human species intrinsically ordered toward the embodied manifestation of the very reason for our existence, namely the *Logos*, the pattern of human existence in its fullest form? Using the word in all its metaphorical richness, Balthasar suggests that it is in his "mask" that "the 'person' both loses and finds himself."[23] The French poet, novelist, and dramatist François Mauriac came to a similar conclusion: "How strange it is that this effort to 'dis-incarnate' oneself in the service of an imaginary story bears such a startling analogy to what the mystics are looking for, to that

---

21 Quoted in Balthasar, *Theo-Drama: Theological Dramatic Theory*, I: *Prolegomena*, 10n6. Emphasis added.
22 Zizioulas, *Being as Communion*, 33.
23 Balthasar, *Theo-Drama: Theological Dramatic Theory*, I: *Prolegomena*, 122.

THE APOCALYPSE OF THE SOVEREIGN SELF

emptiness striven for by those who long to be overwhelmed by God."[24]

We return, therefore, to the tension between the actor as icon of another and the "hysteria of the inexperienced actor," the stage idol appropriating to himself the fascination of his audience. The theater, writes Balthasar, "acts as a brake on all tidy philosophies: it maintains the existential character of existence against all attempts to relativize it," and in so doing, it "is making its own contribution to fundamental theology."[25] "Often actors themselves have been the most profound and existential thinkers about their unique profession, coming up with amazing revelations; like many poets... they sense the uncanny nearness of the religious dimension."[26]

The *person* in the full Christian sense of the term is always sacramental because personhood is always mediated by an other or others, while the *self*, the secular simulation of the person, is inevitably "sacrificial" — in the crude anthropological sense. For the defining claim of a self is autonomy. It is a claim which requires that the truth about the mimetic reality be suppressed, not infrequently by sacrificing the model — literally, socially, or metaphorically — and by the self's ever more exaggerated dramatic impersonations, which tend toward the hysterical. Thus, Rousseau begins his *Confessions* by asserting that he had no predecessor, and Nietzsche insisted on his uniqueness even as he remained haunted throughout his life by Christ. While a self claims to have a will of its own, the "person" in the full Christian sense subordinates his own will to the will of Another. "Not my will, but Thine be done." The scriptural text at the heart of the argument of this book is this from the Gospel of John: "I have come in my Father's name, and you do not receive me; if another comes in his own name, him you will receive" (Jn 5:43).

Christ comes as the Mediator of the Father, and His supreme authority — the deepest source of his personhood — derives paradoxically from precisely the Other-orientation of His existence, His role as Mediator of the Father's love. The person, in the deepest Christian sense of the word, *never comes in his own name*, even though "this world" would be far more predisposed to accept him if he did. Of course, the question arises: In whose name does the person come?

---

24   François Mauriac, "Le mystère du théâtre," in *Journal III*, 113, quoted in Balthasar, *Theo-Drama: Theological Dramatic Theory*, I: *Prologomena*, 10n.
25   Balthasar, *Theo-Drama: Theological Dramatic Theory*, I: *Prologomena*, 20–21.
26   Ibid., 10–11.

The Absolute Opposite of All Hysteria

There is manifest nobility in giving one's life — whether by serving or sacrificing — for one's family, neighbors, fellow countrymen, or hapless victims and so on. But for a Christian all these sacrifices and many others are *in-formed* and ennobled by the sacrifice of Christ. For we are handmaids or manservants of the Lord, whether that core vocation coincides with our worldly responsibilities or merely grounds them in the mystery of our redemption. Such vocations participate, whether consciously or unawares, in Christ's sacrifice on Golgotha. However unbeknownst to the one making these more familiar sacrifices, they draw strength and resolve from the One who taught the world from the ambo of the Cross and died wearing a crown of thorns.

In *God's Gamble* we posed the theoretical question: what might be the most reliable marker for determining the moment when our pre-human ancestors crossed the threshold and became members of our extraordinary species? We answered with a hypothetical: Were we to discover evidence of the first act of non-instinctual self-sacrifice, then we could confidently declare that the one who acted in such a way is a member of our extraordinary species. For this is the birthmark of our humanity, just as the Garden of Eden is the proverbial story of our betrayal of that vocation, when our penchant for evading responsibility and offloading it onto others is so masterfully narrated. Thus is Christ the reconstituting *Logos*, the template according to whom our species was fashioned from the beginning, and in sync with whom we begin to reclaim our cherished birthright. Pope Benedict XVI, quoting the fourth Gospel, beautifully reminded us of this:

> "In the place where he was crucified there was a garden, and in the garden a new tomb where no one had ever been laid" (19:41). John's use of the word "garden" is an unmistakable reference to the story of Paradise and the Fall.... It was in the garden that Jesus fully accepted the Father's will, made it his own, and thus changed the course of history.[27]

The human actor who lives according to the form of Christ, the *Logos*, per-*forms* his unique life as best he can according the *form* of Christ. He keeps his eye on Christ and not on onlookers, should there even be any. It is the saints, argues Balthasar, in whom "Christian love becomes credible." They are "the poor sinners' guiding stars," precisely

---

27 Joseph Ratzinger/Benedict XVI, *Jesus of Nazareth*, Part Two (San Francisco: Ignatius Press, 2011), 149–50.

because "every one of them wishes to point completely away from himself and toward love."[28] We again call the reader's attention to the image on the cover of this book and the other-oriented acts of devotion it depicts.

At this point it is necessary to repeat what we said in the preface: every child of human parents is a person from the moment of conception and worthy of the reverence and respect rightfully due to that noble status. We are, as Hans Urs von Balthasar pointed out, members of "the species whose dignity is that all its members are unique persons."[29] And yet the fulfillment of that ontological status in the life of the person is the great and noble challenge that each member of our species faces. Neither our natural endowments nor the social, historical, or cultural circumstances of our lives are dispositive regarding such a vocation. Not infrequently, a person is called to a task for which he has no noticeable qualifications. If it is in fact a genuine call, then the grace made available upon its acceptance will compensate or more than compensate for whatever natural talents for the task might be lacking. It was Saint Ambrose who reminded us that grace is more efficacious than nature. Whatever one's natural gifts or limitations might be, it is the call, the mission, that is decisive. "Only when we identify ourselves with our mission," wrote Balthasar, "do we become persons in the deepest, theological sense of the word."[30] One could quite confidently say that Christianity exists to help fallen creatures like ourselves discover the mission in the performance of which we fulfill the promise of personhood that is our birthright by *becoming persons in the deepest theological sense of the word.* The word mission can conjure up rather lofty images and not without reason. Every mission in the life of the Church is indispensable, its apparent social or historical insignificance notwithstanding. Even at the most ordinary and natural level, our lives are intermingled in such a way that nothing we do is exclusively private. Dietrich von Hildebrand has nicely captured this mystery:

---

[28] Balthasar, *Love Alone Is Credible*, 120–21.
[29] Hans Urs von Balthasar, *A Theology of History* (San Francisco: Ignatius Press, 1994), 14.
[30] Hans Urs von Balthasar, *Hans Urs von Balthasar on the Ignatian Spiritual Exercises: An Anthology*, trans. Thomas Jacobi and Jonas Wernet (San Francisco: Ignatius Press, 2019), Kindle edition §820.

> Every imitation of a man, even of the greatest, richest, most gifted man, even a genius, would mean giving up of one's individuality, a leveling, a renunciation of personality, not to mention the fact that an absolute, literal imitation of any man is entirely impossible. In relation to Christ, it is quite the opposite. The mysterious truth is that the unique inimitable design of God is fully and ultimately realized in a man only when he is transformed into Christ. Can one find more powerful, more deeply expressed individualities than St. Catherine of Siena, St. Francis of Assisi, St. Augustine, St. Paul, St. Gregory VII?[31]

The person as *personare* is the one through whom what has been given is *enacted, choreographed*, and thus passed on to those for whom it is meant. Both slavish duplication and potentially hysterical efforts to disavow the mimetic influence of the model are prophylactic to the work of the Spirit, that still small voice that must be carefully discerned by those who have felt its gentle stirrings.

Christians *qua* Christians do not have careers; they have missions. Whatever questions may arise for non-Christians, the central question for a Christian is: "By Whom am I called, and to whom am I sent?" The concept of the person cannot be located in the self or in the psychic inventory. Stripped of its deeper Christian meaning, the concept of the person degenerates into the performative and putatively autonomous self from the tedium and insubstantiality of which one eventually flees, often enough into one or another of the pathologies that have appeared so conspicuously in the post-Christian world: sub-clinical hysteria, low-level forms of nihilism, and eventually the crypto-religious delirium — such as Sylvia Plath's desperate longing for a "cause with a capital 'C'" — which is a thinly disguised license to "save the world by breaking shop windows" to which nihilists are especially predisposed.

The ennobling of the status of the human person that the Incarnation inaugurates is accompanied by corresponding responsibilities, among them the necessity of availing oneself of the grace without which those responsibilities cannot be met. The storehouse of that grace is the sacramental resource which it is the privilege and responsibility of the Church to dispense. "Within the drama of Christ," writes Balthasar, "every human fate is deprivatized so that its personal range may extend to the whole universe, depending on how far it is prepared to cooperate

---

31 Dietrich von Hildebrand, *Liturgy and Personality* (Steubenville, OH: Hildebrand Project, 2016), 19.

in being inserted into the normative drama of Christ's life, death and Resurrection."[32] Those whose ontological dignity has been raised by a merely *cultural* exposure to Christ and His Church may know little about how and from whence their aspirations and hopes have been awakened, but these hopes and aspirations will nonetheless be adversely affected by the failure to recognize their religious source. They, more than those who have had no contact with Christianity, will be drawn to pseudo-religious movements and ideologies of the sort that have been the central curse of the late-modern world.

All the world's a stage, but the play that takes place on that stage is both choreographed and improvisational. Its author is the Father, and its central Protagonist is Christ. They send the Spirit into the hearts of the members of the supporting cast, freeing them from preoccupations that would otherwise shackle them and mute the living testimony — both choreographed and spontaneous — that is uniquely theirs to deliver.

> In obeying his calling a person fulfills his essence, although he would never have been able to discover this, his own archetype and ideal within himself, in his nature, by descending into the center of his natural being, his superego, his subconscious or superconscious, by studying his predispositions, yearnings, talents, his potential. Simon the fisherman could have explored every region of his ego prior to this encounter with Christ, but he would not have found "Peter" there; for the present, the "form" summoned up in the name "Peter," the particular mission reserved for him alone, is hidden in the mystery of Christ's soul.[33]

This is true as well even when the name spoken is not a new one. It was only when Mary Magdalen heard her name spoken by the risen Lord that she awakened to the great mystery to which she had been blinded by the exigencies of her life and the depth of her despair. There is a hint of this in the experience of having one's name spoken with genuine affection by another. It is as though one's otherwise shopworn name touches the core of one's being, one's personhood. If one's name spoken by another can have this effect, all the more so is this the case when one hears in his heart his name spoken by Christ. "This personal name uttered by the lips of him who is Eternal Life,"

---

32   Balthasar, *Theo-Drama: Theological Dramatic Theory*, II: *Dramatis Personae: Man in God*, 50.
33   Balthasar, *Prayer*, 60.

writes Balthasar, "is a person's true concept."[34] We hope not to trivialize this precious insight by asking the reader to imagine hearing his name spoken by Christ, in spontaneous response to which spiritual logjams begin to break up and a new form of freedom — the freedom of obedience — awakens.

To better illuminate the Christological innuendo of the word person, we can say that a person is ontologically *sound* to the extent that he allows his life to re-sound the *Logos*, "magnifying the Lord" in the utterly unique way that only this particular person can. Contrary to all the nostrums of individualism, it is in fulfilling one's mission in the christocentric theodrama that a person fulfills the deepest longing of the heart.

The turning point in human history, which is the key for understanding all subsequent history, is the Golgothan scene at the climax of which Christ breathes His Spirit into the world. Thereafter the work of that Spirit arouses and shapes christological missions according to the qualities and temperament of those so aroused as well as the social, communal, and historical circumstances in which they live. Of the person so understood, Balthasar writes: "The stage erected before the world's eyes, to which he is sent as an actor, is always occupied by an ensemble of fellow actors; he is inserted into the ensemble."[35] The admittedly challenging task of discerning one's role in that drama is itself an event of no small importance, requiring the grace of the sacraments, introspection, prayer, and whatever guidance might be available from more experienced and sagacious members of the dramatic ensemble — familial, ecclesial, and cultural — in relation to whom one's personal mission will most fruitfully be choreographed.

Balthasar argues that the actor in the theodrama of salvation history combines "masterly technique and pure inspiration."

> For the human being, this is "living on the knife edge", that is, *between humility and the exhibitionistic loss of self*; thus behind the problem of the actor there emerges the problem of man himself, the conscious subject in search of a role. And ultimately this role cannot be just *any*, interchangeable role but should be his own, unique, "personal" role.[36]

---

34 Ibid., 26.
35 Balthasar, *Theo-Drama: Theological Dramatic Theory*, I: *Prologomena*, 647.
36 Balthasar, *Theo-Drama: Theological Dramatic Theory*, Vol. III: *Dramatis Personae: Persons in Christ*, 532. Emphasis added.

Here again, we meet the analogue of the juxtaposition of the mystic and the hysteric. The hysteric has good reason to insulate himself from absorption into a fascinating model, a pied piper, whose mimetic attraction he struggles to resist. The Christian mystic on the other hand has found a yoke that is easy, a burden that is light. He finds himself on a mission not of his own choosing but one nonetheless that will come alive and become a source of grace to the extent that he has given it his wholehearted assent. In the fulfillment of that mission, his humility will be the necessary ballast for whatever form the "exhibitionistic loss of self" might take in bearing witness to mysteries to which he might have been granted a glimpse. Writes Henri de Lubac:

> The psychological truth is the symbol of one more profound: we must be *looked at* in order to be *enlightened*, and the eyes that are "bringers of light" are not only those of the divinity. Again, does not the *person*, if we take the old original meaning of the word in a spiritual sense, always mean to have a part to play?...The summons to personal life is a *vocation*, that is, a summons to play an eternal role...and it is because the world is a history, a single history, that each individual life is a drama.[37]

As for the "*exhibitionistic loss of self*," David Moss, Associate Lecturer at the University of Exeter, observes: "The most persuasive material for exemplifying the truth of the Christian gospel—one's own life—far from elevating 'my' own spiritual journey becomes the *form* through which the truth of Christian doctrine is grasped and becomes 'followable' in the Church."[38]

The risen Christ said to doubting Thomas: "You have believed because you have seen me. Blessed are those who have not seen and yet believe" (Jn 20:29). This is often misunderstood. The risen Lord is not praising those who believe on the basis of less evidence than was available to those to whom he appeared after his Resurrection. On the contrary, he is speaking, not of insufficient evidence, but of another *form* of evidence, namely, the living witness of believers who have themselves received faith from contact with their predecessors and elders in the faith. A believing Christians can confidently say: I know someone who knew

---

37 De Lubac, *Catholicism*, 331–32.
38 David Moss, "The Saints," *The Cambridge Companion to Hans Urs von Balthasar*, eds. Edward T. Oakes, S.J. and David Moss (Cambridge: Cambridge University Press, 2004), 83.

someone, who knew someone, who knew someone, who knew someone who saw the risen Christ. It is precisely that link with Christ which the sacramental life of the Church mediates and through which grace passes into every Christian in every age. Thus does the authentic Word enter world history and awaken hope. Balthasar has written:

> Grace brings man a task, opens up for him a field of activity, bestows upon him the joy of accomplishment, so that he can identify himself with his mission and discover in it the true meaning of his existence. Grace gives man a center of gravity that, like a magnet, draws all the forces of his nature into a clear and definite pattern that is neither foreign nor cumbersome to the patterns already formed in his nature, but engages them, like idle laborers, in a task that is both pleasant and rewarding. This is the power of the grace of mission.[39]

As for the suggestion that such a task is "both pleasant and rewarding," the dramatic analogy is apropos. The professional gratification that an accomplished actor experiences when he senses that his portrayal has awakened in his audience emotions commensurate with the dramatic situation must not be written off as vanity. On the contrary, in this circumstance the actor has been enriched by the interplay with his audience, just as the audience has been enriched by his performance. Indeed, it is this experience that best explains the authentic appeal of the theatrical vocation, its often-neglected religious dimension.

Most of the modest missions to which we are called in this life require no detailed knowledge about how these missions might fit into the larger drama of which they are but a small part. Nonetheless, it is the degree to which we sense that our lives *are* in fact part of such a drama that we will be fortified against fatigue, surrender, or despair when the immediate circumstances seem unfavorable to any foreseeable promising outcome. As Philip Rieff has written: "Self-confidence is inseparable from submission to the creedal order, and through that order, to the supreme authority expressed in that order.... Without an authority deeply installed, there is no foundation for individuality. Self-confidence thus expresses submission to supreme authority."[40]

"*In Christo*," writes Balthasar, "every man can cherish the hope of not remaining a merely individual conscious subject but of receiving

---

39 Hans Urs von Balthasar, *The Christian State of Life*, trans. Sister Mary Frances McCarthy (San Francisco: Ignatius Press, 1983), 74.
40 Philip Rieff, *Charisma* (New York: Pantheon Books, 2007), 24.

personhood from God, becoming a person, with a mission that is likewise defined *in Christo*."⁴¹ With this in mind, it seems fitting to bring this chapter to its conclusion by recalling a widely circulated, variously recounted, and possibly apocryphal story about a pastor who was serving in the childhood parish of the actor Richard Burton. The pastor was celebrating his fiftieth anniversary as a priest. Burton attended the celebration, and he was enthusiastically acknowledged for his theatrical accomplishments. The old priest asked Burton to recite the Good Shepherd Psalm, Psalm 23, which the priest had once taught Burton to recite when he was a child.

> A strange look came over the actor's face. He paused for a moment, and then said, "I will, on one condition — that after I have recited it, you, my pastor and teacher will do the same." "I," said the old, retired pastor, "am not an actor, but, if you wish it, I shall do so." Impressively the actor began the Psalm. His voice and intonation were perfect. He held his audience spellbound, and, as he finished, a great burst of applause broke from the audience. As it died away, the old pastor rose from his wheelchair and began to recite the same Psalm. His voice was feeble and shivering and his tone was not faultless. But, when he finished, there was not a dry eye in the room. The actor rose and his voice quivered as he said, "Ladies and gentlemen, I reached your eyes and ears, but my old pastor has reached your hearts. The difference is just this: I know the psalm, but he knows the Shepherd."

We earlier said that to consider Dostoevsky's *Brothers Karamazov* as untrue is to adopt an impoverished notion of truth. By the same token, the palpable impact of the last sentence of this story is due to a truth that can in no sense be disparaged by its lack of corroboration. While Burton was a professional actor, a thespian whose special gifts made it possible for him to portray a wide range of characters, his old pastor was an actor in the sense that is of concern to us. His vocation was not only to know the Shepherd but to act and speak in a way that would acquaint his fellow members of the ecclesial ensemble with the Shepherd: to allow the Shepherd's voice to re-sound in his life and his work.

---

41   Balthasar, *Theo-Drama: Theological Dramatic Theory*, Vol. III: *The Dramatis Personae: Persons in Christ*, 220.

24 The Son Can Only Do What He Sees the Father Doing

> For I have not spoken on my own authority; the Father who sent me has himself given me commandment what to say and what to speak. (Jn 12:49)
>
> As in the case of the prophets and lawgivers, what is involved is the razor-sharp discernment of spirits: to see guilt where no one else sees it, to point to expiation where no one else thinks this is possible and, therefore, also to present grace as a requirement.
>
> — Hans Urs von Balthasar[1]

BEFORE EXPLORING THE CIRCUMSTANCES AND resources most favorable to a genuinely personal existence, we pause to note that even the Person who brought the mystery of personhood fully to light was not exempt from such acts of discernment. His very humanity would have been in question had this not been the case. Like us in all things but sin, his mission—known in the mind of God from the foundation of the world—came into focus for him through his engagement with the familial, spiritual, cultural, and religious traditions into which his life had been divinely and providentially inserted. What he sought for in each of these areas of life was one thing: the will of his heavenly Father.

> Truly, truly, I say to you, the Son can do nothing of his own accord, but only what he sees the Father doing; for whatever he does, that the Son does likewise. (Jn 5:19)

Thus did Jesus's mission require him to take a long, hard look at what the Father was doing and had been doing to bring his beloved creature out of bondage. From the moment of his conception in his mother's

---

1 Balthasar, *Tragedy Under Grace*, 20.

womb, Jesus was God incarnate, but this did not exempt him from the task of discerning the nature and meaning of the work which it was his mission to bring to its final consummation. The hope for such a consummation was hardly unknown, but every prior attempt to attain it proved futile. As Balthasar argued:

> The lines from the old covenant do not converge on a single point. And everything that the Jew might have undertaken in order to force something like a convergence, in his longing for fulfilment, showed itself subsequently to be the opposite of convergence; he was an obstacle in the path of God's plans, merely taking up the place that God wanted empty, in order to fill it himself.[2]

The temptations in the wilderness can be seen as Jesus's refusal to "force something like a convergence" by way of the most obvious and familiar worldly stratagems. The elements involved in the redemptive work would be discernable by others only in retrospect, but he who knew himself responsible for accomplishing that work had to bring the task into focus by prayer and by discerning its foreshadowings in the history of his people, especially as the contour of his mission was embodied by his mother and adumbrated by his forerunner John. As Giuseppe Fornari observed: "To credit Jesus with omniscience about what was happening to him would mean not only to absolutize in a way scientifically untenable, but also to abandon the principle of the Incarnation."[3]

Far from being shocked by this idea, we should find it immensely reassuring. For it allows us to draw closer to the inner struggle of the God-man on whose life, death, and resurrection the meaning of the drama of life depends. Since the role of mediators in Jesus's own life is both conspicuous and easily overlooked, we can better reckon with our own mimetic predicament by highlighting the influence of those to whom Jesus looked in bringing his own incomparable mission into sharper focus. Girard is right to say that "true freedom lies in the basic choice between a human or a divine model." But neither can we neglect the indispensable role that human mediators continue to play in orienting our lives toward the *Logos* in person, the very meaning of human existence. Balthasar invites his readers to marvel at the scope of the synthesis

---

[2] Hans Urs von Balthasar, *The Glory of the Lord: A Theological Aesthetics*, Vol. 7: *Theology: The New Covenant*, trans. Brian McNeil C.R.V. (San Francisco: Ignatius Press, 1989), 36.
[3] Fornari, *Dionysus, Christ, and the Death of God*, Vol. II, 251.

that Christ brings about, a synthesis that appears only in retrospect, when the process by which it was accomplished has been completed.

> The numerous images of the Old Testament surround and converge upon a midpoint which remains open and not constructible; through the existence of Christ, this midpoint is occupied, without visible struggling to attain the synthesis; as Christians reflect on this after Easter, it is seen that all fragmentary images order themselves as if automatically towards this midpoint, and contribute a clarification to the unity.[4]

To say that Christ brought together in a stunning way the essential threads running through the Old Testament, and that he did so "without visible struggling" and that the post-Easter Church found that the fragments ordered themselves "as if automatically," is not to suggest that Jesus played no role in bringing about that synthesis. It means, rather, that Jesus allowed his incomparable vocation to take shape in the spirit of his mother's *fiat*. His vocation came fully into view in consequence of his prior surrender to it. As Fornari insists, "we must reject the hagiographic picture of a divine agent suddenly appearing out of the blue, deriving no support from the culture of the age he lived in."[5] No less must we reject any suggestion that Jesus choreographed this convergence. The repeated references to his recourse to solitary prayer make it clear that he awaited — with confidence and patience — the revelation of his Father's will.

The key to his patience in this regard is the influence of his mother, Mary of Nazareth. Perhaps the most distinctive feature of Mary, a feature that would have been formative for her Son, breaks in on us at the Annunciation when Mary responds to the announcement that she, though a virgin, was to bear a Son. "Behold, I am the handmaid of the Lord; let it be to me according to your word" (Lk 1:38). This *fiat* can be regarded as the distinctive feature of Mary's life, her initial surrender to God's will, her consent to allow her life to be used as God in his infinite wisdom saw fit to use it. This reverses the worldly order of things, but it is precisely this to which God had been calling his chosen people throughout the scriptural account of its history. Mary does not ponder the call she is given, nor ask for details; she simply says yes to the open invitation. This is the indispensable first step in discovering

---

4 Balthasar, *The Glory of the Lord*, Vol. 7, 34.
5 Ibid., 95.

the full repercussions of her *fiat*. Fornari helpfully calls attention to "an iconographical detail in the paintings of the Annunciation" in which "Mary is depicted reading the Hebrew Bible when the angel Gabriel appears to her." This, Fornari argues, alludes to the recognition of Mary as the representative of the "*Old Testament as a whole.*"[6]

> Mary provides the key not only to the Gospels but to the interpretation of the Bible as a whole and to the church founded on it. This history of the church and Christianity is incomprehensible without Mary.... In Luke she acts and obeys without question, without understanding, and precisely by so doing she says what nobody before her had said and understands what nobody before her had understood.[7]

The Lord's mother was walking by faith and not by sight a half-century before Saint Paul declared that to be the touchstone of Christian faith. When Fornari makes the rather bold claim that Mary is the key to Christianity, and to the Bible as a whole, and that the "history of the church and Christianity is incomprehensible without Mary," we might ask how and why this is so. One obvious answer is that it was the self-surrendering spirit of his mother that quietly in-formed the young Jesus about living in readiness, exemplifying for him the disposition requisite to his own singular salvific mission.

However pivotal the influence of Jesus's mother, it properly remains shrouded in the intimacies of his childhood. The threshold at which Jesus steps outside the intimate circle of his family occurs, appropriately, when he reached the age at which he was qualified to participate in Jewish religious life. Luke recounts the story of the twelve-year-old Jesus remaining in Jerusalem after he and his parents had gone there for Passover. Of course, this account was written decades after the Ascension and in light of the Passion and Resurrection. We needn't succumb to historical-critical exegesis, however, to recognize what it might have meant for a religiously precocious twelve-year-old, long influenced by so extraordinary a mother, to travel to the sacred center of his religion, there to cross the official threshold into Jewish manhood. There is something quite extraordinary here, especially important for us in our time. Even as a child, Jesus seems to have sensed both that his mission was to fulfill once and for all the promise for which his people had been the

---

6   Fornari, *Dionysus, Christ, and the Death of God*, Vol. II, 272.
7   Ibid., 273, 278.

historical custodian and *therefore* that it was necessary to confer with the official guardians and curators of that promise.

Luke makes it clear that Jesus had crossed the threshold to adulthood, not simply because he had reached the formal age at which he could take part in synagogue proceedings, but because he had stepped outside his family circle to do so. All the most important mediation that he had received from his immediate family, most especially his mother, had occurred. It was now necessary to move outside the domestic milieu in order to learn what he could from his religious elders. The evangelist implies as much when he tells his readers that Jesus made the decision to engage with his religious elders without bothering to tell his parents.

> After three days [his parents] found him in the temple, sitting among the teachers, listening to them and asking them questions; and all who heard him were amazed at his understanding and his answers. (Lk 2:46–47)

Luke calls attention to the amazement his elders experienced at Jesus's answers, but the point we want to bring out is that he was also listening to them, not patronizingly, but with real eagerness to learn. As with his earlier familial — especially maternal — influence, so at this stage: to imagine that in listening to the temple scholars and asking them questions an all-knowing Jesus was engaging in some kind of charade is to abandon the reality of the Incarnation.

Second only to his mother, Jesus's cousin John, the son of his relatives Zechariah and Elizabeth, played an obvious role at the onset of Jesus's public life. Balthasar concurs: "It is probable," he writes, "that Jesus stood for a time in a disciple relationship to the Baptist and that his own mission thereby came in human terms to its own final maturity."[8] Not only did Jesus go to the Jordan to be baptized by John, but a few scriptural passages suggest that Jesus himself performed baptisms. As most editions of the Fourth Gospel note, a subsequent caveat was inserted to suggest that it was Jesus's disciples, not Jesus himself, who performed baptisms.

> Now when the Lord knew that the Pharisees had heard that Jesus was making and baptizing more disciples than John (although Jesus himself did not baptize, but only his disciples), he left Judea and departed again to Galilee. (Jn 4:1–3)

---

8   Balthasar, *The von Balthasar Reader*, 207.

For our purposes, however, that distinction would not call into question the degree of John's influence on the earliest phase of Jesus's public life, even though, in due course, Jesus would recognize the messianic inadequacy of John's mission. For not only did Jesus inaugurate his mission by being baptized by John, but he explicitly followed John's example by retreating to the desert for the scripturally paradigmatic period of prayer and fasting.

Each of the temptations that Jesus underwent in the wilderness represents a dramatic act of the sort that someone with a prophetic or messianic mission might perform to command the attention of his people. Jesus rejected each of these worldly options in turn, and he did so in each case by quoting scripture, thus declaring his fidelity to the tradition for which his mission would be the unsurpassable crowning glory. It was in prayer and fasting that Jesus wrestled with what he had come to see as his singular role in the redemption of his people and, indeed, of the world, past, present, and future. The greater that role became, the more anguishing were the acts of discernment required to bring it into focus.

The chronologies vary between the evangelists, but it is striking that, as Matthew recounts later in chapter fourteen of his Gospel, John had been arrested by Herod for boldly and openly condemning his unlawful marriage to Herodias, the wife of his brother Philip. In consequence of what was a fearless and prophetic act, Herod had John thrown into prison. But it was back in chapter four of Matthew that his readers are told that, immediately upon returning from forty days in the wilderness, Jesus learned of John's arrest by Herod.

> Now when he heard that John had been arrested, he withdrew into Galilee.... From that time Jesus began to preach, saying, "Repent, for the kingdom of heaven is at hand." (Mt 4:12,17)

Here John's influence is both emphasized and nuanced. For in sharp contrast to John's very public condemnation of Herod, Jesus withdrew from the highly charged Judea to the relatively peaceful Galilee. Nonetheless, when he arrived there, he repeated exactly the same words that famously distinguished John's peaching. When John learned of this, he sent his disciples to Jesus, obviously questioning his comparatively less provocative missionary demeanor.

> Now when John heard in prison about the deeds of the Christ, he sent word by his disciples and said to him, "Are you he who

is to come, or shall we look for another?" And Jesus answered them, "Go and tell John what you hear and see: the blind receive their sight and the lame walk, lepers are cleansed and the deaf hear, and the dead are raised up, and the poor have good news preached to them. And blessed is he who takes no offense at me." (Mt 11:2–6)

While John had passionately announced the arrival of the Messiah, Jesus was now quietly performing the deeds by which the true messiah could be recognized. In the face of John's implicit criticism of Jesus's lack of ardor, Jesus replies, "Blessed are those who are not scandalized by me." As mentioned in an earlier chapter, the word *skandalon* means a stumbling block and, as René Girard has convincingly argued, it refers to a situation in which one's model becomes one's rival or when one's rival becomes one's model.

John the Baptist was a man of great zeal and passion. He was on fire with the zeal for moral and religious reform. In Herod's prison he seems to have expected his cousin to take up the prophetic mantle. Sitting in prison for an act he considered consistent with the messianic role he had come to believe his cousin Jesus was chosen to fulfill, John sent his disciples to Jesus to ask what had happened to his messianic passion. By comparison, Jesus had returned to the relative safety of Galilee and had been far less provocative and less eager to challenge the political powers. The question John was posing through his disciples was whether or not Jesus really was the "one who is to come."

In response, Jesus referred to the works of mercy and healing he was performing and to his preaching of the good news. To the implication behind John's question — as to Jesus's comparatively tepid and non-confrontational mission — Jesus replied with an innuendo all his own: the importance of not becoming a *skandalon*, a stumbling block — in other words, a stock player in a social or political melodrama which blinds its participants to their complicity in the very moral outrage of which they believe themselves so innocent. To fall into such a scandal would impede the act of contrition which it was the tacit purpose of the moral outrage to arouse.

Confronting evil directly and courageously will always be necessary in this fallen world, but such confrontations will always run the risk of drawing the protagonists into scandal. When that happens, the protagonists are driven more by antipathy for their opponents than by regard for truth or virtue. The responsibility that falls to mere mortals is such that we may have occasion to run this risk, but Jesus's mission required that he avoid such scandalizing. The Forerunner had allowed himself to be scandalized by Herod, but his failure may well have played a role in alerting Jesus to a danger which he would have to avoid. This was the last and greatest of the messianic clarifications that the Forerunner was to provide.

The need to avoid scandal was marvelously captured by Caravaggio in his famous painting *The Taking of Christ*. In this painting Christ is not even at the center of the painting, but he is the only person in the painting not caught up in the social hysteria of the moment. He alone is not scandalized, for he alone is the incomparable *Dramatis Persona* in the eye of the storm. He is the rejected stone in the very process of becoming the cornerstone of a new way of life. Here Caravaggio, faithful to the artistic revolution in the West, accomplishes what the iconographers of Eastern Christendom achieved according to the principles of their own rich tradition.

By the very act of questioning the messianic mission of Jesus, John was showing how much he remained an Old Testament prophet. Even as he fell back — so to speak — into the Old Testament, John may have helped Jesus understand what his own utterly singular mission would have to avoid. This unintended contribution of the Baptist to the mission of Jesus earned him a unique place in the drama of our salvation. If, as we have expressed it, John "fell back" into an Old Testament paradigm of the fire-breathing prophet, his cousin would bring him into the New Testament. As Balthasar has written:

> John, who himself remains standing at the border of the Old Covenant, is lifted over this border into the New as the "Elias who is come," as "more than a prophet," as the "greatest to be born of woman" (Mt 11:15, 9, 11).... Such a person will not be left behind and forgotten in the work which Jesus will found; as the earthly starter of the mission of Jesus, he enters into it along with him.[9]

The Gospels are filled with references to the prayer life of Jesus. We are familiar with this fact, and it goes without saying that prayer would play a great role in the life of the Person whom the same document declares to have been divine. Nonetheless, each of the evangelists attests to the importance of prayer in Jesus's life.

---

9   Ibid., 209.

> And in the morning, a great while before day, he rose and went out to a lonely place, and there he prayed. (Mk 1:35)
>
> And after he had taken leave of them, he went up on the mountain to pray. (Mk 6:46)
>
> In these days he went out to the hills to pray; and all night he continued in prayer to God. (Lk 6:12)

Jesus had come, after all, to do the will of his heavenly Father, and he repeatedly returned to the wellsprings of his Source.

At the Transfiguration: "he took with him Peter and John and James, and went up on the mountain to pray. And *as he was praying*, the appearance of his countenance was altered, and his raiment became dazzling white" (Lk 9:28–29).

It is worth pausing here to note that the single most important contribution to the spiritual communion that underlies the experience of personhood is the existence of a prayer life. It was true of Christ, and it is no less true for those who live and move and have their being in him. It may be possible to experience a form of personhood based on a communion with others, but without the complement of a personal prayer life the merely social foundation of one's authenticity can run counter to any mission that might fall afoul of social conventions. Investments in the worldly order, even one comprised of the most thoughtful and loving people, will occasionally slacken or otherwise prove unreliable. One's prayer life can wax and wane as well of course, and that is to be expected. The dark night of the soul is a fact of Christian life. But the prayer life remains the most indispensable factor in grounding the experience of personhood. By way of contrast, we may recall the words of Virginia Woolf's Neville: "The brute menaces my liberty," said Neville, "*when he prays.*" This helps explain the fervor of some who, in the aftermath of an unconscionable act of violence, took umbrage at those whose response was to keep the victims and their families in their prayers. Whereas seeing Jesus at prayer inspired his disciples to ask him how to pray, those who have cut themselves off from this source of prayer grow contemptuous of those who retain this indispensable feature of the creature made in God's image.

The fact that the disciples of Jesus asked him to teach them how to pray suggests that they had come to realize that prayer was at the heart of his life and the key to the mystery he embodied. "He was praying in a certain place, and when he ceased, one of his disciples said to him, 'Lord, teach us to pray, as John taught his disciples'" (Lk 11:1). Indeed, as his hour approached, in the garden of Gethsemane, Jesus went back and forth between his disciples and his prayerful communion with his heavenly Father, from earthly to heavenly communion, both of which were indispensable to his mission.

We have touched on evidence suggesting that Jesus continually sought to better understand the mission to which he knew he was being called by his Heavenly Father. It remains to mention the important influence of the mysterious figure referred to as the Suffering Servant, perhaps the most enigmatic figure in the Old Testament. Whatever might have been Jesus's interest in this figure prior to the death of John the Baptist, John's fate may well have brought the Suffering Servant into focus, not least because of the sharp difference between John's provocative condemnations and the silent figure of whom the Suffering Servant songs speak. Indeed, it was to these passages in Isaiah that the first Christians so often turned in their attempt to account for the meaning of Christ's Passion, death, and Resurrection.

Seen against the backdrop of the Suffering Servant songs, the failure of John's prophetic mission would have become apparent. By allowing himself to be scandalized by Herod and the corruption of the Herodian court, John had played a worldly game and lost. It is hardly farfetched to imagine how much John's fate — once bathed in the light of the Suffering Servant songs — contributed to Jesus's understanding of the role he was being asked to play in bringing the story of his people to its unsurpassable conclusion. Passages such as this:

> Surely he has borne our griefs
>   and carried our sorrows;
> yet we esteemed him stricken,
>   struck down by God, and afflicted.
> But he was wounded for our transgressions,
>   he was bruised for our iniquities;
> upon him was the chastisement that made us whole,
>   and with his stripes we are healed. (Is 53:4–5)

What, we might ask, would Jesus have made of these haunting lines? Looking back on his Passion, Christians were not tardy in recognizing them as prophetic of Christ's redeeming act. It is not unlikely that Jesus himself found in the Suffering Servant songs an important clue to the mission he knew had fallen to him to accomplish.

> I gave my back to those who struck me,
>> and my cheeks to those who pulled out the beard;
> I hid not my face
>> from shame and spitting. (Is 50:6)

No less a figure than Benedict XVI insisted that: "This late prophesy is the interpretive key with which Jesus unlocks the Old Testament. After Easter, he himself would become the key to a new reading of the Law and the Prophets."[10]

The point of these reflections has been to suggest that Jesus — notwithstanding his singular and incomparable place in history and his role in the salvation of the world — came to understand the mission to which he was being called thanks to the example — the mediation — of his mother, his cousin, the elders whom he consulted and with whom he debated, his prayerful relationship with his Heavenly Father, and by pondering the meaning of the Suffering Servant songs. In other words, he was like us in at least this respect: he too had to discover his mission by prayer and by reference to the history and traditions of his own people.

There remains the matter of Jesus's exclamation: "My God, my God, why have you forsaken me?" (Mt 27:46). Jesus cried out. He made his abandonment public. In a very real sense, this is the quintessence of the Paschal mystery in all its unfathomability. A great deal of ink has been spilled in the effort to understand this shocking cry. Jesus is quoting Psalm 22, as is well known, but efforts to soften the impact of these words by suggesting that Jesus was invoking the more reassuring verses with which the psalm concludes is not convincing. It is unlikely, in our estimation, that at this nadir of his suffering Jesus would have resorted to literary allusion.

Prayer in the ancient world was not routinely silent. As a common practice, silent prayer would await the developing sense of personhood under the influence of Christianity. This helps us understand, not only why Jesus so often prayed in solitude, but also why he urged his disciples: "whenever you pray, go into your room and shut the door and pray to your Father who is in secret" (Mt 6:6). Whatever might have been the prayers of Christ during his Passion, at its climax he cried out his last, most shocking, prayer. And he did so under circumstances that would

---

10   Benedict XVI, *Jesus of Nazareth*, Part II (San Francisco: Ignatius Press, 2011), 17.

make his cry unforgettable to those present and to all those who would learn of it down through history. Why?

The fact that both Matthew and Mark include an Aramaic translation of this cry of dereliction suggests the consternation it caused as well as its historical authenticity. What concerns us, however, is the need Jesus felt to reveal to those present, and through them to posterity, the real depths of his agony. He had taken on himself the sins of us all, and the ultimate consequence of sin is separation from God. God-man though he was, precisely for that reason he experienced godforsakenness at a deeper depth than anything fallen and sinful humanity can imagine. In the context of our analysis, the point is that Jesus "cried out." Not only did he experience godforsakenness, but he made it public. Had he not done so, who would ever have imagined that, in addition to his physical suffering and social execration, he endured such a shocking and abysmal spiritual deprivation? It was necessary that those for whom he endured these torments be made aware of the price he paid for releasing fallen humanity from the attractive power of sin. He released us from this power by revealing the depths to which he was descending in order to unleash the gravitational power of crucified love. In doing so, he revealed what it means to be a person in the fullest sense. As Balthasar has noted:

> Jesus Christ is *the* Person, in an absolute sense, because in him self-consciousness (of the conscious subject) coincides with the mission he has received from God, a mission that, because of this identity, cannot but be universal, embracing all other possible and partial missions.... There can be other persons within this prime Person: this comes about when conscious subjects identify themselves with the qualitatively unique mission that has been designed for them and that lies within the mission of Christ.[11]

---

[11] Balthasar, *Theo-Drama: Theological Dramatic Theory*, Vol. III: *The Dramatis Personae: The Person of Christ*, 509.

25 "Anthropological Structures Prepared Beforehand"

> The family is one of nature's masterpieces.
> — George Santayana[1]
>
> Without the family there is no first order of affectivity.
> — Paul Kraus[2]

IN ALASDAIR MACINTYRE'S ETHICS IN THE CON-*flicts of Modernity: An Essay on Desire, Practical Reasoning, and Narrative*, the word *desire*, so prominent in the subtitle of the book, appears between its covers more than five hundred times, but not once do the words *imitate* or *imitation* appear. Nowhere does MacIntyre's unquestionably important contribution to moral reasoning betray any familiarity with René Girard's penetrating analysis of mimetic desire. And yet, if MacIntyre fails to formally address this facet of desire, he certainly is cognizant of its operation, as can be seen in a comment early in his book which, though fictional and illustrative, bears a certain likeness to Bob Dylan's early conversion experience. MacIntyre writes:

> Initially I have no particular liking for this kind of music—Tudor madrigals, punk rock, whatever. Then I learn that someone whose judgment I greatly respect not only values this kind of music as a listener but is learning an instrument so as to become a performer. Impressed by this, I start listening carefully to recordings of it, I change my habits, I redirect my attention, and in time I find it rewarding to have done so.[3]

---

1 George Santayana, *Life of Reason, Reason in Society* (New York: Scribner's, 1905), 35.
2 Paul Kraus, "Marxism and the Gender Revolution," *Crisis Magazine*, November 12, 2021.
3 Alasdair MacIntyre, *Ethics in the Conflicts of Modernity: An Essay on Desire, Practical Reasoning, and Narrative* (Cambridge: Cambridge University Press, 2016), 4.

The example MacIntyre uses may be entirely hypothetical, but in the interest of psychological verisimilitude he noted that the person who theoretically aroused his interest in a musical genre has not just shown an interest in it. He has chosen to go to the trouble of learning to become a *performer* of the genre. Thus, the model's interest in the musical style in question was by no means casual. We are invited to surmise that what made the musical genre fascinating enough to change an onlooker's *tastes* was the fact that it had changed the *life* of the admired model; it had inspired someone he respected to become a *performer*, to undertake a new *mission*. The structure of MacIntyre's "conversion" is perfectly analogous to those conversions experienced by the first generation of Christians. They, too, found themselves persuaded by the example of Christ and by those who had in turn been changed by it. On the basis of that example, they changed their lives. Each in his own way became determined to perform his own life as best he could in accord with the way Christ had performed his.

As the etymological roots of the word person suggest, we are actors in a drama that predates us and that will continue to unfold after we pass from "the scene" with which our lives are coterminous. And, as Balthasar has so persuasively argued, the vocation of the person in the full Christian sense of the word is the fruit of a mission accepted and the grace that accompanies that acceptance. If the theatrical language and metaphors we have employed are to be useful in reckoning with our predicament and our challenges, we will need to ask a very sweeping question: What is actually happening in human history? And we will need to ask a very personal question: To what unique role in that drama are we each being called?

As we have tried to show, personhood as the Christian revelation allows us to reckon it is inherently self-sacrificial, but not in some remorseful or romantic sense. Rather it allows our lives to be drawn into the real drama of history, by allowing the grace of the crucified and risen Lord to flow through our lives and into the world, a mystery best captured by the Pauline declaration to which we have alluded repeatedly in the pages above: "I live, now no longer I, but Christ lives in me" (Gal 2:20). "Christology," writes John Zizioulas, "emerges as the only way of fulfilling the human drive to personhood."[4] In other words, as Balthasar observes:

---

4 Zizioulas, *Communion and Otherness*, 108–9.

> The man who concentrates on himself in the attempt to know himself better and thus, perhaps, to undertake some moral improvement, will certainly never encounter God; he will have to start again, from a totally different angle, if he wants to find God's will. But if he earnestly seeks God's will in his word, he will — incidentally, as it were — realize himself and find himself (as far as he needs to).[5]

Balthasar's "as far as he needs to" is an almost playful reminder that there is nothing amiss when one remains something of a mystery to himself. No such parenthesis was warranted for those who inscribed the admonition "know thyself" at the entrance to the temple of Apollo at Delphi, precisely because the pagan world was spiritually incapable of understanding either the meaning of history or the nature of personhood. On the other hand, the grace of mission, Balthasar reminds us, is unabashedly situated in history: "If Christian revelation is to take place in history and be received by the human heart, it must incorporate certain anthropological structures prepared beforehand for this supernatural light."[6] We turn, therefore, to a series of short reflections on those preordained "anthropological structures" that foster the forms of personhood to which we are called and for which we are aided by the sacramental life of the Church.

---

5 Balthasar, *Prayer*, 115.
6 Balthasar, *The Christian and Anxiety*, 23.

26 The Mother's Smile

> The sweetest thing in all my life has been the longing — to reach the Mountain, to find the place where all the beauty came from — my country... the place where I ought to have been born. Do you think it all meant nothing, all the longing? The longing for home? For indeed it now feels not like going, but like going back.[1]
>
> — C. S. Lewis

WHY DOES IT FEEL LIKE GOING BACK? WHY does the longing feel like a sweet and elusive memory? When Paul Evdokimov spoke of the "nostalgia to become a person," he surely had in mind a longing inscribed on the human heart by those "anthropological structures prepared beforehand" of which Balthasar spoke. We long for them because we each have a destiny, a calling, and these antecedent anthropological structures are immensely favorable to the inculcation of the morally ordered, selfless, and generous virtues conducive to the fulfillment of that calling.

The French psychiatrist Jean-Michel Oughourlian collaborated with René Girard on one of the latter's most important books, *Things Hidden Since the Foundation of the World*. In a book Oughourlian published almost forty years later, he argued that the tendency to divide brain function into the cognitive brain and the emotional brain was inadequate, and that a third function — the mimetic brain — deserved to be further investigated. In the course of his argument, Oughourlian spoke of the mother's role in the life of the child in terms that are strikingly congruent with the Balthasarian analysis we are trying to explicate: "This maternal love will in some sense be 'stored' in the second brain to be dispensed throughout the child's life: it will be a source of positive feelings like the capacity for loving, and positive emotions; in all circumstances it will be anxiety-decreasing and reassuring, removing fear."[2]

---

1 C. S. Lewis, *Till We Have Faces* (San Francisco: HarperOne, 2017), 86–87.
2 Oughourlian, *The Mimetic Brain*, 55.

The Mother's Smile

Balthasar was no less insistent on the lifelong effect of maternal affection, especially as communicated by the joy the smiling face of the mother transmitted. Nothing was more important for the child's spiritual maturation than the effect on the newborn infant of his mother's smile, as are its many repetitions in the early stages of an infant's life. By his account, the mother's smile gives the child his first experience of the goodness of existence, and it is the origin of a longing to retain or regain access to the "place where all the beauty came from."

> The little child awakens to self-consciousness through being addressed by the love of his mother... everything — "I" and "Thou" and the world — is lit up from this lightening flash of the origin with a ray so brilliant and whole that it also includes a disclosure of God.... This awareness is joined to the primal experience that one has arrived at participation in the world-fellowship of beings by means of a summons coming from outside one's own "I." It is not through the perfection of one's own power that one has entered this fellowship.[3]

Scientific corroboration for Balthasar's emphasis on the early mother-child relationship was forthcoming from the behavioral psychologist Herbert S. Terrance. Where Balthasar focused on the mother's smile, for Terrance what was uniquely human — from a strictly evolutionary point of view — was the mother's *cradling* of the child. A few citations from Terrance's work will help bring out the salience of Balthasar's more "sacramental" understanding of the early mother-infant relationship. Terrance begins with what is known about human evolution.

> The volume of hominin brains began to increase about 3 million years ago. Once its size exceeded 1,000 cc (in *Homo erectus*), the relatively small size of the birth canal limited the size of an infant's brain. For humans, this meant that most brain development occurred postnatally. In addition to brain volume, the development of the motor system was limited as well. Human infants, unlike other newborn primates, have to be cradled for the first six months of their lives.[4]

---

3   Hans Urs von Balthasar, *Explorations in Theology*, III: *Creator Spirit*, trans. Brian McNeil, C.R.V. (San Francisco: Ignatius Press, 1993), 15, 19.
4   Herbert S. Terrance, *Why Chimpanzees Can't Learn Language and Only Humans Can* (New York: Columbia University Press, 2019), 208.

Terrance points out that cradling "had an unexpected advantage." "Cradling and, in particular, shared eye gaze contribute to a dramatic example of intersubjectivity right after birth. In a classic experiment, [child psychologist, Andrew] Meltzoff showed that infants can imitate another's facial expression a mere 42 minutes after birth."[5]

Perhaps the most fascinating convergence of the behavioral psychologist and Catholic theologian is when Terrance notes: "While being cradled, infants have a close view of the mother's face, of her eyes in particular. Shared eye gaze allows mother and infant to take turns sharing *affect*."[6] The importance of this early experience and the enduring handicaps when the process is impaired come to light when Terrance remarks:

> Visual and auditory expressions of affect have been shown to be highly coordinated in studies of smiling, head turning, moving limbs, touching, vocalization, and so on. Experiments in which that coordination was interrupted reveal a deleterious effect, as, for example, when a mother momentarily exhibits a "still face" while interacting with her infant. During the still-face interval, infants immediately begin to struggle to recapture the reciprocity of affect they normally experience.[7]

There is something heartbreaking about this. So much human anguish is due to our "struggle to recapture the reciprocity of affect." Or in C. S. Lewis's words: "the longing — to reach the Mountain, to find the place where all the beauty came from." Again, this is consonant with the mystery of mother and child on which Balthasar placed so much emphasis. We are capable of love only insofar as we have been loved. Writes Conor Sweeney, lecturer at the John Paul II Institute for Marriage and Family in Melbourne, Australia:

> The occlusion of the mother's smile is the death of sacramental presence. The mother's smile is the kiss of Being, the sign or symbol of all that is gratuitous, all that is gift, and therefore all that is non-calculative, non-mechanical, and non-violent. Its erasure therefore erodes the sacramental foundation of grace.[8]

---

5 Ibid., 115.
6 Ibid., 134. Emphasis added.
7 Ibid., 135.
8 Conor Sweeney, *Sacramental Presence after Heidegger: Onto-theology, Sacraments, and the Mother's Smile* (Eugene, OR: Cascade Books, 2015), 225.

The Mother's Smile

"In the mother's smile," writes Balthasar, "it dawns on the [child] that there is a world into which he is accepted and in which he is welcome, and it is in this primordial experience that he becomes aware of himself for the first time."[9] The mother's smile is, so to speak, nature's sacrament. With it the child enters a world loved and affirmed at the deepest and most ineradicable level. Without it, the most promising mitigating efforts notwithstanding, the child's ontological circumstances will be impaired. As Margaret Turek has argued: "It is the parent's initiative of self-giving, a 'work' of parental love expressed in a manner as simple as smiling at the little child, that induces the child to give himself reciprocally, to smile back at his parent as an answer of love to love."[10]

"All desire," wrote Connor Sweeney, "can thus be said to be rooted in the mother's smile." However the child thereafter expresses his life, directs his desires, and fills out his unique individual existence, the signature of the mother's smile will remain inscribed in his life. Thereafter, the responsibility for preserving this treasure and shielding it from cynicism and skepticism will fall to the person to whom such blessings have been bequeathed. The spiritual and sacramental fruits of this imprinted experience will depend in no small part on the quality of the social, moral, and cultural environment in which the child matures and lives. Writes Sweeney:

> Once the mother's smile has been betrayed, the sacramental glory of creation can no longer attest to the revelation of Jesus Christ.... When this happens, time can no longer mediate an event outside of it. Desire closes in on itself and, denied its authentic longing, becomes narcissistic, destructive, and violent.[11]

In this sense a culture neglectful of religious transcendence renders those under its spell impervious to the great mysteries of human existence, not least the mystery at the heart of Christianity. Indeed, writes Sweeney: "The person who has not experienced or accepted his mother's smile will for that matter have a more difficult time experiencing or accepting the possibility of a 'smile' from the Christian narrative."[12] As Balthasar would argue, the mother's smile is the first intimation of

---

9 Balthasar and Ratzinger, *Mary: The Church at the Source*, 102–3.
10 Margaret M. Turek, *Atonement: Soundings in Biblical, Trinitarian, and Spiritual Theology* (San Francisco: Ignatius Press, 2022), 134.
11 Sweeney, *Sacramental Presence*, 236.
12 Ibid., 237.

the reality revealed by Christ: namely that we are loved by God, in relation to whom it is possible to live and move and have our being with the greatest latitude and peace of mind. In fact, one would not be wrong to see many of the pernicious cultural influences of our age as expressions of a reflexive antipathy for the principles of biblical moral anthropology first adumbrated by the mother's smile.

27 Misconceptions:
ANTINATAL RITES

> Without the family there is no first order of affectivity.
> — Paul Kraus[1]

> Grace and nature are bound to collide once they quit their christological orbit.
> — Douglas Farrow[2]

IN 2015, JOSEPH BOTTUM CITED A PIECE THAT appeared in the *Boston Globe* on Mother's Day of that year. It was written by Kathleen McCartney, the president of Smith College:

> Motherhood is a cultural invention. It reflects a belief adopted by society that is passed down from one generation to the next. In US culture, we hold to the idea that young children are better off when cared for exclusively by their mothers. Mothers are bombarded by this message in the media, especially in programming directed to them.... Mother's Day is a good day to double down on the work required to reconstruct our conception of motherhood.[3]

Bottum noted that the family had been attacked in the past — he mentioned Plato and Schopenhauer and he could have added Karl Marx, Friedrich Engels, Margaret Sanger, Herbert Marcuse, Michel Foucault and their epigones. What struck Bottum was that the current assault on the world's oldest and most trustworthy institution was not accompanied by an alternative. Of course, these despisers of the family are all heirs of Jean-Jacques Rousseau, but Rousseau was at least honest enough to

---

1 Kraus, "Marxism and the Gender Revolution."
2 Farrow, *Theological Negotiations*, 64.
3 Kathleen McCartney, "Time to rethink our social construct of Motherhood," *Boston Globe*, May 6, 2015.

openly declare that the State would henceforth be the alternative to the family and the Church.

―――

Underwritten as it is by instinct and hormones, the maternal bond that is awakened during pregnancy and especially in childbirth is so powerful that suppressing the smile and preventing its lasting effect on both mother and child is no small task. Only a social force of great hypnotic power could seriously subvert the motherly instincts and the feminine gift for nurturing. To succeed, such a power would have to declare itself a moral crusade of great political urgency. Thus, in due course did the legitimate effort to grant women the full panoply of rights and responsibilities, of which they had theretofore been deprived, devolve into a political movement increasingly separated from both moral and anthropological reality. The widespread instrumentalization of sexual relations, and the abortion-on-demand movement that was its all but inevitable sequel, poisoned the cultural well in incalculable ways, and alienated millions of women from their deepest, most personally enriching, and culturally precious sensibilities.

As Carrie Gress has rightly observed: "there must be something more than simple human vice behind the fact that millions of women have betrayed the most sacred and fundamental of relationships, that of mother and child."[4] In Gress's view, the women's movement was roiled from the outset with different expectations on the part of the women involved. This internal conflict within the movement persisted "until they all found one topic to which they could hitch their wagons: *abortion*."[5] That a collection of otherwise acrimonious demands for a more expansive role of women in cultural life overcame internal differences by agreeing on the right to end the life of the child in the womb may seem incomprehensible. As Girard's work shows, however, this is a shockingly explicit return to the most savage forms of the ancient world's sacrificial unanimity.

Once the campaign to instrumentalize conjugal intimacy by the introduction of artificial contraception had severed the marital act from its natural purpose, the next step followed. By convincing mothers that it was morally licit to end the life of their child, the denigration of the

---

4   Carrie Gress, *The Anti-Mary Exposed: Rescuing the Culture from Toxic Femininity* (Charlotte, NC: TAN Books, 2019), xv.
5   Ibid., xi.

feminine was complete. Just as cults often require initiates to demonstrate their allegiance by solemnly affirming or performing acts morally censured by the larger society, so the more radical forms of feminism found in abortion and related transgressions of common decency the litmus test for their "cause with a capital 'C'." Nothing short of this cultic sleight of hand could have convinced women to abandon their most life-affirming instincts, and to do so, if necessary, at a time when maternal emotions were being awakened by hormones of no small emotional magnitude and spiritual promise.

The oldest and most reflexive method for fashioning a consensus where disparate priorities exist is to find an object of execration on which all can unite in transferring their animosity. As the woman's so-called right to abortion moved to the center of the women's movement, the passion and hyperbolic rhetoric of the movement focused on abortion opponents. In a battle against a perceived enemy, acts otherwise regarded as odious become morally acceptable. In short, for the abortion regime to spread as widely as it did, it was necessary to frame it as a fight for women — the very women whose deeply imbedded proclivities the movement was assaulting. This "movement" or cult would need to sublimate motherly instincts in the name of womanly emancipation and champion a "right" to complete autonomy ostensibly threatened by vestiges of moral or legal decency that Christianity had fostered for two millennia. That Christianity remains today the source of the moral and anthropological principle at issue explains why the most radical voices of the women's movement have become explicitly hostile to traditional Christianity, which has opposed abortion for two thousand years.

As for the complicity of the media in the anthropological absurdities that have overwhelmed the commonsense of ordinary citizens and betrayed the most basic moral and anthropological realities, Carrie Gress provides an illuminating instance:

> Sue Ellen Browder, author of *Subverted: How I Helped the Sexual Revolution Hijack the Women's Movement* and former employee at *Cosmopolitan*, said that when she worked at the magazine, she regularly fabricated stories about fictional women known as the Cosmo Girl. "I could make her into anything I wanted her to be — a doctor, lawyer, judge, even a high-priced call girl — but there were two things she could not be if she was going to be glamorous, sophisticated, and cool: a virgin or a mother."[6]

---

6   Ibid., Kindle edition §68ff.

THE APOCALYPSE OF THE SOVEREIGN SELF

A few decades after Sylvia Plath resisted the appeal of domesticity — *The Joy of Cooking* — and renounced motherhood until she surpassed her chief mimetic model, Virginia Woolf — "*No children until I have done it*" — these impulses began manifesting their darker dimension.

Eventually, nothing can expel a religion except another religion, regardless of how anti-religious its zealous converts fancy themselves to be. Gress quotes an article by Mallory Millett, younger sister of the early feminist icon Kate Millett, the author of *Sexual Politics*. Millett describes a meeting in 1969 which might be considered foundational for the sexual revolution. Gress shines a spotlight on one of the earliest and most revealing masterclasses where the self-destruction of the feminine was being ritually celebrated as a feminine triumph and morphing into nihilism in the process. Citing a 2014 article by Millett, Gress writes:

> Twelve (not an insignificant number) highly educated, upper class women sat around a table in New York City and chanted this "litany" to express what they wanted to see happen in the world: "Why are we here today?" the chairwoman asked. "To make revolution," they answered. "What kind of revolution?" she replied. "The Cultural Revolution," they chanted. "And how do we make Cultural Revolution?" she demanded. "By destroying the American family!" they answered. "How do we destroy the family?" she came back. "By destroying the American Patriarch," they cried exuberantly. "And how do we destroy the American Patriarch?" she probed. "By taking away his power!" "How do we do that?" "By destroying monogamy!" they shouted. "How can we destroy monogamy?" "By promoting promiscuity, eroticism, prostitution, abortion and homosexuality!" they resounded. These women had a very clear goal in mind and became the vanguard to what would become the women's liberation movement.[7]

The two categories with which we have associated the apocalypse of the sovereign self are hysteria and nihilism. The 1969 gathering Millett describes is a tangled skein of each: the nihilistic abandonment of all moral norms incompatible with a ritually induced hysterical contagion. We recall the speaker in T. S. Eliot's poem entitled "Hysteria" who feared being drawn into the woman's hysterical laughter by the shaking of her breasts. Alas, the shaking of breasts has only a fraction of the mimetic

---

7 Mallory Millett, "Marxist Feminism's Ruined Lives," *Frontpage Magazine*, September 1, 2014, quoted in Gress, *The Anti-Mary Exposed*, Kindle edition §52ff.

power of the shaking of fists, and what Mallory Millett has described is precisely the mimetic contagion of collective rage confected and propagated by the chairwoman's singsong litany of revolutionary goals. Time and again in recent years this familiar form of street-theater social hypnotism has served to unleash the nihilistic impulses of angry mobs.

Instances of such hysterical rage are common enough today, but most women now involved in the women's movement would be shocked to find that such sentiments were being expressed half a century ago by the founders of their movement. They would be equally shocked to discover how much the movement began with the same crude and mindless sing-song repetition of the chants, slogans, and incantations that have distinguished virtually every act of cultural sabotage since the French Revolution. Girard would have no trouble recognizing this collective chanting as the mind-numbing attempt to inculcate in its adherents a social solidarity cemented, not by genuine concord, but by shared animosity.

Of course, the attack on the family has a long history. Paul Kraus cites a book Karl Marx wrote in the middle of the nineteenth century, but which wasn't published until 1932, *The German Ideology*. Therein Marx argued that sexual difference was at the heart of all oppressive inequality and that liberation from that oppression required the nullification of sexual difference and the dismantling of the nuclear family. Among the twentieth-century disciples of Marx in this regard were Simone de Beauvoir and Shulamith Firestone, the latter of whom Kraus quotes:

> In the case of feminism the problem is a moral one: the biological family unit has always oppressed women and children, but now, for the first time in history, technology has created real preconditions for overthrowing these oppressive "natural" conditions, along with their cultural reinforcements. In the case of the new ecology, we find that independent of any moral stance, for pragmatic — survival — reasons alone, it has become necessary to free humanity from the tyranny of its biology.[8]

Not only is this a sterling example of the nihilism which we have argued is the end stage of the determination to liberate the sovereign self from anything that would infringe on its autonomy, but it reveals one of the persistent specters that the ideologues invoke in justification for the cultural vandalism they champion: planetary survival, which,

---

8   Kraus, "Marxism and the Gender Revolution."

it is argued, demands the dismantling of even the most basic anthropological realities. Of course, it is a conspicuous manifestation as well of the Gnostic impulse, one which the transhuman movement would eventually champion. Moreover, as Kraus perceptively notes:

> The dream of the self-making self and the dream of a world free from the inequality wrought by the gender division is orthodox Marxism. The (un)intended consequence of this war is that *without the family there is no first order of affectivity*; so, love dies in the modern world as well because love is intensely particular and borne from that sexual division of labor and the family that Marxism seeks to eradicate.[9]

The anti-natal animus that solidified the women's movement was easily transferable to ideologically allied movements. As of this writing, a relatively small but by no means insignificant number of mostly young women are renouncing motherhood today out of concern for the future of "the planet." An online group known by its hashtag moniker "#NoFutureNoChildren" has the following heartbreaking slogan on its website:

> *Because even though I want to have children more than anything — what kind of a mother would I be if I brought a baby into a world where I couldn't make sure they were safe?*

How many women down through history knew for certain that the children they were bringing into the world would be safe? Even though a tiny few might have harbored illusions of this sort, the answer is none. What kind of mother would bring children into the world where she couldn't make sure they were safe? Every kind. The bringing of children into the world is the supreme manifestation of hope. A categorical refusal to do so is an unmistakable sign of hopelessness. The renunciation of motherhood by young women who fully acknowledge their desire for children is made even more tragic by the fact that every serious demographer now foresees a catastrophic demographic death-spiral in the twenty-first century and beyond, with very dire consequences for those living in an increasingly childless and aging world.

As we have tried to indicate, the attenuation of Western culture's religious patrimony has been ongoing for centuries. There are reasons to suspect, however, that the abortion on demand regime has been a

---

9   Ibid.

major — arguably *the* major — contributor to the precipitous moral and spiritual decline of American culture that occurred with such breathtaking speed after abortion was legalized in the 1973 Roe v. Wade U.S. Supreme Court decision. To persuade even expectant mothers that hiring medical professionals to kill the child in the womb is morally unproblematic is to inflict irreparable harm on the capacity for rational and moral judgment. Though moral disintegration in once Christian cultures has been ongoing for a very long time, the precipitous decline in both the moral and rational faculties that occurred in the aftermath of the 1973 Supreme Court decision is especially shocking and symbolic of the civilizational crisis in the midst of which we are now living.

Though the Supreme Court overturned Roe v. Wade and returned the abortion debate to the states in the Dobbs v. Jackson Women's Health Organization case, the nihilism and hysteria that has lately characterized the abortion debate continues to roil our public discourse. In August of 2021, two organizations — Judicial Watch and the Center for Medical Progress — released details of a federally funded born-alive organ-harvesting program at the University of Pittsburgh, one of many. We will not subject the reader to the horrors of this program, except to say that it involved organ harvesting on late-term unborn children while their hearts were still beating. This savagery bears mention, however, because what the word *nihilism* often conjures up is crude and senseless destruction by vandals and mobs. Though there is plenty of competition for the distinction, evidence suggests that the most morally and culturally poisonous nihilism today is being carried out and justified by elite corporations, educational institutions, and non-profits: whited sepulchers, run by white-collar and white-coat nihilists.

We have posited throughout that the determined effort to repudiate the Judeo-Christian foundations of Western culture ends in nihilism in one or another of its variations. There are two broad categories into which nihilism might be placed. The first is soft nihilism, which appears to the casual observer to be nothing more than the expansion of "rights" or acceptance of behavior theretofore regarded as improper, incompatible with cultural norms or outright illegitimate. It goes without saying that this form of nihilism is only rarely recognized as such. Indeed, its champions welcome it as the elimination of putative barriers to personal freedom and the legitimation of practices immune to the sanctions or revulsion such practices have long elicited in the inheritors of the Judeo-Christian tradition. The nihilism at the heart of the purported freedom only becomes apparent over time. A more honest and frank form of nihilism — of the Nietzschean kind — revels in the moral offense it gives to those whose ethical and rational faculties it has yet to corrupt. It is the kind of nihilism that Dostoevsky exposed in his novels.

Coincidentally, in the same year that the U.S. Supreme Court established an abortion license the Rumanian philosopher, E. M. Cioran, published a book entitled *The Trouble with Being Born*, an augury of the frank nihilism prefigured by the abortion regime. Written in an aphoristic style, Cioran argues that, since suffering outweighs pleasure in human life, on balance the most compassionate thing we can do for our progeny is to prevent their birth. To reduce life to suffering and pleasure is to ignore what is most ennobling and meaningful: love, empathy, self-sacrifice, and a myriad of other experiences that can in no way be subsumed under the categories of suffering and pleasure.

One of the leaders of the anti-natal movement today is David Benatar, a professor of philosophy at the University of Cape Town in South Africa. The preface of Professor Benatar's 2008 book, *Better Never to Have Been: The Harm of Coming into Existence*, encapsulates his argument and reveals its underlying nihilism:

> Each of us was harmed by being brought into existence. That harm is not negligible, because the quality of even the best lives is very bad — and considerably worse than most people recognize it to be. Although it is obviously too late to prevent our own existence, it is not too late to prevent the existence of future possible people. Creating new people is thus morally problematic. In this book I argue for these claims and show why the usual responses to them — incredulity, if not indignation — are defective.
>
> Given the deep resistance of the views I shall be defending, I have no expectation that this book or its arguments will have any impact on baby-making. Procreation will continue undeterred, causing a vast amount of harm. I have written this book, then, not under the illusion that it will make (much) difference to the number of people there will be but rather from the opinion that what I have to say needs to be said whether or not it is accepted.

It is characteristic of elite nihilists to scoff at those they regard as lacking their sophistication and for being naïve enough to be satisfied with their lives. Benatar exemplifies this perfectly when he declares that life is "worse than most people recognize it to be." Faculty lounge nihilism is hardly rare today, but seldom is it stated so explicitly. Its consequences — both spiritual and cultural — are so horrendous that speaking of them may seem cruel, but in times such as ours, the truth must be spoken. Matthew Schmitz has done so: "More than any previous generation, millennials will die alone: unattended by the spouses they never married, unremembered by the children they never had, unconsoled by thoughts of a God they never knew. Having inherited little, they will pass down less."[10]

---

[10] Matthew Schmitz, "The Life of Julie," *The American Conservative*, February 18, 2022.

28 The Father's Patrimony

> What is happening to America is an excruciatingly painful truth that life without father, Father, and filial piety toward country are not the socially neutral options that contemporary liberalism holds them to be. The sinkhole into which all three have collapsed is now a public hazard.
> — Mary Eberstadt[1]

> I think that we can assign a truly theological meaning to the "death of the father" that a certain Western philosophy demands. In truth, this is about the ancient, destructive desire to receive nothing from anyone so as to owe nothing to anyone.
> — Robert Cardinal Sarah[2]

FEW INFORMED PEOPLE WOULD DENY THE INDISpensability of the mother's role in the life of the infant, notwithstanding the heroic effort of the child's father and others in the absence of the mother. The importance of the father's role in preparing the child for the privileges and responsibilities of personhood has often been less widely recognized. The mother's smile gives the child his first glimmer of God's love and the gifted character of his life. Her smile is the seed that will bear fruit throughout the life of the child, the more so if the father fulfills his role as the guardian and protector of the sanctuaries of home, family, community, faith, and the sundry associations that personalize and enrich the life of his children. In sum, the father's role is to ensure that his children receive their cultural, spiritual, and familial inheritance.

The smile of the mother can awaken the soul and endow it with a longing that nothing in this world can ever fully satisfy. An important

---

[1] Mary Eberstadt, *Adam and Eve after the Pill, Revisited* (San Francisco: Ignatius Press, 2022), 120.
[2] Robert Cardinal Sarah, *The Day Is Far Spent*, trans. Michael J. Miller (San Francisco: Ignatius Press, 2019), 155.

feature of the father's task, one he obviously shares with the mother, is that of gradually turning the longing awakened by the mother's smile upward, so to speak, helping the child to discover in prayer and religious devotion the true and original source of the love which the mother's smile inaugurated. To seek to find something comparable by looking *around*, or by looking *up* only so far as to see those on a higher or more socially prestigious station, will almost certainly disappoint, and it will prevent the most precious spiritual and sacramental fruits of the mother's smile from having their full effect. Not infrequently, moreover, in their effort to awaken a religious acuity in the child, the parents reawaken or deepen — individually and as a couple — their own religious sensibilities.

The mother's influence has priority both temporally and emotionally. And her maternal circumstance has provided her with hormonal and emotional resources for responding to her newborn child with an almost otherworldly love. The father's role vis-à-vis the mother and child is secondary but indispensable. The binary gender specificity of these roles is not absolute, but neither is it insignificant. The mystery to which it gives access is sufficiently delicate to be warped when these intrinsic features are overridden or overlooked.

It is hardly surprising that the abortion regime that has sunk its roots into our cultural life has also played a role in the attenuation of the fatherly responsibilities. Not only has readily accessible abortion on demand encouraged both mothers and fathers to consider this ghastly way of avoiding responsibility, but it has virtually silenced the father's voice in the matter. Some challenges to this situation have recently been made, but for now the decision to abort is left entirely to the mother. Doubtless the decision weighs more heavily on her than on the father of the child, but the bracketing of his opinion in the matter serves to exempt him from responsibility, further depreciating the cultural status of the father, and shattering the integrity of *the* most essential unit of social life, the natural family.

Whereas the mother smiles, the father speaks; initially and archetypally he speaks the child's name. The mother's bond with the child is deeper than speech. She too speaks the child's name, but she does so as one who is always already intimate with the child. The father speaks the child's name from outside the intimate bond of mother and child. He speaks as the archetypal representative of the world beyond that bond: the cultural and social world, at the threshold of which the father stands.

THE APOCALYPSE OF THE SOVEREIGN SELF

In *The Discovery of the Individual 1050 – 1200*, Colin Morris writes: "The training of the child is usually directed to his learning the traditions of the tribe, so that he may find his identity, not in anything peculiar to himself, but in the common mind of his people."[3] Morris cites the advice given to his son by a West African father:

> There is a certain form of behaviour to observe, and certain ways of acting in order that the guiding spirit of our race may approach you also.... If you desire the guiding spirit of our race to visit you one day, if you desire to inherit it in your turn, you will have to conduct yourself in the selfsame manner; from now on, it will be necessary for you to be more and more in my company.[4]

It falls to the father to provide that "continuity with past and future" which Sylvia Plath longed to find. It is surely no coincidence that perhaps Plath's most famous poem is a ferocious attack on her father. Written a few months before her suicide, the poem — "Daddy" — seethes with rage and contempt.

> But they pulsed me out of the sack,
> And they stuck me together with glue.
> And then I knew what to do.
> I made a model of you,
> A man in black with a *Meinkampf* look
> And a love of the rack and the screw.
> And I said I do, I do.
> So daddy I'm finally through.
> The black telephone's off at the root,
> The voices just can't worm through.[5]

For all its savagery, this is a heartbreaking poem, a tour de force of rage and longing. How and why Plath came to hate her father with such fury isn't entirely clear. What is clear, however, is that she felt herself to be deeply wounded by her father's inaccessibility. We mention this poem simply to give some background to her expressed longing for "continuity with past and future." Or, as she says in this poem: "The

---

3 Colin Morris, *The Discovery of the Individual 1050 – 1200* (Toronto: University of Toronto Press, 1972), 1.
4 Camara Laye, *The Dark Child* (New York: Farrar, Straus and Giroux, 1954), 26, quoted in Morris, *The Discovery of the Individual 1050 – 1200*, 2.
5 Quoted in Andrew Spacey, "Analysis of Poem 'Daddy' by Sylvia Plath," *Owlcation*, September 4, 2020.

voices [that] just can't worm through." Whatever Plath might have meant by this, she writes as one deprived of the father's role in mediating the ancestral, familial, and cultural voices that serve to ground one's life within a larger tradition.

Sylvia Plath's life was so troubled that it almost seems inappropriate to cite her experience as in any way indicative of a broader cultural and spiritual problem, but, just as Rousseau, Nietzsche, and others presage the crisis in the midst of which we are living, the depth of Plath's spiritual and psychological torment brings to light in a most palpable way what can happen when the fatherly role is betrayed. Nor can we overlook Plath's plaintive cry, longing to escape from a freedom that had become a prison for her. Everywhere she might have wanted to turn for solace and guidance had been anathematized by the progressive arbiters of culture, as the salient passage from her earlier quoted lament makes clear: the mother's skirts, fatherly guidance, the Church now too liberal and free to turn the eyes upward — leaving only some crude form of self-sacrifice in service to some "Cause with a capital 'C'." Home, mother, paternal directive, Church, each is a facet of what Balthasar called those "anthropological structures prepared beforehand for supernatural light."

All real wisdom is ancient wisdom, and the task of *familiarizing* the child with such wisdom falls — archetypally — to the father. Over time, the father narrates, recalls, and situates the child in history and tradition vis-à-vis his ancestors while inculcating a sense of responsibility for preserving what is healthy in that heritage and rescuing it from whatever historical betrayals might have sullied its memory. In the unique bond she has with her child the mother conveys that he or she is loved and that the love is an unqualified and irrevocable gift. It is a fatherly responsibility, on the other hand, to provide the child with a cultural, moral, and historical patrimony — an inheritance: an appreciation for the transgenerational *drama* in which the child's life is situated. The father prepares the child to *perform* whatever might be his unique role as a bridge connecting his ancestors and descendants. His message is "*You belong*, and this gift of belonging will require something from you, and I am here to help you learn how to meet your responsibilities." For indeed, the most unique among us are those who forswear the desire to be unique, aspiring instead to fulfill the responsibilities commensurate with the mission to which they feel called.

THE APOCALYPSE OF THE SOVEREIGN SELF

In a myriad of ways childless or unmarried women continue to bring the feminine and motherly resources to bear on those whose lives they touch and on the culture at large, often in exceptional ways. And even though the male or fatherly contribution is less underwritten by instinct, single or celibate men, unless otherwise wounded by fathers or father figures, can perform in exceptional ways the task of transmitting cultural traditions and resources. One example of this merits mention.

As an act of reverence for the papal office and often enough out of genuine respect for its occupant, Catholics refer to the pope as the Holy Father. Few popes have fulfilled their paternal role with more distinction than did Saint Pope John Paul II. In the early pages of his first encyclical, *Redemptor hominis*, he left us an example of the fatherly role, albeit in terms of his particular responsibilities as the Roman pontiff. In taking the papal mantle and following tradition, he chose an official name, but his choice and the reasoning he offered for choosing it betoken an exquisite understanding of the fatherly role:

> I chose the same names that were chosen by my beloved Predecessor John Paul I. Indeed, as soon as he announced to the Sacred College on 26 August 1978 that he wished to be called John Paul — such a double name being unprecedented in the history of the Papacy — I saw in it a clear presage of grace for the new pontificate. Since that pontificate lasted barely 33 days, it falls to me not only to continue it but in a certain sense to take it up again at the same starting point. This is confirmed by my choice of these two names. By following the example of my venerable Predecessor in choosing them, I wish like him to express my love for the unique inheritance left to the Church by Popes John XXIII and Paul VI and my personal readiness to develop that inheritance with God's help.
>
> Through these two names and two pontificates I am linked with the whole tradition of the Apostolic See and with all my Predecessors in the expanse of the twentieth century and of the preceding centuries. I am connected, through one after another of the various ages back to the most remote, with the line of the mission and ministry that confers on Peter's See an altogether special place in the Church.[6]

---

6 John Paul II, *Redemptor Hominis*, §2.

This exquisite recognition of one's place in a living tradition stands in stark contrast to the weary effort to distinguish oneself by the thousand and one little rituals of dis-identification that produce the hollow men of our time. It is a vivid reminder of the ennobling power of a venerable tradition.

In light of the etymological and historical affinity between the role of the *actor* and the mystery of the *person* on which we reflected earlier, it is perhaps worth remembering that Karol Wojtyła, the future Saint Pope John Paul II, who was to become an icon of Christian faith, morally dominating the "world stage" at the end of the twentieth century and the beginning of the twenty-first even while succumbing to age and infirmity — and whose first important book was entitled *The Acting Person* — had been an actor, playwright, and director as a young man. To echo Zizioulas, is this mere coincidence? We recall the words of Gabriel Marcel who related the words of scripture "Ye are not your own" to the actor on the stage. This sense of continuity is what every father willing to take up the much-maligned patriarchal task must try to awaken in his children.

The father's responsibility to both the mother and the child is threefold. First, it falls to him to foster and safeguard a peaceful home, one in which the love and promise awakened in the child by the mother's smile can grow into an enduring predicate for the child's life and the life of the family. Then, beyond the task of preserving and protecting the home from whatever forces antithetical to its spiritual tranquility might threaten, it falls to the parents and traditionally to the father of the family to influence to the degree possible the larger social and cultural environments with a determination equal to the proximity and spiritual consequence of these influences. And finally, no less important is the need to familiarize his children with their cultural, religious, and familial heritage — their spiritual patrimony.

Again, there is nothing inherently either masculine or feminine about any of these fatherly tasks save for the average male's physiological advantages in repelling physical danger and in shielding the mother from harsher realities that might distract from the nurturing tasks for which she is uniquely endowed. Nonetheless, the fact that we use the word patrimony for the spiritual treasures received from prior generations should not be dismissed as nothing more than a vestige of gender inequality.

We fully recognize the heroic efforts being made today by many single parents, for whom the complementarity of spousal and parental responsibilities is not available. Indeed, the author of these pages was raised by a single mother, his father having been killed in war, and he is well aware of both the heroism involved in single parenting and of its almost unavoidable disadvantages. Far from suggesting that single-parenthood is comparable to the natural family, the heroic status rightly accorded single-parents bespeaks the inherent disadvantages both for the children involved and for the parent who must try to fill both roles. We can salute the heroism without assigning normative status to the situation that made the heroism necessary.

But what is being demanded today is that we grant normative status to increasingly preposterous alternatives to the natural family. The prospect of medically assisted procreation and the legal recognition of new in vitro fertilization techniques raise the specter of children entirely cut off from any contact with their biological parents. That this can be seriously contemplated indicates how alienated we have become from moral and anthropological commonsense. The Permanent Council of the French Bishops' Conference complained that the most alarming feature of a piece of legislation under consideration would legalize "filiation without a father, or paternal ancestry, and of motherhood through a simple declaration of will, before a notary." The archbishop of Paris, Monsignor Michel Aupetit, decried as monstrous the "act of voluntarily inflicting on children the painful absence of the father."[7] In the years ahead, those shocked or offended by the archbishop's adjective will likely be confronted by evidence of his perspicacity.

As perilous as is the situation we face today, analogues and harbingers of it exist. It is fitting, therefore, to hearken back to a similarly ominous time, one that led one of our finest poets to reflect wisely on his fatherly responsibility and his hope for his newborn child. Two days after the birth of his daughter Anne in 1919, William Butler Yeats wrote his poem "Prayer for My Daughter." The devastation of Europe in World War I was a recent and bitter memory, and the Anglo-Irish War was raging, which seems to the poet to be symbolized by a raging storm. The poem can be read as the ruminations of a new father as he comes to terms with the responsibilities that will fall to him to shelter his child from the coarseness and vulgarity of a world in turmoil.

---

[7] *Info Chretienne*, Bioéthique: Pour Michel Aupetit, archevêque de Paris, «si nous nous taisons, les pierres crieront» January 17, 2020, www.infochretienne.com/articles/bioethique-pour-michel-aupetit-archeveque-de-paris-si-nous-nous-taisons-les-pierres-crieront/.

The Father's Patrimony

> Once more the storm is howling, and half hid
> Under this cradle-hood and coverlid
> My child sleeps on. There is no obstacle
> But Gregory's Wood and one bare hill
> Whereby the haystack and roof-levelling wind,
> Bred on the Atlantic, can be stayed;
> And for an hour I have walked and prayed
> Because of the great gloom that is in my mind.

Yeats frets over his responsibility as father, which he here exercises by speaking an *ordering word* out of a father's innate impulse to fashion a world — domestically, economically, politically, and religiously — in the safety of which the mother's smile can have its full and lasting effect in the life of the child.

Yeats's poem has its timeless appeal because it presents us with a morally principled father, fully aware of his familial responsibilities, coming to realize that the protection of his child from both physical and moral dangers has fallen to him. If the mother's smile is more primary and more indispensable to the flourishing of the child's life, the father's task of insulating his family against forces — physical, moral, and cultural — injurious to the healthy development of his children will be mediated by cultural traditions far more subject to corruption than is the maternal instinct by which the mother's smile is inwardly prompted.

In a subsequent stanza of his poem, Yeats prays that in due course the father of his daughter's children will meet his responsibility to order and safeguard the world around his family.

> And may her bridegroom bring her to a house
> Where all's accustomed, ceremonious;
> For arrogance and hatred are the wares
> Peddled in the thoroughfares.
> How but in custom and in ceremony
> Are innocence and beauty born?
> Ceremony's a name for the rich horn,
> And custom for the spreading laurel tree.

Where either the mother's smile or the father's patrimonial bequests are deficient in one way or another — which is all but inevitable in a fallen world — then to that extent the child's life will be vulnerable to the "arrogance and hatred... peddled in the thoroughfares." To express this in terms of René Girard's anthropological insights, the less "accustomed" and "ceremonious" the life, the more the unfortunate effects of mimetic desire and mimetic rivalry will manifest themselves, leading toward forms of nihilism and hysteria of which we have heretofore spoken.

Over many centuries our civilization, inwardly guided by Christian faith, has gathered about itself impressive instruments for the maintenance of moral and social order: solemn codes of conduct, religious rituals linking contemporaries to their God, their ancestors, and each other, and social memorials expressing gratitude to those from whom cultural blessings have been received — jurisprudential institutions, constabularies, social welfare regimes, political regimes increasingly attentive to the needs and hopes of their members, and so on and so forth. No reasonable person would regard these things as dispensable. And yet today this inheritance is under assault from many quarters.

Christians deepened and enriched the patriarchal principle. Jesus called God Father and taught his disciples to do likewise. The tradition of calling the leader of the Christian community Father was an early one. The appellation would eventually be used for priests. The Church has ever revered the writings and the memory of the Church Fathers, those luminaries of the faith living between the first century of the Christian era and the death of Saint John Damascene in the middle of the eighth century. This reverence for tradition survived largely intact for a millennium. But as Elizabeth Powers has noted:

> Great minds since the eighteenth century have sought to make the self free-standing or to anchor it to art or to a variety of political theories. In doing so, they have succeeded in squandering an immense spiritual inheritance, arduously accumulated since antiquity, that gives substance to the self and makes it whole. Is it any wonder that this legacy, the source of which can be traced back to Abraham, Isaac, and Jacob, should now be anathematized as "patriarchy" by those hoping to usher it off the stage of history?[8]

"The greatest blessing a society can confer on its young," writes Robert Harrison, "is to turn them into the heirs, rather than the orphans, of history."[9]

---

8 Elizabeth Powers, "The Self in Full," *First Things* 97 (November 1999), online at www.firstthings.com/article/1999/11/the-self-in-full.
9 Robert Pogue Harrison, *Juvenescence: The Cultural History of Our Age* (Chicago: University of Chicago Press, 2014), Kindle §79.

> Cultural rejuvenation takes place only if and when a culture acts its age, but a culture cannot act its age unless those who belong to its present learn how old they really are. In revealing our true age to us, education turns us into potential renewers of history. This is above all the case when those who are biologically young acquire an ancient cultural age through their schooling, their reading, or various other means.[10]

Such an education would prepare its beneficiaries for another of the indispensable tasks of preserving and passing on a cultural and spiritual patrimony, namely the task of opposing the corruption of cultural traditions or their replacement by facsimiles antithetical to human fulfillment and happiness. We will return to this theme in our chapter below on the virtue of *pietas*, the duty owed to one's parents, one's country, and one's cultural inheritance.

Before we conclude our reflections on the importance of the maternal and paternal roles in the lives of children, mention must be made of the importance of siblings and the extended network of family relationships that flow from them: aunts, uncles, cousins, and so on. Children can be deprived of these blessings due to circumstances beyond the control of their parents, but both commonsense and widely acknowledged experience suggests that extended families are a source of spiritual and emotional enrichment, and that whatever sacrifices larger families may require of both parents and children, in all but the most troubled of circumstances, all involved will benefit from the greater sense of belonging that large families provide.

---

10 Ibid.

29 The School of Love and Responsibiity

> We do not bring up a child by giving him lectures in morality and deportment, but rather by placing him in an environment having a high tone of conduct and good manners, whose principles, rarely expressed as abstract theories, will be imparted to him by the thousand familiar gestures that clothe them.
>
> — Yves Congar[1]

THE ALARMING NUMBER OF FATHERLESS CHILdren in contemporary western societies has been widely recognized as related to a sharp rise in criminality and other anti-social behaviors among young fatherless males. As disturbing as this must be to anyone who recognizes the emotional and cultural value of family history, it is the final expression of Rousseau's shrugging disregard for parental responsibility and the contempt for the natural family that has been a conspicuous feature of most of the totalitarian regimes of the last two centuries. Rather ominously, a generation ago the poet and critic Richard Howard began a review of a "family memoir" with these words:

> I must acknowledge an interest, or rather a dismay, in discussing this "family memoir," for from experience and from observation I have come to regard the American Nuclear Family in the last 50 years as the enemy of individual determination, of personal autonomy — in short, as a disease.[2]

On the other side of the continent two days after Howard's review appeared in the *Los Angeles Times*, Islamic true believers flew airliners

---

[1] Yves Congar, O.P., *The Meaning of Tradition*, trans. A. N. Woodrow (San Francisco: Ignatius Press, 2004), 22.
[2] Richard Howard, "That Stars Might Sing," *Los Angeles Times*, September 9, 2001. It bears mentioning that Mr. Howard translated the earlier cited 1973 book, *The Trouble with Being Born*, by E. M. Cioran.

into the Pentagon and the Twin Towers of the World Trade Center. 2,977 innocent people were killed in that attack. However intentionally offensive to conventional sensibilities, nothing written by a relatively privileged culture despiser could compare with the evil committed by the Islamic jihadists that day in New York and Washington, DC. Nonetheless, the mind is arrested by the virtual simultaneity of Mr. Howard's rhetorical attacks on the family and the attacks of September 11, 2001. It would be hard to argue that in this case the pen is mightier than the scimitar, but there is nothing tendentious in noticing a certain ideological congruence. The snarling rhetoric of a technically gifted, fashionable, and contemptuous poet left no one dead or injured, though any who might have been inspired by his vitriol may well have come to considerable grief for having done so. At another level, however, one has to recognize that the target of Mr. Howard's rage is far more essential to Western civilization than were the Twin Towers of New York's World Trade Center which the Islamic extremists destroyed two days later. Nor is it possible to argue that the death toll on 9/11 was either more intentional, greater, or more appalling than the thousands of unborn children killed every week in this country, a silent slaughter justified by an ideology of which Mr. Howard's contempt for the family is but one especially vicious variation.

For everyone who openly and consciously holds the natural family in contempt there are thousands who undermine it by defining it out of existence, and — even more astonishingly — by redefining the very meaning of the words man and woman, male and female, husband and wife. Moreover, tinkering with language in such an audacious and irresponsible way — like tinkering with the levers of power or the propagandistic manipulation of "public opinion" — can be a very heady experience. Those who discovered how easily foundational principles and deeply held opinions could be eroded by linguistic legerdemain were spurred by their success to press on to advance ever more radical and ever less plausible revolutions. To date their efforts have been astonishingly successful, though as of this writing healthy signs of a return to sanity are emerging.

Mr. Howard's September 9, 2001 *Los Angeles Times* review was dredged up by Joseph Bottum in a previously cited article highlighting the attack on motherhood by the then-president of Smith College. Mr. Bottum made no mention of the proximity of Howard's splenetic attack on the family to the jihadist attacks that occurred two days later. He did, however, point out that for all his overheated rhetoric, Mr. Howard was not alone in his hostility to the family.

> The family is a premodern arrangement of human life, and the modern turn subjects all premodern things to deconstruction: philosophy, theology, and history; monarchy, nobility, and the Church; culture, art, and society. It just took us this long to dig down to the family. Richard Howard is a late, miniature Voltaire, and the president of Smith College is a tardy, shrunken Jacobin.[3]

Bottum argued that Howard's characterization of the family as a disease relieved him of having to propose an alternative.

> The rage not *for* something new but *against* everything old, hinted at a difference. This was not a messianic promise of having found better ways to live. This was an apocalyptic fury that demands a smashing of the existing ways. The metaphor of disease is telling: We don't propose substitutes for cancerous tumors; we cut them out. Health isn't found in the presence of alternates to disease; it's found in the actual absence of disease. And so the apparent unhappiness of the human condition doesn't need an alternative to family. It just needs to get rid of family.[4]

Such "apocalyptic fury" is an instance of the inevitable nihilism which is the final stage of the resentful determination to destroy any and all obstacles to the will of the sovereign self: the nihilistic hysteria that increasingly characterizes what John Paul II called the culture of death.

The totalitarian horizon of Islam of the strict observance, with its demand for the creation of a worldwide *umma* and the subjection of infidels to dhimmitude status, is widely recognized. What is only today becoming clear is what Bottum implicitly saw in comparing two secular progressives to Voltaire and the Jacobins: the totalitarian spirit at the heart of today's doctrinal secularism, increasingly animated not by a utopian vision but by "apocalyptic fury."

One of Bottum's most important insights deserves special attention, for it helps illuminate the nihilism into which a once buoyant progressivism is collapsing. As the rosy outcome once confidently anticipated by this progressivism encounters the hard realities of the fallen human condition, the dismantling of the past — once rationalized as necessary

---

3 Joseph Bottum, "The Attack on the Family," *Aleteia*, May 25, 2015.
4 Ibid.

to the revolutionary fulfillment — can only feed on the sheer energy of antipathy toward those people and institutions with the temerity to adhere to the perennial anthropological reality enshrined in biblical thought and Christian life.

Nor should we overlook the chief arena in which an anthropological naïveté is degenerating into a raging antipathy for what it thinks is thwarting the consummation of its fantasies. We elsewhere (in *God's Gamble*) noted that the theme of courtly love, derived though it was from non-Western sources, came to full flower only in the Christian West. There we quoted Balthasar to the effect that the "highest realization [of the relationship between the man and the woman] is... an extreme achievement that is made wholly possible only within Christianity."[5] Today, both of the great enemies of the tradition that aspired to this achievement — radical Islam and the sexual revolutionaries now openly at war with the Christianized West — champion a vision of the relationship between the sexes — and between members of the same sex — that is at best arid, barren, and spiritually injurious and at worst heartless, misogynist, exploitative, and oppressive. Inasmuch as the licentious form of this attack is more or less freely chosen, it is doubtlessly preferable to the harshly imposed form found in traditional Islam. The sexual revolutionaries aspire to unrestrained sexual license — destroying thereby the promise of real intimacy — while the heavenly reward that Islam promises the jihadists who die fighting for the worldwide caliphate is a harem of virgins available for their sexual pleasure, a vulgar and inherently misogynist vision to which immature and testosterone-driven males can be expected to be drawn. Both these assaults on the family, however, are deeply corrosive of the human bonds and the moral virtues, without which the West will sink into a pre-totalitarian chaos.

Against that historical backdrop, the emergence in recent years of the Black Lives Matter movement (BLM), among others, represents a further radicalization of the Jacobin spirit. BLM declared in its original manifesto, before some of the more offensive sections were deleted for obvious public relations reasons, its determination to "disrupt the Western-prescribed nuclear family structure" and to "foster a queer-affirming network" free "from the tight grip of heteronormative thinking."[6] That these attacks on commonsense and common decency are related to the

---

5   Hans Urs von Balthasar, *Explorations in Theology*, III: *Creator Spirit*, trans. Brian McNeil, C.R.V. (San Francisco: Ignatius Press, 1993), 17.
6   https://blacklivesmatter.com/what-we-believe/.

themes of hysteria and nihilism, which have occupied us throughout this book, can be underscored by quoting two perceptive observers of contemporary culture. The historian Alan J. Levine has written: "The young field of Critical Race Theory is hyperemotional, even *hysterical*, and utterly unable to grasp the difference between past and present,"[7] while Victor Davis Hanson argued that Critical Legal Theory and Critical Race Theory were "dreamed up by parlor academics to justify the *nihilism*."[8]

As we argued in the first pages of this book, the rise of hysteria and nihilism that has accompanied the dechristianization of a once Christian culture can be traced back to Christ's warning to his own followers: "Abide in me as I abide in you. Just as the branch cannot bear fruit by itself unless it abides in the vine, neither can you unless you abide in me. I am the vine, you are the branches. Those who abide in me and I in them bear much fruit, because apart from me you can do nothing" (Jn 15:4–5).

Not only Christian faith but also the moral, spiritual, and cultural blessings of living in a world under Christian influence are privileges that must not be taken for granted. For when the heightening of human dignity and responsibility that Christianity fosters is neglected or squandered, the result is the nothingness (nihilism) of which the Johannine Christ spoke in his "Apart from me you can do nothing" (Jn 15:5) admonition.

---

[7] Alan J. Levine, "The Critical Flaw in Critical Race Theory," *Chronicles: A Magazine of American Culture,* November 2021, emphasis added.
[8] Victor Davis Hanson, "The Left Got What It Wanted — So Now What?" *American Greatness,* October 10, 2021, emphasis added.

30 Pietas and the Choreography of Forgetfulness

> A society that rejects the past, cuts itself off from its future. It is a dead society, a society with no memory, a society carried off by Alzheimer's disease.
>
> — Robert Cardinal Sarah[1]

> Uprootedness is by far the most dangerous malady to which human societies are exposed, for it is a self-propagating one. For people who are really uprooted there remain only two possible sorts of behavior: either to fall into a spiritual lethargy resembling death, like the majority of the slaves in the days of the Roman Empire, or to hurl themselves into some form of activity necessarily designed to uproot, often by the most violent methods, those who are not yet uprooted, or only partly so.
>
> — Simone Weil[2]

> Often we hear totalitarianism described as something contrary to individualism, but that is not entirely true. Indeed, at its root, totalitarianism is individualism without any relief.
>
> — Russell Hittinger[3]

WHEN FLANNERY O'CONNOR'S O.E. PARKER saw the tattooed man at the fairgrounds, he was "filled with emotion, lifted up as some people are when the flag passes."[4] What makes that mordant remark so funny is that Parker felt that emotion while standing at the back of the tent and glaring slack-jawed at a carnival performer covered with tattoos. That he so comically

---

1   Sarah, *The Day Is Far Spent*, Kindle edition §3168.
2   Simone Weil, *The Need for Roots*, trans. Arthur Wills (London: Routledge, 2002), 47.
3   Russell Hittinger, "Sites of Human Joy: The True Purpose of Intermediate Societies," *Church Life Journal*, December 17, 2021.
4   O'Connor, *The Complete Stories*, 512–13.

squandered the emotion that bespoke a reverence for his native land and its people, alive and dead, hardly suggests that the emotion itself is dubious. O'Connor's allusion to such an emotion works in her short story because it is—or was—an experience common to most people. That Parker still felt such an emotion suggests that some deeply felt allegiance to his country, its people, and its history survived his self-absorption. Being thus "lifted up" cannot be entirely separated from pride in the accomplishments of one's nation, but it is of a different order. It differs from national pride the way that love for one's family differs from the pride one might have for the accomplishments of certain members of one's family or the shame one might feel regarding the misbehavior of a relative.

The virtue of *pietas*, the duty owed to one's parents, one's country, and one's cultural and religious inheritance is key to a survival of a healthy culture. Perversions of this virtue — bellicose nationalism and xenophobia — will always spring up precisely in the arid wastelands where the healthy versions have been mocked as romantic, morally dubious, or insufficiently universal in scope. Whatever form a political order might take, central to its success and sustainability will be the virtue of *pietas*. As Roger Scruton observed:

> Government in turn requires a "we," a prepolitical loyalty that causes neighbors who voted in opposing ways to treat each other as fellow citizens, for whom the government is not "mine" or "yours" but "ours," whether or not we approve of it. This first person plural varies in strength, from fierce attachment in wartime to casual acceptance on a Monday morning at work, but at some level, it must be assumed if we are to adopt a shared rule of law.[5]

This matter is pertinent to the mystery of personhood we are exploring because membership in, and loyalty to, a definable civilization or nation or way of life is one of those "anthropological structures prepared beforehand" on which the healthy development of the human person depends. The loyalty involved can be conceived as the love of one's *country* or one's *nation*. Those nouns are near synonyms, but a subtle difference exists. Christopher Dawson fairly defined love of one's country when he defined the classical virtue of *pietas* as "the cult of parents and kinsfolk and native place as the principles of our being... a moral

---

[5] Roger Scruton, "A Case for Nations," *The Wall Street Journal*, June 3, 2017.

principle which lies at the root of every culture and every religion." It is this sense of belonging to a cultural tradition that inspires a healthy spirit of solidarity and willingness to accept the transgenerational responsibility for preserving this heritage, rectifying those of its past failures for which a workable remedy exists, and passing on this heritage to subsequent generations. Dawson insisted that a society that loses this fundamental sense of belonging "has lost its primary moral basis and its hope of survival."[6] Those bereft of these blessings will, much like the prodigal son, be left to forage for solidarity in a "foreign land" with little or no sense of kinship and shared history with other foragers with whom they are forced to compete. Those lost in this spiritual wasteland will eventually be vulnerable to the siren song of *a cause with a capital "C."*

For as Girard pointed out, the cheapest and easiest way to revive weak relationships of belonging is to find an external enemy. On the other hand: "The more real a group's organic unity, the less that group needs to resort to violence to oppose other groups of the same type, and the more authentically foreign to it violence is."[7]

For René Girard there is an important difference between *patriotism* and *chauvinism*:

> The difference between the two terms corresponds to the two different types of relationships of belonging. The second appears stronger, since it is bellicose, arrogant, and conflictual; in reality, however, it is weaker.... Violence is fueled not by the strength of relationships of belonging but by their weakness. It is precisely because they are collapsing that relationships of belonging try to dress themselves up in a strength they no longer have.[8]

Ian Crowther, the former literary editor of the *Salisbury Review*, expressed a point of view with which many of the sources we have cited would wholeheartedly agree, perhaps most emphatically René Girard and Hans Urs von Balthasar.

> The liberal theory of politics is predicated on the assumption that, essentially, the role of government should be restricted to the management and prevention of conflict, and that a

---

6   Christopher Dawson, *Memories of a Victorian Childhood*, quoted in Fernando Cervantes, "Christopher Dawson and Europe," *Eternity in Time*, ed. Stratford Caldecott and John Morrill (Edinburgh: T & T Clark, 1997), 55.
7   René Girard, "Belonging," *Contagion: Journal of Violence, Mimesis, and Culture*, Vol. 23 (2016): 11.
8   Ibid.

government so restricted guarantees the "minimal state." What the liberal theory fails to contemplate is the possibility that the freedom encouraged by it may generate conflict on such a scale that any state forced to "manage" it will be far from minimal. The early liberal philosophers simply took for granted the existence of a virtuous people, or of freedom as anchored in a closed moral order. They did not envisage, as more pessimistically inclined thinkers did, a government having to cope with the kind of unbridled liberty now exercised in the moral playground which is modern Western society.[9]

In the long line of political regimes, those most consonant with the driving force in human history — the biblical and specifically the Christian revelation — have been those which, more astutely than others, have recognized both the nobility of the human vocation and the sinful condition of human existence. The cultural West is a catalogue of such polities. A great deal of human experience refined that tradition by the time of the American founding, but a point essential to that tradition was still quite operative: an appreciation for the political implications of the Christian doctrine of original sin. This is the realization that, as Aleksandr Solzhenitsyn famously reminded us, the line between good and evil runs through every human heart. Save for the recognition of the inherent dignity of every human person — from conception to natural death — there is no more politically practical principle than the one of which Solzhenitsyn reminded the world.

James Madison acknowledged the political pertinence of this principle when he famously said that if men were angels no government would be necessary. The American republic was fashioned, therefore, by those who clearly recognized the irremediable fact of original sin and who strove to fashion a constitutional order with this uppermost in their minds, notwithstanding the Enlightenment presuppositions with which it was mingled. Of course, the doctrine of original sin was as operative in the lives and arguments of the founders as it was in the quarrelsome people whom they sought to unite as fellow citizens.

Having incorporated into the American founding documents the doctrine of original sin, the founders, under Enlightenment influence, specifically that of John Locke, nevertheless went on to place undue confidence in the countervailing principles of freedom and democracy.

---

9   Ian Crouther, "Introduction," *Permanent Things*, eds. Andrew A. Tadie and Michael H. Macdonald (Grand Rapids, MI: Eerdmans, 1995), xiv–xv.

By the early years of the twentieth century, this principle was morphing into an all-encompassing doctrine of individual freedom. Speaking as a Justice of the Supreme Court, Oliver Wendell Holmes famously said that "if my fellow citizens want to go to hell, I will help them. It's my job." Not even the principle of judicial neutrality permits us to worship so devotedly at the altar of personal freedom. By 1992, as we noted earlier, the worm at the heart of the Enlightenment concept of freedom manifested itself. An heir of Justice Holmes declared: "At the heart of liberty is the right to define one's own concept of existence, of meaning, of the universe, and of the mystery of human life." Thirty years later, four distinguished legal scholars declared: "The notion that the American Republic was created to maximize unbounded individual liberty or autonomy is an egregious, ahistorical anachronism." They drew out the obvious consequences of such a view: "as though we were free to choose genocide or slavery so long as we did it in a democratic way, with the vote of a majority... as though liberty and autonomy were simply good in themselves, regardless of the ends to which they were used."[10]

Understood as an antidote to the ever-recurring dangers of tyranny and oppression, the constitutional guarantee of individual freedom is a precious inheritance that it would be unconscionable to deprecate. But reduced to the rule of the majority and the freedom of the individual, both these treasures will implode under the weight of ungoverned self-will. One of the most balanced and insightful commentaries on the liberationist drift of modern and postmodern political life comes from a review of the political anthropology of John Paul II by the man who was to succeed him on the Chair of Peter:

> In the mind of contemporary man, freedom appears to a large extent as the absolutely highest good, to which all other goods are subordinate. Court decisions consistently accord artistic freedom and freedom of opinion primacy over every other moral value. Values which compete with freedom, or which might necessitate its restriction, seem to be fetters or "taboos," that is, relics of archaic prohibitions and fears. Political policy must show that it contributes to the advancement of freedom in order to be accepted. Even religion can make its voice heard only by presenting itself as a liberating force for man and for humanity.... In contrast, we are inclined to

---

10 Hadley Arkes, Josh Hammer, Matthew Peterson, and Garrett Snedeker, "A Better Originalism," *The American Mind*, March 18, 2021.

react with suspicion to the concept of truth.... The modern attitude toward truth is summed up most succinctly in Pilate's question, "What is truth?"[11]

The history of the modern era, and especially the horrors of the twentieth century and the romance of global governance in the early years of the twenty-first, have led to widespread misgivings, not only about the loss of the virtue of *pietas*, but even of its very virtuousness. In its place there has emerged a romantic idea of a post-national global order tending toward what Giuseppe Fornari has called "globalitarianism," whose precondition is the weakening, if not the outright castigation, of the allegiances and the networks of shared affection and common purpose on which a legitimate social order depends. Veronica Lademan reminds us of one of the anthropological realities that is today ignored in favor of post-national pieties:

> What many globalist idealists cannot accept is that it is in man's nature to love more strongly according to proximity. There are bonds that run deeply within the human heart and mind and are the center of community and cultures. The love and concern of the individual radiates out into a type of charity that is expressed most immediately and intensely to those who are closest to a person; we might think of this as a "charity of proximity." I primarily love myself and my family; this is my first and greatest responsibility in life. This extends out to my communities, my nation, and the world. I have a natural solidarity and obligation to those with a shared homeland, heritage, history, and foundation.[12]

Globalism, on the contrary, writes Douglas Farrow, "serves to *break down identity* and, indeed, requires the breaking down of identity." It necessarily cultivates "a soulless bureaucracy inimical to the maintenance of homes and of homelands."[13] The very title of David C. Schindler's 2019 book — *Freedom from Reality* — highlights the serious shortcomings of a freedom-obsessed governing principle.[14] The dignity properly accorded

---

11 Joseph Ratzinger, *Joseph Ratzinger in* Communio: *Anthropology and Culture*, Vol. 2 (Grand Rapids, MI: Eerdmans, 2013), 147–48.
12 Veronica Lademan, "Rootedness and Refugees," *The European Conservative*, April 20, 2022.
13 Farrow, *1 & 2 Thessalonians*, 100, emphasis added.
14 D. C. Schindler, *Freedom from Reality: The Diabolical Character of Modern Liberty* (Notre Dame, IN: University of Notre Dame Press, 2019).

human freedom arises from the role it plays in the fulfillment of the human vocation, namely, the responsibility for discovering and assenting to transcendent truth and aligning oneself and, to the extent possible, one's culture with that truth. To evade this responsibility is to betray the gift of freedom and to participate in its transformation into license and licentiousness, for which, eventually, an authoritarian solution will seem preferable. As a lodestar for either personal or political life, such an emaciated concept of freedom quickly becomes both morally and culturally catastrophic. In other words, authoritarian solutions appeal to polities based on radical forms of individual autonomy. Drawing on the thought of Hannah Arendt, Augusto Del Noce, and others, D. C. Schindler argued that "the loss of authority is an evacuation of the substance of political existence — indeed, the radical impoverishment of all community from top to bottom."[15] Authority, Schindler argues, is different from — and has a complicated relationship with — power, even as it is inversely related to the need or apparent need for coercion. More to the point of our argument is Schindler's observation that "authority is inseparable from tradition and religion."[16] As distinct from power, authority is itself subject to authority.

The hardiness of a political order depends on the degree to which its underlying anthropological presuppositions conform to the reality of human nature, the human person, and the human predicament. For only by grounding a political regime in anthropological reality will it acquire authority indispensable to legitimate governance. Schindler's warning could not come at a more propitious time, nor be expressed with greater clarity:

> For both Arendt and Del Noce, the only way to avoid the collapse of a political regime — any regime of any style of government, from dictatorship to oligarchy to democracy — into totalitarianism is through the recovery of authority. This is because totalitarianism *is* precisely politics without authority.[17]

Authority, Schindler writes, "has not only disappeared from the political institutions of the modern world but from our memory itself, so

---

15   D. C. Schindler, "Catholic Politics and the Analogy of Authority," *Communio* 48 (Winter 2021): 801–2.
16   Ibid., 805.
17   Ibid., 808.

much so that we cannot even recall the difference between authority and power, authoritarian government and totalitarian government."[18] We glean from Schindler's argument that a well-functioning political sphere — thanks to its reverent and grateful reception by each subsequent generation — enjoys a legitimate degree of "sacrality," understood in anthropological terms. It is a share in the experience of "being filled with emotion, lifted up as some people are when the flag passes," an experience once almost universally felt at some level.

"America," wrote G. K. Chesterton, "is the only nation in the world that is founded on a creed." America, he noted, was "a nation with the soul of a church." In many unmistakable ways, this nation has lost its soul, but it is unchristian to regard lost souls as irredeemable. More than any other nation, America has been conscious of its moral mission, one informed by the Old and New Testament as well as by a rich tradition of political and moral reasoning. That it has betrayed this mission is perfectly obvious, but that it has striven to remedy its betrayals is equally so. The point we are making, however, is both more radical and more explicit, more focused and more expansive: that our political experiment will stand or fall according to the Christ or nothing conundrum. It will adhere to the moral and anthropological principles rooted in the Judeo-Christian tradition, from which its noblest impulses arise, or succumb to either the soft nihilism of antinomian liberalism or the nihilistic hysteria of those determined to find a target for the blind rage that otherwise threatens to consume them. In the middle of the last century, Hans Urs von Balthasar worried that the West was "preparing highly developed civilizations for a degenerate materialistic and nihilistic form of Western thought, which expresses the resentments of the inventors of this secularized Messianism."[19]

These broader cultural and political forces will continue to affect the health and vitality of those living under their influence. Even when we look back with twenty-twenty hindsight on grave shortcomings or even serious crimes of our culture, we would do well to realize that we would likely have been incapable of recognizing these failures had not that same culture awakened in us moral acuities without which the failures of our predecessors would have gone unremarked. On the other hand, thanks to what many call the hermeneutics of suspicion — whose principal agents were Nietzsche, Marx, Freud, Foucault, and Marcuse — we

---

18   Ibid., 810.
19   Balthasar, *The God Question and Modern Man*, 43.

have taught the last few generations to regard their own heritage as irredeemable, and the sad consequence of this cultural sabotage is now everywhere to be seen.

Roger Kimball offers one measure of the loss of common purpose when he compares the poets at the presidential inaugurations of John F. Kennedy in 1961 and Bill Clinton in 1993.

> To get a sense of what has happened to the institution of American identity, compare Robert Frost's performance at John F. Kennedy's inauguration in 1961 with Maya Angelou's performance thirty-two years later. As [Samuel] Huntington reminds us, Frost spoke of the "heroic deeds" of America's founding, an event, he said, that with God's "approval" ushered in "a new order of the ages." By contrast, Maya Angelou never mentioned the words "America" or "American." Instead, she identified twenty-seven ethnic or religious groups that had suffered repression because of America's "armed struggles for profit," "cynicism," and "brutishness."[20]

Commenting on the program for the 2021 presidential inauguration published prior to the inauguration ceremony, Charles Coulombe brought Kimball's lament up to date:

> Where JFK chose the sublime Marian Anderson to sing *The Star Spangled Banner*, Biden has given that honor to Lady Gaga; instead of the venerable Robert Frost intoning his *The Gift Outright*, a paean to American exceptionalism, we'll be treated to 22-year-old Amanda Gorman, whose work "touches on issues of race, feminism, oppression, and marginalization."[21]

Others were no less bewildered by the consequences of the loss of civic concord. The Harvard historian James Hankins surveyed the widespread violence in American cities in 2020 and offered this assessment:

> Toppled statues, an educational culture bent on repudiation of the past, media awash with anti-American propaganda, and more, are bringing one truth hideously into view: The old authors were right when they said that a country without *pietas* will soon disintegrate. Only by recovering that forgotten

---

20 Roger Kimball, *The Fortunes of Permanence: Culture and Anarchy in an Age of Amnesia* (South Bend, IN: St. Augustine's Press, 2012), Kindle §865.
21 Charles Coulombe, "Inauguration Blues," *Crisis Magazine*, January 20, 2021.

virtue can we hope to rebuild the edifice of love and loyalty that shelters our common life.[22]

Amanda Gorman recited her poem at the inauguration ceremony in 2021. Later that year, Bob Dylan released his first album since 2012, *Rough and Rowdy Way*, a treasure trove of biblical and especially Christian allusions, among them these lines from "Mother of Muses."

> Mother of Muses sing for my heart
> Sing of a love too soon to depart
> Sing of the heroes who stood alone
> Whose names are engraved on tablets of stone
> Who struggled with pain so the world could go free
> Mother of Muses sing for me
>
> Sing of Sherman, Montgomery and Scott
> And of Zhukov, and Patton, and the battles they fought
> Who cleared the path for Presley to sing
> Who carved the path for Martin Luther King
> Who did what they did and they went on their way
> Man, I could tell their stories all day[23]

As we said earlier, Dylan expressed heartfelt gratitude for his predecessors. This stands in stark contrast to the fashion among those in whom the spirit of ingratitude has been intentionally inculcated. This indoctrination is not entirely new. The attempt to reorder a culture by disparaging its past has a dark pedigree. The ghost of Rousseau haunts the efforts to vilify the American "experiment in ordered liberty" which Americans have inherited from their predecessors. For Rousseau, the State was to replace the father, and the citizens were regarded as wards of the State or, as British historian Paul Johnson assessed, "the children of the paternal orphanage."[24] In contrast to one's native country, the State hardly awakens affection, which is why the State posing as a sovereign Father, or more recently as a coddling Mother, always substitutes indoctrination for education. Thus, cultural critics from Howard Zinn to Nikole Hannah-Jones try to alter the historical record in order to persuade their gullible readers to adopt a critical — or cynical — attitude toward their cultural inheritance, an act of vandalism that drains the

---

22 James Hankins, "Pietas," *First Things*, November 2020.
23 Bob Dylan, "Mother of Muses," *Rough and Rowdy Ways*, Columbia Records, 2020, compact disc.
24 Paul Johnson, *Intellectuals*, 24.

souls of its recruits. One can hardly read what Paul Johnson said of Rousseau's political project without recognizing its contemporary corollary.

> The educational process was thus the key to the success of the cultural engineering needed to make the State acceptable and successful; the axis of Rousseau's ideas was the citizen as child and the State as parent, and he insisted the government should have complete charge of the upbringing of all children. Hence — and this is the true revolution Rousseau's ideas brought about — he moved the political process to the very centre of human existence by making the legislator, who is also a pedagogue, into the new Messiah, capable of solving all human problems by creating New Men.[25]

Johnson wrote those words in a book published more than thirty years ago. As prescient as he was, he could hardly have anticipated the trend of recent events. So congenial to the spiritual health of the human person is his gratitude for the bounty that is his because of the labors and sacrifices of his cultural predecessors that those who have been badgered into becoming ingrates are left rudderless and vulnerable to the "haystack and roof-levelling wind" which so worried Yeats a hundred years ago.

As both Dostoevsky's Underground Man and Friedrich Nietzsche have shown, the nihilistic impulse arises in those running out of more respectable excuses for unleashing a maniacal lust for destruction. In the end, they succumb to the determination to make the culture both ugly and unworkable, and then to burn it down. As we have repeatedly argued, this nihilism is the inevitable consequence of the dechristianization of Western culture, the manifestation of the "without me you can do nothing" warning of Christ.

Democracy in the twenty-first century, writes Zbigniew Janowski, "is no longer a system that requires responsibility, intellectual alertness, and moral discipline from its participants. It is a realm which promises to fulfill everyone's infantile and unrealistic whims."[26] Moreover, Janowski observes, "nothing but comparison with life under communism can do justice to what life in America is like today."[27] It is the height of moral and cultural irresponsibility to surrender the sexual education of the young to the proudly transgressive experimentation

---

25   Ibid., 25.
26   Zbigniew Janowski, *Homo Americanus: The Rise of Totalitarian Democracy in America* (South Bend: St. Augustine's Press, 2021), 5.
27   Ibid., 7.

conducted by institutions contemptuous of every trace of traditional moral commonsense. The animus against the family — now disdained as "the *traditional* family" — requires that the education of children, very much including the sexual education, should be taken out of the hands of their parents. The goal of such policies, writes Janowski, is "to preclude the possibility of shaping human relationships outside of the ideological framework," and to ensure that "only those which are sanctioned by egalitarian ideology can be said to be legitimate."[28]

Not only in today's world, but throughout history, nations have regularly descended into chaos, driven by social and political passions whose underlying mimetic provenance René Girard catalogued so masterfully. Those who imagined that a post-national governing arrangement would somehow manage to elude these same primordial passions might consider a warning offered by J. M. Smith. What happens, asks Smith, when the lovely post-national one-world government imagined by its serenaders "gets a wild hair for persecution, censorship and genocide. How does one run for the border when there are no borders for which one can run?"[29] Such bracing warnings are apropos, but what has been lost will not be recovered by those driven predominantly by fear. As it did for the fictional O. E. Parker, it is the spontaneous affection for what the flag represents that binds us to both our predecessors and descendants. As Ryszard Legutko has perceptively noted: "People continue to need a community that naturally unites them through a common language, history, social practices, and is cemented by loyalty, love, and even sometimes by the ultimate sacrifice."[30]

As the historian Glenn W. Olsen notes, "if one does not have a preferred language, religion, or set of customs, one probably gravitates to cosmopolitan centers, where — the crowning irony — one can find people like oneself."[31]

> A million things, starting with the raising of children, are easier if one lives with those with whom one agrees. In many historical situations multiculturalism is inevitable, but in certain obvious ways multicultural societies fail humans. Multiculturalism may have a certain short-term attractiveness, but it is doubtful that a civilization or nation can last long without a

---

28 Ibid., 8.
29 J. M. Smith, "Beware of the Pure Heart," *Orthosphere* (blog), February 3, 2022.
30 Legutko, *The Cunning of Freedom*, 156–57.
31 Glenn W. Olsen, *The Turn to Transcendence: The Role of Religion in the Twenty-First Century* (Washington, DC: The Catholic University of America Press, 2010), 48.

fair degree of shared vision of reality. By definition anything more than façade-multiculturalism — I like cappuccino, you like tacos — involves disagreement about reality.[32]

Nostalgia literally means homesickness, and it can be a healthy response to circumstances that have led to loneliness and alienation. Indeed, the experience of spiritual homelessness is perhaps the beginning of a retrieval of one's cultural patrimony. Homesickness will often focus on a familiar and probably familial experience of being a member of a loving and caring community, one ranging from one's family, to one's local community, to one's native country. One grows nostalgic for a community with which one feels a real affinity and affection. Finding no such community, one can at least visit one. But the effect of tourism is precisely to pillage another tradition and incline its legitimate heirs to barter away their cultural patrimony by mass producing the trinkets that trivialize the heritage of which they purport to be proud. Writing of tensions in the western Austrian state of Tyrol where traditional Catholicism remained robust until recently, Tim Parks notes: "What does the globalized world of free travelers feel nostalgic for, if not the closed, traditional community? The more the tourists come, particularly Italian tourists, the more the locals cling to their traditions. And the more they cling to their traditions the more the tourists come."[33]

Alas, *clinging* to one's traditions is a far cry from being animated by them. A living tradition can be distinguished from traditional*ism*. Indeed, though the rise of traditionalism might be an expected response to the loss of tradition, it constitutes yet another contemporary reaction rather than an affectively genuine revival of memory and gratitude. As D. C. Schindler has brilliantly noted:

> It is ironic, but there is perhaps something fitting in the absence of an explicit philosophical theory or account of tradition. A tradition is something we inherit uncritically, without a demand for justification. We feel no need to certify the precise origin of tradition, and, indeed, details about the time and place a tradition was instituted tend to diminish its status as tradition, especially if the origin turns out to be recent and accessible in some way other than its transmission through others. The initiation of a tradition is most properly hidden in the mists of time. Rather than critically assessing it, we are meant to take a

---

32 Ibid., 49.
33 Quoted in Olsen, *The Turn to Transcendence*, 47, n36.

tradition for granted; a kind of spontaneous and unreflective acceptance seems to belong to its essence.[34]

Nothing could be less plausible than the idea that what is truly new necessarily breaks with all that preceded it. Even the greatest apparent breakthroughs seem to create their own precursors, throwing light back on their earlier foreshadowings in the contributions of their predecessors. This applies to the greatest and most singular event in history. The first Christians were quick to find intimations of the unique event of Christ throughout the Jewish scriptures, and later in the ponderings of Hellenistic philosophers. And, as Henri de Lubac noted, the originality of the Apostle to the Gentiles set Christian thought on an amazing voyage of discovery:

> What would remain, for example, of the thought of Saint Paul — who nevertheless so dominated the thoughts of his century — if one cut it off from the thousand roots that, in fact, attached it to the earth of Tarsus and Jerusalem? How can a single one of its essential points be analyzed without constant reference not only to the history of the Hebrew people but also to Greek civilization, to Eastern mysticism, to the Roman Empire? This would be an imaginary transcendence, pure chimera, linked to a no less chimerical ideal of revelation.[35]

The future, writes Robert Harrison, "is born of the past and the past reborn from out of the future, thanks to a mysterious process of transmission."[36] And those who fail to understand this, those who allow the virtue of hope to attach itself to historically untested political projects — or worse, to projects which have been without exception historically catastrophic — will leave their cultural heirs with nothing but devastation. As the French philosopher Rémi Brague observes:

> A deliberate break with the past brings about a loss of civilization and is the harbinger of some form of barbarism, the latter word being understood in the usual meaning as well, that is, as stupidity and cruelty. The historical examples of such a fact are many. Among them, the French Revolution may have pride (or shame) of place.[37]

---

34 D. C. Schindler, "Taking Truth for Granted: A Reflection on the Significance of Tradition in Josef Pieper," *Ressourcement After Vatican II: Essays in Honor of Joseph Fessio, S.J.* (San Francisco: Ignatius Press, 2020), Kindle edition §4460.
35 De Lubac, *Theology in History*, 204.
36 Harrison, *Juvenescence*, 113.
37 Brague, *Curing Mad Truths*, 107.

Harrison expresses it somewhat less dramatically when he writes that "when the new does not *renew* — when it does not *rejuvenate* latent legacies — it gets old in a hurry."[38] So modernity took its time getting old, but postmodernity has gotten old in a hurry.

Today culture is being threatened by the specter of a soulless global governance which is a grim parody of the Christian universalism that quietly undergirded the Westphalian nation-states and made them possible. The Westphalian system was a response to earlier regional and doctrinal fissures within Western Christendom, and these fissures continued to jeopardize the mutual bonds that might have otherwise prevented the rise of the bellicose nationalism that wreaked such havoc on the twentieth century. As we have noted, one of the chief reactions to the twentieth-century crisis of nationalism has been the dream of an anthropologically untenable post-national globalism, a novel arrangement allegedly less parochial and putatively more tolerant, inclusive, and diverse — adjectives that are now saturated with perfidy. The perennial truth of the matter was stated by the American historian Wilford McClay:

> "Citizenship" means a vivid and enduring sense of one's full membership in one of the greatest enterprises in human history: the astonishing, perilous, and immensely consequential story of one's own country. Today, we must redouble our efforts to make that past our own, and then be about the business of passing it on.[39]

Happily, we can conclude these sobering reflections on a more hopeful note. It would be naïve to regard one Supreme Court decision as a sign that recent trends are losing their grip on American culture. But we have reason to take heart. For we concur with Mary Eberstadt's assessment of the larger implications of the Court's decision in the Dobbs v. Jackson Women's Health Organization. "Hamilton, Madison, and Jay came through. The federalism that remains one of the wonders of the political world came through. It came through in a way that many since *Roe* had despaired of ever happening again."[40]

---

38 Harrison, *Juvenescence*, 113. Emphasis added.
39 Wilford McClay, "Recovering Our Legacy: The Many Uses of the American Past," *Imaginative Conservative*, March 8, 2020.
40 Mary Eberstadt, "What the Nurses Knew."

31 Mother Church

> Happy are those who from childhood have learned to look on the Church as a mother! Happier still are those whose experience, whatever it might have been, has confirmed them in this truth! Happy are those who have been gripped (and are gripped more and more) by the inconceivable richness, inconceivable depths of the Life communicated to them by this mother!
> — Henri de Lubac[1]

> Jesus was not "missed" by the generation that came after, because "God's love has been poured into our hearts through the Holy Spirit which has been given to us" (Rom 5:5); it is for this reason that Paul no longer wishes to know Jesus "in the flesh" (2 Cor 5:16).
> — Hans Urs von Balthasar[2]

THANKS TO THE MOTHER'S SMILE AND THE MYStery of intercommunion that it inaugurates, a child will have experienced something about love and wonder and longing. If the paternal task of acquainting the child with his spiritual and cultural inheritance and the responsibilities that fall to him to enrich and ennoble that heritage is adequately performed, the child will be blessed indeed. But these blessings alone will not provide the sufficient wherewithal for living out the human vocation, for fulfilling the promise of personhood. The question remains: Will the seeds of a sacramental disposition awakened in childhood by the mother's smile find sufficiently rich soil in which to sink roots and bear fruit? However bountiful the child's maternal and paternal patrimony, the greatest fruits of this heritage await the moment when the child's gaze is turned *upward*, so to speak.

---

1 Henri de Lubac, S.J., *The Church: Paradox and Mystery*, trans. James R. Dunne and Anne Englund Nash (San Francisco: Ignatius Press, 2021), 15.
2 Balthasar, *Love Alone Is Credible*, 89.

Arguably, the least appreciated factor in any assessment of human fulfillment is the existential difference between a person who has a real prayer life and one who does not. Much of Martin Buber's exposition of the I-Thou relationship is a testimony to this difference. Almost as elusive, even for Christians, is how unique Christian prayer is. For Christians pray to a God who is not only an inconceivable mystery beyond our capacity to imagine, but a God who has known, and does now know, all the exigencies of human existence, a God who is like us in all things but sin. To have a prayerful relationship with the Christian God, whose inner-Trinitarian communion is quite literally the fountainhead of love itself, is to enjoy the greatest possible protection against the pernicious forms of mimetic contagion. One becomes a person most truly by being in a prayerful relationship with God-in-Christ who calls each of us by name. Yves Congar has expressed this most remarkably:

> What would I be, what would my faith, my prayer, be if I were given the Bible and thereafter left to my own devices? Indeed, what would be the point of having a Bible at all? I have received everything from and in the Church.... I am only a moment out of an *immense life that has been personalized in me* (and this aspect is magnificent!) but which includes and surpasses me, which existed before me and which will survive me. It is not mine![3]

The new humanity the Church has been commissioned to awaken involves a new form of subjectivity, one that was fully enfleshed in Christ and limned in the lives of the saints, which the Church raises up as models of the Christlikeness that fulfills the deepest longing of every human heart, "the inborn nostalgia to become a 'person.'" The Church alone has the tools — both the time-tested and those we are here trying to espouse — for recovering the mystery of the human person, for which John Paul II called in his early writings. With tools that are both ancient and still in the process of being forged, the Church can offer an account of personhood that is both anthropologically sound and christologically grounded. For, as paragraph 22 of the Second Vatican Council document *Gaudium et Spes* declares: "the revelation of the mystery of the Father and His love, fully reveals man to man himself and makes his supreme calling clear." Henri de Lubac expressed this

---

3   Quoted in de Lubac, *The Church: Paradox and Mystery*, 21, n11, emphasis added.

with equal audacity when he argued that the abysses of man's nature open only "on impact with Revelation."[4]

While she shares with other cultural institutions her commitment to political and economic justice, the Church's sacramental obligations are uniquely her own. These obligations must never be subordinated, therefore, to more worldly responsibilities, however legitimate these may be. As urgent as it is to provide political protection and economic security to those suffering from injustice and however practicable to this purpose the vocabulary of autonomy and individual rights might be, the justice the Church seeks begins with the person rightly understood.

From the Church's earliest era, the faithful have thought of the Church as the Mother Church, one that is analogous to the role of the mother's smile in the life of the child. For in her capacity as the minister of her sacraments, the Church dispenses grace, and grace is as elusive and efficacious in the lives of the faithful as is the mother's smile in the life of the child.

Moreover, the Church is the custodian and curator of a five-thousand-year-old patrimony recounted in the Bible and in two millennia of doctrinal, catechetical, moral, and theological reflection on the event at the center of the New Testament. For those fortunate enough to know the Church as one's "spiritual native country," as Henri de Lubac expressed it, "nothing which concerns her will leave him indifferent or detached.... It will be from her that he learns how to live and die."[5] As Dietrich von Hildebrand perceptively observed, the ecclesial and sacramental grounding that the Church exists to foster will help inoculate her faithful not only against the hyper-individualism of late modernity but also against the spiritual pandemics which are spreading so rapidly in the postmodern period.

> That liberal conception which considers the "solitary" man as the great, profound human being is the logical outcome of the understanding of communion as something peripheral in its nature. Of course, a true personality is, in one sense, solitary among average men, because this personality is alone in his knowledge of that deep communion to which average men have not awakened; he is not satisfied with the superficialities of mere interest or pleasure and seeks a profounder link;

---

4 De Lubac, *Theology in History*, 314.
5 De Lubac, *The Splendor of the Church*, 242.

he does not inwardly accept the communion offered by the average. But a true personality is never solitary in the sense of being isolated from others in the depths, in the sense of indifference or hostility; he is not unalive to that ultimate, triumphant unity with his brother, whom he sees in the place where each man in truth stands before God, whether he is aware of it or not.[6]

We have spoken of the human vocation, using the singular noun, even as we have emphasized the utter uniqueness of each person's expression of that vocation. The vocation to which one is uniquely called will necessarily be situated within the ensemble of vocations with which it will be in a choreographic relationship. To exemplify this, de Lubac shared a poignant example of the "we" of the Christian communion:

> The story is told of a priest who, shortly after apostatizing, said to a visitor who was about to congratulate him: "From now onward I am no more than a philosopher — in other words, a man alone." It must have been a bitter reflection, but it was true. He had left the home outside which there will never be anything save exile and solitude. Many people aren't aware of it, because they live in the passing moment, alienated from themselves, "rooted in this world like seaweed on the rocks." The preoccupations of daily life absorb them; "the golden mist of appearances" forms a veil of illusion around them. Sometimes they look in a hundred and one different places for some substitute for the Church, as if to deceive their own longings. Yet the man who hears in the depths of his being the call which has stimulated his thirst for communion — indeed, the man who does no more than sense it — grasps that neither friendship nor love, let alone any of the social groupings that underlie his own life, can satisfy it.[7]

While the priest in de Lubac's story became an apostate willingly and knowingly, countless people today have been absorbed by, and absorbed into, an increasingly apostatizing culture, under the influence of which their drift into spiritual alienation has gradually occurred. René Girard observed that the faithful themselves are not immune to de facto apostasy.

---

6 Hildebrand, *Liturgy and Personality*, 31–32.
7 De Lubac, *The Splendor of the Church*, 237.

What's most pathetic is the insipidly modernized brand of Christianity that bows down before everything that's most ephemeral in contemporary thought. Christians don't see that they have at their disposal an instrument that is incomparably superior to the whole mishmash of psychoanalysis and sociology that they conscientiously feed themselves. It's the old story of Esau sacrificing his inheritance for a plate of lentils.[8]

To be a believing Christian is to recognize Jesus of Nazareth as the incarnate Word of God — the definitive and final revelation of the Divine *Logos*, the life-sustaining *Blueprint*, the ontological DNA of the entire created order, and the Living *Script* of the Theo-drama whose first intimations were limned by the priests, prophets, and psalmists of ancient Israel. Bringing this panorama of the Christocentric Theo-drama into focus was the burden of *God's Gamble: The Gravitational Power of Crucified Love*.

It is in this theodramatic context that an individual Christian's vocation is properly situated. It is here where we Christians best discern the character of our unique missions. This discernment will always involve reckoning with the particular setting in which we find ourselves and the moral responsibilities that arise from it. It is by the people closest to us and by the daily situations we face that our missions will be largely determined. Though our mission will require us to love the most familiar people in the most ordinary of circumstances, our ability to perform that mission with poise and serenity will be enhanced by a more conscious awareness that everything we see and do is better seen and better done as the work of one "taken into service" — a handmaid or manservant — of Christ.

The royal access to Christ is neither exegetical, philosophical, nor mystical. It is sacramental. It is by way of the Church's sacramental mediation that we are offered proximity to Christ and participation in his mystery. We enter into that mystery via baptism, confirmation, penitential contrition, and most intimately in the Eucharist. Such sacramental mediation involves a graced indwelling of the Spirit of Christ which, though it largely eludes sensory detection, nonetheless remains operative in the depths of the sacramental recipient. The fruits of the sacrament are more likely to become palpable, writes Ratzinger, when "we see before us the transcendence that has already occurred in the

---

8 *Conversations with René Girard: Prophet of Envy*, ed. Cynthia L. Haven (London: Bloomsbury Publishing, 2021), 77.

world of faith, which, as it were, lets itself be contemplated there and invites our participation."⁹

> Doubtless, this contact with already existing Christian experience was more obvious to man in the past than it is today; man lived then in a world that bore the stamp of faith. Today, the Church as a place of accumulated experience is for many an alien world. Nevertheless, this world continues to be a possibility, and it will be the task of religious education to open the door to this place of experience that is the Church and thus to encourage participation in the experience she has to offer.¹⁰

As we noted much earlier, Joseph Ratzinger mused on how Tertullian was able to formulate the deepest mystery of Christianity — "three persons in one God" — with an "almost somnambulistic assurance." Balthasar detected something similar with respect to the Church's overall doctrinal deposit: "Dogmatic formulations are often a step ahead of the full philosophical 'ownership' of a new way of thinking: with the assurance of a sleepwalker, the Church coins a formula that only later on reveals all the dimensions of its meaning."¹¹

As Balthasar argued more than half a century ago, everything of value in secularism is taken from the treasury of Catholic resources. Everything, that is, except the most essential: the Church's "unbearable claim to absolute truth." Indeed, to the extent that the Church has the faith and fortitude to proclaim this absolute truth, "she will be completely isolated and alone."¹² Balthasar was not naïve. He knew well that both the Church's hierarchy and her unwary members would succumb to the temptation to reassure the secular world that the Church was in complete agreement on all the important issues of the day. The truth of the matter, however, was not lost on Balthasar: "Since it is a well-known fact that the herd-man is afraid of getting mixed up with the 'party' of an isolated minority that is likely, and even certain, to be attacked, a progressive 'defection of the masses' from the Church can be prophesied with corresponding certainty."¹³

---

9   Ratzinger, *Principles of Catholic Theology*, 351.
10 Ibid.
11 Hans Urs von Balthasar, *Cosmic Liturgy: The Universe According to Maximus the Confessor*, trans. Brian E. Daley, S.J. (San Francisco: Ignatius Press, 2003), 211.
12 Balthasar, *The God Question and Modern Man*, 81.
13 Ibid., 87.

32 The Osmosis of Sanctity

When reading the accounts of the patriotic deeds of French heroines, especially the Venerable Joan of Arc, I had a great desire to imitate them; and it seemed I felt within me the same burning zeal with which they were animated, the same heavenly inspiration. Then I received a grace which I have always looked upon as one of the greatest in my life.
— Thérèse of Lisieux[1]

There is an osmosis between souls, today as always, whose mystery is sometimes revealed when we meet certain persons or find ourselves in certain settings. Moreover, we even have a need for this mystery and are constantly slaking our thirst from this source by reading, conversations, prayers.
— Pierre Emmanuel[2]

Ignatius was passionately fond of reading worldly books of fiction and tales of knight-errantry. When he felt he was getting better, he asked for some of these books to pass the time. But no book of that sort could be found in the house; instead they gave him a life of Christ and a collection of the lives of saints written in Spanish.... While reading the life of Christ our Lord or the lives of the saints, he would reflect and reason with himself: "What if I should do what Saint Francis or Saint Dominic did?"
— From the life of Saint Ignatius from his own words by Luis Gonzalez[3]

A S SO MANY CHRISTIANS BEFORE HER, THÉRÈSE of Lisieux experienced a special grace, not only from the example of her elder sister Pauline, but after entering the convent, and

---

[1] St. Thérèse of Lisieux, *Story of a Soul*, 72.
[2] Quoted in de Lubac, *Theological Fragments*, trans. Rebecca Howell Balinski (San Francisco: Ignatius Press, 1989), 18.
[3] From the life of Saint Ignatius from his own words by Luis Gonzalez (Cap. 1, 5–9: *Acta Sanctorum*, Julii, 7) [1898], 647.

more strikingly, when reading about Joan of Arc. Whereas her childhood desire to enter the convent was awakened by the rather obvious example of her own sister, the profound effect the story of a fifteenth-century warrior-martyr had on her could hardly have been predicted. Joan of Arc was a model whose historical situation and personality could not have been less like those of the cloistered Carmelite, who never left her motherhouse and who died of tuberculosis at the age of twenty-four. The Church would beatify and later canonize Joan some years after Thérèse's death. For Thérèse, as for many of her fellow Frenchmen, Joan was known for her military valor and for being burned at the stake as a heretic, hardly the profile of someone with whom a cloistered Carmelite would become so enamored.

As radically different as were these moments of mimetic attraction, Thérèse records an experience not unlike what Bob Dylan felt in the presence of Buddy Holly and what the fictional O. E. Parker felt in the presence of the tattooed man at the fairgrounds. When reading of Joan of Arc, Thérèse seems to have had a similar awakening. In her childhood, as we have noted, Thérèse modeled herself on her older sister, a Carmelite nun, declaring: "I too will become a religious." In effect, her response to the example of Joan was analogous: "I too will become a martyr." But what might martyrdom look like for her? The French Revolution and the martyrdom of many priests and nuns was in the distant past. What Thérèse saw in Joan was the self-sacrificial core of the Christian vocation. "Joan of Arc was not her favorite saint for nothing," writes Balthasar of Thérèse, "she was the one with whom she competed in spirit, with whom she compared her mission, whose part she played so enthusiastically in a theatrical piece, as photos we still possess can attest."[4]

Another example of the mimetic dimension of what Catholics call the communion of saints was eloquently recollected by Henri de Lubac. It concerns the Renaissance philosopher Giovanni Pico and the esteem in which he held the prolific third-century Alexandrian theologian Origen. De Lubac explains:

> More than any particular doctrine, more than the depth or any particular characteristic of Origen's thought — which... he could have known only rather poorly [since he had only a Latin translation of the Greek texts of Origen] — what undoubtedly seduced the young thinker was the spiritual impulse he had received from it. In him was renewed that kind of miracle that

---

4 Balthasar, *The von Balthasar Reader*, 399.

> is ascertained down through the centuries: between his soul
> and the soul of the great Alexandrian, a spark had flashed.[5]

Like faith itself, such a transmission is a gift that cannot be entirely explained by the theological or literary accomplishments of the person who serves as the conduit of the gift. Indeed, it can be awakened as often by the simplest and humblest model as by a spiritual or intellectual giant. The most important facet of this mystery of transmission was brought out by the twentieth-century German bishop, Klaus Hemmerle (1929 – 1994). "I am only playing Mozart well if Mozart is still Mozart," Hemmerle wrote, "But when I play really well, Mozart becomes more Mozart-like, and I become more myself."[6]

Were we to substitute for Mozart the Christian saints to whom the faithful look for inspiration and example, Hemmerle's analogy is perfectly apt. Paradoxically, when we allow the example of a saint to awaken an analogous ardor in us, we become more fully ourselves. It follows that those who most faithfully explored and proclaimed the living Parable at the center of Christian faith became themselves living parables. Indeed, every person who strives to be worthy of the name Christian is a living parable. He is admonished to put his lamp on the lampstand but not to be anxious about how the world responds.

Some years ago, in an essay on the anthropological element in theology, then-Cardinal Joseph Ratzinger reminded his readers that "a very simple person who bears within himself a sense of values and, thus, a sensitivity toward others, toward what is right and beautiful and true, is immeasurably more learned than the most experienced technocrat with his computer brain."[7] The example that Cardinal Ratzinger gave was that of Saint Augustine. If at the moment of his conversion the prodigal son turned toward his father, Augustine turned toward his saintly mother, on whose prayers he had — unbeknownst to himself — long depended.

> Augustine experienced this in the case of his mother while he, with his friends, all of whom came from the academic world, struggled helplessly with the basic problems of humanity, he was struck again and again by the interior certainty of this simple woman. With astonishment and emotion, he wrote of

---

5   De Lubac, *Theology in History*, 65 – 66.
6   Klaus Hemmerle, *Theses Towards a Trinitarian Ontology*, trans. Stephen Churchyard (Brooklyn, NY: Angelico Press, 2020), 42.
7   Ratzinger, *Principles of Catholic Theology*, 341.

her: "She stands at the pinnacle of philosophy." Anyone who has ever met such a simple person — a person who lets himself be inwardly permeated by the strength of the Christian faith — has experienced the same thing and will be unable to think of that person without the greatest respect.[8]

As we have said earlier, Jesus, as the Son, is the *sun* at noonday, who lights up the world and everything in it, but whose light is blinding to the mortal eye. For the author of the Letter to the Hebrews, Jesus is the pioneer and perfecter of faith, whom we are able to follow thanks to the example of the "great cloud of witnesses," in whose lives the otherwise blinding light of Christ is refracted and thereby made more followable.

The Church in her wisdom canonizes saints, thereby holding them up as models worthy of imitation. But, as the examples above show, uncanonized saints walk in our midst largely unnoticed. Their sanctity suffuses their lives more mysteriously to the extent that it is both unaffected and unsung. "I know of no more convincing proof for the faith," wrote Joseph Ratzinger, "than precisely the pure and unalloyed humanity that the faith allowed to mature in my parents and in so many other persons I have had the privilege to encounter."[9] As Pope Benedict XVI, Ratzinger expressed this gratitude to a papal audience in 2011:

> Actually I must say that also for my personal faith many saints, not all, are true stars in the firmament of history. And I would like to add that for me not only a few great saints whom I love and whom I know well are "signposts", but precisely also the simple saints, that is, the good people I see in my life who will never be canonized. They are ordinary people, so to speak, without visible heroism but in their everyday goodness I see the truth of faith. This goodness, which they have developed in the faith of the Church, is for me the most reliable apology of Christianity and the sign of where the truth lies.[10]

Echoing this, de Lubac observes that "faith has its own light, which can be far brighter in the intellect of a simple believer than in that of the finest theologian."[11] The poet and priest Gerald Manley Hopkins famously concurred:

---

8   Ibid.
9   *The Essential Pope Benedict XVI: His Central Writings and Speeches*, eds. John F. Thornton and Susan B. Varenne (San Francisco: Harper, 2007), 208.
10 Benedict XVI, *General Audience: Holiness* (April 13, 2011).
11 De Lubac, *The Mystery of the Supernatural*, 165.

THE APOCALYPSE OF THE SOVEREIGN SELF

> Christ plays in ten thousand places,
> Lovely in limbs, and lovely in eyes not his
> To the Father through the features of men's faces.[12]

In 1911, the French poet Charles Péguy challenged a theological interlocuter, M. Fernand Laudet, with these words:

> If Mr. Laudet had any idea of the meaning of communion, the Church, Christianity and Christendom, he would know that the communion of saints is, in one of its meanings, precisely that direct access that we Christians have not only to saints of the fifteenth century but to all saints in all centuries, and to those of the first century and of that most eminent group who knew Jesus in person just as much as to any others. Through prayer and the sacraments, through grace, through the merits of Jesus Christ and the saints, we have immediate, instantaneous, atemporal, eternal access without having to engage in any archeology of the soul.[13]

At first, wrote then-Cardinal Ratzinger, faith is "as it were, a kind of borrowed faith ... a secondhand faith."[14] We receive it from others. Faith is a mission that begins with a trans-mission. Only those who love God know God. And, inasmuch as God is not alone but rather the Trinitarian communion, no one can truly love God or know God other than in communion with others. In this regard, perhaps one of the most haunting passages in the New Testament is from the First Epistle of Saint John: "Beloved, we are God's children now; it does not yet appear what we shall be, but we know that when he appears we shall be like him, for we shall see him as he is" (1 Jn 3:2).

We are brought back, not only to the power of mimetic attraction, but arguably to its eschatological meaning. We have reason to hope, as we argued at some length in *God's Gamble*, that the postmortem experience of finally seeing Christ *as he is* will be such an overwhelmingly osmotic event that only by an act of towering rebellion would one be able to avoid being drawn into the salvific mystery of which he is the essence, thereby fulfilling the promise of personhood by an act of kenotic self-surrender of which Christ is the supreme paragon and his mother the unique human manifestation. "Thus we can say, in the end," writes

---

12 Gerard Manley Hopkins, "As Kingfishers Catch Fire," *A Hopkins Reader* (Garden City, NY: Image Books, 1966), 67.
13 Cited in de Lubac, *Theological Fragments*, 22.
14 Ratzinger, *Principles of Catholic Theology*, 351.

Henri de Lubac, "that we are fully persons only within the Person of the Son, by whom and with whom we share in the circumincession of the Trinity."[15] When the scales fall from our eyes and we see him as he is, our mimetic disposition will achieve its ultimate purpose. Short of a monumental act of rebellion, we will begin the purification and rectification process required for entry into the Trinitarian life for which we were made. "We will be like him, for we will see him as he is." "By these words," St. Augustine remarked, "the tongue has done its best; now we must apply the meditation of the heart."[16]

In the *meantime*, however, where can we go to train our eyes and our hearts for that decisive act of recognition? A related question is: What is the nature and structure of the ongoing theodrama in the midst of which we find ourselves, and in choreographic sync with which we might *truly* find ourselves?

---

15   De Lubac, *Catholicism*, 342.
16   From the *Tractates on the first letter of John*, Tract 4 (PL 35:2008–9).

33 The Eucharistic Meta-drama

> The cup of blessing which we bless, is it not a participation in the blood of Christ? The bread which we break, is it not a participation in the body of Christ? (1 Cor 10:16)

> And by virtue of the grace of the continuation of that drama after Christ in the mission of the Church, the individual has the chance of being inserted into that same drama.
> — Hans Urs von Balthasar[1]

> Sheltered in the liturgical ritual of the Church, the human being encounters Christ in the readings and the gospel and in the most personal form in the real presence of the Eucharist. In this each person understands in the deepest sense possible his or her own identity and purpose.
> — Emery de Gaál[2]

IT IS SURELY OBVIOUS BY NOW THAT BASING A POLity on the rights of its individuals is a recipe for instability, confusion, and internal strife. For the sundry rights asserted will inevitably conflict with other rights, whose claimants will be no less zealous in defending and asserting them. The rights discourse will quickly become a struggle for the levers of power by which some rights claims will be countenanced at the expense of others incompatible with them. What we need more than rights that protect us from others are *rites* which bring us into communion with one another precisely by acknowledging our mutual dependence on God's mercy and grace. Any enumeration of human *rights* not subtended by the social, cultural, and ecclesial *rites*— which draw us into the overarching drama of human history and that bring us into communion with one another regardless of the differences of race, class, ethnicity, or religion—will succumb in the end to the sectarian pressures corrosive of any sense of common purpose.

---

1 Oakes, *Pattern of Redemption*, 224.
2 Emery de Gaál, *The Theology of Pope Benedict XVI: The Christocentric Shift* (New York: Palgrave Macmillan, 2010), 298.

The Eucharistic Meta-drama

For history to have any serious meaning, there must be a thread that runs through it, constituting its leitmotif and prefiguring its consummation. To be a Christian, especially a Catholic Christian, is to see that thread in the Golgothan tableau, the crucified Christ, the Passion drama, its remoteness in time more than overcome by the sacramental mystery of its repristination in the Eucharistic liturgy, the source and summit of the Church's life. The mother's smile is to the life of the child what the elevation and later reception of the consecrated Body and Blood of Christ is to the Eucharistic liturgy: a moment when the most extraordinary and mysterious communion takes place, of the true consequence of which the faithful — like the infant gazing at the mother's smile — remain only tenuously aware, even as they are being inwardly transformed by it.

Writes Yves Congar: "Nothing is more educative for man in his totality than the liturgy."

> The sort of Christian produced by an enlightened and docile participation in the liturgy is a man at peace and unified in every fiber of his human nature, by the secret and powerful penetration of faith and love in his life, throughout a period of prayer and worship, during which he learned, at his mother's knee and without effort, *the Church's language*: her language of faith, love, hope and fidelity. There is no better way of acquiring "the mind of the Church" in the widest and most interior interpretation of this expression; it is something quite different from an instinctive obedience.[3]

We have spoken in Balthasarian terms of the theodramatic character of the Christian revelation, which is nothing less than the drama of cosmic time and the created order itself. To characterize this theodrama as having been revealed is to acknowledge that it could have become recognizable only in the way that it did: in the Incarnation, life, death, and Resurrection of Christ, made intelligible by its adumbrations in the history of the Jewish people. The scandal of this view is that the event that revealed it happened at one moment in the very history which it claims to have brought to fulfillment, at least in the sense that no subsequent revelation will add to or alter what is revealed in the canonical Scriptures and reprised in the sacramental life of the Church, most especially in the Eucharistic liturgy. Like the scandal of the Cross itself,

---

3 Congar, *The Meaning of Tradition*, 138.

this is one of those scandals that are "bound to occur" (see Mt 18:7).

Even those who are ignorant of the theodrama of which Balthasar has written can play an important role in that drama. Cyrus the king of Persia who returned the Israelites to their homeland is the classic example, but many others, less honorably remembered, could be named: Judas, Pilate, Herod and so forth. But the role these latter players in the drama perform, though essential, conduces to a condemnation from which only a postmortem encounter with Christ might rescue them. For it is those who have some general sense of the contours of the historical theodrama who will play their unique roles in that drama with the requisite intentionality, perseverance, and grace.

In Christ, Balthasar writes, "the end, the *eschaton*, is on the scene."[4] And not only "on the scene" in ancient Galilee and Judea but equally on the scene wherever the Eucharistic liturgy is celebrated. That Liturgy, writes Dietrich von Hildebrand, "combines holy sobriety with the greatest ardor, eternal calm with the deepest emotion.... It awakens us to that true, ultimate consciousness of communion, that ultimate, victorious union in love which is the very opposite of all human relationships of boisterous good-fellowship."[5] When this is not the case, an examination of conscience is in order — for the faithful in the pews as well as for the presiding priest. Roiled as the Church is today by non-negligible differences, boisterous good-fellowship may seem a consummation devoutly to be wished, but even when such fellowship is genuine, it is highly unstable. The more sociological this sense of participation is, the less reliable and spiritually efficacious it will be.

Christ left the Church the Eucharist thereby providing each of his followers down through history with access to the central event in history: Christ's assault on sin and death at its very heart, accomplished by his suffering, death, descent into the underworld of sin and despair, and his Resurrection on Easter morning. Inasmuch as the Eucharistic liturgy re-presents the central event of history — Christ's self-offering unto death and his raid on the otherwise impregnable fortress of annihilation — those who are sacramentally drawn into that drama will tap into theretofore unrealized resources of grace and, by cooperating with that grace, become beacons of hope to others. Indeed, they may thereby come to realize that Christ is not part of their life-story, but that they are part of his. "You did not choose me, but I chose you" (Jn 15:16).

---

4   Balthasar, *The von Balthasar Reader*, 120.
5   Hildebrand, *Liturgy and Personality*, 27.

34 The Acting Person:
NOT IN ONE'S OWN NAME

> It is not as if the very terminology of theology has not always been deeply indebted to the theater, especially in the use of *persona* as applied to the individuations of the Trinity.
> — Edward T. Oakes[1]

> For the human being, this is "living on a knife edge," that is, *between humility and the exhibitionistic loss of self*; thus behind the problem of the actor there emerges the problem of man himself, the conscious subject in search of a role.
> — Hans Urs von Balthasar[2]

> I also remember that my apparent self — this clown or hero or supernumerary — under his grease-paint is a real person with an off-stage life. The dramatic person could not tread the stage unless he concealed a real person.
> — C. S. Lewis[3]

MARTIN LUTHER KING, JR. FAMOUSLY SAID THAT he dreamt of a day when his children "will not be judged by the color of their skin but by the content of their character." It is one of the felicities of our language that the word *character* is commonly used when speaking of a performer in a drama, suggesting that the very nature of one's character is intertwined with the fact that, whether we realize it or not, we play a role in the drama of history, which Christians understand as the drama of world reclamation whose archetypal perturbations are recorded in the Old and New Testaments. It is not enough to explicate the truth that this tradition reveals; it must

---

1 Oakes, *Pattern of Redemption*, 221.
2 Balthasar, *Theo-Drama: Theological Dramatic Theory*, Vol. III: *Dramatis Personae: Persons in Christ*, 532, emphasis added.
3 Lewis, *Letters to Malcolm*, quoted in Oakes, *Pattern of Redemption*, 228.

be exemplified as well. Significance requires a signifier—not an idol who attracts attention to himself, but an icon who redirects attention to another. One's role in that drama will be a source of grace to the extent that one realizes its religious provenance and avails oneself of the requisite catechetical and sacramental resources.

Giuseppe Fornari captured an essential feature of Girard's apocalyptic apprehensions when he spoke of "the loss of all credible mediations,"[4] the evidence for which we have presented above. The adjective *credible* is aptly chosen. We are awash in mediations. There is water, water everywhere, and hardly a drop to drink. What is rare indeed are mediations that are credible in the etymological sense, from the Latin *credibilis*, meaning worthy of belief. A mediation or mediator is credible in this sense, not just when it gives rise to imitators, but when it awakens an act of "faith," a desire consonant with the imitator's true vocation. So fractured and divisive has our communal life become, and so preoccupied are many today with ever more minuscule and superficial differences, that we have forgotten the destiny we humans share by virtue of the fact that, as Henri de Lubac reminds us, "we all have the same essential finality."[5]

Of Christianity, then-Cardinal Joseph Ratzinger wrote: "It is not primarily the discovery of some truth; rather, it is the activity of God himself making history. Its meaning is, not that divine reality becomes visible to man, but that it makes the person who receives the revelation into an actor in divine history."[6]

As we have repeatedly stressed, each person has a vocation, a role to play in life, however lofty or humble it might be. To have a vocation is not only to be called, as the etymology of the word indicates, but to be called and sent. Our vocations intertwine with those of other members of our extraordinary species. No two vocations are the same, even though our vocations are almost always awakened by the example of others. As unavoidably mimetic as we humans are, finding no credible mediations at hand, we default to incredible ones, models who function for us as a pied piper, leading us away from the unique calling that is ours alone. We saw this with the fictional Willy and Hap Loman and the sundry characters in Virginia Woolf's *The Waves*, among others we have discussed.

---

[4] Fornari, *Dionysus, Christ, and the Death of God*, Vol. II, 421.
[5] De Lubac, *The Mystery of the Supernatural*, 63.
[6] Joseph Ratzinger, *Truth and Tolerance: Christian Belief and World Religions* (San Francisco: Ignatius Press, 2004), 42.

The Acting Person

In an earlier chapter we paused to notice the controlled — indeed, exquisitely choreographed — hysteria of the writer Camille Paglia, whom we included in our reflections on mystics in the primitive state. We now want to acknowledge Paglia's penetrating insight into the questions that have occupied us throughout this book. Emily Esfahani Smith began her 2019 *City Journal* article "The Provocations of Camille Paglia" with this fascinating assessment:

> The word "person" captures a concept so fundamental to Westerners that it can be jarring to discover that it once had a different meaning. Etymologically, "person" comes from the Latin word *persona*, which means "mask." To be a person is to wear a mask, act out a role — what people today might call being fake.
>
> But to Camille Paglia, the dissident social critic, a mask does not conceal a person's true nature; it helps reveal it. This is why Halloween was her favorite holiday as a child. It was "a fantastic opportunity," she told an interviewer recently, "to enact one's repressed and forbidden self — which in my case was male." When she was five, she dressed up as Robin Hood; at seven, she was a Roman soldier; at eight, Napoleon; at nine, Hamlet. "These masks," Paglia told me in Philadelphia recently, "are parts of myself."[7]

Here Paglia sees the dramatic nature of human personhood, but, lacking a master model capable of giving coherence to the various mimetic enticements, the models she finds appealing serve only to bring out parts of herself. Without that organizing principle and the Master Model in whom it is incarnated, the mimetic capacity of the individual actor slides from one model — one *persona* — to another in a helter-skelter, multiphrenia fashion, from Robin Hood, a Roman soldier, Napoleon, Hamlet, and leading in the end to what René Girard called the crisis of undifferentiation, where the most incontestable differences are blurred, and moral and cultural chaos ensues.

The best use to which Paglia can put her insight into the link between masks and personhood is to see the mask as "a fantastic opportunity to enact one's repressed and forbidden self." The enactment required an audience but appears not to have burdened the actor with a corresponding responsibility vis-à-vis that audience. The performance was

---

7   Smith, "The Provocations of Camille Paglia."

not to make the words and actions of the character being represented "come alive" for the edification of others, but an opportunity for the self-expression of the actor.

At seven, Paglia was a Roman soldier. Her contemporary, Bob Dylan, also played a Roman soldier as a child. Notwithstanding the similarity with Paglia's childhood Halloween experiences, Dylan's first experience as a performer seems to have left a lasting mark on him. He reminisced about it in 2004:

> My first performances were seen in the Black Hills Passion Play of South Dakota, a religious drama depicting the last days of Christ. This play always came to town during the Christmas season with professional actors in the leading roles, cages of pigeons, a donkey, a camel and a truck full of props. There were always parts that called for extras. One year I played a Roman soldier with a spear and helmet — breastplate, the works — a nonspeaking role, but it didn't matter. I felt like a star. I liked the costume. It felt like a nerve tonic ... as a Roman soldier I felt like a part of everything, in the center of the planet, invincible.[8]

That experience stayed with Dylan and his reference to it in an autobiographical work attests to its enduring importance for him. Whereas Paglia experienced sundry "parts of herself" each Halloween, Dylan felt himself to be *part* of a larger and more important drama. "It felt like a nerve tonic... I felt like a part of everything, in the center of the planet, invincible." It is this latter experience that resonates with what John Zizioulas meant when he said the actor onstage experiences "a certain taste of freedom, a certain specific 'hypostasis,' a certain identity," becoming a *person* "albeit for a brief period." In light of what we know of Dylan's spiritual journey, the broader significance of this recollection should not be overlooked. As Dylan realized in retrospect, the part he played in the drama "didn't matter." It might have been any part. What mattered was the drama in which he was given a small but non-negligible role to play. He may have felt like a star, but the exhilaration he felt derived from the significance of the drama far more than from the part he played in it.

In light of his career since his 1979 album, *Slow Train*, Dylan's recollection of his childhood role in a Passion Play may not have been

---

8   Bob Dylan, *Chronicles*, Volume One (New York: Simon & Schuster, 2004), 124–25.

as offhanded as it seemed. It is, arguably, the buried lede. In a 2017 interview with Bill Flanagan, Dylan was asked if he had been inspired by any films. Of the five films he mentioned, the first three were based on biblical characters and themes. In the order in which he listed them they were: *The Robe, King of Kings*, and *Samson and Delilah*.[9] It bears noting that the first film Dylan mentioned was *The Robe*, the elaborate story of a "Roman soldier" drawn by circumstances into the Passion of Christ and brought thereby to faith in Christ.

More evidence for this intriguing suggestion can be found in a number of lyrics in Dylan's 2020 album *Rough and Rowdy Ways*. The album is suffused with Christian themes and tropes. It is hard not to see unmistakable signs, not just of Dylan's debt to Christianity, but, more plausibly, his deeply Christian cast of mind.

> Mother of Muses, unleash your wrath
> Things I can't see, they're blocking my path
> Show me your wisdom, tell me my fate
> Put me upright, make me walk straight
> Forge my identity from the inside out
> You know what I'm talking about
>
> Take me to the river, release your charms
> Let me lay down a while in your sweet, loving arms
> Wake me, shake me, free me from sin
> Make me invisible, like the wind
> Got a mind that ramble, got a mind that roam
> I'm travellin' light and I'm a-slow coming home.[10]

After this plea to be awakened and freed from sin, the next song of the album, "Crossing the Rubicon," picks up what is an unmistakable allusion to the Jordan, the baptismal river, and, some have surmised, perhaps even the Tiber. Dylan drives the theme of fateful decision by punctuating each of the nine stanzas with the same line:

> I've painted my wagon, abandoned all hope
> And I crossed the Rubicon...
> I prayed to the cross, I kissed the girls
> And I crossed the Rubicon...
> I pawned my watch, I paid my debts

---

9   Q and A with Bill Flanagan, March 22, 2017, www.bobdylan.com/news/qa-with-bill-flanagan/.
10 Dylan, "Goodbye Jimmy Reed," *Rough and Rowdy Ways*.

> And I crossed the Rubicon…
> I poured a cup, I passed it along
> And I crossed the Rubicon.[11]

We invite the reader to ponder the meaning of the line "I pawned my watch." For this writer, it is a magnificent reference to the poet's escape from the fashionable tropes of revolutionary progress with which Dylan's earliest lyrics were suffused: the times they are a-changin', and so on. Whatever hints of catholicity we might discern in Dylan's songs, they are balanced by lyrics of a more Protestant tenor. From a song dedicated to the Blues musician from the mid-twentieth century, "Goodbye Jimmy Reed," we find these lines:

> Give me that old time religion, it's just what I need…
> For thine is kingdom, the power, the glory
> Go tell it on the mountain, go tell the real story
> Tell it in that straightforward, puritanical tone
> In the mystic hours when a person's alone.[12]

For our purposes, the confessional meaning of Dylan's allusion is less important than the palpable sense that he has come to see himself as someone who, as Balthasar would say, *has been taken into service*. He is living on that "knife-edge" *between humility and the exhibitionistic loss of self*. He has come to realize that his life belongs more to an Other, whom he must now re-present, than was the case when, as he says in *False Prophet*: "I opened my heart to the world and the world came in."[13] Among the many places in his 2020 album that hint at an experience of Paul's "It is no longer I who live, but Christ who lives in me," perhaps the most explicit is the title of one of the songs on the album: "My Own Version of You."

> I'm gon' bring someone to life, someone I've never seen
> You know what I mean, you know exactly what I mean.
> …
> You can bring it to St. Peter
> You can bring it to Jerome
> You can bring it all the way over
> Bring it all the way home
> Bring it to the corner where the children play

---

11   Ibid., "Crossing the Rubicon."
12   Ibid., "Goodbye Jimmy Reed."
13   Ibid., "False Prophet."

> You can bring it to me on a silver tray
> I'll bring someone to life, spare no expense
> Do it with decency and common sense.[14]

It appears from these latest iterations of Dylan's musical and poetic testimony that, while Buddy Holly served as the mimetic icon for Dylan's musical career, it was the seemingly insignificant role he played as a child in the Passion Play that came slowly to flower in his mid-career conversion, his carefully encrypted but heartfelt Christ-centered sensibility.

In contrast to the "individual" whose private rituals of dis-identification remain within permissible subclinical limits, and the hysteric whose strategies for resisting the unwelcome mimetic allure of a model has attracted the attention of clinicians, the actor is fully authorized to subordinate himself (if temporarily) to another in accord with his professional responsibilities. By playing a part in a larger drama, the actor discovers forms of both freedom and dignity beyond anything he might achieve by foreswearing the apparent constraints on his freedom that the role may have demanded.

In the theodrama of which Balthasar has written, the analogue of the inner-Trinitarian collaboration is that between the playwright, protagonist, and casting director. It is the latter — the inscrutable Spirit — who coaxes potential members of the supporting cast by calling each to an utterly unique role, one that depends in part on the capacities of the one called no less than on the historical and circumstantial conditions to which a Christian response is required. The grace commensurate with the demands of the role is available in proportion to the willingness of the one who responds to the inner call. What is astonishing about this is that the role each actor in the theodrama is asked to play requires more creativity on his part than do the roles which appear to give him more latitude.

As Father Roch Kereszty has insisted, "we do not become carbon copies of Christ but rather, by our conformity to Christ, we realize our most authentic and individual selves."[15] Lucien Richard expressed this boldly and beautifully: "Vicariousness is not something esoteric, rather, it is the fundamental principle of all personal life."[16] A vicarious life

---

14   Ibid., "My Own Version of You."
15   Roch Kereszty, O. Cist., "The Body and the Bride of Christ," *Communio*, Vol. 46, no. 2 (Summer 2019): 275.
16   Lucien Richard, *Christ: The Self-Emptying of God* (New York: Paulist Press, 1997), 176.

or a vicarious mission is the life of a vicar, a deputy or proxy, one who acts and speaks on behalf of—and in the name of—a superior authority.

As his dying gift, Christ breathed out his Spirit on fallen humanity, as he breathed on the apostles after the Resurrection. The goal of the Christian life is to allow the Spirit that Christ sent into the world and into our hearts to have access to our natural endowment in all its uniqueness, trusting that our lives will be fulfilled to the degree that the Spirit of Christ passes through them as unimpaired as possible by sin and self-will. "And when they bring you to trial and deliver you up, do not be anxious beforehand about what you are to say; but say whatever is given you in that hour, for it is not you who speak, but the Holy Spirit" (Mk 13:11).

In the fallen world Christians are always being brought to trial in one way or another, and no defense we might muster out of our own moral, intellectual, or rhetorical resources will suffice. We must "take a deep breath" and allow the Spirit to speak through us. In allowing the Spirit access to his faculties, the "actor" becomes a person. As we noted earlier, the Hebrew prophets gave the world the first adumbration of this intersubjective mystery, and both Bob Dylan and the poet and singer Leonard Cohen have brought the Jewish prophetic persona into a profound engagement with its Christian extension. In his ominously apocalyptic song, *The Future*, Cohen allows the biblical Spirit to speak through him. He speaks vicariously.

> You don't know me from the wind
> you never will, you never did
> I'm the little jew
> who wrote the Bible.[17]

The Mystery that gave rise to the Bible makes use of the frailties no less than the strengths of those who allow themselves to become instruments of its proclamation. If those who are "brought to trial" before the bar of worldly indignation take a deep breath of the Spirit to which their social precariousness gives them privileged access, they can "resonate" (re-sound) with the world's most powerful and healing truth. Such an "actor" unites both with the Source — the still small voice — and with his fellow actors in the drama into which his performance is being dramatically inserted and sacramentally choreographed.

---

17 Leonard Cohen, *The Future*, Columbia Records, 1992, compact disc.

Together this chorus re-sounds with a symphonic truth that can be adequately acclaimed in no other way.

Julián Carrón has provided another apt analogue of this mystery: "Following has nothing to do," writes Carrón, "with obeying user instructions or doing what others tell us to do. It is engagement with a living event, which causes another person's heart to start vibrating within our own."[18] That living event has a Golgothan structure, and the power of one's witness will depend on how close to the center of that event one allows himself to be drawn. In one way or another, every sincere Christian is brought to trial and handed over. For he is charged with the task of proclaiming the enigmatic mystery at the heart of his faith, a mystery which demands the Yes or No of which Balthasar has so provocatively spoken.

The Amazon jungle is a cacophony of bird calls, but each bird is keenly and primarily alert to the call of those of its own species. Admittedly a crude comparison, but the analogous point is that we are ordered to the call — the *Logos* — that is cognate with the mystery of our existence. We, like the birds, are called, and amid the pandemonium that is our life in this world, we are endowed with an acuity that disposes us to respond to the call that comes from Christ. This call comes through countless inadequate transmitters without losing its integrity. This mystery was expressed with great clarity by David L. Schindler in his introduction to Henri de Lubac's *The Mystery of the Supernatural*:

> On the one hand, if grace did not somehow — always already — touch the soul of every human being, the Christian fact would remain an essentially "private" matter of urgent concern only to those who were already believers. On the other hand, if the order of grace were not essentially gratuitous — that is, did not really add something to nature that could not be anticipated or claimed by nature itself — then the Christian fact would lose its newness and its proper character as divine gift.[19]

The burden of de Lubac's argument, Schindler writes, is "how human persons in the natural order can be interiorly directed to the order of grace that fulfills them, without in the least possessing this grace in

---

18   Julián Carrón, *Disarming Beauty: Essays on Faith, Truth, and Freedom* (Notre Dame, IN: University of Notre Dame Press, 2017), 222.
19   David L. Schindler, introduction to de Lubac, *The Mystery of the Supernatural*, xvi.

anticipation, and without being able at all to claim it for themselves."[20] Suzanne Siauve restates this mystery quite beautifully:

> The radically new idea that Christianity introduces, one that is not found in any other religious conception, is that the baptized person, by the fact of his free gift from Christ — and not because he is a saint or spiritual leader, a great yogi or bodhisattva — has the actual power to transmit to his neighbor what he has himself received, to reach the other person through the intermediary of those channels of life that run through all the mystical body, even though most often nothing about this transmission is directly perceptible.[21]

According to Balthasar, the inner drama of history after Christ involves the mutual intensification of the Yes and the No to Christ and his Church. This correlates with the Jacques Maritain observation often cited by Girard: "with the passing of time there is always more good and more evil in the world."[22] With Balthasar, Girard saw this "mutual intensification" as the key to understanding history after the Golgothan revelation. Balthasar provides an extremely timely recognition of this when he writes:

> One may imagine that one could advocate human dignity without believing in God's person, indeed precisely by denying it. But the logic of history will again level, either existentially or collectivistically, the persons who have thus been absolutized. It will turn them into cannon fodder and the objects of experiments, into manure for evolution.[23]

---

20   Ibid., xvii.
21   Suzanne Siauve, *Axes* (December 1970): 41–42, quoted in de Lubac, *Theological Fragments*, 34.
22   Girard, *Evolution and Conversion: Dialogues on the Origin of Culture*, 220.
23   Balthasar, *The von Balthasar Reader*, 194.

35 All the World's a Stage

> God had written, not so much a poem, but rather a play; a play he had planned as perfect, but which necessarily had been left to human actors and stage-managers, who have since made a great mess of it.
> — G. K. Chesterton[1]

> Christianity is not only to be received in faith, nor only preached, but *performed*.
> — Hans Urs von Balthasar[2]

> All the world's a stage,
> And all the men and women merely players.
> — William Shakespeare (*As You Like It*, II: vii)

THE FAMOUS SOLILOQUY THAT SHAKESPEARE PUTS into the mouth of his character Jacques trails off into a mournful lament about the stages of life. But the first line of the famous seven ages of man speech invites two understandings of the word stage: a theatrical one and a temporal one. All the world is a *stage* on which we the actors take our place and play our parts, but it is a world with a prologue and a future, and we live at one moment, at one unique *stage* in an ongoing historical drama in which we "find ourselves" and in the midst of which we each have a small, undefined, but non-negligible role to play.

In summarizing Balthasar's theodramatic understanding of the Christian vocation, Edward Oakes argues that, for the Swiss theologian, the artist, and by extension, the Christian, is most free when "no longer trapped in a slum of infinite possibilities or caught up in the indecision of having to decide among a number of 'neutral' possibilities for the execution of his work." This spiritual vagrancy ends, Oakes avers, if and when one "is finally 'possessed' by the idea inspiring him and *surrenders*

---

1   Chesterton, *Orthodoxy*, 74.
2   Balthasar, *Convergences*, 40–41. Emphasis added.

himself completely to its imperious and peremptory demands."[3] Hardly could such a vision of Christian personhood be more germane to the current cultural situation.

To which we would only add one qualification: However reflexively we may fit into the larger historical story going on around us, we do so in choreographic sync with our fellow actors, who share our moment in time and our cultural milieu. Those with whom we share this moment in time and this particular historical predicament are *given* to us, as we are to them, as members of an ensemble responsible for playing our parts in ways that put us in touch with the mystery of our existence. Of this mystery, the Christian is generally more cognizant than are his secularized neighbors, for whom he therefore bears a corresponding responsibility. C. S. Lewis has beautifully captured the reality of which the Christian is invited to become conscious:

> I cannot, in the flesh, leave the stage, either to go behind the scenes or to take my seat in the pit; but I can remember that these regions exist. And I also remember that my apparent self — this clown or hero or supernumerary — under his grease-paint is a real person with an off-stage life. The dramatic person could not tread the stage unless he concealed a real person.[4]

No one can completely avoid being affected by the spirit of the age, nor should we, though Saint Paul was surely right to warn against the danger this involves. Our historical and cultural moment supplies the circumstances and challenges that may well frame the role we play in life. Nor, however, should the accident of our birth and cultural situation become the exclusive criterion for discerning the life to which we are called. What distinguishes Christians is that their faith has made them aware of the broad outlines of the ultimate story of human and cosmic history. Thus, they can more readily find their own unique part to play in that story, which they understand, or are encouraged to understand, as a *mission*. It is the mission, Balthasar stresses, that is constitutive of the person. For a Christian, each vocation will have a theodramatic dimension, the core essence of which will be to live one's life and face one's death in ways that make God's love, Christ's Incarnation of God's love, and the saving gift of Christ's life to humanity

---

3 Oakes, *Pattern of Redemption*, 219.
4 Lewis, *Letters to Malcolm*, quoted in Oakes, *Pattern of Redemption*, 228.

more tangible and credible, and to perform that role with all the freedom and spontaneity that grace affords.

> If I had the wings of a snow-white dove
> I'd preach the gospel, the gospel of love
> A love so real, a love so true
> I've made up my mind to give myself to you.[5]

---

[5] Dylan, "I've Made Up My Mind to Give Myself to You," *Rough and Rowdy Ways*.

36 Stage Fright

> And it is no less curious that many of these traditionalists are so volubly and intransigently hostile to both the last century's *ressourcement* movement and the inaptly named *nouvelle théologie* with which it was often associated. Both of these latter, after all, were attempts to return to and learn from the deepest, most ancient, and most enriching wellsprings of Catholic tradition.
> — David Bentley Hart[1]

> The modern image of the world does not in the least refute the faith. But it does demand a quite different armory of spiritual power than the Middle Ages, for example, or the apostolic age.
> — Reinhold Schneider[2]

> Our age does not appreciate the power and the necessity of the nation, a natural community in which we seek habits of virtue and ordered liberty.
> — Jakub Grygiel[3]

Accommodations between the Church and the world that might be possible and fruitful at one stage in the historical theodrama may well be entirely counterproductive at another. For instance, Saint Paul's Areopagus debates demonstrated, not the complete incompatibility of Christianity and the noblest aspirations of pagan thought, but that in the mid-first century an adjudication of their points of contact was premature and untimely. In the fourth century Augustine was in a better position to try to bring elements of the Platonic tradition into an engagement with Christian thought. And by the thirteenth century, Thomas Aquinas would brilliantly and boldly find points of engagement with the Aristotelian corpus. In the following

---

1 David Bentley Hart, *Tradition and Apocalypse: An Essay on the Future of Christian Belief* (Grand Rapids, MI: Baker Academic, 2022), 16.
2 Quoted in Balthasar, *Tragedy Under Grace*, 271.
3 Jakub Grygiel, "Miracle on the Dniepr," *First Things*, March 7, 2022.

century, Dante would perform a poetic reconnoiter of the Greco-Roman tradition on a broader front. Thus, the terms of the engagement between Church and world change from one epoch to another. In each age the Church must recognize the unavoidable chasm that must exist between worldly assessments and Christian thought. It will always be necessary for Christianity to work out how best to present to its worldly interlocuter the Truth it exists to profess, and to do so without betraying the deposit of faith that has been entrusted to the Church.

This is no task for the fainthearted, as Henri de Lubac reminded his readers in his magnificent *Catholicism: Christ and the Common Destiny of Man*: "In examining this entirely secularized concept of society, which at the present time dominates men's minds everywhere and only degrades what it has inherited of the historical and social character of our Faith, we must have the courage to show ourselves resolutely reactionary."[4]

But in being "resolutely reactionary" with respect to that assortment of ideological secular creeds that are corrupting the culture built on Christian faith, we must resist the hope of restoring the Church-state relationship found workable at an earlier stage in the historical interplay between the Church and the world. No accommodation will ever eliminate the inherently agonistic character of that relationship. Indeed, the congeniality of a putatively more harmonious relationship might well be accomplished by obscuring the mutual intensification of the "Yes" and the "No" to the crucified and risen Christ. For, as Balthasar has argued and we have stressed:

> We are not free to decide whether we want to say "Yes" or "No" or not.... If a man does not want to say "Yes" he has already said "No." If he thinks it impossible to say "No," he has said "Yes," if not to the historical Christian revelation, which he may fail to understand, at least to a possible word from God and the obligation to obey it.[5]

For such a response to be dispositive, it must be a free decision. No merely cultural assent can dispense a Christian from uttering the Yes that inaugurates the life of faith — the source of personhood in its full religious sense. Any attempt to revive a Christian culture by substituting a cultural Yes for a personal one would eviscerate both the faith and the act essential to personhood properly understood. The Christian character

---

4 De Lubac, *Catholicism*, 357.
5 Balthasar, *The God Question and Modern Man*, 72.

of a culture will flow from the bottom, not the top. It will result from the gradual Christianization of the members of that culture. Whatever gratitude we might feel for the historical and ecclesial benefits of Constantine's conversion, the top-down Christianization of cultures is no longer either possible or preferable.

The fluctuations in the historical drama will continue, and the faith of Christians in the final triumph of Christ will be sorely tested even in epochs more tolerant of Christian faith. Today, when faith is weak even in once highly Christianized cultures, two somewhat related temptations have arisen, each made plausible by some feature of the Christian cultural heritage, a secular one and a religious one, namely: post-national globalism and pre-modern integralism. Each is a misunderstanding of the actual *stage* of history at which we now stand. The globalist dream, secretly drawing its appeal from Christian universalism, is as anthologically naïve as it is potentially tyrannical.

Pre-modern integralism, on the other hand, pines for an accommodation between God and Caesar that was workable for a while under historical circumstances that no longer exist and are not likely to return. Meanwhile, as the Catholic political philosopher Daniel J. Mahoney has perceptively noted: "For all its imperfections the modern nation-state provides a home for political freedom, an obstacle to sentimental cosmopolitanism, and an alternative to the ferociously tyrannical vision of a 'universal and homogenous state.'"[6]

Globalism is championed today by the most powerful political and economic institutions, whose technocrats and plutocrats regard, not without some reason, popular plebiscites as too cumbersome to meet the crises of the moment — real and imagined. The challenge as these globalists see it is to prevent national loyalties — *pietas* — from interfering with bureaucratic management by the qualified elite, whose authoritarian predilections are conspicuous.

The new integralism, on the other hand, is no less appalled by the "entirely secularized concept of society" toward which de Lubac declared himself "resolutely reactionary." This is how Father Edmund Waldstein, O. Cist. has defined integralism:

> Catholic Integralism is a tradition of thought that, rejecting the liberal separation of politics from concern with the end of human life, holds that political rule must order man to his

---

[6] Daniel J. Mahoney, "Between Marx and Aquinas," *Claremont Review of Books*, Fall, 2022.

final goal. Since, however, man has both a temporal and an eternal end, integralism holds that there are two powers that rule him: a temporal power and a spiritual power. And since man's temporal end is subordinated to his eternal end, the temporal power must be subordinated to the spiritual power.

Understood in broad terms, there is nothing problematic about this statement, any more than one can fail to sympathize with the words of Pope Pius XI: "When once men recognize, both in private and in public life, that Christ is King, society will at last receive the great blessings of real liberty, well-ordered discipline, peace and harmony."[7] Thus understood, integralism is an eschatological, not practical, aspiration, which is underscored by Pius's phrase: "at last." To expect to achieve "real liberty, well-ordered discipline, peace and harmony" in this life is, frankly, utopian, and Christians, especially Catholic Christians, have a well-earned reputation for eschewing utopian dreams. Like the blessed condition of heavenly life, such a seamless concord of Church and world is an eschatological vision, not a strategy for achieving it in this life. The social furniture that would have to be broken, and the betrayals — seen and unseen — that its attainment would require, would amount to the Church's implicit confession of the failure of its evangelical mission, namely, to bring about the subordination of temporal power to spiritual power in the old-fashioned way, by relying on the living testimony of Christian exemplars, champions, and martyrs.

Writing almost forty years ago about the nostalgia for a throne and altar integralism among those bemoaning the attenuation of Catholic faith and practice following Vatican II, Joseph Ratzinger expressed himself no less forcefully than did de Lubac when speaking of contemporary sterile secularism. But he did so with his characteristic nuance and sense of balance.

> Among the more obvious phenomena of the last years must be counted the increasing number of integralist groups in which the desire for piety, for the sense of mystery, is finding satisfaction. We must be on our guard against minimizing these movements. Without a doubt, they represent a sectarian zealotry that is the anthesis of Catholicity. We cannot resist them too firmly. But we must likewise ask ourselves, in all earnestness, why such contradictions and distortions of faith and piety have such an

---

7   Encyclical letter *Quas Primas* §19.

> effect and are able to attract those who, by basic conviction as well as by personal inclination, are in no way attracted by sectarianism. Why have they lost the feeling of being at home in the larger Church? Are all their reproaches unfounded? Is it not, for example, really strange that we have never heard bishops react as strongly against distortions in the heart of the liturgy as they react today against the use of a Missal of the Church that, after all, has been in existence since the time of Pius V? Let it be said again: we should not adopt a sectarian attitude, but neither should we omit the examination of conscience to which these facts compel us.[8]

The link that the future Benedict XVI recognized between the appeal of integralism and the widespread banalization of the Eucharistic liturgy was typically prescient. It is hardly surprising that those who lament the increasing marginalization of the Mass of the Ages find the romance of Catholic integralism attractive. It is easy as well to empathize with the integralist reaction to its secular parody whereby Christian denominations are expected to morally and doctrinally "evolve" by sanctioning or tolerating social and moral fashions deeply at odds with traditional Christian faith and biblical anthropology.

On the eve of the last Council, Balthasar foresaw the danger facing the Church and the temptation to adopt the tolerance and inclusion ruses that now ring so hollow. "Religion disappears from public life," he wrote, and "*if* it is still mentioned ... it is something that demands to be officially tolerated, and hence must itself make *toleration* its supreme law."[9]

These words were written many decades before the secular tolerance and inclusion movement, having commandeered — and then betrayed — the empathy for victims (the premier source of which is the Christian scriptures), came to dominate American popular culture. However pathetic it is for the Church to give credence to that act of moral prestidigitation, and however legitimate, when properly understood, the aspiration to subordinate worldly concerns to eschatological ones, this can properly be accomplished only by the power of Christian witnesses. "It is not our mission to make truth triumph," wrote Henri de Lubac, "but to testify for it."[10]

---

8   Ratzinger, *Principles of Catholic Theology*, 389–90.
9   Hans Urs von Balthasar, *The God Question and Modern Man* (New York: Seabury Press, 1967), 75, emphasis added.
10 Henri de Lubac, *Paradoxes of Faith* (San Francisco: Ignatius Press, 1987), 72.

It is passing strange, moreover, that at the moment when the sitting Roman Pontiff routinely appears to be more in sync — and in sympathy — with the aspirations of today's post-national globalists than with the Church Fathers, no small number of those eager to restore the Church's authority dream of an integralism which, under the present and foreseeable ecclesial circumstances, might well compound the worldly compromises from which the integralist seeks to free the Church. Indeed, the proponents of integralism appear to have contracted the latest variant of the political virus for which integralism is declared to be the efficacious vaccine. Aidan Nichols, O.P., wisely warned against "a false internationalism [which] suppresses love of homeland, and a false pacifism [which] makes men overanxious and war more likely."[11] If the state or the global superstate is to be superintended by the Church, it will be the Church's saints and not her governing hierarchs who occasion some semblance of that blessed state of affairs.

> The decision for or against God can only be made by individuals.... No one can make his own decision on behalf of his brethren, relieving all others from their obligation to make theirs. For *at this stage*, when religion has come to mean essentially this decision, everything depends on this, that each individual, representing the whole, should personally decide for God.... The slightest compulsion would at once, and rightly, be felt and opposed as "religious fascism."[12]

It is of course perfectly proper and necessary for those with social and political responsibilities to work to pass laws and shape society in conformance with the natural law and its specification in the ten commandments and the "law of freedom" in the New Testament. As John Paul II insisted, the Christian way is to propose, not impose, and Christians have the advantage of having a very attractive proposal to make. Challenging though it is, it is ennobling and edifying. It needs only to be proclaimed in the spirit with which it is suffused.

Wary of the "exaggerated traditionalism which neglects the man of today and tomorrow in its enthusiasm for a magnificent ecclesiastical past," Balthasar cites Reinhold Schneider's dictum: "faith triumphs even on the funeral pyre of mockery."[13] The faith of which we speak,

---

[11] Nichols, *The Word Has Been Abroad*, 125.
[12] Balthasar, *The God Question and Modern Man*, 76, 77. Emphasis added.
[13] Balthasar, *Tragedy Under Grace*, 88, 71.

of course, began by triumphing on that funeral pyre at Golgotha. With the help of D. C. Schindler's perceptive analysis, we spoke in an earlier chapter of the enigma of power and authority, which is at the heart of the Christian revelation itself. Stated straightforwardly, we can say that power, properly understood, is the rightful exercise of authority. But the paradox is that real authority originates in the renunciation of power.[14] As Balthasar stresses: "Wherever the Church rejects the powerlessness of the Cross, which is offered her and imposed upon her, she reaches out to take hold of power, and the face of Satan glimmers in her."[15]

Far from depriving the Church and the world of the blessing of the integralism of an earlier age, its rejection today is the precondition for the retrieval of this blessing.

> The medieval kingdom has crumbled away, the knightly Orders and the sociological forms of the feudal system have disappeared. But no bourgeoisie can suffocate the Christian knighthood: the man who follows Christ to the full, who denies himself and dies to himself and to the world in poverty and chastity and obedience, in order to clothe himself in the mind of Christ and to take up the weapons of the Spirit, can never, ever be a "bourgeois." He does not strive on his own behalf (like the bourgeois), but on behalf of the will and for the glorification of Another.[16]

In other words, not only does chivalry survive the passing of the "sociological forms of the feudal system," the superannuation of those forms is the precondition for the revival of a properly Christian chivalry, one that draws its attractive power from its relative powerlessness.

The place from which the gospel is most effectively preached is the Cross, whether the one proclaiming it is on the Cross or at the foot of it. Thus, the dream of achieving what non-Christians would recognize as a Christian victory is a wan fantasy. For that would not be the victory of the Cross. De Lubac has captured this in two aphoristic observations which appear next to one another in his first collection of paradoxes.

---

14 For a more sustained treatment of this enigma and the anthropological roots, see our *God's Gamble: The Gravitational Power of Crucified Love*, 11–30.
15 Balthasar, *Tragedy Under Grace*, 212.
16 Ibid., 248.

Will [success] be obtained when everybody will have been pleased, when everybody will have understood, and when no astonishment or scandal greatly risks being merely the mark of ineffectiveness. Nothing strong, nothing new, nothing urgent penetrates man's mind without crossing resistance. Or would you think that Christian preaching should no longer be "scandal" and "folly" in the eyes of the world?[17]

The very success of an extreme popularization is sometimes, in religious matters, a disaster. Mr. X, for example, a brilliant professor, attracts a large audience to his classes and thus sheds, as everyone sees and acclaims, Christian influence. But on each occasion a few young men and girls, less docile, more demanding, not daring perhaps to stand opposed to the enthusiastic atmosphere, clench their fists in silence.[18]

---

17   De Lubac, *Paradoxes of Faith*, 76–77.
18   Ibid., 77.

37 "I Live, Now No Longer I, But Christ Lives In Me"

> Christianity is thus throughout the Revelation of Personality....
> For a Person came, and lived and loved, and did and taught, and died and rose again, and lives on by his Power and his Spirit forever *within* us and *among* us.
> — Friedrich von Hügel[1]

> We are fully personal only within the Person of the Son, by whom and in whom we have a share in the exchanges of the trinitarian life.
> — Henri de Lubac[2]

THE SUBTITLE OF THIS BOOK IS: RECOVERING THE *Christian Mystery of Personhood*. Inspired by the catholicity of René Girard's anthropological genius and the humility of his Catholic faith, we have explored the other-oriented structure of personhood and its manifestation in Christian thought and faith. In conclusion we must now say a few words about the unique form of personhood that Christian faith inaugurates in the believer, and which he thereafter has an opportunity to bring to fruition. In sync with de Lubac and so many of his precursors down through history, we conclude with a few reflections on personhood in its full theological and christological sense.

Everyone conceived by human parents is a person from the moment of conception, as we have repeatedly stressed. Nonetheless, each of us is inwardly summoned thereafter to the fulfillment of that noble vocation according to whatever might be one's God-given resources, opportunities, and handicaps and, not least, our attentiveness to the subtle summons that serves to bring these things into a fruitful harmony. "*In Christo*," writes

---

1 Quoted in de Lubac, *Catholicism*, 439, emphasis added.
2 Henri de Lubac, *At the Service of the Church*, trans. Anne Elizabeth Englund (San Francisco: Ignatius Press, 1993), 192.

Balthasar, "every man can cherish the hope of not remaining a merely individual conscious subject but of receiving personhood from God, becoming a person, with a mission that is likewise defined *in Christo*."[3]

An important factor in fulfilling the promise of personhood is the degree and clarity with which one knows at least the outlines of the actual drama in which his life is situated. There are countless examples of people who have given their lives to merely fanciful or even patently ridiculous "causes" or fashionable, unexamined presuppositions with an admirable degree of sincerity, dignity, and selflessness. However commendable such lives might be, neither the moral rectitude of the actor nor the genuine fruits of his efforts completely compensate for the dubiousness of the worldview in furtherance of which such efforts were expended, and their fruits harvested. There always remains something sad about the imbalance between the romanticism or naïveté of a cause and the sincerity and ardor of its champion.

Notwithstanding the earnestness of the actor and the zeal of his commitment to the drama in which he imagines himself to be performing his part, the fulfillment of his human vocation will largely depend on how closely the story about the meaning and purpose of his life operating in the background of his imagination accords with the actual situation of his existence, of the world in which he lives, and not least with what Henri de Lubac calls his "essential finality." This latter consideration is especially important, for without a *telos* — a sense of the ultimate destiny of a life or of the cosmic order itself — the adventure of life easily succumbs to fashions and urgencies more likely to squander one's human agency than to make it fruitful. To fail to reckon with one's essential finality, or to harbor an illusion about it or dismiss the matter as irrelevant to the challenges immediately at hand, is to expose oneself to the passing allure of merely fortuitous events.

Fulfilling the promise prefigured in the Old Testament prophets, those who had a consequential encounter with Jesus during his years on earth became persons in an incomparable way, as did those who became Christians on the evidence that these first-hand witnesses bequeathed to them by word and deed. Jesus was and is the *Truth in Person* (see Jn 14:6). Persons, in the deepest Christian sense, are awakened by an encounter with the Person of Christ, observably by the intermediate mediation of a Christian exemplar and more elusively and yet more profoundly by

---

3 Balthasar, *Theo-Drama: Theological Dramatic Theory*, Vol. III: *The Dramatis Personae: Persons in Christ*, 220.

the sacramental mediation of Christ himself, for which the Church was founded and commissioned. In either case, Henri de Lubac insisted, faith is "not the simple knowledge or the simple affirmation of an impersonal truth," rather it is "the impulse of a personal commitment to a Person."[4] Whatever the circumstances that leave this christological watermark on one's life, it may fade or mature, according to one's circumstances, resolve, and inner disposition. But the decisive point is that it is not thereafter *extinguishable*.

"Deep in human nature (and so in every man)," de Lubac writes, "the image of God is imprinted... a kind of secret call to the Object of the full and supernatural revelation brought by Christ."[5] Thus every person "has an organic link with Christ — and has it in such a way that he cannot lose it."[6] If this inner summons fails to elicit a fully conscious — even if tentative — "Yes," it risks succumbing to the serial idolatry of the hysteric or being swept toward a nihilistic "No," and "the raging fire that is to burn rebels" (Heb 10:27) — examples of which we have surveyed and which abound in our world today.

Alternatively, the light of the *Logos* "plays in ten thousand places... through the features of men's faces" without arousing idolatry. To catch a glimpse of this light is to awaken to the entirely unique personal existence to which Christ invites us, which can thereafter bear fruit in choreographic sync with our fellow actors in the particular theodramatic setting of one's life and historical circumstances.

> The grace which the Father gives us is christoform: it assimilates us to the Son without violating us as human beings — for the Son himself became a human being.... Paul calls this "putting on Christ" (Rom 13:14, Gal 3:27), "putting on the new nature" (Eph 4:24; Col 3:10), "Put on then, as God's chosen ones, holy and beloved, compassion, kindness, lowliness, meekness, and patience.... Let the word of Christ dwell in you richly" (Col 3:12–16).[7]

"I live, now no longer I, but Christ lives in me," wrote one of the most unique men who ever lived (Gal 2:20). And yet, as the Apostle to the Gentiles insisted, his role in the redemptive drama was no more essential than were the roles to which each of his fellow Christians were called:

---

4 Quoted in de Lubac, *Theology in History*, 329.
5 De Lubac, *The Church: Paradox and Mystery*, 102–3.
6 Ibid., 103.
7 Balthasar, *Prayer*, 58, 59.

"I Live, Now No Longer I, But Christ Lives In Me"

> Now there are varieties of gifts, but the same Spirit; and there are varieties of service, but the same Lord; and there are varieties of working, but it is the same God who inspires them all in every one. To each is given the manifestation of the Spirit for the common good. To one is given through the Spirit the utterance of wisdom, and to another the utterance of knowledge according to the same Spirit, to another faith by the same Spirit, to another gifts of healing by the one Spirit, to another the working of miracles, to another prophecy, to another the ability to distinguish between spirits, to another various kinds of tongues, to another the interpretation of tongues. All these are inspired by one and the same Spirit, who apportions to each one individually as he wills. (1 Cor 12:4–11)

That toward which we have been awkwardly gesturing in these concluding and inadequate remarks is the reality to which Yves Congar gave witness when he spoke of that "immense life that has been personalized in me." Congar was quick to insist of this immense life that "it is not mine."[8] As it was with Paul, so it was with the French Dominican. It was Christ alive in him. The paradigmatic Christian form of personhood, therefore, is not strictly speaking selfless. In Balthasar's remarkable formulation, previously cited, it is "living on the knife edge *between humility and the exhibitionistic loss of self*." By living on such a knife edge, one does not forfeit either the vitality of his own unique personhood nor his responsibility to exercise his own agency. Quite the contrary. It simply means that the person in the deepest Christian sense of the word *does not come in his own name*. Such a person is spared none of the confusion and anguish of his age and temperament, but he has the ballast that will steady him when facing the perennial storms of human existence.

> Even in these times of intoxication mingled with anxiety, amidst the most pressing necessities, it is the role of the Christian, a man among his brother men, buoyed up by the same aspirations and cast down by the same anxieties, to raise his voice and remind those who forget it of their own nobility.[9]

Christ is both the mediator of salvation and its exemplar and adjudicator. It is through an encounter with him — mediated though it inevitably is by any number of intermediate models — that one is made

---

8 Quoted in de Lubac, *The Church: Paradox and Mystery*, 21, n.11.
9 De Lubac, *Catholicism*, 357–58.

aware of the insubstantiality of one's pre-conversion existence and given a glimpse of what a genuinely holy life might be. As we argued at length in *God's Gamble,* the only outstanding question is whether this encounter occurs in this life, when its fruits might be harvested for oneself and others and a corresponding reorientation might begin, or, on the contrary, it occurs at the "moment" of death, with a magnitude disproportionate to one's preparation for it. There is no guarantee that the transforming power of such an unexpected postmortem encounter with Divine Love will compensate for a lifetime based on premises incompatible with it, otherwise the urgency of the evangelical mission would lose its force. For, as Balthasar has warned: "As the naked freedom of man appears, the abyss of being eternally lost is open."[10]

---

10   Balthasar, *The God Question and Modern Man,* 128.

POSTSCRIPT

As we conclude our "mosaic of highly anecdotal snapshots of the postmodern self and its besetting distresses" to which we referred in an early chapter, we leave the patient reader with a beautiful image of the Christian mystery of personhood. The image is from the pen of one of the finest poets of the twentieth century, Richard Wilbur. The poet is here celebrating precisely the uncelebrated life of someone who has performed her modest role in the theodrama of salvation with selflessness and nobility. It is our hope that the poem will remind the reader of the christological underpinnings of the person, to which Saint Paul testified when he declared: "I live, now no longer I, but Christ lives in me." The reader is invited to join this writer in reading Wilbur's poem, not only as a tribute to just such a person, manifestations of which, praise God, can still be found among us, but also as an allusion to a love for the concrete reality of the Church manifested in the perennial determination to keep the exigencies of time and cultural neglect from occluding its inner mystery.

> . . . It is seventeen years
> Come tomorrow
> That Bruna Sandoval has kept the church
> Of San Ysidro, sweeping
> And scrubbing the aisles, keeping
> The candlesticks and the plaster faces bright
> And seen no visions but the thing done right
> From the clay porch
> To the white altar. For love and in all weathers
> This is what she has done.
> Sometimes the early sun
> Shines as she flings the scrubwater out, with a crash
> Of grimy rainbows, and the stained suds flash
> Like angel-feathers.[1]

---

[1] Richard Wilbur, *Collected Poems 1943–2004* (Orlando: Harcourt, 2004), 318.

INDEX

Alacoque, Marie, 177
Al-Ghazali, 64
Allen, Joe, 171–72
Andrew Spacey, 248n5
Anthropological Structures, 231–32, 249, 262
Apocalypse, 3, 21, 23, 39, 95, 126, 139, 170, 175, 183–84, 240
Arendt, Hanna, 267
Arkes, Hadley, 265n10
Armitage, Duane, 93
Arnold, Matthew, 55
Auerbach, Erich, 25, 79
Augustine, 2, 23, 28, 64–70, 79–80, 86, 99, 178, 211, 284, 287, 304
Aupetit, Monsignor Michel, 252

Bahr, Hermann, 206–7
Bailie, Gil, 21
Bakalar, Nicholas, 113n3
Barron, Robert, 74
Baudelaire, Charles, 141–43, 145
Bell, Rudolph M., 173–76
Benatar, David, 244
Benedict XVI, 4, 63, 90, 167n33, 201–2, 209, 227, 285, 288n2, 308
Berdyaev, Nicholas, 160
Bertonneau, Thomas F., 76
Betz, John, 76
Borch-Jacobsen, Mikkel, 119–20, 123
Bottum, Joseph, 56–57, 237, 257–58
Brague, Rémi, 49, 74, 157, 164, 274
Braudy, Leo, 80
Browder, Sue Ellen, 239
Buccellati, Giorgio, 182
Burrell, Brian David, 129
Burton, Richard, 216

Caravaggio, Michelangelo, 224
Carrón, Julián, 299
Cary, Phillip, 67
Catherine of Siena, 173–75, 177, 211
Charcot, Jean-Martin, 129–30, 177
Chesterton, G. K., 2, 62, 82, 268, 301
Cioran, E. M., 244, 256n2
Clare of Assisi, 173–75
Claretie, Jules, 147
Clayton, Alison, 112, 168
Clinton, Bill, 269
Cohen, Leonard, 298
Congar, Yves, 256, 277, 289, 315
Coulombe, Charles, 269
Crews, Frederick, 112, 130
Crowther, Ian, 263

Dandy, 47, 140–44
Davis, William N., 174–76
Dawson, Christopher, 262–63
de Gaál, Emery, 288
de Lubac, Henri, 7, 11, 21–22, 48, 67, 71, 93, 96–97, 100–2, 104, 111, 160, 172, 177–80, 185, 188–90, 199–200, 205, 214, 274, 276–79, 282–88, 292, 299–300, 305–8, 310–15
Del Noce, Augusto, 267
de Rougemont, Denis, 22
Descartes, René, 23, 62–66, 68–78, 82, 86, 91, 98–99, 124, 131–32, 142–43, 154, 168, 191
Dostoevsky, Fyodor, 105–8, 110, 119, 126, 159–60, 177, 187, 216, 244, 271
Du Saulle, Henri Legrand, 177
Dylan, Bob, 11–12, 14–17, 32, 122–23, 229, 270, 283, 294–98, 303

Eberstadt, Mary, 154, 184, 189, 246, 275
Eliot, T. S., 43–44, 53, 55, 135–39, 157–58, 164, 240
Emerson, Ralph Waldo, 87
Emmons, Libby, 169
Engels, Friedrich, 237
Esfahani Smith, Emily, 145, 293
Eucharist, 280, 288–90, 308
Evdokimov, Paul, 6, 232

Farrow, Douglas, 76–77, 82, 188, 200–1, 237, 266
Fornari, Giuseppe, 91, 95, 103–4, 185n9, 199, 204–5, 218–20, 266, 292
France, Peter, 83, 85
Franks, Angela, 155
Freud, Sigmund, 23, 35, 72, 83, 86–88, 95, 98, 102, 112–17, 119–25, 131–32, 136, 139, 147–51, 157, 160, 168, 174, 177, 268

Gans, Eric, 21, 28
Gergen, Kenneth J., 160–68, 182–83
Gide, André, 97
Gillespie, Michael Allen, 64, 69–70, 77
Girard, René, 3, 6, 13, 19, 21–26, 30–34, 38–39, 46–47, 51–52, 54–55, 59, 68, 78, 85, 88, 92–93, 95, 100–2, 104–5, 114–15, 117, 126, 133, 138, 142–43, 150–51, 155, 162, 168, 173, 175–77, 199, 218, 223, 229, 232, 238, 241, 253, 263, 272, 279–80, 292–93, 300, 312
Globalism, 266, 275, 306
Goebbels, Joseph, 186–87
Goldman, David, 125, 149, 152
Gorman, Amanda, 269–70
Gress, Carrie, 238–40
Grygiel, Jakub, 304
Guardini, Romano, 5, 28, 192–93, 198n1

Hammer, Josh, 265n10
Hankins, James, 269–70
Hanson, Victor Davis, 260

Harrison, Robert Pogue, 254, 274–75
Hart, David Bentley, 304
Haven, Cynthia L., 24n7, 280n8
Healy, David, 98, 150
Healy, Nicholas J., 3n6
Heimel, Cynthia, 162
Hemmerle, Klaus, 284
Hendershott, Anne, 169–70
Hill, John Lawrence, 151–52
Hittinger, Russell, 261n3
Hodak, Max, 171
Hoffman, Susanna, 60
Hölderlin, Friedrich, 133
Hopkins, Gerard Manley, 285–86
Hovat, John, 146n19
Howard, Richard, 256–58
Hughes, Robert, 143–44

Ian Crouther, 263–64
Imitatio Christi, 114, 178
Integralism, 306–10

Janowski, Zbigniew, 271–72
Joan of Arc, 177, 282–83
John Paul II, 15, 234, 250–51, 258, 265, 277, 309
Johnson, Paul, 80, 88–89, 270–71
Jung, C. G., 112, 126, 131–32

Kendall, Paul Murry, 178–79
Kennedy, Anthony, 2–3, 167
Kennedy, John F., 269
Kereszty, Roch, 297
Kierkegaard, Søren, 95, 102
Kimball, Roger, 269
King, Helen, 127
Kirke, Michael, 61
Kraus, Paul, 229, 237, 241–42

Lademan, Veronica, 266
Laye, Camara, 248n4
Legutko, Ryszard, 140, 272
Levine, Alan J., 260
Lewis, C. S., 232, 234, 291, 302
Lifton, Robert Jay, 166

Index

MacIntyre, Alasdair, 10, 229–30
Mahoney, Daniel J., 306
Manegold, Catherine S., 145–46
Marcel, Gabriel, 4, 7, 23, 190, 206, 251
Marcuse, Herbert, 237, 268
Marion, Jean-Luc, 135, 190, 196–97
Marx, Karl, 72, 145, 164, 237, 240–42, 268
Mary of Nazareth, 219
Mauriac, François Charles, 207–8
Mauss, Marcel, 4
McCartney, Kathleen, 237
McClay, Wilfred M., 60, 275
McHugh, Paul R., 155–57
Merrill, Trevor Cribben, 54, 85n19
Micale, Mark S., 113–15, 119–20, 127–28, 147–48, 150–51, 156
Miller, Arthur, 24–26, 28–30, 32, 34n9, 52, 183, 194n11
Millett, Mallory, 240–41
Miłosz, Czesław, 160–61
Milton, John, 191
Mimesis, 22–23, 26, 29, 32, 36, 59, 83, 114, 119, 138–39, 143, 177
Momigliano, Arnaldo, 79n2
Morandé, Pedro, 195–96
Morris, Colin, 248
Moss, David, 214
Mother's Smile, 232–36, 246–47, 251, 253, 276, 278, 289
Mullarkey, Maureen, 3
Multiphrenia, 18, 160, 163, 168, 182–83, 293

Newman, John Henry, 173
Nichols, Aidan, xin1, 1, 11, 54n4, 63, 309
Nieman, Susan, 97
Nietzsche, Friedrich, 62, 64, 70n23, 72, 82, 84, 91–104, 106, 108, 169, 176, 179, 187, 193, 195, 208, 244, 249, 268, 271
Nihilism, 1–3, 22, 35, 54–55, 64, 95, 105, 111, 128, 177, 179, 187, 195–97, 240–45, 254, 258, 260, 268, 271

Oakes, Edward T., 78, 154n26, 214n38, 288n1, 291, 301–2
Ockham, William, 63–64, 72, 75–76
O'Connor, Flannery, 16–20, 153, 261–62
Olsen, Glenn W., 7, 272–73
Origen of Alexandria, 200, 283
Oughourlian, Jean-Michel, 85, 115, 124, 132–33, 158, 179, 206, 232

Paglia, Camille, 144–45, 293–94
Paul, Saint, 52, 65, 84, 122, 178, 220, 274, 302, 304, 317
Pelikan, Jaroslav, 69
Percy, Walker, 56, 148
Peterson, Matthew, 265n10
Picard, Max, 147
Pickstock, Catherine, 28
Pietas, 255, 262, 266, 269–70, 306
Plath, Sylvia, 182, 184–85, 188, 194, 211, 240, 248–49
Postmodern, 23, 26, 39, 42, 51–52, 82, 109, 115, 142, 145, 157, 160–63, 165, 190, 192, 265, 275, 278, 317
Potential Mystics, 177–78, 185–86
Powers, Elizabeth, 254
Prodigal Son, 74, 189–94, 197, 202, 263, 284

Radcliffe-Brown, Alfred, 5
Ratzinger, Joseph, 3, 67–68, 74–76, 124, 167, 193n9, 198, 201, 205, 209n27, 235n9, 266n11, 280–81, 284–86, 292, 307–8
Redemptor Hominis, 250
Ralf, Georg Reuth, 186
Richard, Lucien, 297
Rieff, Philip, 115, 215
Robbins, Jane, 153–54
Ropper, Allan H., 129
Rosenstock-Huessy, Eugen, 62, 73, 82
Rothblatt, Martine, 168 70
Rousseau, G. S., 95–96
Rousseau, Jean-Jacques, 23, 79–90, 95, 98–102, 109–10, 140–41, 152, 168, 179, 208, 237, 249, 256, 270–71

321

Rowland, Tracey, 10
Rudolph M. Bell, 173–75
Ruysbroek, John, 188

Sanger, Margaret, 237
Santayana, George, 145, 229
Sarah, Cardinal Robert, 246, 261
Sass, Louis A., 58, 141–43
Schindler, D. C., 8n16, 266–68, 273–74, 310
Schindler, David L., 3n6, 299
Schmitz, Kenneth L., 6, 75
Schmitz, Matthew, 245
Schneider, Reinhold, 95, 304, 309
Scruton, Roger, 262
Scull, Andrew, 128–31
Senior, John, 49–50
Shakespeare, William, 29, 31, 36–38, 43, 109–10, 165, 301
Shorvon, Simon, 126, 133
Showalter, Elaine, 118, 124, 148, 150–51
Shrier, Abigail, 151
Siauve, Suzanne, 300
Smith, J. M., 111, 272
Smith-Rosenberg, Carrol, 113
Snedeker, Garrett, 265n10
Solomon, Robert, 65, 81, 194
Sontag, Susan, 144–45
Sotillos, Samuel Bendeck, 113
Spretnak, Charlene, 54
Stallybrass, Peter, 120–21, 151
Stout, Jeffery, 66, 75, 77
Sweeney, Conor, 234–35

Taylor, Charles, 69–70
Temple, William, 74
Teresa of Avila, 177
Terrance, Herbert S., 233–34
The Acting Person, 152
Theodrama, 205, 213, 280, 287, 289–90, 297, 301–4, 314, 317
Thérèse of Lisieux, 15–16, 32, 183, 282–83
Transgender, 151, 153–54, 168–70, 172, 175–76
Transhuman, 151, 168–72, 242
Turek, Margaret M., 235

Underground Man, 106–10, 119, 140–41, 146, 168, 185–87, 271

von Hildebrand, Dietrich, 210–11, 278, 290
von Hügel, Friedricha, 312
von Rad, Gerhard, 4–5

Warhol, Andy, 142–44, 146
Weil, Simone, 9, 261
White, Allon, 120–21, 151
Widmer, Gabriel, 199
Wilbur, Richard, 185–86, 317
William of Ockham, 63–66, 72, 75–76
Williams, James G., 33n8, 100n23, 105, 108
Wittels, Fritz, 98, 148

Zinn, Howard, 270
Zizioulas, John D., 65, 203, 205–7, 230, 251, 294
Zweig, Paul, 81, 98, 141

www.ingramcontent.com/pod-product-compliance
Lightning Source LLC
Chambersburg PA
CBHW031428160426
43195CB00010BB/650